PRAISE FOR *THE ULTIMATE YANKEE BOOK*

"*The Ultimate Yankee Book* is really the one-stop, has-it-all book that will give Yankees fans and baseball historians their entire fill of nothing but Yankees baseball."

—**BRADFORD H. TURNOW,** owner of UltimateYankees.com

"Yankee fans will want to keep Harvey Frommer's *The Ultimate Yankee Book* right next to their chair alongside the peanuts and Cracker Jacks. Surprising nuggets of Yankees lore adorn each page."

—**GLENN STOUT,** author of *The Selling of the Babe* and series editor, *The Best American Sports Writing*

"It's all here. Everything you ever wanted to know about the most storied sports franchise in American history. Even Red Sox fans should get in on this so they'll know all about the enemy."

—**DAN SHAUGHNESSY,** sports columnist and author of *The Curse of the Bambino*

"I guarantee you this: *The Ultimate Yankee Book* is the most valuable guide the Bronx Bombers Baseball Almanac will have in its research library."

—**SEAN HOLTZ,** owner of www.baseball-almanac.com

"A must-read for Yankee fans and Yankee haters alike. No team anywhere has this kind of history, and Harvey Frommer is the perfect tour guide for a stroll down memory lane."

—**LEN BERMAN,** broadcaster and author

"Stan Musial once said, 'Baseball records? The Yankees had 'em all.' Harvey Frommer's book proves it."

—**DAVE KINDRED,** author of *Sound and Fury*

The
ULTIMATE
YANKEE BOOK

FROM THE BEGINNING TO TODAY: TRIVIA, FACTS AND STATS, ORAL HISTORY, MARKER MOMENTS AND LEGENDARY PERSONALITIES—A HISTORY AND REFERENCE BOOK ABOUT BASEBALL'S GREATEST FRANCHISE

HARVEY FROMMER

Author of the *New York Yankees Encyclopedia* and *Remembering Yankee Stadium*

PAGE STREET
PUBLISHING CO.

PAGE STREET
PUBLISHING CO.

First published in 2017 by
Page Street Publishing Co.
27 Congress Street, Suite 1511
Salem, MA 01970
www.pagestreetpublishing.com

Distributed by Macmillan, sales in Canada by The Canadian Manda Group.

23   6

ISBN-13: 978-1-62414-433-2
ISBN-10: 1-62414-433-0

Library of Congress Control Number: 2017935500

Cover and book design by Page Street Publishing Co.
Photography credits:
Associated Press: cover (left and right), pages 95, 122, 142, 146, 148, 149, 150, 151, 152, 154, 155, 156 (left and right), 157, 162, 186, 187 (bottom), 222
The David Atkatz Collection: pages 22, 23, 35 (top), 38 (bottom), 44 (top right), 52 (top), 54 (left), 84, 105, 124, 128, 131, 132 (top), 136 (left and right), 138, 140, 198
Paul Doherty: pages 14, 15
Robert Edward Auctions: pages 33, 34, 50 (center and far left), 59, 60, 81, 96, 141, 164, 195 (top and bottom), 208, 233, 245, 275
Library of Congress: pages 2 (top), 8 (top), 24, 27, 28, 43 (bottom), 63 (right), 102, 125, 126, 133, 170, 187 (top), 197, 220
National Baseball Hall of Fame and Museum: pages 25, 32, 35 (bottom), 38 (top), 39, 40, 43 (top), 44 (top left), 45, 46, 47, 48, 49, 50 (far right), 52 (left), 54 (top), 55 (top and bottom), 56, 57, 58, 61, 62, 63 (left), 64, 65, 66, 68, 69 (top and bottom), 70, 71, 72, 73, 75, 78, 79, 82, 83, 90, 100, 101, 104, 106, 108, 110, 113, 114 (left and right), 115, 117, 119, 120, 129, 132 (bottom), 167, 174, 176, 183, 189
David Spindel: pages 2 (bottom), 9 (bottom), 10 (top and bottom), 11 (top), 20, 206
Brad Turnow: page 16
Underwood Archives: pages 8 (bottom), 9 (top), 11 (bottom), 19, 172, 192, 218

Printed and bound in China

For Myrna.

THE GOLDEN CHANCE
I NEVER LET PASS ME BY.

CONTENTS

Author's Note - 13

Prelude - 18

OWNERS AND PLAYING FIELDS - 21

From Farrell and Devery and Hilltop Park to the Steinbrenners and New Yankee Stadium

LEGENDS, LEADERS AND LUMINARIES - 33

The Babe, the Iron Horse, Marse Joe, Joltin' Joe, the Old Perfessor, Donnie Baseball, Mr. October, Mr. November, A-Rod and more

EPIC MOMENTS, STREAKS AND FEATS - 123

Yankee Stadium opens: April 18, 1923; DiMag, 56-game hitting streak, 1941; Reggie Jackson, three homers on three consecutive swings, October 16 to 18, 1977; and other great moments in Yankee history

YANKEE MONIKERS AND NICKNAMES - 165

Noms de plume, aliases, sobriquets, catchwords—nicknames, all time, all ways for Yankees

NUMEROLOGY: YANKEES BY THE NUMBERS FROM 0 TO $3.4 BILLION - 173

The numbers, stats and figures that are a staple of Major League Baseball

YANKEE DOODLE DANDIES - 193

Assortment of all things Yankee—talkin' Yankees, oddities, spring training, greatest and worst team, uniform and logo, monuments, "meet me at the bat," Old-Timers' Day, apocryphal, lists and factoids

ULTIMATE YANKEE QUIZ - 207

150 provocative questions and answers with some sure to be daunting even for the most extreme Yankee diehards

MARCH OF YANKEE TIME - 219

Dates to remember from 1903 to 2016

Appendices - 247

Selected Sources - 276

Acknowledgments - 280

About the Author - 281

Other Books by Harvey Frommer - 282

Index - 284

Captions for previous pages:

Page 8, top: Yankee ballplayer is tagged out at home; bottom: Mickey Mantle steals second in the 11th inning of a game against the Minnesota Twins, 1961.

Page 9, top: Joe DiMaggio in the dugout during the first game of the 1937 World Series against the New York Giants; bottom: A classic image of the Yankee Stadium entrance reflects the power and majesty of the ballpark in the Bronx, 2009.

Page 10, top: Teams lined up for Old-Timers' Day, 1990s; bottom: Derek Jeter homers the Yankees into the playoffs.

Page 11, top: Teams lined up at Yankee Stadium for a 9/11 tribute; bottom: Baseball fans waiting in line to buy tickets for the World Series, c. 1938.

AUTHOR'S NOTE

The great novelist Bernard Malamud wrote: "The whole history of baseball has the quality of mythology." He was right about that, and his words apply especially to the New York Yankees.

The Ultimate Yankee Book is the culmination of decades of watching the games of the greatest franchise in sports through so many years of my life. It involved being there at the ballparks they have played in, listening on the radio, watching on TV and following the doings on the Internet.

Through the years I have written hundreds of articles about the New York Yankees and more than half a dozen books on the team. I recall once promoting one of my Yankee books at the Staten Island Mall and hearing a voice shout out from the rear of the audience: "I remember you from the old neighborhood in Brooklyn. You were never a Yankees fan. You were that crazy Cardinals fan."

My former neighbor was right: For a brief time I was "that crazy Cardinals fan." But mostly my fanatical feelings about baseball were all about the Yankees of New York. That feeling is underscored in these pages by some personal reminiscences about the Yankee personalities I have come into contact with.

The idea for *The Ultimate Yankee Book* has always been a big project I wanted to delve into. For authors as well as fans, "Yankeeology" is a serious subject. Choosing Yankee leaders, luminaries and legends to write about, and selecting epic events to focus on, was easy. Eliminating so many from both categories was the hard part. My team on "the bench," my son Fred Frommer, the ultimate Yankee expert Paul Doherty, the wise and steeped-in-all-things-Yankee Brad Turnow and others all contributed mightily by advising me all along the way.

It was a great pleasure to research and write this book. It is, in my view, a special book for fans of the New York Yankees. It is also a book that will prove to be a treat for all sports fans.

—HARVEY FROMMER, LYME, NEW HAMPSHIRE, 2016

ORAL HISTORY VOICES

- **MEL ALLEN,** famed Yankee announcer

- **RED BARBER,** famed Brooklyn Dodger and Yankee broadcaster

- **JOHNNY BLANCHARD,** one-time Yankee backup catcher and super-sub

- **RON BLOMBERG,** as a Yankee became the first designated hitter to bat

- **DON CARNEY,** one-time vice president for sports and special events, WPIX-TV

- **JOE CARRIERRI,** former Yankee batboy

- **FRED CLAIRE,** former Los Angeles Dodger executive, 1969 to 1998

- **JERRY COLEMAN,** Yankee star who partnered with Phil Rizzuto in top double-play combination

- **MARIO CUOMO,** one-time New York State governor

- **DOM DIMAGGIO,** brother of Joe, longtime star center fielder for the Red Sox

- **PAUL DOHERTY,** Yankee expert extraordinaire

- **MICHAEL DUKAKIS,** former governor of Massachusetts and 1988 presidential nominee

- **SAL DURANTE,** caught the ball Roger Maris hit for his 61st home run

- **JOE FLYNN,** one-time New York Giants ticket taker

- **WHITEY FORD,** Yankee Hall of Famer

- **BILL GALLO,** former sports editor and top cartoonist, *New York Daily News*

- **RUDY GIULIANI,** big-time Yankee fan and former mayor of New York City

- **RALPH HOUK,** player, coach, manager and executive for Yankees

- **FRANK HOWARD,** one-time standout home run hitter

- **JEFF IDELSON,** president of the Baseball Hall of Fame, former Yankee media relations director

- **MONTE IRVIN,** Hall of Famer, one of the first to break baseball's color line

- **"BIG" JULIE ISAACSON,** businessman and good friend of Roger Maris

- **ROGER KAHN,** standout baseball author and newspaperman

- **IRV KAZE,** one-time Yankees media relations head

- **LEONARD KOPPETT,** famed one-time sportswriter and author

- **DON LARSEN,** pitched a perfect game for the Yankees in 1956 World Series

Yankee sage Paul Doherty at the stadium. He has been there through the decades and seen it all.

- **PHIL LINZ,** former Yankee infielder

- **STAN LOMAX,** longtime fixture in New York City sportscasting

- **EDDIE LOPAT,** star southpaw hurler for the Yankees in 1940s and '50s

- **JOHN McNAMARA,** grew up near Yankee Stadium in the 1920s

- **WALTER MEARS,** former AP editor

- **JON MILLER,** San Francisco Giants broadcaster

- **BOBBY MURCER,** once top Yankee outfielder and broadcaster

- **MEL PARNELL,** star Red Sox pitcher who competed against the Yankees a great deal

- **LOU PINIELLA,** Yankee player, coach, manager and executive

- **WILLIE RANDOLPH,** former star Yankee second baseman

- **BOBBY RICHARDSON,** former star Yankee second baseman

- **ARTHUR RICHMAN,** longtime fixture on the New York sporting scene

- **PHIL RIZZUTO,** Hall of Fame shortstop

- **BROOKS ROBINSON,** Hall of Fame third baseman

- **PETE SHEEHY,** longtime Yankee clubhouse fixture

- **BOB SHEPPARD,** the "Voice of God" and of the Yankees

- **BILL SKOWRON,** slugger supreme in Yankee dynasty years

- **MIKE STANLEY,** one-time Yankee, 1990s

- **CASEY STENGEL,** great Yankee manager, 1949 to 1960

- **RON SWOBODA,** one-time Yankee, 1971 to 1973

- **JIM THOMSON,** stadium superintendent director and ticket director

- **BRADFORD TURNOW,** webmaster for Ultimateyankees.com

"Voice of God," beloved announcer Bob Sheppard, whom every kid dreamed would announce his name as he stepped onto the field in his pinstripes at Yankee Stadium.

Yankee guy extraordinaire Brad Turnow with his son Gehrig at old Yankee Stadium. Brad is the owner of the Ultimate Yankees website, a lifelong keeper of all things Yankees in his memory and online.

MARIO CUOMO: *Growing up in Queens in the 1930s, you had to be a Yankee fan. If you were Mario Cuomo, and they had a guy by the name of Joe DiMaggio, not to mention Frankie Crosetti and Phil Rizzuto, but mostly Joe DiMaggio, then you were for all time fated to be a Yankee fan. The first baseball game I ever saw was with Joe DiMaggio. That's the kind of fan I was. I was absolutely mesmerized by the New York Yankees. They were everything and always were.*

RUDY GIULIANI: *My first game was between the Yankees and the Red Sox, with Joe DiMaggio playing for the Yankees and Dominic DiMaggio playing for the Red Sox. I found that fascinating—that brothers would be on two different teams. I asked my father: "How come they're playing for different teams—are they angry at each other?"*

LEONARD KOPPETT: *By the 1950s, the Yankees are the lords of baseball from Babe Ruth to Lou Gehrig to Joe DiMaggio to Mickey Mantle. They win, win more than anybody. Everybody hates the Yankees except die-hard Yankee fans. They happen to be in the Bronx but it is not a local Bronx thing since they are the aristocracy—a lot of the people who move to the suburbs remain Yankee fans.*

"What visions burn, what dreams possess him, seeker of the night. The packed stands of the stadium, the bleachers sweltering with their unshaded hordes, the faultless velvet of the diamond. The mounting roar of 80,000 voices and Gehrig coming to bat."

—THOMAS WOLFE

"The essence of the Yankees is that they win. From in front or from behind, they win. And that's why the history of the New York Yankees is virtually the history of baseball."

—DAVE ANDERSON, the *New York Times*

"Where have you gone, Joe DiMaggio? A nation turns its lonely eyes to you."

—PAUL SIMON AND ART GARFUNKEL

"A white streak left Babe Ruth's 52-ounce bludgeon in the third inning of yesterday's opening game at the Yankee Stadium. On a low line it sailed, like a silver flame, through the gray, bleak April shadows, and into the right field bleachers. And as the crash sounded, and the white flash followed, fans arose en masse . . . in the greatest vocal cataclysm baseball has ever known."

—GRANTLAND RICE, *New York Tribune*

"Yankee Stadium is something else, a law unto itself. It has earned the right to look any way it pleases and I would not change a seat of it. . . . It is particularly dream worthy because not so long ago the World Series used to turn up there as regularly as Wimbledon. I once sneaked out to center field myself as a youth to see how things looked from Mickey Mantle's point of view and felt the same tingle some people get from Civil War battlefields."

—WILFRID SHEED

"On a chilly Sunday in 1939 I went to see my first game of the year. The sports pages had been full of stories about Lou Gehrig. He was not himself, they said. Something was wrong. The Yanks won with ease. But Gehrig was sluggish, he swung without power. He was no veteran slowing up. His reflexes were so far off, you could not but observe the fact. I didn't know it was to be one of Gehrig's last games."

—JAMES T. FARRELL

"Yankee Stadium has not been the classic ballpark, the 'House That Ruth Built,' since it was remodeled in the 1970s. The old Yankee Stadium was one imposing structure, but when it comes to this one, I don't think we are losing something of great architectural note. We are getting rid of an architectural mishmash. Sometimes new is better."

—ROGER KAHN

"Have faith in the Yankees, my son."

—ERNEST HEMINGWAY, *The Old Man and the Sea*

"There has never been anything like it. Even as these lines are batted out on the office typewriter, youths dash out of the AP and UP ticker room every two or three minutes shouting, 'Ruth hit one! Gehrig hit another one!'"

—PAUL GALLICO

"All literary men are Red Sox fans. To be a Yankee fan in literary society is to endanger your life."

—JOHN CHEEVER

"The majority of American males put themselves to sleep by striking out the batting order of the New York Yankees."

—JAMES THURBER

PRELUDE

From a stumbling start back in 1903, from owners that since then in the main have set a top-drawer tone and a high standard, from managers who asserted their will pushing players to perform beyond their abilities, who established winning ways setting the pattern for others to follow, from stars and superstars and a support staff on the field, behind the scenes and in the broadcast booths, the song of the New York Yankees has captivated and thrilled their fans. No franchise in the history of sports can lay claim to what the Yankees of New York have accomplished. "Most" and "more" and "ultimate" are the operative words.

The Yankees have been in more World Series and won more world championships than any other team in baseball history. They have 27 championships, 18 division titles and 40 pennants—all Major League records.

The Yankees have bragging rights to the five top players ever in World Series history in runs scored and RBIs and total bases, and the top three in World Series home runs and slugging percentages.

The Yankees have the most retired numbers, the most ever inducted into Cooperstown. Forty-four Yankee players and 11 managers are now in the Hall of Fame and more are on the way—another Major League record.

The roster of managers who have been leaders of the franchise from the Bronx have contributed mightily to the team's image and success. Although a few have been indolent or slow, there have been others who have been head and shoulders above their contemporaries.

Chief among them are Miller Huggins, Joe McCarthy, Charles Dillon Stengel, Billy Martin and Joe Torre.

The eighth manager in franchise history was the self-effacing Miller Huggins, the little man who was arguably the first great skipper in Yankee history. Weighing 140 pounds soaking wet with boots still on, and standing at 5-foot-6, he moved the Yankees from middling to mind-boggling.

Joe McCarthy was in the dugout from 1931 to 1946, sixteen years. His Yankees of 1936 to 1939 won four straight World Series. "Marse Joe" was dedicated, obsessive and tuned in to the culture and success of the New York Yankees. His Yankee teams won 1,460 games and compiled a record .627 winning percentage. Although McCarthy played fifteen seasons in the minors and never a game in the big leagues, he ranks as the winningest Major League Baseball manager of all time.

Charles Dillon Stengel was a piece of work. He was an unlikely manager for the Yankees; his time from 1949 to 1960 was an era of true Yankee greatness, a time his teams won five straight world championships. Just once in those dozen years did a Stengel team fail to win more than 90 games. His record as Yankee manager was 1,149–696, .623. In his time as skipper, Stengel was not that young, he mangled the English language and spiced it up with profanity, he could be outlandish and crass and cruel and egotistical, but he could manage a ball club, getting the most out of every player on his roster.

Disagreeable, driven, disliked by many, Bill Martin seemed to be in pinstripes as player and manager forever. In reality, it was his comings and goings, his five stints (1975–1978, 1979, 1983, 1985, 1988) as skipper, his histrionics and his tabloid exposure that seemed never-ending that kept him in the public eye for better or worse. Martin's record as Yankee manager was 556 wins, 385 defeats. His clubs won but one world championship and two American League titles.

With 1,000 career losses as a manager, Joe Torre was a peculiar selection to take over as skipper of the fabled franchise. When he arrived in 1996, it was the right time, the right place, the right circumstances for him. The first Yankee manager to be born in the New York City area, the calm Joseph Paul Torre was a skilled communicator, a diplomatic handler of players. He and team owner George Steinbrenner presided over a magical time for the New York Yankees, winning six pennants and four world championships. He was selected Manager of the Year in 1996 and 1998.

And then there are the players.

The Yankees of Babe Ruth and Lou Gehrig, Joe DiMaggio, Mickey Mantle, Whitey Ford, Yogi Berra, Reggie Jackson, Ron Guidry, Thurman Munson, Derek Jeter and others through the long decades who stepped up and left their mark on the shining story of the team from the Bronx.

The little Willie Keeler hitting 'em where they ain't; the Iron Horse Lou Gehrig playing in pain, playing on; the Babe, boisterous, bold, bigger than life; the reserved Yankee Clipper, Joe DiMaggio, one to be counted on; the solid Lawrence Peter Berra, a rock and a sage, through all those seasons a star player, coach and manager; Eddie Lopat with his junk balls, mystifying batters; the live wire Phil Rizzuto; the elegant Jerry Coleman and Willie Randolph; Ron Guidry, honed in on the mound; the composed and fearless Mariano Rivera, grace under pressure; the monster home runs of Charlie Keller, Bill Skowron, Roger Maris, Mickey Mantle, Chris Chambliss, et al., bringing the crowd to its feet; in dirty uniform, the driven Thurman Munson blocking home plate . . .

The oddballs and characters: Lefty Gomez, Mickey Rivers, Phil Linz, Joe Pepitone and Goose Gossage.

The tough and dependable ones: Bill Skowron, Hank Bauer, Tommy Henrich, Ralph Houk, Allie Reynolds, Elston Howard and Jorge Posada.

The fiery, sometimes moody ones: Bob Meusel, Billy Martin, Sparky Lyle, Paul O'Neill, Joe Page, Roger Maris and Thurman Munson.

The truly gifted ones: Derek Jeter, Mickey Mantle, "Catfish" Hunter, Joe Gordon, Graig Nettles, Ron Guidry and Herb Pennock.

The "Core Four" of Andy Pettitte, Mariano Rivera, Derek Jeter and Jorge Posada.

Those with a touch of class and quiet elegance: Elston Howard, Willie Randolph, Lou Gehrig, Earl Combs, Bobby Murcer and Bernie Williams.

Heritage, mystique, ritual, magic, aura, tradition and ghosts—all have all been a part of the package for the New York Yankees.

And so have Casey Stengel, racking up the English language and other teams; Joe McCarthy, pushing all the right buttons; DiMag hitting in 56 straight; Bucky hitting the f***ing home run in Fenway; Chris Chambliss, taking Mark Littell deep; larger-than-life Larsen tossing the perfect game; and David Wells and David Cone.

It is all those pennants and world championships, the standing-room-only crowds, the Bleacher Creatures, the Ballantine Blasts, the White Owl Wallops, the Southern voice of Mel Allen exclaiming, "How about that?" and the New York accents of Phil Rizzuto shouting "HOLY COW!" and John Sterling's "Sterlingese."

It is the Babe blasting the ball, Reggie Jackson smacking home run after home run after home run into the chilly World Series night, Mickey Mantle ripping the mammoth clouts and Derek Jeter becoming "Mr. November."

Then there are one-liners passed down from generation to generation:

Waite Hoyt: "It's great to be young and a Yankee."

Joe DiMaggio: "I'd like to thank the Good Lord for making me a Yankee."

Casey Stengel: "I'll never make the mistake of being 70 years old again."

Roger Maris: "If all I am entitled to is an asterisk—that will be all right with me."

Lou Gehrig: "I consider myself the luckiest man on the face of the earth."

Col. Jacob Ruppert: "Yankee Stadium was a mistake, not mine but the Giants."

Buck Showalter: "Every kid growing up has dreamed of lining up at Yankee Stadium and having Bob Sheppard announce his name."

Derek Jeter: "God, I hope I wear this jersey forever."

Frank Sinatra (singing John Kander and Fred Ebb's): ". . . If you can make it there, you'll make it anywhere . . ."

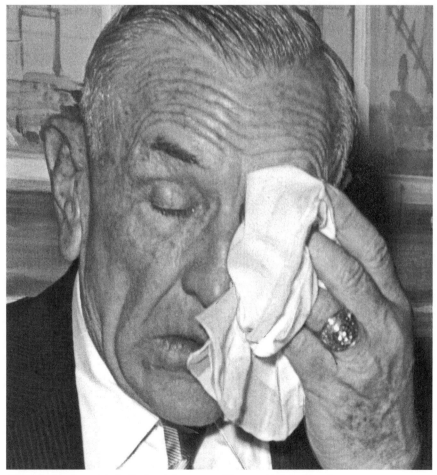

The end of the line with the Yankees brings tears to 70-year-old Casey Stengel.

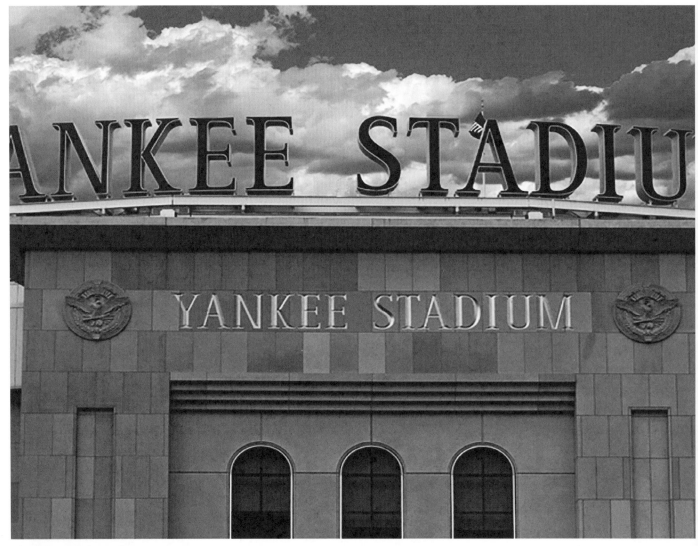

The edifice at Yankee Stadium.

One

OWNERS AND PLAYING FIELDS

From Farrell and Devery and Hilltop Park to the Steinbrenners and New Yankee Stadium

- William Stephen Devery and Frank J. Farrell ... 21
- Tillinghast L'Hommedieu Huston and Col. Jacob Ruppert ... 25
- Jacob Ruppert Estate ... 29
- Daniel Topping, Del Webb and Larry MacPhail ... 30
- CBS ... 30
- George Steinbrenner ... 30
- Hal Steinbrenner and Hank Steinbrenner ... 31

All kinds of personalities have had their turn owning the New York Yankees, and all with a few exceptions have been the better for it. This chapter is a survey of those men—some legendary, some ordinary. Then there are the playing fields; interestingly enough, there have been very few of them that the Yankees have played on in their long history.

It has been estimated that more people have dreamed of owning the New York Yankees than any other franchise in sports. George Steinbrenner declared: "It's like owning the Mona Lisa, you never want to sell it." Dan Topping said: "I'm going to buy the Yankees. I don't know what I'm going to pay for them, but I'm going to buy them."

Incredibly, even though the franchise has been around for such a long time, the number of people who have been "principal owners" is very few. And of that select group, a couple of very long tenures characterize that ownership. Two dozen years for Colonel Jacob Ruppert and a whopping 35 years for George

Steinbrenner and by extension to the Steinbrenner family—almost 45 years.

On the whole, dedicated, intelligent, involved and interested individuals have held the power and the purse strings of the New York Yankees, arguably the most legendary and successful of all sports teams ever. All have come from different backgrounds, with very different personalities, and owned with different styles. What follows is a primer on ultimate baseball power—a look at those who have been fortunate enough to be the owners of the New York Yankees and the ball fields their teams have played on.

Ownership matters. It certainly has mattered when talking Yankees.

WILLIAM STEPHEN DEVERY AND FRANK J. FARRELL, 1903 TO 1913

Known as the Baltimore Orioles during the 1901 and 1902 seasons, the franchise went out of business and left their American League brethren much distressed. Ban Johnson, American League president, sought balm for

the wound—new ownership for the franchise and relocation to the major market of New York City.

Despite his energetic efforts, no takers surfaced as the 1903 season loomed. Enter William Stephen Devery, a former New York City police commissioner, and Frank J. Farrell, a professional gambler. The duo was the last and least of choices as owners.

A former bartender and prizefighter, "Big Bill" Devery made a lot of money from shrewd real estate investments that he oversaw from his estate in Far Rockaway, Queens. He also did quite well, it was said, from graft, corruption and his affiliation with the New York City Police Department. He moved up the ranks and wound up being the first police chief. Along the way, when he was a police captain, he allegedly told his men: "They tell me there's a lot of grafting going on in this precinct. They tell me that you fellows are the fiercest ever on graft. Now that's going to stop! If there's any grafting to be done, I'll do it. Leave it to me." The word was correct that he was skilled in the art and science of collecting "honest graft" in saloons, brothels, betting parlors, gambling dens and dance halls. Protection was a big part of the daily work of those under him.

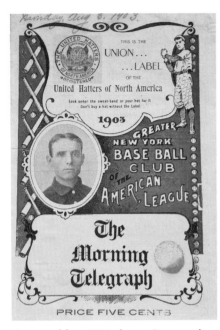

A scorecard from 1903, the year Devery and Farrell bought the Baltimore franchise.

The other half of the ownership duo was Frank J. Farrell, who was immersed in the New York City gambling world, owning pool halls and a casino. He was called the "Pool Room King" because he controlled over 250 pool halls or "gambling dens," most of them located in lower Manhattan. The short and stocky Farrell shared a love of baseball with his Tammany Hall cohorts.

Devery and Farrell were friends, and they made millions through their assorted and sordid ventures and services to Tammany Hall. A news account of that time described one of them this way:

"Mr. Frank Farrell is a gambler, the chief gambler of New York City, we suppose. The business to which he owes his bad eminence, and in which he gains his living is carried out in violation of the law. His gambling places have enjoyed the protection of the law [because] he is an intimate, personal friend of Mr. W. S. Devery, the Deputy Police Commissioner of New York."

Suppressing his misgivings about Farrell and Devery, Ban Johnson, founder

of the American League, allowed the pair to purchase the Baltimore franchise for $18,000 on January 9, 1903. With the sale, the new owners were expected to move the team to New York City and build a new ball field for it.

On the twelfth day of March, 1903, Johnson presided over a press conference announcing that New York City would have a new team in his American League. Owners Frank J. Farrell and William S. Devery were not identified as the new owners; surprisingly, they were not even present. In Albany, a few days later, incorporation of the team took place. Again, Frank J. Farrell and William S. Devery were not part of the program.

It was no wonder Ban Johnson chose to keep the twosome in the background when and while he could. It was crystal clear they were not the types he sought as owners. But something was better than nothing, and Johnson had not been overwhelmed with ownership offers.

A property tract in the Washington Heights section of upper Manhattan owned by the New York Institute for the Blind, situated between 165th and 168th Streets and Fort Washington Avenue and Broadway, was chosen as the site for the new ballpark to house the new team. It was located ten blocks north of the Polo Grounds, the home field of the New York Giants.

Over $200,000 was spent excavating the rocky site that the park was being built on. It was said that 12,000 cubic yards of rock were pulled out of the ground at a cost of $15,000. Construction had to be a rush job, and it was. The ballpark was far from ready for the team's inaugural season of 1903. A swampy area in right field was in need of rock fill. There was very little grass in the outfield. The planned grandstand was still incomplete. The clubhouse needed a lot of work. Players wound up dressing at their hotel rooms.

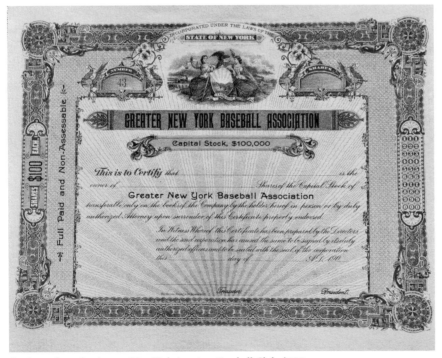

Stock certificate for the new New York American Baseball Club, $100.

Mediocre at best was the politest way to characterize the entire playing surface and structure. The ballpark was initially called American League Park, but its name was changed to Hilltop Park because it was located at one of the highest points in Manhattan. The new playing field featured a grandstand and bleachers that held close to 16,000 fans. Hundreds more would be allowed to stand just outside the first and third base foul lines, or several men deep behind the outfielders.

Joseph Gordon was appointed the team's first president by Farrell and Devery. He was there to add a badly needed touch of class and legitimacy to the whole operation. A former coal-mining executive, Gordon was genial and also a former state assemblyman. He had at one time been on the corporate board of the New York Giants. He was well connected.

Gordon was the one who suggested the team be called Highlanders because of the "high land" it would play on. It was said Gordon was also influenced by a crack British regiment named Highlander that was touring the United States at the time. Their commander, no relation, was also named Gordon.

In addition to Highlander, other printable names the team was called included Hill Dwellers, Porch Climbers, Burglars, Cliffmen, Hilltoppers, New Yorkers, Invaders and Americans. The favorite of the press in New York City was Yanks or Yankees.

When Hilltop Park was finally completed, a single-tier wooden covered grandstand extended from the third base dugout to home plate and around to the first base dugout. Uncovered grandstands spread out to both foul poles. There was very little parking space until 1906, when lots were set up inside the grounds behind the grandstand for carriages and cars.

The hastily put together wooden ballpark took six weeks to be constructed on the roughly cleared site. On April 30, 1903, the first home game of the Greater New York Base Ball Club of the American League took place: Highlanders versus Washington Senators. Each of the 16,243 in attendance that pleasant Opening Day of the brand-new American League franchise was given a small American flag.

Many entered Hilltop Park through its main entrance that faced Broadway. A seat in the single deck-covered wooden grandstand that extended from first base to third base cost 50 cents. Bleacher seats were 75 cents, box seats a dollar. Fans who sat behind home plate could see the Hudson River and the New Jersey Palisades. Ban Johnson was at the ballpark for the first pitch, seated next to Devery in a front row box very close to the Highlanders bench. Johnson had seen to it that the team's roster had bragging rights to some high-level talent—future Hall of Fame outfielder Willie Keeler, first-rate infielder Wid Conroy and a pitching staff anchored by standouts Jack Chesbro and Jesse Tannehill. Guiding the team would be astute pitcher-manager Clark Griffith.

With a playing field surface of dirt on rock, or dirt on dirt, the ballpark featured an unappealing hollow in right field that was roped off. A player hitting a ball past the ropes was awarded a double. In June of that first season, a fence was placed in front of the hollow. A ball hit over the fence would be awarded a home run. The dimensions were vast: left field was 365 feet from home plate, center field was an enormous 542 feet and right field was 400 feet.

At 3 p.m., both teams marched from the outfield to home plate and stood at attention as the 69th Regiment band played the "Washington Post March"

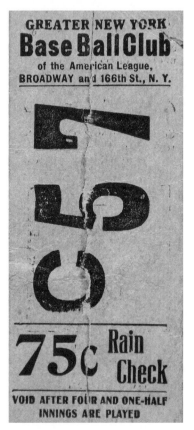

Hilltop Park ticket stub, 1903, when bleacher seats were 75 cents.

A pocket schedule from 1903, the year Hilltop Park was completed.

and then the "Star Spangled Banner." Ban Johnson threw out the first ball and the first game in Highlanders (Yankee) history began. Jack Chesbro was the winning pitcher as the Highlanders beat Washington, 6–2. The franchise's first home game was in the history books.

That first season the Highlanders finished in fourth place (7–2), 17 games out of first. It was not a bad beginning for the new team in town; however, problems were evident. Attendance was a disappointment, and the New York Giants of the established National League were fan favorites.

"We made money," Gordon insisted. Not a lot, but "enough to know that our investment is a good one and that next year we will do better." The Highlanders' home attendance of 211,808, however, was only half the 422,473 drawn by its nearest geographic American League competition in Philadelphia, which outpaced the league in attendance.

The 1904 season was better for Farrell, Devery, Gordon and their team. Paced by Jack Chesbro's century-best 41 wins, the Highlanders matched up against Boston for the American League pennant. An ill-thrown Chesbro spitball gave the pennant to Boston. Nevertheless, there was excitement aplenty in Highlander world. Attendance surged that season to 438,919, double that of the previous year. Not one to shirk publicity and attention, Farrell made sure their standing in the sport grew. Most press coverage of the Highlanders routinely identified him as the owner of the team.

There were good days and bad days and many muddling along days for the Highlanders up to the 1908 season, a season that was a disaster for them; they suffered through 103 losses in a 154-game schedule.

For 1909, Bill Devery, hoping to change the team's fortune and image, changed the Highlander logo. He adopted a "NY" insignia that was on a medal of honor for policemen shot in the line of duty. The new interlocking NY would go on to become the most recognizable logo in all of sports. In the first year the

Yankee owner Frank Farrell, bottom center, looking at the camera, in his box seat at the Polo Grounds, c. 1903.

"NY" appeared on the uniform, the team improved to a 74–77 record.

As the 1912 season was set to begin, the relationship between Big Bill Devery and Frank Farrell was at an ending point. Over their years together, they had grown to hate each other. And their team's failures on the baseball field were just part of the problem. No longer on speaking terms, and no longer consulting each other on baseball decisions, Farrell spread the word that he was seeking a buyer for Devery's share of the Yankees.

The 1912 season was a disaster. The Yankees finished in last place, losing 102 games, winning 50. Not one pitcher had a winning record. Attendance was subpar—just 242,194 paid admissions, less than half the total that had been at Hilltop Park just three seasons before. However, another home uniform design change was in place that season: a touch of pinstripes foreshadowing the future was now standard fare.

That 1912 season was also the last one of the ten-year-lease on Hilltop Park. The Institute for the Blind was not willing to extend it. Farrell and Devery had some frantic moments. However, it all worked out . . . sort of.

Farrell promised that his team's stay at the Polo Grounds would be brief—only until a new ballpark at Kingsbridge Road was completed. He promised June 1, 1913, would be the date. Unfortunately, his promises, like many others he had made through the years, did not come true. The Yankees played all their home games of 1913 at the Polo Grounds.

They also played all of their games in 1914 at the Polo Grounds, winning 70 games, losing 84 games, and finishing in sixth place. Attendance was 359,477. The season was a microcosm of their ownership.

For the unsavory Farrell and even more unsavory Devery, success was a sometimes thing. Under their watch, their team's total won-lost record was 861–937. The two owners took all the profits they could. They plowed nothing back into the team. Mismanagement was always on parade.

The overall lack of success on the field, the disappointments at the gate and the failures that forced them to close other business operations drained and diminished Farrell and Devery. Their run was over. The word on the street was that they were obliged to sell. Lengthy meetings and negotiations for the purchase of the Yankees got underway. Farrell's asking price for the franchise was $500,000.

The American League president was all in as a broker. All kinds of back and forthing involved Tammany Hall types, other baseball team owners and the American League office. The paramount issue for all of them was the need to replace the Yankee ownership with new and stable people and ensure a successful team in New York City.

On January 11, 1915, Farrell and Devery sold the team to Tillinghast L'Hommedieu Huston and Jacob Ruppert for $460,000. Nineteen days later the official transfer took place. The sellers received twenty-five times more than what they had originally paid for the franchise.

Devery would live on for five more years. Farrell would die in 1926.

TILLINGHAST L'HOMMEDIEU HUSTON, 1915 TO 1922, AND COL. JACOB RUPPERT, 1915 TO 1939

"I never saw such a mixed-up business in my life," Col. Jake Ruppert complained right off the bat. "Contracts, liabilities, notes, obligations of all sorts. There were times when it looked so bad no man would want to put a penny into it. It was an orphan club without a home of its own, without players of outstanding ability, without prestige."

It was a team whose average annual attendance was 345,000. Subpar seasons at the gate and on the field were a way of life. But Jake Ruppert, the man they would later call the "Master Builder in Baseball," would change all that.

A friend of Ruppert, Tillinghast L'Hommedieu Huston was a big-bodied, self-made man who began his working career as a civil engineer in Cincinnati. He was a captain during the Spanish-American War and went on to make a fortune bringing the sewerage system and harbor of Cuba into the modern age. He was called "Cap" or "the Man in the Iron Hat" because of his derby hat, which was generally crumpled. The hat matched his suits, always crumpled and rumpled.

Ruppert, on the other hand, was born into wealth and an heir to millions. The son and grandson of beer tycoons who founded the Ruppert breweries, he was an aristocrat all the way. He inherited the brewing company Knickerbocker Beer from his father

A serious-looking Tillinghast L'Hommedieu Huston, one of the first owners of the New York Yankees and one of the great baseball names.

and became president of the business in 1915, the same year he purchased the Yankees. He was also president of Astoria Silk Works. His personal fortune was estimated at $50 million.

In the beginning of his ownership time, Ruppert, the "Prince of Beer," wanted to rename the Yankees "Knickerbockers" after his best-selling beer. The marketing ploy failed. He could not get approvals from the American League. Additionally, it was said, the name was too long for newspaper headlines. Years later it would be short enough for basketball's New York Knickerbockers.

The challenge to turn around the Yankees was enormous, but both new owners were more than up to the challenge. They had deep pockets, a great deal of business acumen and many important connections. And both were beguiled by baseball and making money.

Early on, Ruppert lost almost as much money as was paid to purchase the Yankees. But the team gradually improved on the playing field, finishing fifth in 1915 and fourth in 1916, its first time out of the second division since 1910.

As a beer baron, Ruppert was hands-on for every aspect of his business. That same behavior pattern transferred over for him and the New York Yankees. He had a personal and deep interest in each player. He knew them all and was always up-to-date on their capabilities, shortcomings, foibles and performances. However, the Yankee owner rarely hung out "with the boys," Rud Rennie wrote in the New York Herald-Tribune. "For the most part, he was aloof and brusque. . . . He never used profanity. 'By gad' was his only expletive."

The Colonel's idea of a wonderful day at the ballpark was any time the Yankees scored 11 runs in the first inning, and then slowly pulled away. "Close games make me nervous," he

said. The Colonel was also fond of saying, "There is no charity in baseball, and I want to win every year." With that goal in mind, he went on to create what became known as the "Ruppert effect." Members of his team received first class treatment. For the Yankees, this especially showed itself in the sleeping accommodations he arranged on trains. Most other teams gave players berths, upper or lower, dependent on seniority. The players on the New York Yankees all slept in upper berths. The whole traveling operation generally took up two cars at the end of the train. And there was many a summer day that players, wearing only underwear, lounged about, engaging in long conversations, playing cards and enjoying each other's company and the food; rest and recreation made them perform better on the playing field.

In 1919, now hitting his stride as the driving force behind the New York Yankees, Jacob Ruppert made arguably the best purchase in baseball history. He acquired George Herman "Babe Ruth" from the Red Sox. That deal transformed the Yankees into the first great dynasty in American sports. With the Babe in pinstripes, the "Ruppert Rifles," as some called them, would win seven World Series championships and 10 pennants during an 18-year span.

The Colonel bragged, "They're coming out to see me in droves." From 1920 to 1922, the Yankees, with G. H. Ruth on board, drew more than three million fans into the Polo Grounds. The New York Giants had never drawn a million fans in a season. Astonished, angered and annoyed at the great success of Babe Ruth and Company, the Giants informed the Yankees that they were no longer welcome as tenants at the Polo Grounds and should look around for other baseball lodgings.

The Yankees had been playing in the shadow of the Giants at the Polo Grounds since 1913. Now all

the glamour and glitz, the power and pop, had moved over to the Yankees. With Ruppert's team outdrawing the Giants in their own ballpark, it was an embarrassment to the proud National League franchise.

Ruppert and Huston's first reaction was a suggestion to the New York Giants that the Polo Grounds be demolished and replaced by a 100,000-seat stadium. It was a visionary idea. The new playing field then could be used by both teams and also host other sporting events. The Giants, however, were not interested. They were not even interested in collecting the $65,000 in annual rent from the Yankees. They were only interested in seeing the end of the American League team in their ballpark as unwelcome tenants.

So Ruppert and Huston began the adventure of creating a new and novel ballpark, the greatest and grandest edifice of its time, one to be shaped along the lines of the Roman Coliseum. "The Yankee Stadium," as it was called at the start, was envisioned as a structure that exuded a feeling of permanence lacking in many big league parks. Unlike the builders of older ballparks, the Yankee owners would not fit their fields of play into the contours and configurations of city streets. They planned to place their structure on open land.

One idea was to build a stadium or an amphitheater over the Pennsylvania Railroad tracks along the West Side near 32nd Street. The War Department nixed the idea because that space was reserved for anti-aircraft gun emplacements. The Hebrew Orphan Asylum, at Amsterdam Avenue and 137th Street, was a serious contender for the new ballpark site. A contract was actually drawn up, but the deal fell through. A lot in Long Island City in Queens was also given some consideration. Nothing happened.

Finally, Ruppert and Huston settled on a former lumberyard in the west Bronx, City Plot 2106, Lot 100, a

Yankee owner Jake Ruppert, fourth from left, with Governor Al Smith to his right on April 18, 1923, Opening Day, the first game played in the new stadium.

10-acre mess of boulders and garbage. The cost for the land obtained from William Waldorf Astor's estate was $675,000. It was located directly across the Harlem River from Coogan's Bluff and the Polo Grounds. That was one of the major reasons Ruppert chose that site, knowing how it would irritate his former landlord. Another plus was that the IRT Jerome Avenue subway line snaked its way virtually atop the stadium's right-field wall, providing ease of transportation for fans.

The land had been a farm owned by John Lion Gardiner prior to the Revolutionary War.

JOE FLYNN: *It was all farmland. It was beautiful. You could get fresh milk and vegetables there.*

But critics blasted Jake Ruppert for his location choice, which was not at all close to the center of New York City. Some called the concept "Ruppert's Folly," claiming that fans would never venture to a Bronx-based ballpark. "They are going up to Goatville," barked John J. McGraw, manager of the Giants. "And before long they will be lost sight of. A New York team should be based on Manhattan Island."

The Yankees put out a press release indicating the new stadium was to be shaped like the Yale Bowl, that towering battlements enclosing the entire park would make it impossible for those without tickets to see any of the baseball action, just the way Jake Ruppert liked it.

The determined "King of Beer" and co-owner Huston moved ahead with their plans. Osborn Engineering Company of Cleveland, Ohio, was responsible for the design. The building

of the ballpark would be done by the White Construction Company of New York. A demanding taskmaster, a man who was used to getting the results he wanted, Ruppert insisted the ambitious project be completed "at a definite price" of $2.5 million, be built in just 185 working days and be up and running by Opening Day 1923.

It would actually be completed in a record 184 days. Some 500 men turned 45,000 barrels of cement into 35,000 cubic yards of concrete. Bleachers were constructed out of 950,000 board feet of Pacific Coast fir that came to New York by boat through the Panama Canal. The mainly solid concrete structure, with its massive triple-deck stands—the first ever—would have 60,000 seats.

"Ruth Field" was a name many suggested for the edifice. It was argued that his powerful presence and performance as a Yankee made the

Opening Day 1923, Colonel Ruppert and President Warren Harding in the stadium's brand-new box seats.

entire concept possible. Ruppert rejected the idea. He wanted to have the new playing field named for himself and his best-selling "Ruppert beer." That idea was resisted. His fallback position was "The Yankee Stadium." It would be the first ballpark to be called a stadium.

While some argued with the nickname "The House That Ruth Built" for Yankee Stadium, it was in truth "The House That Was Built for Ruth." It was situated so that the late-afternoon Bronx sun would set in left field, not right field, sparing the Sultan of Swat the glare that would hamper him.

On May 5, 1922, ground was broken. Sixteen days later, Ruppert would buy out Huston's share of the Yankees for $1.25 million ($17,360,840 in today's dollars). "Cap" Huston had done his thing—supervising all aspects of the building. Some said Huston's knowledge of construction was why Ruppert partnered with him to purchase the Yankees and build a ballpark. Whatever, there were no tears shed for Huston, who made a nifty profit on his original investment.

On April 18, 1923, a massive crowd showed up for the proudest moment in the history of the South Bronx. It was Red Sox versus Yankees. Boston owner Harry Frazee walked on the field side-by-side with Yankee mogul Jake Ruppert. The teams followed the marching beat of the Seventh Regiment Band, directed by John Phillip Sousa, to the center field flagpole, where the 1922 pennant and the American flag were raised. Many wore heavy sweaters, coats and hats. Some sported dinner jackets. The announced attendance was 74,217, later changed to 60,000. More than 25,000 were turned away and some lingered outside in the cold listening to the sounds of music and the roar of the crowd inside the Yankee Stadium. And Colonel Jacob Ruppert, proud as a peacock, boasted: "Yankee Stadium was a mistake—not mine, but the Giants."

In 1929, it was Ruppert who came up with the idea of numbers on the uniforms of Yankee players. "Many fans," he explained, "do not attend games on a regular basis and cannot easily pick out the players they have come to see."

Truly one of the most significant figures in New York Yankees history, Jacob Ruppert deserves all credit given to him. A fixture at his Yankee Stadium, which he insisted on keeping so immaculate that sometimes he even swept it himself, Ruppert had a private box. He invited the celebrities of the day to join him there. He was not an owner, though, who came to the park to be seen. His interest was in seeing his team triumph.

His two dozen years as Yankee owner saw him build the team from a rag-tag and near-moribund franchise into a baseball powerhouse. He was the man who not only built Yankee Stadium but also the Yankee Empire, who transformed a baseball franchise that was stumbling to one that was soaring. His building blocks included hiring gifted Hall of Fame managers like Miller Huggins and Joe McCarthy; coming up with the vision and then executing the plan for the fabled Yankee Stadium; putting in place executives like business manager Ed Barrow and farm director George Weiss to "mind the store" that was the New York Yankees; and to acquire the franchise players for the Yankees through trade, purchase or from their fabled farm system.

The star of stars and the engine behind Ruppert's Yankees was Babe Ruth. The Colonel was the only one to conduct salary negotiations with the "Sultan of Swat," sometimes in the "Prince of Beer's" brewery office, sometimes in Florida. George Herman Ruth was a valuable commodity and the Yankee owner treated him as such. The pair disagreed at times privately and publicly about contracts; nevertheless, Ruppert and Ruth were personal friends with a relationship that some described as love-hate.

Frugal to a fault, Ruppert gave orders to the Yankee front office to always monitor Babe Ruth's expenses. Incredibly, deductions from Ruth's salary were made for a $3.80 train ticket for Mrs. Ruth and a $30 "uniform deposit."

In the 1930s and 1940s, Yankee Stadium was rented by the Black Yankees of the Negro National League when the Yankees were on the road.

MONTE IRVIN: *I played there as a member of the visiting Newark Eagles. It was being on hallowed ground. But we didn't get into the Yankee dressing rooms. We all had to dress together with the Black Yankees in the visitor's dressing room.*

The Yankees of New York ruled baseball as the 1930s neared its end. Normally vigorous, the Yankee owner who was sitting on top of the world, Ruppert attended just two games at Yankee Stadium during the 1938 season. He followed his beloved Yankees from his sickbed, listening to games on the radio for the first time. The medium so influenced him that he arranged for all Yankee home games to be broadcast on radio. That was his last official act for the franchise.

On Friday morning, January 13, 1939, the 71-year-old suffered a heart attack, slipped into a coma and passed away. Ruppert's death ended a 24-year ownership of the team and ended an era. At the time of his death, the Yankees were valued at $7 to $10 million dollars, underscoring Jake Ruppert's incredible impact on the franchise.

Babe Ruth was one of the last to see the Yankee owner in his hospital bed before he died. The funeral was held at St. Patrick's Cathedral. Public dignitaries, political big shots and more than 500 Ruppert employees, fans and

family were part of the assemblage. Also in attendance were Lou Gehrig, Babe Ruth, Yankee manager Joe McCarthy, general manager Ed Barrow, farm system director George Weiss, members of the 1939 Yankees including Tommy Henrich and Johnny Murphy, chief scout Paul Krichell, Boston Red Sox manager Joe Cronin, Chicago White Sox manager Jimmie Dykes and star players like Honus Wagner and Eddie Collins. More than 10,000 people were outside the cathedral. Honorary pallbearers included a who's who of the baseball, business and political worlds.

The estate left by Jacob Ruppert was initially valued at $40 million and later corrected to around $6 million, and a vast part of it went to three women. Three equal shares went to two nieces and a former chorus girl, Helen Winthrop Weyant, 37. She lived on 55th Street in Manhattan with her mother. Described in newspapers as a "ward," as "formerly a chorus girl," and by *The Sporting News* as "a former showgirl friend," Weyant claimed she had met the Colonel about 14 years before his death. She told reporters that she had "no idea why he left her so much money."

JACOB RUPPERT ESTATE, 1939 TO 1945

The actual operation of Jacob Ruppert's two principal businesses, the brewery and the ball club, was turned over to a board of directors with Ed Barrow as president and George Weiss and Ruppert's brother George as members. The Yankees functioned nicely under that operation. There were reports, however, that the brewery was mismanaged.

The estate itself began having difficulty. It needed funds in order to pay estate taxes. Their only option at the time was to sell.

DANIEL TOPPING, DEL WEBB AND LARRY MACPHAIL, 1945 TO 1964

With bragging rights to 15 pennants and 10 World Series titles in 20 seasons, it is doubtful that any baseball franchise will ever best the record of owners Daniel Topping and Del Webb, who along with Larry MacPhail, acquired the Yankees in 1945 from Jacob Ruppert's estate for $2.9 million. MacPhail was bought out in 1947.

Topping and Webb's Yankees went on to win six of the next seven World Series and 10 of the next 16, including five straight from 1949 to 1953. Their Yankee teams made up arguably the greatest dynasty baseball has ever seen, with multiple Hall of Fame players and managers spread over 20 seasons.

The millionaire Webb was born in Fresno, California, in 1899. After MacPhail departed, Webb shared equal partnership of the New York Yankees with the millionaire Dan Topping, who was born in 1912 in Greenwich, Connecticut. Webb's business acumen enhanced his image as one of baseball's movers and shakers. Although neither had worked closely with a business partner before, and Webb was a Westerner and Topping was an Easterner, they had a pretty easy rapport and division of power and influence on the Yankees. The day-to-day operations and workings of the team were handled by Topping. Webb watched out for Yankee interests by being very involved in American League matters.

Topping and Webb ended their run as owners in August 1964, selling the Yankees to CBS. Topping and Webb divided up the $11.2 million sale price. In 1945, they had purchased the Yankees for $2.9 million, so they had quite a ride financially and franchise-wise.

CBS, 1964 TO 1973

On November 26, 1964, CBS paid $11.2 million for 80 percent ownership of the New York Yankees. Webb and Topping kept minority ownership shares for a time. The network had made a $41 million profit the year before. The purchase of the Yankees seemed to fit into its plans to remove cash off its books by diversifying holdings.

The owner of five stations outright, the most allowed by federal law, CBS also had bragging rights to 250 affiliates. Focusing on entertainment properties and putting money in Broadway shows, CBS turning to purchase the Yankees seemed a natural progression of what they were doing. Unfortunately, the best-laid plans of mice and men, and CBS, did not work out. At the outset, the media giant was excited about the Yankees, who had incredibly been in the World Series 14 of the previous 16 seasons. But sadly and truthfully, CBS looked upon the Yankees as another holding in its business portfolio.

In eight seasons under CBS ownership, the Yankees would finish as high as second place only once. The fabled franchise would finish lower than fourth place five times. Yankee Stadium attendance dropped under one million for the first time since 1945. It was truly a ride down the elevator shaft, a fall from grace for the Yankee Empire.

At the January 1973 press conference at which Steinbrenner was announced as the new owner, CBS executive Michael Burke said, "I think CBS suffered some small embarrassment in buying a club at its peak and then having it fall. The bottom fell out. The Yankees no longer fit comfortably into CBS's plans."

PAUL DOHERTY: *The story was that Burke was fired; he actually resigned a few months after Steinbrenner bought the team due to incompatibility with "the Boss." Gabe Paul took over as president and eventually as GM. Burke remained as a limited partner and eventually was bought out completely by Steinbrenner.*

GEORGE STEINBRENNER, 1973 TO 2010

On January 3, 1973, an investment group headed by George Steinbrenner purchased the New York Yankees from CBS. "I won't be active in the day-to-day operations of the club at all. I can't spread myself too thin. I've got enough headaches with my ship building company," he said.

That was short-lived. The tumultuous time of the man they called "the Boss"—and he was all of that—was a merry-go-round of managerial (23 managers in 20 seasons) and general manager changes (11 times), of highly publicized and expensive free agent signings.

The 1970s had many marker dates for the Steinbrenner Yankees. One was New Year's Eve of 1974. Free agent pitcher Jim "Catfish" Hunter signed on for five years. That move by Steinbrenner opened the gates for the cash flow out of the team's treasury and into wallets of other free agent stars. "The Boss" got a lot of flak. The Yankees were put down by critics as "the best team money could buy."

When Steinbrenner bought the Yankees in 1973, the team had already won 20 championships but hadn't won a World Series in a decade. By contrast, Steinbrenner's ownership of the Yankees spanned seven championships,

11 American League pennants and two dynasties. The outlandish and controversial Bronx Zoo era (1977–1981) was a time of two world championships and three World Series appearances. It was also a time of feuds with players, inflated egos and headline-grabbing comments by "the Boss."

Then there were George Steinbrenner's illegal campaign contributions to Richard Nixon's presidential campaign. There was the suspension from baseball for consorting with small-time gamblers. There was the alleged fight with two Dodgers fans in an elevator in a Los Angeles hotel. George Steinbrenner said he enjoyed "creative turmoil," and there was plenty of that. He also said, "A ship that sails on a calm sea gets nowhere." His experience with the Yankees proved that. Most of the time, his Yankee ship was never on a calm sea, and most of the time it got where it needed to go to the delight of its fans and the consternation of its opponents.

In 2009, the new Yankees Stadium opened, a tribute to the perseverance and imagination of George Steinbrenner. With a seating capacity of 52,325, located one block north of the original stadium, the exterior pre-cast facade evoked the original Yankee Stadium with a replica of the original copper frieze. When the Yankees moved to the new Yankee Stadium, a new Monument Park was built beyond the center field fences. Everything was transported over. Monument Park, established in 1974–1975 during the makeover of the original Yankee Stadium, housed the flagpole and a collection of monuments, plaques and retired numbers to honor distinguished members of the Yankees. When the stadium was originally built, the flagpole was in play, over 450 feet from home plate to the left of straightaway center field. After manager Miller Huggins's death, a monument dedicated to him was positioned in front of the flagpole. That started the whole tradition and celebration of Yankee lore and legends. George Steinbrenner took great pride in the franchise's history and heritage.

"The Boss" was at the first game in 2009 at the new stadium, smiling and signing autographs, in his glory. A little more than a year later, on July 13, 2010, in Tampa, the day of the 81st All-Star Game, 80-year-old George Steinbrenner suffered a massive heart attack and died. His New York Yankee teams during his 38 years as their iconic owner had racked up more victories than any other team in baseball. He had lived out his creed: "Winning is the most important thing in my life, after breathing. Breathing first, winning second."

HAL STEINBRENNER AND HANK STEINBRENNER, 2008 TO PRESENT

Hal Steinbrenner, George's son, took over the running of the team as owner in 2008. He is principal owner, managing general partner and co-chairman. "It's a different world [than] it was 15, 20, maybe even 10 years ago," he said in 2016 after Yankee veterans were traded away for young talent. "There's a lot of teams out there that now have the wherewithal to spend money on the free agents. . . . There's a lot of competition, where my dad, there was less."

Hank Steinbrenner is part-owner and co-chairman of the New York Yankees. He is the older of the two brothers by about 13 years.

A very young Joe DiMaggio and Yankee owner Jake Ruppert. One was at the start of his becoming a legend and the other was near the end of a fabled run as owner of the New York Yankees, 1930s.

Two

LEGENDS, LEADERS AND LUMINARIES

*The Babe, the Iron Horse, Marse Joe, Joltin' Joe, the Old Perfessor, Donnie Baseball,
Mr. October, Mr. November, A-Rod and more*

- Mel Allen ... 34
- Red Barber ... 36
- Ed Barrow ... 37
- Hank Bauer ... 39
- Yogi Berra ... 39
- Chris Chambliss ... 42
- Spud Chandler ... 43
- Hal Chase ... 43
- Jack Chesbro ... 44
- Roger Clemens ... 44

- Jerry Coleman ... 46
- Earle Combs ... 47
- Frank Crosetti ... 48
- Bill Dickey ... 48
- Joe DiMaggio ... 49
- Bob Fishel ... 51
- Whitey Ford ... 52
- Lou Gehrig ... 53
- Lefty Gomez ... 54
- Joe Gordon ... 55
- Goose Gossage ... 56
- Ron Guidry ... 56
- Tommy Henrich ... 57

- Ralph Houk ... 58
- Elston Howard ... 60
- Waite Hoyt ... 62
- Miller Huggins ... 63
- Catfish Hunter ... 65
- Reggie Jackson ... 66
- Derek Jeter ... 68
- Wee Willie Keeler ... 69
- Charlie Keller ... 69
- Paul Krichell ... 70
- Tony Kubek ... 70
- Tony Lazzeri ... 71
- Eddie Lopat ... 71
- Sparky Lyle ... 72
- Larry MacPhail ... 74
- Mickey Mantle ... 76
- Roger Maris ... 79
- Billy Martin ... 80
- Hideki Matsui ... 81
- Don Mattingly ... 82
- Joe McCarthy ... 83
- Bob Meusel ... 84
- Thurman Munson ... 85
- Bobby Murcer ... 85
- Johnny Murphy ... 86
- Graig Nettles ... 86
- Paul O'Neill ... 87
- Joe Page ... 88
- Gabe Paul ... 89
- Herb Pennock ... 89
- Andy Pettitte ... 90

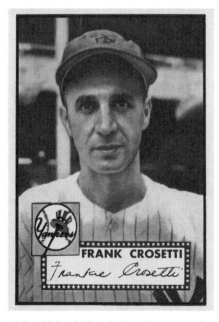

Collectible baseball card of Frank Crosetti, who had 37 straight seasons as player and coach in a Yankee uniform.

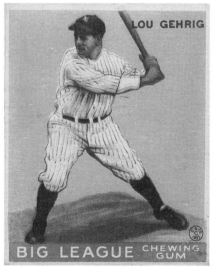

1933 baseball card of Lou Gehrig, the first Yankee to win the Triple Crown.

(Continued)

Baseball card of MVP Wee Willie Keeler, who in 1903 earned the highest salary in baseball, $10,000.

Baseball card of Mickey Mantle, of whom Casey Stengel said, "I never saw a player who had greater promise."

- Lou Piniella ... 90
- Jorge Posada ... 91
- Willie Randolph ... 91
- Vic Raschi ... 92
- Allie Reynolds ... 92
- Bobby Richardson ... 93
- Dave Righetti ... 93
- Mariano Rivera ... 94
- Phil Rizzuto ... 95
- Alex Rodriguez ... 98
- Red Rolfe ... 99
- Red Ruffing ... 99
- Babe Ruth ... 100
- George Selkirk ... 103
- Bob Shawkey ... 103
- Pete Sheehy ... 103
- Bob Sheppard ... 105
- Bill Skowron ... 107
- George Steinbrenner ... 107
- Casey Stengel ... 109
- Mel Stottlemyre ... 112
- Dan Topping ... 113
- Joe Torre ... 114
- Del Webb ... 115
- George Weiss ... 116
- Bernie Williams ... 118
- Dave Winfield ... 120

Stars galore, luminaries without limits, leaders excelling—all of this has been part and parcel of the Yankee magic and mystique. An entire book could be devoted to this subject, as these legendary individuals have through the decades been the backbone of the franchise's success. Consider what follows as a star-studded sampling.

MEL ALLEN

"I guess I was in the right place at the right time."   *—Mel Allen*

I had the very good fortune in 1990 to visit the legendary Mel Allen at his home in Greenwich, Connecticut. I was there to collect memorabilia for the "Stars of David: Jews in Sports" exhibit that I was the curator and executive producer for at the Klutznik Museum in Washington, D.C.

My wife, Myrna, came along with me, and Mel had his sister Esther at the ready. I had driven out from Long Island in my Toyota Celica. The thinking was that I would spend a few hours, collect whatever Mel Allen offered and go back home. It wound up as a virtually all-day affair. My car was too small and the time was all too brief.

Talking sports, talking Jews in sports, receiving precious photos, artifacts, guides, record books and magazines—I was so impressed with the warmth, kindness and intelligence of Mel Allen. His hospitality and that of his sister, who provided the food and beverages, was a kindly gesture to strangers in their midst.

When I was growing up in Brooklyn, his was the "voice" I had listened to those long-ago summer days and nights that so splendidly spun the tales of New York Yankee baseball. It was that pleasing Southern voice that got me interested in writing about sports, especially baseball, especially the Yankees.

At the top of his game as a broadcaster, Mel Allen received in excess of a thousand letters a week. The son of Russian Jewish immigrants, born in Johns, Alabama, near Birmingham on February 14, 1913, he enrolled at the University of Alabama at age 15. The highly intelligent and ambitious Allen

Some lucky fan took this marvelous snapshot of Babe Ruth at bat, 1926.

is Mel Allen!" He created nicknames: "Joltin' Joe" DiMaggio, "Scooter" for Phil Rizzuto, "Old Reliable" for Tommy Henrich and many more.

Allen's signature phrase, "How about that!" originated in 1949, when Joe DiMaggio slammed three home runs in three games coming back from a severe heel injury. Each DiMaggio home run call was punctuated by Allen with a "How about that!" The exclamatory phrase caught on with the Yankee audience and became a battle cry for top Yankee plays and also home runs. "Going, Going, Gone!" was Allen's trademark call for a homer, and his description of a four-bagger as "Ballantine Blasts" and "White Owl Wallops" was a nod to sponsors.

went on to earn degrees in political science and law and passed the bar. And he joked, "I took a class with the great football coach Bear Bryant and earned all A's. I was absent all the time."

Remaining close to home, working as a speech instructor and covering football for a radio station in Birmingham, Allen went to New York City in 1936 with friends for a Christmas vacation break. On impulse, he stopped at CBS for an audition. The rest, as they say, is history.

By 1939, he was announcing home games for the network of the New York Giants and New York Yankees. By 1940, he held forth as the main voice on radio and then TV for the Yankees. His incredible time in the Yankee booth started in the sad days of the end of Lou Gehrig and ended in the final failing days of the Yankee Empire of the 1960s. If you were a fan of the Yankees, chances were you loved him. Chances were that if you were anti-Yankee, you were anti-Allen.

EDDIE LOPAT: *He was accused of being prejudiced for the Yankees. One year we won thirty-nine games in the seventh, eighth and ninth. He had to get riled up.*

JERRY COLEMAN: *I worked with Mel Allen, who was the personification of the great broadcast voice. He was magnificent in what he did and how he did it. And he could talk forever.*

DON CARNEY: *Mel was the "Voice of the Yankees." He changed the whole style of broadcasting. Announcers before Mel were pretty much straight reporting than dramatizing events. He lived and breathed baseball, and he made fans feel what he felt.*

The articulate and enthusiastic Mel Allen brought the game to millions in a cultivated, resonant voice. He began broadcasts with "Hello, everybody, this

MONTE IRVIN: *Mel Allen had that golden voice. We thought he used to root more than anybody. Red Barber did less rooting. Mel was strictly a homer, but he was a truly fine announcer.*

Hall of Fame broadcaster Mel Allen was known for his signature phrase "How about that!"

Allen's resume included announcing 20 World Series and 24 All-Star Games, being there for nearly every major Yankees event: Joe DiMaggio's 56-game hitting streak in 1941 at the stadium, Mickey Mantle's tape-measure shots, Roger Maris and his quest for 61 home runs. Allen had introduced Lou Gehrig at his July 4, 1939, farewell and Babe Ruth at his sad final Yankee Stadium appearance in 1948.

Suddenly, strangely, when the 1964 season ended, the great "Voice of the Yankees" was let go by the team.

MEL ALLEN: *They never even held a press conference to announce my leaving. They left people to believe whatever they wanted—and people believed the worst.*

RED BARBER: *He gave the Yankees his life and they broke his heart.*

Pained, angered and confused, Mel Allen moved into the shadows for a time, and disappeared from public view and consciousness. But then he returned. In 1965, he announced for the Braves in their last season in Milwaukee. He broadcast Cleveland Indians games in 1968, called 40 Yankee broadcasts annually on SportsChannel from 1978 to 1985. He had a long run starting in 1977 as the voice of *This Week in Baseball*. And he became the host of the MSG Network program *Yankees Magazine* in 1986.

It was George Steinbrenner who was generally credited with bringing him back into the Yankee family, hiring Allen to do games on cable TV and emcee special events at Yankee Stadium. "The minute I bought the Yankees," Steinbrenner said, "I wanted to know where Mel Allen was and I immediately brought him back to the organization."

PAUL DOHERTY: *Mel's return to the Yankees organization actually occurred six years before George's arrival in January 1973. His first return to the Yankees was to call the Old-Timers' Day Game on the field at the stadium in 1967. After the return, Mel came back to the stadium to do the play-by-play on field for most all of the Old-Timers' Day games for the next two decades. He also received a nice pat on the back from the Yankees brass when they had him call Mickey Mantle from the dugout on Mantle Day, June 9, 1969. So his exile from the Yankees didn't last very long.*

The long broadcasting run of Mel Israel Allen came to an end on June 16, 1996. The "Voice of the Yankees" was finally stilled. He passed away at his home in Greenwich, Connecticut. The heart trouble that had afflicted him for several years was the cause of death. Fittingly, the 83-year-old Mel Allen had just finished watching a Yankee game on television.

RED BARBER

"Red was perhaps the most literate sports announcer I ever met." —Vin Scully

Walter Lanier "Red" Barber passed away at the age of 84 from complications after emergency surgery on October 22, 1992. His 33-year career as a play-by-play broadcaster had many acts, most notably as the top man announcing Brooklyn Dodgers baseball for 15 years and then as part of the Yankee team with Mel Allen for a dozen seasons.

The "Old Redhead," the pride of Brooklyn, had his relationship with "Dem Bums" severed when he was fired or resigned in 1953. One story that circulated was that Barber's outlandish salary demands triggered his departure. Another was that he was too critical of the team at times in his calls.

No matter. The Yankees scooped him up quickly and paired him with Mel Allen, the most famous sports announcer anywhere. The two men had contrasting styles but they worked well, even complemented each other, though their personalities and approaches were very different. Allen was hot, and Barber was cool. Both would be the first broadcasters inducted into the National Baseball Hall of Fame's broadcasting wing.

The new announcing job with the Yankees was quite a comedown for Barber after 20 years as the main man in Cincinnati and then in Brooklyn. It was in Brooklyn that he introduced such folksy expressions like "tearin' up the pea patch [winning streak]," "rhubarb [fight]" and "catbird seat [being in charge]." Barber's role with the Yankees was pregame and postgame shows on televised home games, working a few innings of play-by-play. He traveled with the team occasionally. Despite the downsizing, the soft-spoken Southerner accepted his role. "Mel," Barber said, "accepted me as an equal. He could not have been nicer to me either then or all through the years we worked together."

When Barber joined the Yankees, many of the colorful expressions he had used broadcasting Dodgers games belonged mainly to the past: "Oh-ho, Doctor! [Wow oh, wow!]," the home run call—"Back, back, back, back, back, back." He was more restrained, more objective, and highly accurate, even though he was no longer the "main man."

In 1966, the Yankees were owned by CBS and were a dismal last-place team. During a home game on Thursday, September 22, the first for CBS executive Mike Burke as team president, only 413 fans were scattered around the huge ballpark. It was a makeup game against the White Sox that most thought would be rained out. The TV cameramen were under strict instructions from CBS media relations not to transmit images of foul balls into empty seats. Red Barber, truthful to a fault, described the scene on air. A week later, Red Barber was invited to a breakfast meeting. Burke snapped out the news that the legendary announcer would not have his contract renewed for 1967. In the space of just a couple of seasons, two incredible baseball announcers were let go by the Yankees. It was a sad time for those who appreciated the great narratives of Yankee baseball they had provided.

PAUL DOHERTY: *Mike Burke inherited the Red Barber situation, a situation made apparent long before this ill-attended game versus the White Sox. Dan Topping [who had just sold his interest in the Yankees completely to CBS] left it for Burke to deal with as Red's option was coming due at the '66 season's end.*

A non-renewal of Barber's contract was also pushed by the head of broadcast for the Yankees, Perry Smith, a former NBC executive, and a big Joe Garagiola backer [Joe Garagiola had joined the Yankees as Mel Allen's replacement for the 1965 season]. Red's bitterness over former-athletes-as-announcers did him in, nothing else. His testiness on air with fellow broadcasters Garagiola and Phil Rizzuto won him no fans within the organization, let alone with his fellow announcers and Smith.

Nevertheless, the "Old Redhead" kept busy in the post-Yankee years, authoring seven books and many articles and reviews, and serving as a voice in a few documentaries. In 1981, he joined National Public Radio's Morning Edition as a regular commentator.

Red Barber was another of my inspirations—listening to him spin the story of Brooklyn Dodger and then New York Yankee baseball made me love and understand the game, and write about it. Through the early years of my writing sports books, Red Barber was a constant. I called on him perhaps more than I should have for interviews and to read, review and supply blurbs for my work. He always came through. I am in his debt.

Walter Lanier Barber had quite a run, broadcasting thirteen World Series and four baseball All-Star Games, and hosting so many other major sports events. He was there when Jackie Robinson broke the color barrier in 1947, when Roger Maris hit the 61st home run in 1961 and through all the marker events before and after those.

RED BARBER: *"I worked day and night to learn my business and I respected it to the end. I didn't win 20 games or hit .350, but I worked harder at my trade than any announcer I knew about."*

ED BARROW
"The Yankee Empire Builder."

Before Ed Barrow came over from the Boston Red Sox in 1920 as business manager—read general manager—the Yankees had never won a pennant. They won their first in 1921. Barrow, at 52, was a man who had held virtually every executive position in baseball. He would be the engine driving the Yankee dynasty. It was back in 1894 that he began in baseball, teaming up with Harry Stevens to operate concessions for the Pittsburgh Pirates. From that humble beginning, he served in all kinds of executive baseball positions: minor league manager, owner, president of the Eastern League. "Cousin Ed" and "Cousin Egbert," as some called him, managed the Red Sox to a world championship in 1918. He also had some help from a young and talented southpaw pitcher whom he converted to an outfielder, George Herman Ruth.

Barrow and Yankee owner Jacob Ruppert were driven men and made a terrific team. It was the beer baron owner who cheerfully signed off on one of Barrow's first significant moves, hiring Red Sox coach Paul Krichell as a Yankee scout who would become a major figure in the creation of one of the top baseball scouting systems in all of baseball. Under Barrow, the Yankees had arguably the top assemblage of scouts in place at one time. Outworking, trumping the competition, Barrow's scouts identified top minor league players and made offers to owners of the teams they played for that were difficult to turn down.

It was the business and baseball partnership of Ruppert-Barrow that elevated the Yankees of New York above all the competition. In the 1930s, Ruppert wanted and Barrow created the biggest and best farm system in baseball. It was to Barrow's credit, and his ability to delegate, that he picked George Weiss to run the farm system empire.

Ed Barrow had instincts for doing and saying the right thing. As Miller Huggins was told early on by Barrow: "You're the manager, and you'll not be second guessed by me or the owner. Your job is to win; mine is to get you the players you need. I'll make the deals—and I'll take full responsibility for every deal I make."

Barrow was a man who frowned on ballpark promotions and looked down on night baseball. The industrious Barrow held sway over all things New York Yankees. Working out of both Yankee Stadium and his office on 42nd Street in Manhattan, Barrow, if not the most liked of men by his rivals, nevertheless had their respect. He sat in his mezzanine box observing all that took place on the field. If there was anyone doing what he was not supposed to do—lolling around,

Business manager Ed Barrow, one of the great Yankee builders, created the biggest and best farm system in baseball.

chairman of the board and stripped of most of his powers.

In 1947, Edward Grant Barrow retired. It was the end of nearly a quarter century of success as the Yankees' top guy, the first Yankee executive to win The Sporting News Major League Executive of the Year Award.

In 1950, "Ed Barrow Day" was staged at Yankee Stadium. In 1953, Barrow was elected to the Baseball Hall of Fame. And in 1954, a plaque honoring him was dedicated at Yankee Stadium.

In his tumultuous time as king of the hill with the Bronx Bombers, Ed Barrow was called many things, but the phrase that fit him best was "The Yankee Empire Builder."

snoozing, eating—"Cousin Egbert" got on the phone. Yankee order had to be maintained. And Barrow was an expert in blending profanity with annoyance and using questions like, "What the hell do you think we are paying you for?"

Ed Barrow was born in a covered wagon in Springfield, Illinois, on May 10, 1868. A boxer in his youth, he still had the fighter inside him. He was also quick to use his fists, and angered quickly. Innovative and bold, and always involved, Barrow went into places his peers shied away from.

When others were fearful of giving minor league second baseman Tony Lazzeri a chance because he was an epileptic, Barrow was not. Despite the price tag of $50,000 and five players, lots of money back then, the Yankee boss man opted for Lazzeri. Some teams shied away from Joe DiMaggio because of a knee injury, dubbing him damaged goods. Barrow took the chance.

The Yankee 1927 world championship team featured many top-drawer players—first baseman Lou Gehrig, catcher Pat Collins, second baseman Tony Lazzeri, shortstop Mark Koenig, outfielders Bob Meusel and Earl Combs, pitcher Wilcy

Moore—all on the recommendations of Ed Barrow's scouts. Bill Dickey, Joe DiMaggio, Frank Crosetti, Lefty Gomez and more would literally follow the pathway of the stars to the Bronx.

Ed Barrow was the power behind the New York Yankee dynasties of the 1920s, 1930s and 1940s—a fabulous time for the team, winners of 14 pennants and 10 World Series. But in 1939, the end of a Yankee era took place. Jacob Ruppert passed away. Barrow was moved up to the role of team president by the executors of the estate and also still ran the organization as general manager.

"This was a great day for me," the man once known as "Cousin Egbert" said, beaming. "And I must say that I was proud. Mrs. Barrow and I had an extra cocktail that night before dinner." Jacob Ruppert had been dead for four days.

In 1945, Ruppert's heirs sold the Yankees to Larry MacPhail, Dan Topping, and Del Webb. Barrow was appointed chairman of the board. However, he and the new owners had many differences. Now 76, considered very old-school, at odds with the new ownership on various matters, Barrow was kicked upstairs, given the title of

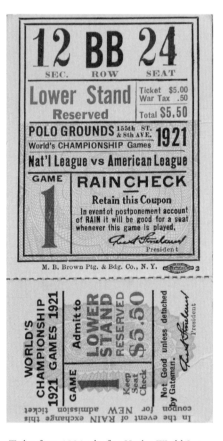

Ticket from 1921, the first Yankee World Series, won a year after Ed Barrow joined the team as business manager.

HANK BAUER

"Bauer taught me how to dress, how to talk—and how to drink." —Mickey Mantle

Hank Bauer was born in East St. Louis, Illinois, on July 31, 1922. The tough and gritty Bauer was a Marine in the Second World War and saw action in the battle of Okinawa. "We went in with 64," he recalled, "and six of us came out." He won quite a few battle stars for his combat in the Pacific.

Signing with the Yankees after the war, the rugged Bauer climbed up the minor league rungs. In late 1948, he was promoted from Kansas City. He was 26, old for a rookie. Busting it in one game in the outfield, which was his way, he took notice of center fielder Joe DiMaggio glaring at him in a not-too-friendly manner.

"Did I do something wrong?" a puzzled Bauer asked.

"No, you didn't do anything wrong," DiMaggio responded. "But you're the first son of a bitch who ever invaded my territory."

Bauer never invaded the Yankee Clipper's territory again.

Casey Stengel often platooned him in the outfield. "I didn't like it," Bauer said. "But there wasn't much I could do about it. He was the boss. Later on I finally realized he probably prolonged my career a couple of years." His favorite expression was "Don't mess with money!" When he saw a teammate he thought was not putting out as much effort as he believed was required, Bauer used that phrase as a wakeup call. A Yankee for 1,406 games spread over a dozen seasons, a three-time All-Star and one of Casey Stengel's favorites, Bauer didn't make mental mistakes and became testy when his teammates did.

Hank Bauer's time with the Yankees ended in 1960 when he was shipped off to Kansas City in a big trade that brought Roger Maris to the Yankees. It ended a Yankee career that spanned the

Outfielder Hank Bauer (right) and manager Casey Stengel (left). Even though Stengel often platooned him in the outfield, Bauer recognized that it probably prolonged his career a couple of years.

end of the DiMaggio era through the rise of Mickey Mantle.

"Dependable," "selfless" and "honed in" were just a few of the ways he was described. Famed cartoonist Willard Mullin chose Henry Albert Bauer, who had a rugged handsomeness, as the model for the prototypical Yankee. Oddly enough, Hank Bauer does not have a plaque in Monument Park.

YOGI BERRA

"Mr. Berra is a very strange fellow of very remarkable abilities." —Casey Stengel

"Talking to Yogi Berra about baseball, is like talking to Homer about the gods."
—Bart Giamatti

The kid who grew up in St. Louis eating banana sandwiches with mustard ended up being one of the legends of New York Yankees baseball. Born on May 12, 1925, Lawrence Berra was raised in "The Hill," the Italian section of St. Louis. One of his neighbors and friends was future big league catcher and broadcaster Joe Garagiola.

Berra's parents were Italian immigrants. His father was a bricklayer

and construction worker. The young Berra dropped out of school without completing the eighth grade. The story was he needed to work to help support his family financially. Of course, in his spare time he played American Legion baseball.

There are many versions that have been passed down explaining how Lawrence Peter Berra came by the nickname "Yogi." The Baseball Hall of Fame is on record with this one. After attending an afternoon movie that showed a "yogi" practicing yoga, his friend Jack Maguire noted how his buddy resembled the "yogi." Maguire said: "I'm going to call you Yogi." And as it turned out, so did millions of others.

Berra could have played for the St. Louis Cardinals, but Branch Rickey blew it. After a tryout, he offered Berra a $250 bonus, unsure whether the youngster was big league material. His friend Joe Garagiola, Berra knew, was offered $500. For the canny Berra, it worked out well, as most things in his life did. He waited for a better offer. Enter the Yankees and $500. His first stop was the Norfolk Tars of the Class B Piedmont League. There, at age 18, Yogi briefly left organized baseball and enlisted in the Navy. "I was just a young guy doing what he was supposed to do back then, joining the Navy, serving my country, fighting the war. I wasn't a baseball player on that boat. I was a sailor."

As a second-class seaman on a six-man rocket boat, Berra took part in the D-Day invasion at Omaha Beach and manned a machine gun providing cover fire. He also served in North America and Europe and was awarded a Purple Heart.

With the war over, Berra was assigned in 1946 to a team in New London, Connecticut, for a few games and then it was up to the top Yankee farm team, the Newark Bears of the International League. In 77 games, splitting time between catcher and outfield, he batted .314 with 15 homers, and batted in 59 runs. The Yankees had seen enough. They called him up.

As the story goes, the first day Berra came into the Yankees clubhouse, he was in his Navy uniform. The clubhouse manager barely took notice of him. He "didn't even look like a sailor, no less a Yankee player," said the clubhouse manager. When Larry MacPhail, Yankee president, spotted him for the first time, he was also was not very impressed with

the 5-foot-7 squat rookie. MacPhail said Berra reminded him of "the bottom man on an unemployed acrobatic team."

Perhaps it was because of comments like these that Berra played in overdrive. In his first Major League game in 1946, he slammed a home run. The next day he hit another one. He started that way and never let up. Although he shared time as Yankee catcher with others, he batted .280, slammed 11 home runs, and drove in 54 runs in 1947, his rookie season.

Dogged, driven, determined and highly capable, the young Berra showed off what he was made of and what he would become in a game against the St. Louis Browns in 1947. An inexperienced catcher, he jumped out for a bunted ball, tagged the batter and tagged the runner coming home from third on a squeeze play. "I just tagged everything in sight, including the umpire," he explained.

Manager Casey Stengel fell in love with him right from the start, calling him "Mr. Berra" and "my assistant manager." When Stengel was asked why Yankee pitching was so excellent, he replied: "Our catcher, that's why. He looks cumbersome, but he's quick as a cat."

In 1949, Stengel's "quick as a cat"

catcher and "assistant manager" broke a finger. No matter. Berra played a part of that season with one finger outside of his catcher's mitt. Berra began the practice that would be adopted by most catchers.

The great Bill Dickey, a Yankee coach and former legendary catcher, put in much time with Lawrence Peter Berra. As his mentor and his pupil observed, uttering what would become one of his most famous "Yogi-isms," "Bill is learning me all his experiences." Yogi was a very quick learner, and he went on to become an accomplished heads-up catcher. A celebrated bad-ball hitter, Berra swung at quite a few balls that were not strikes. He smashed them anyway.

PHIL RIZZUTO: *I saw him hit them on the bounce; I've seen him leave his feet to hit them.*

"He had the fastest bat I ever saw," said his one-time Yankee teammate Hector Lopez. "He could hit a ball late, that was already past him, and take it out of the park. The pitchers were afraid of him because he'd hit anything, so they didn't know what to throw. Yogi had them psyched out and he wasn't even trying to psych them out."

He was a remarkable clutch hitter, highly intelligent and durable, incredibly productive. He was the engine, the force, the constant. He was always somehow obscured by the Yankee legends he played with. But Yogi had the goods.

The stats are truly amazing. A three-time Most Valuable Player, Berra caught 14,387 innings, 1,699 games behind the plate, throwing out almost half of those who attempted to steal on him. He had ten straight seasons with at least 20 home runs. Five seasons he recorded more home runs than strikeouts. From 1947 to 1965, Yogi

One-of-a-kind Lawrence Peter Berra, the son of Italian immigrants, never finished eighth grade but has more memorable quips than anyone in baseball history.

averaged about 500 at bats a season, never striking out more than 38 times each year. He played in 15 straight All-Star games, on 14 pennant winners and on 10 world championships, more than anyone in history. Known as "Mr. World Series," Mr. Yogi holds records for games played (75), at bats (259) and hits (71) and is tied with Frankie Frisch for the record in doubles (10). "Mr. Berra" for his career batted .285, slammed 358 home runs and batted in 1,430 runs. Incredibly, he averaged just fewer than 5.5 strikeouts per 100 at bats and whiffed just a measly 414 times in 2,120 games. Berra played 15 seasons in which he took 300 plate appearances and received MVP votes in every one of them, once putting together a six-year run of MVP finishes of first, fourth, second, first, first and second. He is one of two players who hit 350 home runs without striking out 500 times. The other is Joe DiMaggio.

As the decade of the 1950s passed into history and another took its place, Yogi Berra was in his middle thirties, a tough time for most catchers. Talented backstop Elston Howard was the future. Casey Stengel realized that, as did Yogi. Always a team player, Berra returned to the outfield, winning two more World Series rings and playing the outfield more than he caught.

In 1964, his momentous and remarkable playing career over, Berra replaced Ralph Houk as Yankee pilot. It was a team that had a great deal of talent and had ripped off a string of four straight pennants. But for Berra and his players, there were lots of struggles for a good part of the season. Rumors made the rounds that Yogi was disrespected by some of his players.

It was dog days of August. The Yankees had dropped four straight to the White Sox and 10 of their last 15 games. They were on a bus headed to the airport.

PHIL LINZ: *I sat in the back of the bus, which was stuck in heavy traffic. It was a sticky, humid Chicago summer day. I was bored. I pulled out my harmonica. I had the Learner's Sheet for "Mary Had a Little Lamb." So I started fiddling. You blow in. You blow out.*

Yogi Berra came from the front of the bus and told Linz to tone it down. There was a slap directed either at Linz or the harmonica or both. Whatever the slap was directed at, that incident was a game changer for the Yankee season. Berra got new respect. Linz was elevated to starting shortstop due to injuries to Tony Kubek.

The "Harmonica Incident" momentum propelled the Yanks to a 22–6 record in September, victory in a close pennant race over the White Sox. The only negative was a seventh game World Series defeat at the hands of the Cardinals. That cost Berra his job. Many, however, claimed the Yankee legend was already on the way out when the "Harmonica Incident" took place, no matter how the season finished.

Bounce-back-Berra, never out of work for long, moved on to the woeful Mets in 1965. Casey Stengel was the manager, and at the very tail end of his storied career. By 1969, Stengel was gone, replaced by Gil Hodges as manager. Yogi Berra was still in place as the first base coach. The "Miracle Mets" defeated the Reds in the World Series and became the darlings of New York City baseball.

In 1972, when Gil Hodges died, Berra became manager. In 1973, he brought the Mets within a game of winning another world championship. In 1975, restless management pulled the trigger on their manager. On August 6th, with the Mets in third place, and the team having lost five straight, Yogi Berra was fired.

Resilient and reliable, the workaholic Berra bounced back again as a Yankee coach in 1976. In 1984, George Steinbrenner moved him up as manager, replacing Billy Martin, another dizzying move in a revolving door of Yankee pilots over those years. The 1984 Yankees went 87–75 under Berra, good enough for third place. Steinbrenner reportedly told Berra in spring training in 1985 that he was his manager that season no matter what happened.

"No matter what happened" was forgotten as "the Boss," after just 16 games of the season had passed, said, "Goodbye, Yogi" and "Hello again, Billy Martin."

More than the firing by Steinbrenner, what really infuriated Berra was that Steinbrenner sent general manager Clyde King to deliver the news of the termination. Hurt and disgusted with the Yankee owner, the prideful Berra announced he would never return to Yankee Stadium as long as George Steinbrenner ran the show. The promise was kept for fourteen years. Berra was not even there in 1988 when plaques honoring him and Bill Dickey were added to Monument Park.

Rapprochement finally was effected in 1999. Steinbrenner visited Berra in New Jersey and apologized, bringing the great Yankee back into the family. Reports were that "the Boss" told Berra: "I know I made a mistake by not letting you go personally. It's the worst mistake I ever made in baseball."

I had two meetings with the unassuming and lovable Lawrence Peter Berra. One took place in the late 1980s, when he was a coach for Houston, working for his friend, Astros owner John McMullen. I was interviewing for my autobiography of Nolan Ryan. Entering the Astrodome very early, thinking no one else would be there, I moved into the dugout to organize myself for pregame interviews. Yogi Berra was already there, sitting silently, looking odd in the outlandish Crayola uniform of the Astros. We greeted each other and then he uttered a Yogi-ism: "You know, if it rains, we won't get wet." He had gotten off much better ones, but I laughed and agreed with him. We talked a little baseball and then got on with our day.

I didn't think of reminding him of another time we had met in a different dugout—at Shea Stadium in 1975—when he managed the Mets. That time my publisher had given me a letter that said something about extending all professional courtesies to "Dr. Harvey Frommer" (a reference to my PhD). Yogi had looked at the letter, smiled and said, "It's always good to have another doctor around. People get sick. What can I do for you?"

He did so much for me and for so many others through all those Yogi Berra seasons. Number 8 was part of the "greatest generation"—real, wise, human, talented, truly one of a kind.

Accolades and honors deservedly came Yogi Berra's way. He was elected into the Baseball Hall of Fame in 1972. And his plaque in Monument Park, the ceremony for which he didn't attend, carries the line: "It ain't over 'til it's over."

It was over for him at age 90. He passed away on Tuesday, September 22, 2015, the 69th anniversary of his Major League debut. The man is gone, but not his words.

SELECT YOGI-ISMS

JERRY COLEMAN: *Yogi got four hits in four at-bats in a game. The next day he was upset looking at the box score that listed him going 3–5. He was told that it was a typographical error. "Bullshit," Berra said. "It was a clean single up the middle."*

- *"I never said most of the things I said."*
- *"A nickel ain't worth a dime anymore."*
- Asked if Yoo-Hoo chocolate drink was hyphenated, he allegedly replied, *"No, ma'am, it isn't even carbonated."*
- *"If you can't imitate him, don't copy him."*
- *"It ain't over 'til it's over."*
- *"Nobody goes there anymore because it's too crowded."*
- *"You can observe a lot just by watching."*
- *"You've got to be very careful if you don't know where you are going because you might not get there."*
- *"We made too many wrong mistakes."*
- *"Baseball is 90 percent mental. The other half is physical."*
- *"How can you hit and think at the same time?"*
- *"I always thought that record would stand until it was broken."*
- *"If people don't want to come out to the ballpark, how are you going to stop them?"*
- *"I'm a lucky guy and I'm happy to be with the Yankees. And I want to thank everyone for making this night necessary."*
- *"It's like déjà vu all over again."*
- *"Never answer an anonymous letter."*
- *"The future ain't what it used to be."*
- *"If you don't know where you are going, you might wind up someplace else."*
- *"Pair up in threes."*
- *"Why buy good luggage? You only use it when you travel."*
- *"Bill Dickey is learning me his experience."*
- *"I don't know. They had bags over their heads."*
- *"I'm not going to buy my kids an encyclopedia. Let them walk to school like I did."*
- *"In baseball, you don't know nothing."*
- *"It ain't the heat, it's the humility."*
- *"I think Little League is wonderful. It keeps the kids out of the house."*
- *"So I'm ugly. I never saw anyone hit with his face."*
- *"Take it with a grin of salt."*
- *"The towels were so thick there I could hardly close my suitcase."*
- *"You should always go to other people's funerals, otherwise they won't come to yours."*
- *"When you come to a fork in the road, take it."*
- *"I usually take a two-hour nap from 1 to 4."*
- Introduced to Ernest Hemingway at Toots Shor's and told he was a writer, Berra asked: *"What paper do you work for?"*
- *"I never blame myself when I'm not hitting. I just blame the bat, and if it keeps up I change bats. After all, if I know it isn't my fault that I'm not hitting, how can I get mad at myself?"*

CHRIS CHAMBLISS

"For a while it was strange picking up the papers and seeing my name on top in RBIs. I'm more used to seeing my name ninth or tenth among the leading hitters."

—Chris Chambliss

He was steady, calm, classy: a man who sharply stood apart from the hyper, conceited teammates he played with in the time of the Bronx Zoo. Acquired from Cleveland on April 27, 1974, Chambliss was a Yankee dandy for only six seasons. He is not forgotten and neither is his graceful southpaw swing and his hitting the ball where it was pitched.

The stocky athlete was a model of reliability. Chambliss was a key component of Yankee pennant winners in 1976, 1977 and 1978, when he drove in a minimum of 90 runs each season. The native of Dayton, Ohio, hit .304 in 1975 and began a string playing in 150 or more games for four straight seasons.

He was an All-Star in 1976, and worked at becoming the top defensive first baseman in the American League. He was a Gold Glove winner in 1978.

Perhaps the most memorable moment for Chris Chambliss came in the last game of the 1976 championship series against Kansas City. His homer put the Yankees into the World Series against Cincinnati and gave the Yankees their first American League championship in a dozen years.

In his time as a Yankee, Chambliss recorded 954 hits and 79 home runs. In the 1990s, the classy Chambliss became a Yankee as batting coach and was key in helping the Yanks cop four world championships in five seasons.

SPUD CHANDLER

"He's got five pitches. He's got that fastball. He's got the curve. He's got the slider. He's got the fork ball. He's got the screw ball. You can call for any one of them at any time."
—Bill Dickey

His mouthful full name was Spurgeon Ferdinand Chandler. He was born September 12, 1907, in Commerce, Georgia. He spent his growing-up years working on a farm. A terrific all-around athlete, Chandler played baseball and football at the University of Georgia. He signed with the Yankees, turning down opportunities to play professional football.

It took him until May 6, 1937, to make his big league debut. He was 29 years old. The winning hurler in the 1942 All-Star Game, Chandler pitched two complete game victories in the 1943 World Series against the Cardinals, yielding but one run. He was the first and only Yankee pitcher ever to win the MVP award.

The 1943 season was Chandler's year of years. Recording 20 complete games and 5 shutouts, he yielded just 46 earned

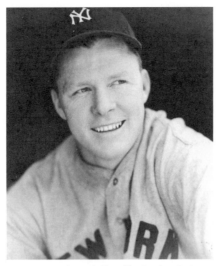

Spurgeon Ferdinand Chandler, Yankee Stalwart hurler, was the first and only Yankee pitcher ever to win the MVP award.

runs in 253 innings. Chandler led all American League pitchers in victories, complete games and shutouts. He had a glittering 1.64 ERA, the lowest in the American League in 24 years.

Chandler enlisted early in the 1944 season for military duty, returning a couple of years later. In 1946, he won 20 games for the second time, and posted a 2.08 ERA. He was 39 years old.

A four-time All-Star and a three-time World Series champion, Chandler notched 26 career shutouts, compiled 109 wins and a .717 winning percentage. No wonder Bill Dickey was so impressed with him.

HAL CHASE

"Could he really have existed, or was he perhaps invented by Robert Louis Stevenson, along with the Master of Ballantrae, Long John Silver and the good Dr. Jekyll? Hal Chase is remembered as a shining, leering pock-marked face, pasted on a pitch-dark soul; there is some evidence to say that he appeared in the flesh, but I lean more toward the invention theory." —The Bill James Historical Baseball Abstract (2003)

An enigma, a celebrated and talented baseball player, an unsavory character—all of these were labels that characterized Hal Chase. He was born in 1883 and grew up in the Santa Cruz Mountains, a place where his father operated a sawmill. He excelled in baseball in the minor leagues, and the Highlanders signed him to a contract.

His big league debut was April 14, 1905. From the start, he stood out from the rest and was dubbed "Prince Hal" because of his elegant bearing. It was standard practice back then for first basemen to stand on the bag and be ready for throws. Playing off the bag, Chase was adroit enough to charge bunts, tag runners and throw out a runner attempting to advance a base. He could field. He could hit. He had a lively personality, and he was his own man. All of that contributed to making Hal Chase both a popular and a controversial figure.

Baseball card of Hal Chase, who had a reputation for consorting with gamblers and was banned from baseball for life for being involved in the Black Sox scandal.

There were claims that he threw games and bet against his own team. He was charged with being involved in the Black Sox scandal, which resulted in his being banned from baseball for life. His reputation for consorting with gamblers prompted fans to chant, "What's the odds?" And Yankee manager Frank Chance griped: "He's throwing games on me." *The Sporting News* claimed: "He can play first base as it never was and perhaps never will be played is a well-known truth. That he will is a different matter."

But the record also shows that Chase was one of the most popular players of his time and that he revolutionized the way first base was played; he still ranks high on the all-time Yankee stolen base list and set various fielding records. What he did around first base at times was fairly amazing. On September 21, 1906, he tied the Major League record for putouts by a first baseman in a nine-inning game with 22. In two other games, he had 21 putouts.

Captain of the Yankees from 1909 to 1912, Harold Homer Chase, one of the first of the long run of Yankee stars, batted .284 in 1,059 games for the Highlanders/Yankees from 1905 to 1913. He brought fans to their feet with his fielding around first base. Both Babe Ruth and Walter Johnson selected Chase as the best first baseman. Warts and all, he had the goods.

JACK CHESBRO
"Happy Jack"

He was the starter (and loser) for the first game played by the New York Highlanders/Yankees on April 22, 1903, yet he ended the season as a 21-game winner.

Stocky, out of North Adams, Massachusetts, Chesbro was known as "Happy Jack" because of his pleasant ways. He was a mainstay of the Highlander hurler crew from 1903 to 1909.

"Happy Jack" Chesbro, Yankee early days pitching legend, was the first pitcher to win 40 games in the modern era.

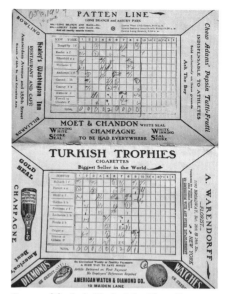

Scorecard for Jack Chesbro's "wild pitch" game, October 10, 1904, first game of a doubleheader.

His stardust-filled season was 1904. It is the best one he ever had, one of the best any pitcher ever put together. Chesbro was the master of a spitball (it was a legal pitch then) that he said he could make a ball drop from 2 to 3 inches to more than a foot and a half. That pitch was his bread and butter, and caviar, too.

Chesbro explained the pitch as the "most effective ball that possibly could be used." That 1904 season he won 41 games, pitched 48 complete games in 51 starts, 454 innings, and to boot the right-hander posted an amazing 1.82 ERA. He was the first pitcher to win 40 games in the modern era.

His dream season unfortunately turned into a nightmare on its last day. His team was in need of a sweep of a doubleheader with Boston to claim first place. Chesbro, shooting for his 42nd win, took the mound in the first game. Charged with a wild pitch with two out in the ninth inning, Chesbro was blamed for the loss that gave the American League pennant to the Red Sox. It was said he was haunted

by the wild pitch for the rest of his career and was never the same pitcher. Nevertheless, in 1946, John Dwight Chesbro was admitted into the Baseball Hall of Fame.

ROGER CLEMENS
"Rocket is remarkable." —Joe Torre

"Roger is in another world when he's pitching. He's there, but he's not there." —Derek Jeter

He came to the Yankees from the Blue Jays in a trade involving David Wells on February 18, 1999. His Major League debut was back on May 15, 1984, with the Boston Red Sox and he was a big part of the rivalry between the two teams.

Clemens was quoted in the *New York Times*: "He is the one who gave me a chance to get to the World Series. This is where I wanted to be all along. We had a couple of nice offers from other teams, but I tied my agents' hands. I told them I wanted to be a Yankee."

BRADFORD TURNOW: *He had to wear uniform number 12 when first arriving to the Yankees because his longtime number 21 was worn by Yankees legend Paul O'Neill. By mid-season, he switched to number 22.*

From the beginning, before each start he made at Yankee Stadium, Roger Clemens would exit the bullpen, wipe the sweat from his brow and gently touch the head of Babe Ruth while passing his monument. That was the ritual that helped him get good luck and connect with the glory of Yankee times past, he explained.

Yankee fans who had hated him, loved him. Red Sox fans who had loved him when he starred for their team, hated him. "It's been said before," sportswriter Sean McAdam wrote. "But it's true: For Red Sox fans, watching Clemens thrive as a Yankee is the equivalent of watching your ex-wife marry your sworn mortal enemy—then live happily ever after."

Imposing on the mound and off it, 6-foot-4 and 220 pounds, Roger Clemens had all the equipment: a nearly unhittable forkball, a four-seam fastball, a slider. And perhaps best of all, he was a throwback to old-time pitchers—he had no compunction about firing his 95 mph fastball inside if he had to.

BRADFORD TURNOW: *But after many years, it was the splitter that Clemens relied on most when he needed it. Batters would see the pitch as a fastball and then realize after it was too late the pitch was indeed a splitter that dropped out of the zone and buckled their legs as they swung away. Too many batters were embarrassed to be swinging at a pitch that usually ended up in the dirt, but it was Clemens who could disguise his splitter so well.*

The first of five World Series rings came to Clemens in 1999. The second one came in 2000, but what stays in the memory of so many is his performance in the ALCS. The Rocket was brilliant—a one-hit, 15-strikeout, complete game shutout at Seattle. It was the first complete-game one-hitter in ALCS history.

More fireworks were on parade a week later. In Game Two of the World Series, Clemens was a winner against the Mets, fanning nine in eight innings. His confrontation with Met catcher Mike Piazza in the first inning cast him in the role of one of the bad guys. A Clemens pitch shattered Piazza's bat. Clemens tossed the bat fragment in the direction of Piazza. Benches cleared; calm was restored. Clemens was fined $50,000 for what he did.

GAME CALL, GARY COHEN, WFAN: *"Broken bat, foul ball off to the right side. And the barrel of the bat came out to Clemens and he picked it up and threw it back at Piazza! I don't know what Clemens had in mind!"*

"When he threw the bat, I basically walked out and kept asking him what his problem was," recalled Mike Piazza. "He really had no response. I was trying to figure out whether it was intentional or not. I was going to ask him. If it was, then obviously he really had no response. I was more shocked and confused than anything."

"There was no intent," Clemens said at the post-game press conference. "I was fired up and emotional and flung the bat toward the on-deck circle where the batboy was. I had no idea that Mike [Piazza] was running. I guess it came close to him. I came back into the dugout and I said I've got to get control of my emotions and calm down."

The fire in the belly, the total into-the-game mentality was part of Roger Clemens's makeup as one of the best pitchers of his era. And he constantly strutted his stuff.

On April 2, 2001, on Opening Day for the Yankees, Roger Clemens passed Walter Johnson, becoming the American League career strikeout king. That season, he won his 15th straight game, setting a new Yankee record. He also turned heads by becoming only the second hurler in MLB history to start a season with 19 wins in his first 20 decisions.

"Rocket is remarkable; 19–1 is one thing," Joe Torre said. "But 39 years old is another thing. To still be the power pitcher, the dominant pitcher that he is, is remarkable."

In 2001, he led New York to their fourth consecutive AL pennant, posting a 20–3 record, fanning 213 and winding up the season with 280 career wins. On November 15, 2001, Roger Clemens won his record sixth Cy Young award. At 39-plus, he became the third-oldest recipient.

Roger Clemens, always with something on the ball, was a big part of the rivalry between the Yankees and the Red Sox.

Insight into Roger Clemens's work ethic, mind-set and the dedication to his craft comes from Sportswriter Bob Klapisch on ESPN: "If there's one iron-law in the Yankee clubhouse, it's that you won't find Roger Clemens at his locker days between starts. He's not signing autographs, he's not making TV appearances and he's certainly not in the players' lounge eating pizza. Instead, the Rocket is in the weight room, consumed by a four-day ritual that he's convinced has kept his elite-caliber fastball in the mid- to upper-90s, and has actually prolonged his career."

He lit up the scoreboard playing with the New York Yankees, but he excelled at his craft with other teams, too. All told, Roger Clemens won seven career Cy Young Awards, more than any other pitcher in the history of baseball.

Longevity, durability and excellence marked his 24-year MLB career. The best pitcher of his generation, one of the top hurlers ever, William Roger Clemens, however, is not enshrined in the Baseball Hall of Fame.

Jerry Coleman, known as "The Colonel," a true Yankee gentleman and American hero, was never the same ballplayer after returning from active duty in Korea in 1953.

BRADFORD TURNOW: *His reputation and image was tainted later in his career by charges of his use of Performance Enhancing Drugs [or PEDs]. It should be noted that even though Roger was accused of using PEDs, he never once tested positive for drugs and was found not-guilty on all 6 counts of lying to Congress in 2008. Though these shadows linger, it is hard to forget about the impact "Rocket" had on the Yankees and all of baseball during his playing career.*

JERRY COLEMAN

"The Yankees were not our team, they were our religion." —Jerry Coleman

He was hooked on baseball, he told me, from the time he could walk. In 1942, Coleman was signed off the California sandlots by the Yankees and sent to Class D Pony League, the Wellsville Yankees.

World War II interrupted his baseball career. He became a 19-year-old fighter pilot who, over three years, flew 57 bombing missions in campaigns over the Solomon Islands, Guadalcanal and the Philippines. Coleman was awarded two Distinguished Flying Crosses and seven Air Medals. When the war ended, in 1946, Coleman began to climb his way up through the Yankee farm system.

JERRY COLEMAN: *Spring training of 1948 I was trying to make the Yankees. I was the last man cut. I played for the Newark Bears in the International League and came up to the Yankees at the end of the season.*

On April 20, 1949, Coleman made his rookie debut as the regular Yankee second baseman. He led all who played his position in fielding that season through 1951. He was selected third as the Sporting News and Associated Press American League Rookie of the Year in 1949.

"The best second baseman I ever saw on the double play," according to his manager Casey Stengel, Coleman played nine seasons for the Yankees and with Phil Rizzuto formed a celebrated double-play combination.

Going north from spring training, we'd pass through small towns and people would be out there early in the morning as the train went by, waving to us. I don't know how they got the word, but we'd be having our breakfast in the diner and they'd be there.

Arguably Coleman's top season was 1950, when he batted a career best .287, and set a team record for double plays by a second baseman. An All-Star that 1950 season, the adroit infielder was the World Series Most Valuable Player.

In May 1952, Coleman was called back to active duty and transferred to Korea to the 323 Marine Attack Squadron. Flying 120 missions, earning six more Air Medals, he was promoted to the rank of lieutenant colonel.

The Yankees staged a day for him September 13, 1953, when he returned from active duty. Nearly 50,000 showed at the stadium. Back as a Yankee, the time in Korea had taken something out of him, as he admitted. Coleman was never the same ballplayer.

His playing career ended, the "Colonel" joined the Yankees front office after the 1957 season and then moved into the Yankees broadcast booth from 1963 to 1969. A member of six Yankee pennant winning teams, the man also graced baseball broadcast booths for decades. Jerry Coleman is the only Major League Baseball player who was in combat duty in two wars. He truly was an officer, a gentleman and a splendid baseball player despite losing so many seasons out of his nine-year Yankee career to military service for his country.

EARLE COMBS

"I think he was the best lead-off man of all time"   —Ed Barrow

Possessed of a great eye at bat and exceptional speed, Earle B. Combs was the table setter, the leadoff batter for the terrific Yankee teams of the 1920s and early 1930s. He averaged almost 200 hits and 70 walks a season during his prime.

Combs hailed from Pebworth, Kentucky, and it was when he was playing for and showing off his tremendous base-stealing skills at Louisville in the minors that the Yankees purchased his contract for $50,000.

Combs made his big league debut with the Yankees on April 16, 1924. In his first two dozen games, he batted .400. A fractured ankle sidelined him for the rest of the season. He came back to hit .342 with 203 hits and 117 runs scored for the seventh place 1925 Yankees.

In the minors, the former one-room-schoolhouse teacher was dubbed the "Mail Carrier" for his speedy ways on the base paths. Yankee skipper Miller Huggins told him: "Up here, we'll call you the waiter." Huggins was referring to his waiting for Ruth or Gehrig, Meusel or others to hit home runs.

Combs batted .299 in 1926 and each of the next eight seasons batted over .300. It was Combs who gave the '27 Yankee team the nickname "Five O'clock Lightning" for their late inning rallies. That season, the graceful Combs was first in the American League in hits with 231 and batted .356. His loyal fans presented him with a gold watch.

Earle Combs, one of the greatest Yankee center fielders, was considered a first-class gentleman for his poise and elegance.

A churchgoer, nonsmoker and nondrinker who never cursed, his poise, class and elegance set him apart from most of his contemporaries. Babe Ruth said of him: "Combs was more than a grand ballplayer. He was always a first-class gentleman. No one ever accused him of being out on a drinking party and you'd laugh at the words he used for cussing. Often he'd sit in his room and read the Bible, for he came from a strict mountaineer family. But Earle was all man, and a great competitor."

Combs especially excelled at World Series time, hitting .357 in 1926, .313 in 1927 and .375 in 1932. A line drive hitter, a deadly ball hawk in center field and a speed demon in the field and on the bases, Combs was part of 11 pennant-winning teams and nine World Series championships during his dozen seasons with the Yankees. The man they called "The Kentucky Colonel," the lefty-swinging Combs finished with 1,866 hits and a .325 batting average. The triple was his forte. He slashed three in a 1927 game, led the American League in triples three times and collected 154 in his career.

A fractured skull, sustained crashing into an outfield wall, changed him forever as a player. He played his final season as a Yankee in 1935. Then as a coach he passed on to rookie Joe DiMaggio all of his tricks of center field play.

When Earle Combs was inducted into the Baseball Hall of Fame in 1970, Arthur Daley wrote in the *New York Times*: "The gentleman from Kentucky will add a touch of class to the Hall of Fame."

Earle Combs said: "I thought the Hall of Fame was for superstars, not just average players like me."

Always self-effacing, the Kentucky Colonel was anything but average. He is yet another Yankee luminary who is not honored in Monument Park. After a long illness, Earle Bryan Combs died on July 21, 1976, in Richmond, Virginia, at age 77. Weary of receiving so many World Series rings, "he would take cameras and shotguns in their place," former Yankee third baseman Andy Carey remembered. "If he had only kept all the rings he would have had a small fortune."

FRANK CROSETTI
"The Crow"

Frank Peter Joseph Crosetti was born on October 4, 1910, in San Francisco. He would play shortstop for the Yankees for 17 seasons, from 1934 to 1948. He earned $8,000 in his rookie season and $500 less in his final season. All told, he earned approximately $173,000 as a player for the team from the Bronx.

The Yankees paid the San Francisco Seals $75,000 for his contract. He came to the Yankees on April 12, 1932, Babe Ruth's last year on the team. He stayed until 1968 as player and coach; all told, 37 straight seasons in a Yankee uniform—a team record.

Listed at 5-foot-10 and 165 pounds, Crosetti possessed much more strength than it appeared. His surprising power at the plate was reflected in the stat that four times he had double-digit home run seasons. Three times he paced American League shortstops in putouts and double plays.

A very heady player, always looking for any edge, he led the American League eight times in being hit by pitches. He was a threat on the baseball field in so many ways, even called the master of the hidden ball trick and one the great baseball sign-stealers.

His playing career done, Crosetti remained in place after 1948 as the Yankee third-base coach for 20 years, and participated in 15 more World Series. He made it clear: "I wouldn't manage for any amount of money. I have the best job in baseball right here, and my only ambition is to remain as third-base coach of the Yankees. Anyone who says different is nuts."

A baseball lifer, as player and coach for the New York Yankees, Crosetti was a member of 17 World Championship teams and participated in a record 23 World Series overall, from 1932 to 1964. His kind will probably never be seen again in any sport.

BILL DICKEY
"This boy will be better than Muddy Ruel, better than Wally Schang, better than any of them."   —Miller Huggins

The first of a fabulous fivesome of Yankee catchers that would include Yogi Berra, Elston Howard, Thurman Munson and Jorge Posada, Bill Dickey became a Yankee in 1928 and went on to become one of the greatest of catchers in the history of baseball. Early on, the right-handed thrower and left-handed hitter out of Bastrop, Louisiana, strained to show he belonged and tried perhaps a bit too much.

Shrewd Yankee manager Miller Huggins advised the highly praised 21-year-old rookie: "Stop unbuttoning your shirt on every pitch. We pay one player here for hitting home runs, and that's Babe Ruth. So choke the bat and drill the ball."

Oh, did the sweet southpaw swinger drill the ball. Eleven times he batted over .300, including .362 in 1936. An 11-time All-Star, Dickey's lifetime batting average was .313, with 202 career home runs and only 289 strikeouts in 6,300 at bats.

"A catcher must want to catch," Dickey said. He never played a single game at another position. The impressive southerner had a way with pitchers, and he had a strong and accurate throwing arm. He could hit but he was something else behind the plate. According to the Society for American Baseball Research, he led the league in putouts three times, assists twice and fielding percentage once.

Outwardly amiable, low-key, dubbed the "Man nobody knows" for his blandness, the rugged Dickey was one tough cookie. In 1932, Washington's Carl Reynolds of Washington slid hard into him at home plate. An

Bill Dickey, catcher extraordinaire, never played a single game at another position.

outraged Dickey socked Reynolds in the jaw, broke it and was given a 30-day suspension and a $1,000 fine.

After his illustrious playing career was over, Dickey settled into his role as coach from 1949 to 1957 and again in 1960, according to Yankees.com, all those seasons under Casey Stengel. In 1954, William Malcolm Dickey, who as player and coach was part of 17 Yankee pennant winners, was inducted into the Baseball Hall of Fame. "It was the nicest thing ever to happen to me," he said.

In one of baseball's most interesting ironies, the Yankees retired Uniform No. 8, worn by both Dickey and Berra, on August 21, 1988. The plaque honoring Dickey in Monument Park at Yankee Stadium reads: "First in Line of Great Yankee Catchers. The Epitome of Yankee Pride."

JOE DiMAGGIO

"Joe didn't sweat; he perspired."
—*Sportswriter Red Foley*

"I would like to take the great DiMaggio fishing, the old man said. They say his father was a fisherman. Maybe he was as poor as we are and would understand." —*Ernest Hemingway, The Old Man and the Sea*

The eighth of nine children, born to Rosalie and Giuseppe DiMaggio, a crab fisherman émigré from Sicily, on November 25, 1914, in Martinez, California, Joseph Paul DiMaggio was supposed to follow in his father's footsteps.

The youth had other plans that mainly concerned baseball. He honed his skills on the streets and playgrounds of San Francisco whenever he could and worked on hitting skills using a broken oar from a fishing boat.

In 1933, with the San Francisco Seals of the Pacific Coast League, DiMag hit safely in 61 straight games. The Yankees took notice. They also took more

Joe DiMaggio, always making it look easy, had his season of seasons in 1941 with his epic 56-game hitting streak.

notice when he hit .341 and injured his knee the next season.

Yankee scouts Joe Devine and Bill Essick, injury notwithstanding, recommended his signing and general manager George Weiss cut the deal—$25,000 and five players.

"You've bought yourself a cripple," Bill Terry of the New York Giants said. Was he ever wrong!

George Weiss said many times: "Getting him was the greatest thing I ever did for the Yankees." In the first game the young DiMaggio played, an exhibition contest, he collected four hits. Later in spring training his father sent him a telegram. "Come home, Joe. The fish are running. Give up this game of baseball. It is for loafers."

The 21-year-old's first Major League game took place May 3, 1936, at Yankee Stadium against the St. Louis Browns. In his first time at bat, he hit the second pitch into left field for a single. He had another single and then a triple to left field. The youngster DiMaggio played 138 games that rookie season: batted .323, with 29 home runs and 125 runs batted in.

MONTE IRVIN: *DiMag held the bat back, and didn't stride very much, maybe 4, 5 inches. I watched that. I became a pretty good hitter because I watched Joe. In later years I told him that I copied him.*

In DiMag's first four seasons (1936–1939), the Yankees were winners of four straight World Series; they also lost a total of just three Series games. A lot of that was the Joe DiMaggio impact.

As the seasons moved on, as the Yankee superstar became more secure, as he took pride in knowing that he was one of the greats of his era, he guarded his image, the way he looked, the way people looked at him. Silliness was out; seriousness was in. His highly polished shoes, the crafted fit of his impeccably tailored clothes, were integral parts of his package. Discipline, focus and extremely high standards in everything were paramount.

JERRY COLEMAN: *I was raised in San Francisco. I knew more about him than any player that lived. He was the god, the icon. He was it. He was baseball. My first spring training was '48. He was there. It was thrilling, the magnitude of the man. I didn't go up to him and say, "Hi, Joe, I'm so-and-so." Billy Martin tried to cozy up to him. That lasted about a week.*

PHIL RIZZUTO: *There was an aura about him. He walked like no one else walked. He was immaculate in everything he did. Kings of State wanted to meet him and be with him. He carried himself so well.*

Only his teammates saw him sit alone in front of his locker after the Yankees had suffered a tough loss or when he thought his performance in a game was below the standards he had set for himself.

A signed photo by Joe DiMaggio and Mickey Mantle; they played in the outfield together in 1951.

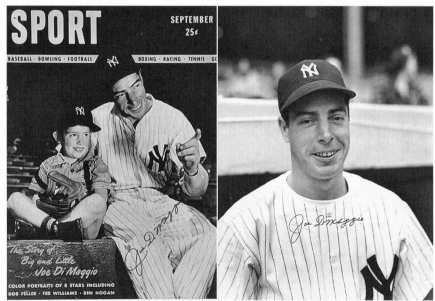

Joe DiMaggio signed cover of Sport *magazine, which did a feature story on him in 1946.*

In 1941, the great DiMaggio had his season of seasons. Batting .351, leading the league with 125 RBIs, he slashed 30 home runs. He also struck out a mere 13 times. But his incredible bragging rights that epic season was his matchless 56-game hitting streak.

Nothing made Joe happier than to do well in a big series and help the club win. He was a winner in the finest sense of the word. He was simply the greatest ballplayer I ever saw and it's not easy for a man to carry that burden. Joe carried it with class and dignity.

On February 7, 1949, the man they were calling "the Yankee Clipper" signed a contract for $100,000, the highest sum for a player in baseball history to that point in time.

The great *New York Post* sportswriter Jimmy Cannon wrote: "If you saw him play, you'll never forget him. No one ran with such unhurried grace. His gifts as an athlete were marvelous because they were subdued. Here was an outfielder who followed a fly ball with a deft serenity as though his progress had been plotted by a choreographer concerned only with the defeat of awkwardness."

"Joe did everything so naturally," Casey Stengel said, "that half the time he gave the impression he wasn't trying. He made the rest of them look like plumbers. I wish everybody had the drive he had. He never did anything wrong on the field. I'd never seen him dive for a ball, everything was a chest-high catch, and he never walked off the field."

Joe DiMaggio had a career average of .325, 361 home runs, eight World Series home runs, and two batting championships. He also won three Most Valuable Player awards. He was also named to the All-Star team every season he played.

One can only wonder what he would have accomplished if military service and injuries had not limited the great DiMaggio to just 13 years in pinstripes, a time the Yankees won 10 pennants and nine world championships.

A very young Mickey Mantle played in the outfield with Joe DiMaggio in 1951. In the World Series, Casey Stengel said to the "Mick," "Take everything you can get over in center. The Dago's heel is hurting pretty bad."

The Yankee Clipper's long home run brought fans to their feet in that World Series, and the Yankees won the '51 world championship. Not long afterwards, "the Dago" retired at age 36.

"I feel like I have reached the stage where I can no longer produce for my club, my manager and my teammates," he said. "I had a poor year, but even if I had hit .350, this would have been my last year. I was full of aches and pains and it had become a chore for me to play. When baseball is no longer fun, it's no longer a game."

Elected to the Hall of Fame in 1955, the Yankee Clipper passed away on March 8, 1999, at age 84.

BOB FISHEL

"He and his department handled everything from player interviews to Old-Timers' Day to the Yankees' annual yearbook to fan mail." —Paul Doherty

On the job as a Yankee official for two decades, just a shade over five feet tall, accustomed to wearing a white shirt and conservative tie, Bob Fishel more than capably manned all public relations details for the Bronx Bombers. He came to work in New York after stints with the Cleveland Indians, St. Louis Browns and Baltimore Orioles. In 1954, he joined the Yankees as public-relations director and rose to the vice presidency.

A bachelor, a man whose job was his life, the Cleveland-born Fishel was highly popular among past Yankee players and those who played for the team during his tenure. He was called a newspaperman's best friend if there was a need for anything Yankee.

In 1974, Fishel left the Yankees, becoming special assistant to American League president Lee MacPhail. He was promoted from that position to executive vice president. In 1981, the Robert O. Fishel Award was established and has been an annual honor given to the outstanding Major League publicist.

The legendary Bob Fishel passed away in 1988. The next year, the Yankee Stadium pressroom was renamed the "Robert O. Fishel Press Room."

Whitey Ford, "Chairman of the Board," the backbone of the Yankee powerhouse teams of the 1950s and 1960s.

Yankee Stadium from overhead in 1951, the year Mickey Mantle made his debut with the Yankees.

WHITEY FORD: *When I was nine years old, I went to my first Yankee game and sat in the center field bleachers. Growing up in Astoria, Queens, I'd be taken to Yankee Stadium by my father or my uncles. We'd sit in the bleachers. I never dreamed of pitching there. I wasn't even playing baseball. There were no baseball fields in Astoria.*

Out of high school, I pitched for the 34th Avenue Boys in Queens and we ended up winning the New York City Sandlot championship in 1946 at the Polo Grounds, right across the river from Yankee Stadium.

Yankee super scout, Paul Krichell, spotted the youngster playing first base at a tryout in 1946 and signed him to a contract, switching his position to pitcher. Krichell said, "I never saw a kid with a curveball like his. It just came natural to him."

WHITEY FORD

"I came here in 1950 and was wearing $50 suits. And I'm leaving wearing $200 suits, and I'm gettin' 'em for $80. So I guess I'm doing all right." —Whitey Ford

"If you had one game to win and your life depended on it, you'd want him to pitch it."
—Casey Stengel

Edward "Whitey" Ford was born in New York City 10 days before Halloween, 1928.

WHITEY FORD: *Teams were bidding for my services. I signed at the Stadium in the fall of '46 for $7,000. The Yankees were playing Philadelphia. Paul Krichell, the famous head of scouting, had me sitting in the front row there next to the dugout.*

"I want you to meet somebody," Krichell said. "He just came up from our Newark Bears farm team."

He says: "Larry Berra, this is Eddie Ford."

That was how Yogi and I were first introduced to each other. I never thought I would be pitching to him through all those great times.

Always a crafty southpaw, always a guy who was New York smart, Ford was also always nervy. As the story goes, Casey Stengel received a phone call telling him that his best chance of winning the pennant was to bring up Whitey Ford from the minors. Casey always insisted that it was Ford who made the call.

Brought up to the Yankees in June 1950, Ford won his first 9 decisions on his way to becoming the "Chairman of the Board," the backbone of the Yankee powerhouse teams of the 1950s and 1960s. With the native New Yorker doing his thing, the Yankees won 11 pennants and seven World Series.

BRADFORD TURNOW: *He was called "Whitey" because of his bright blond hair while in the minor leagues. Casey also liked to call him "Slick" or "Whiskey Slick."*

"I don't care what the situation was," his buddy Mickey Mantle said, "how high the stakes were—the bases could be loaded and the pennant riding on every pitch. It never bothered Whitey. He pitched his game. Cool. Crafty. Nerves of steel."

A stylish pitcher, a gifted all-around athlete, Ford rapped out 177 Major League hits. But it was what he did on the mound that the Yankees paid him for. He was into every game, every pitch that he threw at different speeds to different locations through 3,170 career innings.

"You kind of took it for granted around the Yankees that there was always going to be baseball in October," Ford noted. "I never had a lucky glove or a lucky uniform. A glove was nothing but a glove to me. They bronzed the glove I wore the day I broke Babe Ruth's scoreless inning World Series record, but I still don't know why. People think there's something special about the glove a pitcher wears, but I don't. The glove I had on that day was just another glove, that's all. The glove doesn't throw the ball."

Ford paced the American League in victories three times, in ERA and shutouts twice. He holds many World Series records, including 10 wins, 33 consecutive scoreless innings and 94 strikeouts. There were 45 career shutouts, eight 1–0 victories. He thrived on pressure.

Ford pitched for two Yankee managers: Casey Stengel and Ralph Houk. Casey often saved him to face the best competition and also rested him. Starting in 1961, Houk, not "saving" Ford, slotted him into the rotation and pitched him every fourth game.

"Whitey didn't begin cheating until late in his career," former American League umpire Bill Valentine confirmed. It was said he used his wedding ring and belt buckle to gouge into the baseball. "Elston Howard would make believe he had lost his balance and would go down in the dirt," Valentine said. "He would scratch up or muddy up the ball for Ford."

"I didn't cheat when I won the twenty-five games in 1961," the outspoken Ford let it be known. "I don't want anybody to get any ideas and take my Cy Young Award away. And I didn't cheat in 1963 when I won twenty-four games. Well, maybe a little. I never threw the spitter, well maybe once or twice when I really needed to get a guy out real bad."

On May 30, 1967, after getting off to a 2–4 start, Edward Charles "Whitey" Ford decided he had had enough. Enough was a golden resume:

16 seasons in pinstripes, 236 wins, the all-time Yankees leader in wins, innings pitched, strikeouts, shutouts, a Cy Young award in 1961, a .690 career winning percentage, best ever for pitchers with at least 200 wins and a career ERA of 2.74. Well-earned Hall of Fame admission came for him in in 1974.

LOU GEHRIG

"Gibraltar in cleats." —Jim Murray

"He just went out and did his job every day."
—Bill Dickey

He was born Heinrich Ludwig Gehrig II on June 19, 1903, in New York City to German immigrant parents of very modest means. He grew up excelling at the game of baseball. Playing for his Commerce High School team in a "national championship" game at Wrigley Field in Chicago, the 17-year-old clubbed a ninth inning grand slam home run. He earned the nickname "Babe Ruth of the Schoolyards."

Yankee super scout Paul Krichell was in the stands to watch a Columbia-Rutgers baseball game. "I did not go there to look at Gehrig," Krichell said. "I did not even know what position he played, but he played in the outfield against Rutgers and socked a couple of balls a mile. I sat up and took notice. I saw a tremendous youth, with powerful arms and terrific legs. I said, here is a kid who can't miss."

Gehrig's mother, who said, "Louie was always a good boy," protested to no avail. He gladly accepted the $1500 bonus the New York Yankees offered him. Early on he was viewed as a "mama's boy," reportedly a virgin, very uncomfortable in the presence of women, a young man who enjoyed fishing by himself for eels and living in an apartment with his parents.

As a Yankee he batted fourth in the powerful lineup behind Babe Ruth and wore Number 4 for his position in the batting order. Total opposites, Ruth and Gehrig would be the most feared one-two punch in baseball history. In 1927, they combined to slug 107 home runs—a quarter of the league's total production.

In 1927, Lou Gehrig was picked as the Most Valuable Player in the American League and the path ahead of him as superstar was clear. His .363 average in 1934 gave him the batting championship. There were 13 straight seasons of 100 RBIs, seven seasons of more than 150 RBIs. His power came from his big shoulders, broad back and powerful thighs.

A two-time MVP, a three-time home run king, a five-time RBI champ, Gehrig was the first Yankee to win the Triple Crown. His career batting average was .340. Three times he batted higher than .363. The powerful first baseman was a major part of seven pennant winners and six world championships.

"I had him for over eight years," manager Joe McCarthy said. "And he never gave me a moment's trouble. I

Lou Gehrig, Iron Horse, in a familiar pose; despite being diagnosed with a fatal disease at age 36, he considered himself "the luckiest man on the face of the earth."

guess you might say he was kind of my favorite. He came through in the clutch above all others."

On May 2, 1939, Wally Pipp, the player who Gehrig had replaced in the Yankee lineup those long years back, made the trip from his home in Michigan to watch a Tigers-Yankees game. Unbelievably, the Iron Horse, the highest paid player in all of baseball, had taken himself out of the lineup.

On June 19, 1939, the day of his 36th birthday, Lou Gehrig walked out of the Mayo Clinic in Minneapolis with a sealed envelope. The document inside read: "Mr. Gehrig is suffering from amyotrophic lateral sclerosis. This type of illness involves the motor pathways and cells of the central nervous system and in lay terms is known as a form of infantile paralysis. The nature of this trouble makes it such that Mr. Gehrig will be unable to continue his active participation as a baseball player."

In December 1939, the Baseball Hall of Fame waived the mandatory five-year waiting period for Lou Gehrig. On June 2, 1941, exactly 16 years to the day that he replaced Wally Pipp at first base, Gehrig passed away, and on

the Fourth of July 1941, a monument honoring him was erected in center field at Yankee Stadium.

LEFTY GOMEZ

"Gomez's zaniness set him apart from the decorous Yankees of the 1930s. He once held up a World Series game, exasperating manager Joe McCarthy (as he did with some frequency), to watch an airplane pass by."
—Writer Mark Gomez

"GOOF"—The license plate on his car

"El Goofo," "Goofy," "Singular Señor," "The Happy Hidalgo," "Yankee Doodle Zany," "Gay Castilian" and "Gay Caballero" were just a few of the nicknames attached to the fearless, fun-loving Vernon Louis Gomez out of Rodeo, California. He was all one-liners, quick quips, self-deprecating humor and wild antics.

"Maybe the name 'Vernon' that my folks gave me caused me to go off on tangents," Gomez said. "I never liked that name. And it wasn't my father's choice either. When I was born back in 1908, my Irish mother asked my Spanish father what I should be called. My father

"Iron Horse" Lou Gehrig poses with a lucky young fan, July 8, 1935, before the All-Star game.

Lefty Gomez, one of the great characters and pitchers in Bronx Bomber history, had four 20-win seasons.

bent over the cradle, took one look at me, and then said to my mother 'Let's call it quits.' Ma liked Vernon better."

The Yankees liked Vernon Gomez, too, so much so that they paid a hefty price of about $39,000 to the San Francisco Seals of the Pacific Coast League for the right to his services. His first full season for the New York team was 1931. His salary was $4,000. He was worth every penny, winning 21 of 30 decisions and pitching 17 complete games. It was the first of his four 20-win seasons.

It was manager Joe McCarthy who changed his pitching style from throwing sidearm style to a straight overhand delivery, transforming Gomez into one of baseball's top pitchers in the 1930s.

The tall and slight southpaw helped the Yanks win five American League pennants and world championships. Featuring a high leg kick and a dazzling fastball, Gomez was money in the bank for most of the 1930s for the Yankees. He was especially at the top of his game in All-Star play, five starts, three wins and

in World Series play—six wins and no losses with a 2.86 ERA.

Married to Broadway star June O'Dea, the zany southpaw, the happy-go lucky and amazingly outgoing Gomez was best of friends with the reserved, elegant superstar Joe DiMaggio.

The voluminous collection of Lefty Gomez one-liners included:

"The secret of my success was clean living and a fast outfield."

"I talked to the ball a lot of times in my career. I yelled, 'Go foul. Go foul.'"

"I'm throwing twice as hard, but the ball is getting there half as fast."

Third all-time in the Yankee record book in wins, second in complete games, fourth in shutouts and strikeouts among all Yankee hurlers, Gomez finished his career at 189–102. The Yankees gave him a plaque in Monument Park. Oddly enough, for a player of his accomplishments, his Number 11 is not retired.

In 1972, Vernon Gomez was admitted into the Baseball Hall of Fame. In his speech, he said, "I want to thank all my teammates who scored so many runs; Joe DiMaggio, who ran down so many of my mistakes and Johnny Murphy, without whose relief pitching I wouldn't be here."

JOE GORDON

"The greatest all-around player I ever saw, and I don't bar any of them, is Joe Gordon." —Joe McCarthy

The scenario was one that had been and would be a part of New York Yankee history—one star leaving and another star ascending. In this case it took place on April 18, 1938—Joseph Lowell 'Flash' Gordon took over second base for the great Tony Lazzeri.

The acrobatic, multi-dimensional athlete in his two years at the University of Oregon played baseball, was a running back in football, excelled in soccer, was a star long jumper and a skilled violinist.

Yankee scout Bill Essick signed him, writing in his report: "At his best when it meant the most and the going was toughest."

Number 6 was key in helping the Yankees win four World Series. A nine-time All-Star, in 1942, he won the American League MVP award, batted .322 and drove in 103 runs. He was the rarest of second baseman, possessed of wide range in the field and power at bat. He still has the American League record for second basemen for most career home runs (246). He was fond of explaining the difference between hitting and fielding. "What is there to it? You swing and if you hit the ball, there it goes. Ah, but fielding. There's rhythm, finesse, teamwork and balance."

The story made the rounds that his manager Joe McCarthy called "Flash" Gordon over and asked: "Joe, what is your batting average right now?"

"I don't know," was the reply.

"What about your fielding average?"

"Hell if I know," was the reply.

McCarthy at that point stopped asking questions, but remarked: "That's why I like him. All he cares about is winning."

Joe Gordon, one of the top second basemen in Yankee franchise history, was enshrined in the Baseball Hall of Fame in 2009.

During World War II Joe Gordon, like quite a few Major Leaguers, was away on military duty. It seemed he was not the same player in 1946, batting a subpar .210.

After playing in a thousand games and recording a thousand hits for the Yankees, in a flash, Gordon was shipped off to Cleveland for fire-balling hurler Allie Reynolds in a trade that Joe DiMaggio encouraged.

Gordon's time as a Yankee is well remembered. In 2009, he was enshrined in the Baseball Hall of Fame. His Yankee plaque in part praises Joseph Lowell Gordon as "An acrobatic second baseman with tremendous power."

GOOSE GOSSAGE

"I gave them their money's worth."
— *Goose Gossage*

Why not Gossage? The outspoken hurler late season 1978 torqued the Yankee charge to catch up to the Red Sox. It was Gossage who saved the one-game American League East playoff game against the Red Sox. That was how he started, and he stayed in that rhythm despite challenges for seven Yankee seasons.

IRV KAZE (FORMER YANKEE MEDIA DIRECTOR): *Gossage was this big hulking guy who would get out of this little Toyota with pinstripes on it coming in from the bullpen for the Yankees. It seemed he unfolded as he came out of the car. After his first season in 1978 with the team he had grown that Fu Manchu mustache—and there he was 60 feet away with seemingly the ability to throw a ball through a wall. But he was a gentleman.*

Number 54 was a superstar in the years of the "Bronx Zoo" who twice saved more than 30 games for the Yankees. His mouth, some said, was even quicker than his pitches that could reach 100 miles per hour.

In 1980, the "White Gorilla" Gossage led the American League in saves, but is probably remembered most for "the homer" he gave up to George Brett, which iced KC's sweep of the Yanks in the ALCS.

George Brett–"Goose" Gossage was an item again in 1983 in the "Pine Tar" Game trading unpleasantries.

PAUL DOHERTY: *He came back to the Yankees for 11 games in 1989. And he didn't have the mustache in his first Yankee season, 1978.*

Through a lot of that time of great success on the Yankees there was also his running feud with its owner whose facial hair policy he deeply disapproved. To protest, the "Goose" grew the Fu Manchu mustache.

And on more than one occasion, Gossage's riotous rants appeared in the New York tabloids: "I want out. I'm sick of everything that goes on around here.

Goose Gossage, reliever par excellence, saved the American League East playoff game against the Red Sox.

I'm sick of all the negative stuff and you can take that upstairs to the fat man and tell him I said it."

The "fat man" (George Steinbrenner) heard those words and others. In 1983, Gossage's half dozen plus Yankee seasons ended. He went on to play with other teams over what would amount to a 22-year Major League Career.

Happily entering the Hall of Fame with a Yankees cap on his head in 2008, all the bitterness from long ago put away, Gossage has become a regular at Old-Timers' Days. He was part of the ceremonies closing Yankee Stadium. At Old-Timers' Day 2014 in the new Yankee Stadium, a plaque honoring him was unveiled.

Sometimes annoying, obnoxious, out of line, outspoken, always his own man, Gossage recorded a 2.14 ERA in pinstripes, a won and lost record of 42–28 and an average of almost a strikeout an inning. He was a piece of work on and off the mound.

RON GUIDRY

"Winning 25 games in the big leagues is easy, it's losing only three games that's hard."
— *Ron Guidry*

A man of many talents, Ron Guidry was proficient on the drums and kept a trap set at Yankee Stadium where he played away with the same verve and drive he performed with on the baseball field. There was a time when he was part of a post-game concert with the Beach Boys. However, it was as a pitcher that he truly excelled.

Number 49 wore Yankee pinstripes for 14 seasons—his season of seasons, however, was 1978. A winner in 25 of 28 decisions for a percentage of .893, one of the best ever, Guidry posted an ERA of 1.74. He fanned a franchise record 248 strikeouts. He also won the American League Cy Young Award and finished second in MVP voting.

Five-time Gold Glove winner Ron Guidry was called "Louisiana Lightning" for his speed on the field.

A couple of highlights of the magical 1978 season for the man they called "Louisiana Lightning" included winning his first 13 decisions, 18 strikeouts against the Angels and tying Babe Ruth's American League record for a lefty hurler with nine shutouts. His final victory of the season came in the Yankees' epic victory over the Red Sox in a tie-breaker to crown the AL East champion.

The year was no fluke. In his prime years of 1977 to 1985, "Gator" (in tribute to his Lafayette, Louisiana roots) was among the best of the best. With a sharp fastball complemented by a rattlesnake-like slider, Guidry stormed through the opposition. His won-lost record was 154–67 with a 5–2 career posts record and 3–1 in the World Series competition. From 1982 to 1986, he won Gold Gloves five times.

Ronald Ames Guidry had his number retired by the Yankees on August 23, 2003. Up to that point, the franchise had retired sixteen numbers, but only one other pitcher, Whitey Ford, was so honored. It was a perfect moment for the wiry Guidry, who was so thin at 160 pounds that Yankees manager Billy Martin at first had doubts about him and wanted to trade him. But Guidry, who did not count Martin among his favorite people, said: "If you approach Billy Martin right, he's okay. I avoid him altogether."

No one can avoid recognizing what "Louisiana Lightning" meant to those Yankee teams he starred for.

TOMMY HENRICH

"He's a fine judge of a fly ball. He fields grounders like an infielder. He never makes a wrong throw, and if he comes back to the hotel at 3 in the morning when we're on the road and says he's been sitting up with a sick friend, he's been sitting up with a sick friend."

—Casey Stengel

The New York Yankees signed Tommy Henrich for an estimated $25,000 after he was ruled a free agent by Baseball

Tommy Henrich, dubbed "Old Reliable" by Mel Allen for his dependability, lived up to his nickname during his time in pinstripes.

Commissioner Landis for being hidden illegally in the farm system of the Indians. Out of Massillon, Ohio, he made his debut in right field on May 11, 1937.

Together with Joe DiMaggio and Charlie Keller, Henrich would be a part of one of the most praised outfields before and after Second World War injuries and three years with the Coast Guard kept his production down, but he still managed a memorable eleven years on the Yankees. Henrich batted .282 on his Yankee career and was a four-time All-Star. His time in pinstripes had many epic moments.

In 1949, he bashed a ninth inning home run off Brooklyn Dodger ace Don Newcombe in Game One of the World Series, winning the game, setting the stage for another Yankee world championship. Another moment was the World Series of 1941 against the Dodgers, Game 4.

GAME CALL, MEL ALLEN: *"Casey goes into the windup. Around comes the right arm, in comes the pitch. A swing by Henrich . . . he swings and misses, strike three! But the ball gets away from Mickey Owen. It's rolling back to the screen. Tommy Henrich races down toward first base. He makes it safely. And the Yankees are still alive with Joe DiMaggio coming up to bat."*

"That ball broke like no curve I'd ever seen Casey throw," Henrich mused later. "As I start to swing, I think, 'No good. Hold up.' That thing broke so sharp, though, that as I tried to hold up, my mind said, 'He might have trouble with it.'"

Catcher Mickey Owen did have trouble with the ball and was charged with a passed ball. The flub opened the door for the Yankees to score four times, to win the game 7–4. The next day they clinched another world championship.

These Henrich moments and others led to Mel Allen nicknaming Henrich "Old Reliable" for a railroad train that was always punctual that ran from Cincinnati through the Yankee announcer's Alabama birthplace state. Henrich was also called "The Clutch."

The classy defensive outfielder who was Yankee pride personified began as a 24-year-old in 1937 earning $5,000 and finished in 1950 earning $40,000. At the time of his death in 2009 in Dayton, Ohio, at age 96, Tommy Henrich was the oldest living Yankee.

RALPH HOUK

"He was the best manager I ever played for."
—Mickey Mantle

Houk led the Yanks to a 109–53 record in his rookie managerial year, capping it off with the World Championship. 1961 was, of course, the year of Mantle and Maris. Houk did make a few very huge decisions, though.

He basically scrapped Stengel's platoon system. Now that Gil McDougald had retired, he went with Richardson at 2B, Kubek at SS and Boyer at 3B, which turned out to be a fine defensive infield. He put Mantle behind Maris in the lineup. Casey did so, but Houk continued it, in order to "protect" Maris. Maris had no intentional walks in his 61 HR season as a result. Yogi continued his move to LF, and platooned with Hector Lopez. Elston Howard was now the full-time catcher, due to Yogi turning 36.

But most importantly, Whitey Ford now pitched every fourth day instead of being saved for certain teams. Prior to 1961, Ford pitched over 226 innings in a season just once. In 1961 he threw 283 innings and won the Cy Young Award. Ford was never a 20-game winner before. In 1961 he went 25–4, 3.21. Ford's best two seasons, 1961 and 1963, were under Houk.

RALPH HOUK: *Yankee Stadium for me was a home away from home without a doubt. Those were really the best years of my life. The first time I saw it I could hardly believe it was a place to play baseball in. It was so big and awesome. I was born in Kansas and raised on a farm and I had played in the Kansas City ballpark a little bit. But I never expected anything like the Stadium.*

It was especially amazing to me when I walked out on the field and saw the people sitting in the high stands looking down and the trains going by outside right field. The women were all dressed up and the men all wore hats and jackets. It just didn't seem where you ought to be playing baseball. When I began, I was one of three catchers along with Robinson and Yogi. I was catching against left-handers, Aaron was catching against right handers, and Yogi was playing right field.

My locker from the start was right next to the manager's office. I can always remember DiMaggio coming in on the other side and going down to the end, and equipment manager Pete Sheehy bringing him a cup of coffee. He didn't ask for one—Pete always knew when he wanted one.

DiMaggio became one of my better friends on the club, believe it or not. He knew I had been in the war. I was pretty quiet then, and he was more of a loner. He invited me to dinner a few times. In those days, my best friend was anyone who wanted to see me.

Mickey Mantle, Ralph Houk and Roger Maris; as a manager, Houk put Mantle behind Maris in the lineup in order to "protect" Maris.

Born in Kansas on August 9, 1919, the son of a farmer, Ralph George Houk excelled in all the high school sports he played, especially baseball. The Yankees signed him as a catcher in 1939. He was a minor leaguer for three seasons, then joined the Army. He began as a private and after officer candidate school became a lieutenant. Like Yogi Berra, he saw action on June 6, 1944, in the D-Day invasion of Normandy. He was at Omaha Beach. Houk also fought with the Rangers in the Battle of the Bulge.

When he was discharged with the rank of Major at war's end, a shade under six feet tall and 200 pounds, Houk went back to the states with a memento of his time in combat: a helmet he had worn at Omaha Beach. It had holes in the front and back. He kept it around as a reminder of the bullet that almost finished him off. For his heroic efforts in WWII, the former Kansas farm boy was awarded the Silver Star, Purple Heart and Bronze Star.

The Yankees of his era were loaded with talent in the majors and minor leagues. So Houk's Yankee debut came late in the game, as a 27-year-old on April 26, 1947. His salary that year was $3600. Yogi Berra was very much there and superstarring it so Houk managed to play

in parts of eight seasons for a total of 81 games. He hit no home runs and admitted he spent most of his time in the bullpen.

RALPH HOUK: *I used to sit out there with pitchers who weren't in the starting rotation, and I learned exactly what went through their minds.*

In 1955, playing career over, Houk took over as manager of the Denver Bears in the American Association, the top minor league club of the Yankees. Dan Topping, Yankees owner, was grooming Houk for one day managing the team. Houk was part of a very successful stint at Denver for three seasons, guiding such future Yankees as Johnny Blanchard, Tony Kubek, Don Larsen, Bobby Richardson, Ralph Terry and Ryne Duren. In 1957, he steered Denver to the Little World Series championship, and came back to the Yankees as a coach in 1958.

When the Yankees fired popular Casey Stengel as manager after the 1960 season, Houk was selected to replace him. General Manager George Weiss

was succeeded by his top aide, Roy Hamey. For the "lifer" in the Yankee organization, it was a pressure-filled situation. Houk was taking over for a legend, winner of 10 pennants and 7 World Series. "There's only one Casey Stengel," he said. "I'm Ralph Houk."

RALPH HOUK: *I moved into the manager's office in 1961, and the great clubhouse guy Pete Sheehy had everything ready for me. It had all I wanted: a room, a desk, a place to keep my records. Most of my memories of that office was bringing guys in and telling them things they didn't want to hear. I was usually down at one end of the Yankee dugout managing from a standing position with one leg up. I stood rather than sit on the bench. I was always moving.*

From the start Houk was his own man, making changes, asserting his style. He was a very positive influence on the team. For him there were no elaborate rules, no curfews, no paybacks. It was a more open environment.

Collectible baseball card of Ralph Houk, who said playing for the Yankees were the best years of his life.

RALPH HOUK: *I was on the player's side. I don't think you can humiliate a player and expect him to perform.*

He encouraged Mickey Mantle to assume more of a leadership role, made Bobby Richardson and Clete Boyer everyday players and placed Whitey Ford, who was "saved" by Casey Stengel, into the regular rotation, pitching every fourth day.

Ralph Houk, Yankee manager, was not too shabby. He did have the talent, but he knew how to handle it. The Yankees won three straight American League pennants and two World Series championships in his first seasons.

A widely distributed story then was about when Houk was readying to manage in a World Series game for the first time. It was a game against the Cincinnati Reds in 1961. A reporter asked Houk: "Are you nervous?"

"Why, is somebody going to be shooting at me?"

The 1961 Yankees took the Reds apart in five games in the World Series. For the rookie manager, in the organization from the time he was 19 years old, it was top-of-the-world time. In 1962, Houk notched his second straight pennant and world championship. But in 1963, the Dodgers swept the Yanks in the World Series. The Yankees were held to a miserable .171 batting average. That World Series defeat was disappointing, but Houk had made managerial history—along with Hughie Jennings he was the only manager to finish in first place in each of their first three seasons.

PAUL DOHERTY: *The season of 1963 over, Ralph Houk was appointed by owner Dan Topping as the Yankees' Vice President and General Manager. He replaced Roy Hamey who was retiring [Hamey had replaced his boss George Weiss in November 1960]. With Houk bumped up to GM, Yogi Berra was promoted from player/coach to field manager for 1964. In early May 1966, Houk, after a disastrous 1965 and early 1966 season, fired Johnny Keane, who had replaced Berra as field manager after the 1964 World Series. Houk then resigned as GM, replaced Keane, and commenced his second stint as Yankee manager.*

During the 1973 season, his first as owner, George Steinbrenner terrorized Houk in the meddlesome style he later became notorious for. Houk, who under Mike Burke and Lee MacPhail's management was used to almost total autonomy, soon tired of George's bullying and innuendos. He packed it in at season's end. Houk's eight-year record as a Yankee manager was 944-805. He moved to Detroit to manage the Tigers for his friend, GM Jim Campbell.

In July 2010, less than two weeks after the deaths of PA announcer Bob Sheppard and owner George Steinbrenner, the "Major" passed away just 19 days before his 91st birthday.

ELSTON HOWARD

"A man of great gentleness and dignity."
—On his plaque in Monument Park

"He deserves credit and where would I be without him? Phew! He can give me a job in the outfield and he can catch, too. Good kid, too. He's good." —Casey Stengel

The Yankees scouted Elston Howard playing in the Negro Leagues for the Kansas City Monarchs. He was signed to a minor league contract and broke in with Muskegon, Michigan, in 1950 in the Class-A Central League. His playing there was interrupted by two years of Army service. In 1953, Howard played for Kansas City of the American Association, the Yankees' top farm team. He did well, hitting .286, collecting 10 home runs and driving in 70 runs.

There was much clamoring for the Yankees to promote Howard to the Major League roster and finally have their first African-American player. No dice. In 1954, the Yankees assigned him to Toronto in the International League, outside their organization. More controversy. Charges of Yankee prejudice and discrimination were in the news. Frustrated but determined, Howard batted a robust .330, hit 22 home runs, drove in 109 runs and led the league with 16 triples.

MONTE IRVIN: *Howard, like me, bided his time. By the time he made the Yankees, he was 26. He also had to suffer through the indignity in that first spring training of not being able to stay with the rest of the team at their hotel in segregated St. Petersburg; he had to be put up by a family in the black section of town. He bore up under this, too.*

Elston Howard batted a robust .330, hit 22 home runs, drove in 109 runs and led the league with 16 triples.

On April 14, 1955—almost eight years to the day that Jackie Robinson broke the color barrier—the Yankees called up catcher Elston Howard. He had been in the team's farm system since 1950, won the International League's Most Valuable Player in 1954 and could have been the regular catcher for most Major League teams.

Manager Casey Stengel appreciated Howard's versatility and that rookie season, one in which he earned $10,000, with Yogi Berra still quite "the man," Howard caught nine games and played 75 games in the outfield.

The Yankees had been under pressure for years to break their own baseball color line and Elston Howard, affectionately known as "Ellie," was a wise choice. He had the goods. Much has been made of the fact that Casey Stengel said: "When I finally got me a nigger, I got one who could not run." Those who knew Casey knew the comment was another example of his running his mouth, an old habit that was hard to break. The "Ol' Perfessor" was also very much aware that although the first black Yankee was not swift afoot, he was a tremendous athlete, dangerous as a hitter, a very capable handler of pitchers and a class act all the way around. And it was the St. Louis born Howard who made the point: "No one in the Yankee organization made me conscious of my color." And he fit in and flourished in the winning culture of the New York Yankees.

Clear evidence of his acceptance was visible a month after his Major League debut on May 14th. Howard slashed a triple in the bottom of the ninth inning with two outs, two runners on and the Yankees trailing the Tigers 6–5. The three bagger vaulted the Yankees to a 7–6 victory. Entering the clubhouse, Howard was touched by the carpet of white towels Collins and Mantle had laid out from his locker to the shower.

Casey Stengel utilized Howard from 1955 to 1957 in the outfield and as catcher. An American League All-Star nine straight seasons (1957–1965), a two-time Gold Glove catcher, Howard batted over .300 three times. Number 32 had a heck of a career, not the least of which included being a major part of ten pennant winners and four World Series champion teams and winning the MVP award in 1963, the first black player to be so honored in the American League. A jubilant Howard said: "I've just won the Nobel Prize of baseball."

When Ralph Houk became manager in 1961, Howard finally became the regular catcher. The 36-year-old Yogi Berra went to left field. "Ellie" had the season of his life, hitting .348. He also rapped 21 homers and drove in 77 runs. In 1964, he won his second Gold Glove, and led American League catchers with a .998 fielding mark, as the Yankees won their fifth straight pennant.

Inventive, interested in all things baseball, Howard pioneered the hinged glove, which made possible one-handed catching and a catcher being able to place his exposed hand behind his back, protecting his "meat" hand. Howard also invented the weighted donut swung by some batters in the on-deck circle.

In 1967, Howard was traded to Boston. A few years later he came back to the Yanks as the first black coach in the American League. He was a vital and respected member of the coaching staff for eleven years. A solid catcher who played 13 years for the Yanks, "Ellie" was in nine World Series. He was strong and solid in the clubhouse, a guy who everyone could count on.

Tragically, "Ellie" passed away from a heart attack on December 14, 1980. He was only 51 years old. At the time, Red Barber said: "The Yankees lost more class than George Steinbrenner could buy in ten years."

Elston Howard, the first black Yankee and one of the greatest catchers in franchise history.

WAITE HOYT

"It's great to be young and a Yankee."
—Waite Hoyt

Waite Charles Hoyt is one of the more interesting characters in the history of the New York Yankees. And although he pitched in the big leagues for seven different teams in his 20-year career, it was with the team from the Bronx that he made his mark.

Out of Brooklyn, New York, with a father who was a professional minstrel, Hoyt tossed three no-hitters for Erasmus Hall High School. He also pitched for batting practice at the Polo Grounds at age 15. Never at a loss for words, the young Hoyt asked to be paid for his labors. Tough John J. McGraw, Giant manager, had Hoyt's father sign for the youngster. A five-dollar bill was the payment. A precocious and ambitious hurler who was called "Schoolboy" became one of the youngest players ever to turn professional.

Hoyt pitched in only one game for the Giants on July 24, 1918. And then it was on to the Red Sox where he and Babe Ruth became friends. What followed were a couple of below-par

"Schoolboy" Waite Hoyt, out of Brooklyn's Erasmus High School, made his Yankee debut at age 22 in 1921.

New York Yankees team picture, 1926, the year they won the pennant.

seasons for Hoyt with the team from Boston. The Yankees picked up the 22-year-old before the 1921 season. Like others before him and after him, he blossomed in pinstripes, posting just one losing season.

Sophisticated, always looking to increase his income—the most he made in any one season was $16,000—Hoyt added to his earnings in odd ways during the off-season. In the late 1920s he sang and danced in vaudeville, even earning a few gigs at Manhattan's Palace Theater. He opened up a business as a mortician and bragged: "I'm knocking 'em dead on Seventh Avenue while my partner is laying 'em out up in Westchester."

As a Yankee the sturdy right-hander was an anchor for the pitching staff from 1921 to early 1930. He was a winner of 157 games, instrumental in his team winning six pennants and three World Series and ranks among the Yankee all-time leaders in shutouts, complete games, winning percentage, wins and innings pitched. In 1969, he was elected to the Baseball Hall of Fame.

PAUL DOHERTY: *Hoyt went on for many years [1942–1965] after his active playing days as a very successful and entertaining announcer for the Cincinnati Reds. In fact, even Red Barber, who did not like ex-jocks in the broadcast booth, was quite positive about Hoyt's work. He's considered by many the best broadcaster in Cincinnati baseball history.*

MILLER HUGGINS

"There was one great little fellow. A great fighter but always square and sportsmanlike. I always entertained the highest regard for Miller Huggins as an able leader and as a man."

—*John McGraw*

He was an unlikely Yankee, an unlikely hiring, a little man with a lot of pride who thought assuming command as manager of the team would be a step down for him. Yet, it all worked out for Miller Huggins and the franchise.

One owner of the Yankees, Colonel Tillinghast L'Hommedieu Huston, was overseas fighting in WWI. The other,

Jake Ruppert, was intent on hiring a new manager for the 1918 season. Huston favored Wilbert Robinson of Brooklyn. Ruppert did not. He had his eye on Huggins.

At their first meeting, the Yankee dandy owner was very unimpressed with Huggins. He later remarked about "the worker's clothes, the cap perched oddly on Huggins's head, the smallness of the man." Nevertheless, always able to judge character and talent, Ruppert was able to look beyond appearances.

Huggins would be the new Yankee manager. And despite initially thinking the Yankees would be a demotion from his five years as St. Louis Cardinal skipper, the 40-year-old Huggins came on board. Ruppert and Huggins would be the duo dedicated to creating Yankee greatness and their pairing would be a marker moment in the history of the franchise.

According to Ruppert: "Huggins had vision. Getting him was the first and most important step we took toward making the Yankees champions. Huggins had constructive ideas and far-seeing judgment. He planned on a big scale."

Manager Miller Huggins, "the Mighty Mite" (right), was a little man who did big things for the Yankees.

Huggins had a law degree from the University of Cincinnati. One of his professors was future President William Howard Taft. Just 5-foot-6 and 140 pounds, known as "Hug" or the "Mighty Mite," Huggins had been a scrappy second baseman for the Reds and Cardinals from 1904 to 1916.

As the 1918 season began, Huggins took his place as the eighth manager in the franchise's 16-year history. At first "Hug" was unhappy with his situation. "New York is a hell of a town. Everywhere I go in St. Louis or Cincinnati, it's always 'Hiya Hug.' But here in New York I can walk the length of 42nd Street and not a soul knows me."

Like a schoolteacher, training players, modifying their behavior, Huggins held sway. Players had to report for games at 10:00 at the Stadium—to sign in, not to practice, a move designed to reduce late-night merriment. Backslapping was frowned upon. Flamboyance was discouraged. Razzing of opponents was not permitted. In the dugout, attention to what took place on the playing field was paramount. Players were expected to keep track not only of the score and the number of outs, but of the count on the batter.

"Miller Huggins was a good manager," the opinionated Mark Koenig observed, "although he was a nervous little guy who moved his feet a lot in the dugout. But he didn't have to be much of a strategist. Lots of times, we'd be down five, six runs, and then have a big inning to win the game."

"Hug" may have been small in frame and possessed of a law degree, but he could hold his own with anyone. He was always to the point direct in giving his player's directions. For pitchers, he used "Coive him! Coive the busher!"

The Yankees finished in fourth place in 1918 and in third place the next two seasons. In 1921, the Yankees won 98 games and their first American League pennant. They lost to the Giants in the World Series.

"Huggins," a delighted Ruppert said, "is one of the smartest men in baseball, besides being one of the finest personally. He has gone about his work quietly and you hardly ever see him but you see the results of his planning and his keen baseball mind. He is a little marvel."

The little marvel was just beginning to assert himself. The 1926 Yankees won the 91 games and the pennant. In 1927, there was another world championship. In 1928, Miller Huggins steered the Yankees to their third straight pennant, sixth in eight seasons. A four-game sweep over St. Louis gave the Yanks a string of eight straight World Series game victories.

Those two World Series sweeps and the half-dozen pennants in just eight years, were record setting. The "Mite Manager" was the mighty manager. Self-effacing to a fault, Huggins said: "Great players make great managers."

Dubbed "the unhappy little man," and the "Mighty Mite," Huggins always seemed to have a short-stemmed pipe in his hand or jutting out of his mouth. He would suffer over his stock market investments although he played the game with great skill and enthusiasm and at times invested for players, turning a profit for them.

In 1928, the Yankees finished in second place. The little manager would not be there at the end. On September 20th, he checked himself into the hospital. He had been bothered by what he thought was just a boil under his eye. It was a form of blood poisoning. On September 25, 1929, Miller James Huggins passed away at age 51.

A monument honoring the late Yankees skipper was placed in center field

and dedicated on May 30, 1932. Miller Huggins became the first in a long line of Yankees greats honored in what became Monument Park. His plaque reads: "A Splendid Character Who Made Priceless Contributions to Baseball and On This Field Brought Glory to the New York Club of the American League." Baseball Hall of Fame admission came to Miller Huggins in 1964.

CATFISH HUNTER

"Just walking through Yankee Stadium, chills run through you." —Jim Hunter

"The sun don't shine on the same dog's ass all the time." —Jim Hunter

James Augustus Hunter was born on April 8, 1946, in Hertford, North Carolina, into a sharecropping family. Throwing baseballs at a hole in his father's barn door taught him the pinpoint control that enabled him to star in high school and American Legion competition.

A good ol' farm boy, Jim Hunter learned his famous control from his older brothers and rose to prominence dazzling scouts who visited his high school in Perquimans.

With Oakland, Hunter had reeled off four consecutive years with at least 20 wins, four World Series wins with no losses and a 1974 league-leading earned run average of 2.49. On December 31, 1974, Hunter signed a $3.75-million, five-year deal plus a one million dollar signing bonus with the Yankees making him the highest paid pitcher in baseball. In his first season in New York, Catfish went 23–14, and managed to keep his down home sense of humor and style. "The same crazy stuff" he said, "happens in Oakland and New York. But in Oakland there weren't as many reporters to write about it."

With Hunter on board the Yankees racked up three straight pennants in 1976 to 1978.

Star pitcher James Augustus "Catfish" Hunter, who, in George Steinbrenner's phrase, "taught the Yankees how to win."

"Catfish Hunter was the cornerstone of the Yankees' success over the last quarter century," Yankees owner George Steinbrenner said. "We were not winning before Catfish arrived…He exemplified class and dignity and he taught us how to win."

In March 1978, Hunter was diagnosed with diabetes. He still, however, won 12 games and was the winning pitcher in New York's 7–2 World Series, clinching victory over the Los Angeles Dodgers in Game 6.

Too many pitches, too much strain on his arm and the sapping effects of diabetes finally caught up to the star hurler. In 1979, at the age of 33, Hunter retired.

Catfish went back to his roots, farming in North Carolina.

In 1987, Hunter was elected to the Baseball Hall of Fame. "I was probably the first player who broke it open for other players to be paid what they're worth," he said.

His record included a Cy Young award, a perfect game and five consecutive 20-win seasons and five seasons in the pressure cooker of the Bronx Zoo when he anchored most things Yankee.

"I didn't think I would make it," he admitted. "I figured I wasn't good enough. I figured the people in there were like gods." Hunter resisted pressure from the Yankee and Athletics and went into the Hall with the insignia of neither team on his cap.

In 1998, Hunter was diagnosed with Lou Gehrig's disease. On September 9, 1999, he passed away at age 53.

REGGIE JACKSON

"He'd give you the shirt off his back. Of course, he'd call a press conference to announce it." —Catfish Hunter

"Off the record, he's a piece of shit."
—Billy Martin

He spent only five years as a Yankee in a 21-year Major League career. But what those five years were like . . .

Reggie Jackson in pinstripes seemed an appropriate match. In November 1976 he announced that he came to the Yankees because "George Steinbrenner outhustled everybody else. Certain things have a lot more meaning than money. It was easy to see I could become a rich man. Some clubs offered several thousand more; there was even the possibility of seven figures more."

The Yankees won the 1976 AL East pennant in a romp, squeezed through to win the American League title and were swept by Cincinnati's "Big Red Machine" in the World Series.

A ticked-off George Steinbrenner first signed free agent Don Gullet of Cincinnati for $2.09 million. Then he signed Reggie Jackson, the most prized free agent of all, to the highest salary contract in baseball at the time.

Steinbrenner's first offer was $2 million, then raised to $2.9 million with an extra sweetener of $60,000 for Jackson to purchase a Rolls-Royce. Waiting for several hours in the Hyatt

at O'Hare Airport, "the Boss" was determined. He got his man. Details of the contract were scribbled on the back of a cocktail napkin as was the signature of Reggie Jackson who wrote on the napkin: "I will not let you down. —Reginald M. Jackson."

Born on May 18, 1946, in Wyncote, Pennsylvania, Jackson was one of six children. He showed off his athletic talents from the start. In high school, he was a four-sport varsity athlete. He starred in football and baseball at Arizona State. After his sophomore season, he was scooped up by the Kansas City Athletics with the number two pick of the 1966 draft. Incredibly, the New York Mets had the number one pick and passed on Reggie Jackson.

By 1967, he was in the big leagues. Owner Charley Finley moved Jackson and other talented youngsters and the team to Oakland. There were five straight AL West titles from 1971 to 1975 that Jackson was a big part of, as well as three World Series and an MVP award. With free agency for Jackson on the horizon, Finley traded him to Baltimore. After one year with the Orioles, enter George Steinbrenner!

The talent was always there for Reggie Jackson and so was the big mouth. A self-promoter and a deprecator of others, he bragged, "I didn't come to New York to be a star. I brought my star with me."

He came to the Yankees with lots of baggage, the verbal kind. Many on the Yankee roster and in the media thought he went too far with his running commentary that included lines like:

"God do I love to hit that little round sum-bitch out of the park and make 'em say, 'Wow! Hitting is better than sex.'"

"In the building I live in on Park Avenue there are ten people who could buy the Yankees, but none of them could hit the ball out of Yankee Stadium."

"The only difference between me and the other great Yankees is my skin color."

"You know this team . . . it all flows from me. I've got to keep it going. I'm the straw that stirs the drink . . ."

"After Jackie Robinson, the most important black in baseball history is Jackson, I really mean that."

He had the mouth. He also had the goods. In Reggie Jackson's first season as a Yankee, he led the team to its first world championship in 15 years.

"The writers were never late that year," recalled Phil Rizzuto, "because something was always going on. A lot of egos were vying for the headlines."

The headline of headlines belonged to October 18th, 1977, as Reggie Jackson became "Mr. October." The Yankees were up three games to two against the Los Angeles Dodgers and Jackson literally took over game six. He hit a home run on the first pitch in the fourth, fifth and eighth innings.

The controversial slugger was on fire in that World Series, batting a blazing .450 with a record five homers. Jackson also recorded the highest slugging average in a six-game Series (1.250), most total

Reggie Jackson, signed by George Steinbrenner in 1976 to the highest salary contract in baseball at the time.

bases in a six-game Series (25), most runs (tied with 10).

George Steinbrenner's signing of Jackson paid off big time. There was joy in the Bronx for most. "Mr. October" was what Reggie Jackson was called for his post-season heroics. "Mr. Obnoxious" was what he was called for his over-the-top arrogance.

One can only wonder about the comments made by Jackson about Steinbrenner after the 1977 World Championship: "I was happy for George because George wanted it so bad. I said to myself, 'Now he can really have fun at the 21 Club. He'll go around and give rings to his friends and he'll be able to talk about this one as long as he lives.'"

Reggie maintained if he played in New York, a candy bar would be named for him. He called the shots. Opening Day 1978 at the Stadium was "Reggie Bar" giveaway day. Catfish Hunter described the orange wrapped candy this way: "Open it and it tells you how good it is." The crowd received free samples. Reggie blasted a three-run homer. Thousands of the orange-wrapped candies were thrown out onto the field. It was a marketing and public relations disaster, an embarrassment. Chicago pitcher Wilbur Wood, who gave up the home run, was beside himself. There was annoyance among the press, some outrage among players.

"It's not called for," the generally calm White Sox manager Bob Lemon said, agitated. "Let them throw them when he's in right field," Lemon said. "See how he feels. People starving all over the world and 30 billion calories are laying there."

It was called "the Bronx Zoo" and other earthier phrases, that general environment around the Yankees. There was always something going wrong, some annoyance magnified big time.

A case in point took place on Saturday afternoon June 18, 1977, in a game against the Red Sox at Fenway Park. Reggie was the centerpiece, some would say the catalyst, for what happened.

The game was on national TV. The Yankees were being blown out by the Red Sox. In the sixth inning, Boston's Jim Rice lifted a ball into short right field. Playing deep for the slugger, who had power to all fields, Jackson got to the ball after it landed. Poor judgment on his part, he later claimed.

An annoyed—always annoyed, it seemed, with Jackson—Billy Martin sent reserve outfielder Paul Blair running out to right field. Jackson went berserk—never had he been taken out of a game in his long career. Later he would tell writers that Martin's negative handling of him had racial overtones.

A furious Jackson jogged in towards the dugout, heading straight for his manager, who was in the right corner. Two Yankee immortals, strong men, former catchers Yogi Berra and Elston Howard, had taken up positions and were ready for Jackson.

"You never wanted me on this team in the first place," Jackson yelled.

"I ought to kick your ass," Martin shot back.

The strong man Howard contained Jackson. Berra got into it, too. "Once that little guy gets his monkey claws on you, you ain't goin' nowhere," Ron Guidry said.

All the histrionics ultimately ended. The Red Sox and their fans left Fenway happy. The home team won, 10–4, smashing five home runs.

Afterward Billy Martin said: "When they don't hustle, I don't accept that. When a player shows the club up, I show the player up."

For the Yankees and Billy Martin and Reggie Jackson, it was just another wacky day at the ballpark.

Later that 1978 season, a slumping Jackson was used as a designated hitter by Billy Martin. Reggie was not pleased. He shared his displeasure with anyone who would listen including owner George Steinbrenner. In one game, Martin gave Jackson the sign to swing away. He bunted. Martin suspended him for five games.

The hot-tempered trio of Steinbrenner-Jackson-Martin was big news in all the New York media. Especially publicized was Martin's rant: "One's a born liar [Jackson]; the other's convicted," a reference to the Boss's conviction for illegal campaign contributions. That comment got Martin fired and it seemed Reggie was back in vogue.

Jackson belted 41 homers to tie for the league lead and hit .300 in 1980. But in the strike-shortened 1981 season, Jackson batted just .237 with 15 homers in 94 games.

On January 22, 1982, irritated and fed up with Steinbrenner putdowns, Reggie Jackson severed his ties with the Yankees and signed as a free agent with the California Angels. After five years of tumult in the Big Apple, the controversial and cocky outfielder was back out west. Steinbrenner later said that letting Jackson go was "the worst decision of my career."

When Reggie Jackson was elected to the Hall of Fame in 1993, he went in as a Yankee even though lots of bad blood passed between him and management, ownership and teammates. The Yankees retired his uniform, Number 44, on August 14, 1993. Reggie Jackson is currently a member of the Yankees' special advisory group.

"Mr. November," Derek Jeter, most everybody's favorite Yankee, always dreamed of playing shortstop for the Yankees.

DEREK JETER

"Most likely to play shortstop for the New York Yankees." —Jeter's junior high school yearbook

"When I come back, I want to come back as Derek Jeter." —George Steinbrenner

"Here is a guy who turns away millions of easy dollars in endorsements each off-season so he can go down to Tampa and train every day at the Yankee minor league complex to improve himself for the upcoming season." —David Cone

The kid that was born on Wednesday, June 26, 1974, in Pequannock, New Jersey, who grew up dreaming of a career with the New York Yankees, got his dream fulfilled many times over.

Derek Jeter is the franchise's career leader in hits (3,465). He leads all Yankees in career games played (2,747), stolen bases (358), and at-bats (11,195). He was an All-Star shortstop 14 times, a Gold Glove and Silver Slugger award winner five times. He is the twenty-eighth player to become a part of the three thousand hit club. Baseball Almanac lists him as the 13th captain in Yankee history.

George Steinbrenner said of the honor of being a Yankee captain in 2003: "I have always been very, very careful about giving such a responsibility to one of my players, but I cannot think of a single player that I have ever had who is more deserving of this honor than Derek Jeter. He is a young man of great character and has shown great leadership qualities. He believes, as I do, what General [Douglas] MacArthur said, that 'there is no substitute for victory.' To him, and to me, it's second only to breathing."

Other Yankee legends have been lavish in their praise of the 17th player in franchise history to wear Number 2:

"In big games," Reggie Jackson said, "the action slows down for him where it speeds up for others. I've told him, 'I'll trade my past for your future.'"

"This kid, right now," his manager Joe Torre said, "the tougher the situation, the more fire he gets in his eyes. You don't teach that."

Ritual and respect for Yankee tradition underscored the shortstop's time. After the passing of Bob Sheppard, Jeter still had his name announced by a recording from the legendary public address announcer. The Yankee star also had a selection of different kinds of music played when he stepped up to the plate at Yankee Stadium, like Beanie Sigel/Freeway's "Roc the Mic," Black Rob's "Whoa," Eminem's "Without Me," Fat Joe's "What's Luv" featuring Ashanti, Nelly's "Hot in Herre" and Notorious BIG's "Juicy."

He is just one of a half-dozen big leaguers who played for the same team when he was 20 years old and also as a 40-year-old. It was as if he had a career that was preordained. Growing up as a youngster in Kalamazoo, Michigan, he spent summers with his grandmother in New Jersey. And there so many times they would go on weekends and sit in the bleachers watching Yankee baseball

at the Stadium. The one constant was Jeter's dream of playing shortstop for the Yankees.

He was the sixth selection in the 1992 free-agent draft, and he was on his way. In 1994, Jeter was "Minor League Player of the Year." On May 29, 1995, the 20-year-old Jeter wearing Number 2 made his Yankee debut at shortstop.

Jeter's first and rookie season was Joe Torre's initial campaign as Yankee manager. The kid from Kalamazoo batted .314 with 10 homers and 78 RBIs. Making the big and spectacular plays in the field, leading by example, he won the American League Rookie of the Year award.

His first five seasons (1996–2000) in the big leagues were story book stuff. The Yankees were victors in four World Series. No Major Leaguer in that time span had more hits than the 996 hits he recorded. He was only the third Yankee who strung together three straight 200-hit seasons, joining Lou Gehrig and Don Mattingly.

He came to play. "God," Jeter said, "I hope I wear this jersey forever."

On Opening Day in 2002, Jeter, just 27 years old, signed a contract that extended through the 2010 season, then the second largest contract in sports history. He was worth every penny of it. There were all those Jeter magic moments.

October 14, 2001. Yankees facing elimination, two outs, seventh inning, Game 3 of the ALCS, Oakland's Jeremy Giambi was plodding home ready to tie the score. The "air-mailed" throw from the outfield by Shane Spencer came into the infield. Jeter, about 20 feet up the first baseline, went all out cutting off the throw, did a back-hand flip of the ball to a stunned Jose Posada who tagged Giambi out. The din at the Stadium was incredible. Mike Mussina got his 1–0 victory.

"The kid has great instincts," Joe Torre said. "That was obviously the play of the game."

Oakland manager Art Howe was effusive about the young shortstop: "I guess that's the reason he's wearing so many rings. This kid is as good as they come. Whenever they need a big play, he's there to make it. Whenever they need a big hit, he gets it."

In addition to "the flip moment," there were so many more that included: the Jeffrey Maier moment in Jeter's rookie season; the "Mr. November" moment just after the clock struck midnight on November 1, 2001; his leadoff home run in Game 4 of the 2000 Series against the Mets who doomed the team from Flushing; his chasing down a foul ball in July 2004, winding up bloodied but with the ball; his 3,000th hit, a towering homer off David Price; and Derek Jeter Day, his final game.

"Captain," "Captain Clutch," "Mr. November," they called him. His instincts, his intangibles, his athleticism made him get the job done. Jeter played 158 postseason games, basically an entire season. He racked 20 home runs, most of them clutch, when his team needed them.

The "Captain," a Yankee from May 29, 1995, to September 28, 2014, was graceful, driven and highly competent.

WEE WILLIE KEELER

"The most wonderful hitter that ever lived."
—*Sportscaster Bill Stern*

"I keep my eyes clear, and I hit 'em where they ain't." —*Wee Willie Keeler*

Born William Henry O'Kelleher, the surname evolved into Keeler. He was just 5-foot-4 and 140 pounds. But he was a sweet southpaw-swinging marvel. His lack of size was more than made up for with his will to win, incredible bat control and fine running speed.

Star Sam Crawford said this about "Wee Willie" Keeler's bat that was just 30 inches long, the shortest ever used in the majors: He choked up so far that "he only used half his bat."

"Wee Willie" Keeler, the "Hit 'Em Where They Ain't" guy, compiled a lifetime average of .341 and recorded 2,932 hits.

The son of a Brooklyn trolley switchman, Keeler was a member of the famed Baltimore Orioles. In 1903, he jumped from the National League to the New York Highlanders of the American League—the lure was the offer of the highest salary in baseball, $10,000.

Bunting the ball accurately and precisely was one of his skills. Another was executing the "Baltimore chop" and smacking the ball in front of home plate off hardened dirt. Another specialty of the little man was rapid wrist action and a punching of the ball over infielders' heads. He was a magician with a bat.

A third baseman transformed into an outfielder, Keeler also had longevity, playing 19 seasons in the Major Leagues. He batted over .300 for 16 seasons, compiled a lifetime average of .341, recorded 2,932 hits. For seven straight seasons he also had an on-base percentage that was above .400.

His best season came in 1897 when he batted .424, which is the highest average for a left-handed hitter in baseball history. He led the American League with 239 hits in only 129 games. Keeler posted a .294 batting average over his seven seasons (1903–1909) with the Highlanders.

Called by sportscaster Bill Stern, "The most wonderful hitter that ever lived," in 1939, Keeler was inducted into the Baseball Hall of Fame. The New York Yankees were listed as his primary team.

CHARLIE KELLER

"He wasn't scouted, he was trapped."
—*Lefty Gomez*

Just 5-foot-10 and 185 pounds, but muscular, Charlie Keller made his debut as a Yankee on April 22, 1939. With Newark, he had won the International League batting crown and Minor League Player of the Year honors in 1937. But in those days with so much talent on the big club, Keller had to wait his turn to get into "the Show."

That rookie season Keller split time between right field and left field and batted .334, fifth best in the American League. In the 1939 World Series against the Reds, the southpaw slugger powered the Yankee sweep—batted .438, hammered three homers and drove in six runs in 16 at-bats.

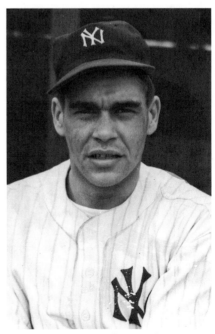
"King Kong" Charlie Keller was a five-time All-Star and a fan favorite.

His career year was 1942, with career highs in runs and walks, third in the league in homers, RBIs, home run ratio and total bases. The talented Keller paced another Yankee pennant run. For much of his time in pinstripes, Keller together with Joe DiMaggio and Tommy Henrich formed one of the top outfields in the history of the Yankees. A five-time All-Star, the muscular Yankee was a big part of half a dozen Yankee pennants and three world championships for the team from the Bronx.

Charlie Keller was called "King Kong" because of his powerful physique, his hairy body, and his thick, bushy eyebrows. A very quiet and private person, one who rarely made public appearances, he never responded to this nickname he disliked.

Back problems and nearly two seasons lost to World War II service impacted Keller's career. He played from 1939 to 1943 and 1945 to 1949. He also played briefly for the Tigers in 1951 and 1952. By age 30 he was a part-timer. Five years later he was retired into thoroughbred horse breeding in Maryland. He founded "Yankeeland Farm" and became a successful horse breeder. His time as a Yankees player obviously had an influence on his breeding business as some of his horses were named "Fresh Yankees," "Handsome Yankee," "Yankee Slugger" and "Guy Yankee." Keller passed away at his Frederick, Maryland, farm in 1990 at age 73.

PAUL KRICHELL

"I did not go there to look at Gehrig, I did not even know what position he played."
—Paul Krichell

Hired in 1920 at 37 by general manager Ed Barrow, for whom he had worked for in the minors and at Boston, Krichell became the first great Yankee scout. Early on he found a slugger at Columbia University. He signed him. That signing

made Krichell's reputation. The player's name was Lou Gehrig.

He was still on the Yankee payroll 37 years later when he passed away, having added Johnny Murphy, Tony Lazzeri, Phil Rizzuto, Whitey Ford and more to the list of players who enriched and empowered the New York American League franchise. Another who could have been a Krichell "signee" was not to be—Hank Greenberg and his parents were tempted. The realization that Lou Gehrig was one of the Yankee cornerstones and their rock as first baseman, convinced Greenberg to sign with Detroit. Paul Krichell was a legendary "scout" in every sense of the word. There are many of the opinion that without Paul Krichell in the organization, the Yankees would never have become what they became.

TONY KUBEK

"Here's a boy who sits on the bench without opening his mouth. So you don't know which side he's on. But when he goes out on the field, you know." —Casey Stengel

Signed a month before his seventeenth birthday in September 1953 by the Yankees, handsome Tony Kubek's versatility and strong arm attracted Casey

Tony Kubek, Yankee standout from 1957 to 1965, played in 1,092 games for the Yankees.

Stengel's attention in spring training 1957. Always a manager with an eye for talent, Stengel made the decision to move the youngster onto the big club's roster.

On April 20, 1957, just 21 years of age, Tony Kubek played in his first big league game. The mild-mannered rookie would play 50 games in the outfield, 41 at shortstop, 38 at third base, one game at second and bat .297. He helped the Yanks record another pennant, and his efforts helped the Wisconsin native to be named Rookie of the Year.

TONY KUBEK: *Bobby Richardson and I were astonished that Jerry Coleman and Gil McDougald went out of their way to help us for we were ultimately to take their jobs. It was typical of Yankee pinstripe loyalty. There was such an atmosphere of helping on the club. The Mantles, the McDougalds, the Careys, the Colemans were eager to help out. They had been through it and were there to show the way. It was a fun time.*

EDDIE LOPAT: *We had a loyalty to the organization. It was part of the Yankee way. There was always a responsibility to the new players coming up. If there was some technique we could teach the young players to improve, we did it and they learned it. If they didn't they were gone.*

It was Yankees versus Milwaukee Braves in the 1957 World Series. It was showtime for Kubek, playing before his hometown folks. It was Kubek everywhere—he started games in left field, third base and center field. In Game Three he homered two times, making the highlight reel of the 12–3 Yankee mashing of Milwaukee. But Milwaukee defeated the Yankees in the series. In 1958 against the team from

Wisconsin, Kubek started at shortstop and the Yankees won the series.

Season to season, day by day, with Casey Stengel's feel for juggling, Tony Kubek, Number 10, sometimes never knew where he was going to play. No matter. He played in 1,092 games for the Yankees. Wherever he played, he did the job.

A two-time All-Star, a player on seven Yankee pennant winners and three World Champions, he and second baseman Bobby Richardson formed one of baseball's best double-play combinations for eight seasons. Incredibly sure hands and remarkable range helped Kubek pace all shortstops in total chances in 1961. Two seasons later he put up the fifth best fielding percentage by a Yankee shortstop, .980.

Still young at 29, still a major baseball talent, it all came crashing down for Tony Kubek on January 25, 1966. A Mayo Clinic assessment in 1965 showed that he had fused vertebrae in his back. If he continued playing baseball, he was informed, a collision could paralyze him.

Tony Kubek announced his retirement. There were many who believed he should be considered one of the better shortstops in Yankee history. Kubek played his last game just nine days before he turned 30. He homered in his final at bat.

TONY LAZZERI

"I've seen a few better second basemen, but not many. He has a phenomenal pair of hands, a great throwing arm and he covers acres of ground."

—*Miller Huggins*

On August 6, 1946, the baseball world was saddened to learn of the death in San Francisco of Tony Lazzeri at age 42. He fell down the stairway in his home.

The son of a blacksmith, Anthony Michael Lazzeri was born on December 6, 1903, in San Francisco. Lazzeri carried the memory of his growing-up years with him: "I was a pretty tough kid," he said.

"The neighborhood wasn't one in which a boy was likely to grow up a sissy, for it was fight or get licked, and I never got licked."

Playing for the Salt Lake City Bees in the Pacific Coast League in 1925, assisted by the altitude and the almost 200-game schedule, Lazzeri pounded 60 home runs, drove in 222 more and scored an amazing 202 runs.

The Yankees knew he was an epileptic, but they also knew he could play ball. For $55,000 and five players, the quiet second baseman became a Yankee. He debuted April 13, 1926. That rookie season of 1926, the 22-year-old batted .275, hit 18 home runs and drove in 114 runs.

Seemingly aloof, in reality it was his epilepsy that made him almost painfully quiet. But Lazzeri's talent spoke for itself. He was a clutch hitter with power, a deadly combo that fit the mix of six Yankee "Murderers' Row" pennant-winners.

Lazzeri was a favorite of the many Italian fans at Yankee Stadium who would scream out "Poosh 'em up, Tony," exhorting him to hit home runs.

The main right-handed power hitter on the '27 Yankees, five times a .300 hitter, Lazzeri drove in over 100 runs seven times. From 1927 through 1930, and again in 1932, Lazzeri batted .300 or better.

There were so many stars on the Yankee teams Lazzerri played on that his being overlooked was not new to him. In 1927, he hammered 18 home runs, good for third in the league. Ruth was first with 60 and Gehrig was second with 47.

On June 3, 1932, Lazzeri hit for the cycle, capping the day with a grand slam homer. Not that many took notice of the super second baseman's terrific accomplishment for in that same game Lou Gehrig slammed four home runs.

On May 24, 1936, Tony Lazzeri became the first Major Leaguer to hit two grand slams in one game and set a still-standing AL record with 11 RBIs. Tony Lazzeri appeared in six World Series in a dozen Yankee seasons and

Tony Lazzeri, one of the greatest of New York Yankee second basemen, was the Yankees' first Italian-American superstar.

played in the very first All-Star game. Fellow Italian and San Franciscan Frankie Crosetti was his teammate since 1932. Joe DiMaggio, another Italian and San Franciscan, joined him on the Yankees in 1936. But it was Lazzeri who was the first Italian-American superstar.

In 1991, the Veterans Committee finally put Lazzeri in The Hall of Fame.

EDDIE LOPAT

"The Yankee clubhouse had a bell. It rang five minutes before the game started. We went through the door. We were ready. The Yankees were always ready."

—*Eddie Lopat*

The sports columnist Red Smith once said that Lopat's pitches "never exceeded the speed limit," and Lopat once explained how he was successful with Ted Williams of the Red Sox, the best hitter at the time: "I never threw the same pitch twice and never to the same spot twice and he didn't like it."

Hitters called him "the Junkman" and worse for the baffling and wide variety of pitches he could throw—everything but real fastballs.

Eddie Lopat, "Steady Eddie" and "The Junkman," and as a pitcher he was all that.

He was born Edmund Walter Lopatynski.

EDDIE LOPAT: *As a kid growing up in New York City, I was always a Yankee fan. I wondered what made them tick.*

Even when I was with the White Sox, I wondered. My main purpose was to make a hitter off-stride. "I couldn't overpower hitters, so I had to operate from a different angle.

After four seasons with the White Sox, Lopat was traded to New York before the 1948 season. It was the first deal trader George Weiss made. Southpaw Lopat fit the Old Yankee Stadium perfectly—especially the deep left center field and center field dimensions. He became part of the pinstriped line lefty hurlers that includes Pennock through Gomez through Ford through Guidry through Pettitte through Sabathia.

It was said that Lopat was able to pitch three different ways: slow, slower and slowest. Free swingers were frustrated against him.

In 1949, first-year manager Casey Stengel sandwiched the southpaw in the Yankee pitching rotation between right-handed power pitchers Allie Reynolds and Vic Raschi, creating the "Big Three." The move was a brilliant one, making Lopat's slow stuff appear even slower than it actually was.

A Yankee stalwart from 1948 to 1955, Lopat made 202 starts for the Yankees and was 113–59 with a 3.19 ERA. He was an important component of the Yankee dynasty.

World Series time was Eddie Lopat time. In five series, 52 innings pitched, he won 4 games and lost but one and nailed down a 2.60 ERA. In the 1951 World Series, Lopat pitched complete game victories in Games Two and Five, giving up just one earned run in eighteen innings.

For five straight seasons Eddie Lopat wound up with a winning percentage between .667 and .800. They may have called him "Junkman," but the Yankees and their fans knew him best as "Steady Eddie."

SPARKY LYLE

"Your attention, please. Ladies and gentlemen, coming up to pitch for the Yankees, number 28, Sparky Lyle, Number 28!"

—*Bob Sheppard*

"Why pitch nine innings when you can get just as famous pitching two?"

—*Sparky Lyle*

His mother nicknamed him "Sparky" because she believed he was "a sparkling child." The "sparkler" in his time with the New York Yankees as a closer was a piece of work. He came to New York in the spring of 1972 in a trade with the Red Sox. He brought along a devastating slider, a pitch Ted Williams had pushed him to master.

"It's the only pitch," the Sox legend said, "the only pitch I couldn't hit when I knew it was coming."

Manager Ralph Houk knew he had an ace for the bullpen. That 1972 season, in 59 games and 107⅔ innings, Lyle posted a 1.92 ERA and the most saves in the league. In 1974 to 1975, in a new venue, Shea Stadium, Lyle had just 15 saves—he wasn't getting that many opportunities. He did go 9–3 with a 1.66 ERA.

PAUL DOHERTY: *Lyle was off-stride in 1975, saving just 6 games, his only relative poor year with the Yankees other than 1978 would be with Gossage there.*

On the mound, he showcased his superior and wicked slider with excellent results. At other times the lively southpaw was a source of laughs for his Yankee teammates: bare-ass sitting on birthday cakes, self-deprecating jokes and pranks, exiting from a coffin, sitting around nude, coming to spring training with his limbs in casts.

"Some people say you have to be nuts to be a relief pitcher," the man they were calling the "Count" said. "But the truth is, I was nuts before I ever became a relief pitcher."

All jokes aside, Lyle was a major franchise asset on an improving Yankee squad that had added Graig Nettles, Chris Chambliss and Catfish Hunter. Billy Martin was now (for a time) top man in the ever-revolving manager musical chairs game. In 1972, New York competed until early September. Lyle was an All-Star and led the league in saves.

The '77 season, the rubber-armed, free-spirited Lyle had the time of his life out of the bullpen, appearing in a league-high 72 games, pitching a career-high 137 innings. The heavy use did not lead to any ineffectiveness; in fact, he was brilliant with a 2.17 ERA, 26 more saves, numerous holds and bailouts. There were some fine starters in

Star southpaw reliever Albert Walter Lyle, best known as "Sparky," did his thing for the Yankees from 1973 to 1978.

the team's rotation that year, but Sparky was the star of pitching stars. Martin believed in Lyle. Lyle believed in Lyle. He was the first reliever in history to win the Cy Young Award. He added a win in the World Series as the Yankees trumped the Dodgers in six games.

"I wanted to find out if the diamond was for real on the World Series ring we got. So I cut the glass on my coffee table with it. Then I found out that the coffee table was worth more than the ring."

Paul Doherty, a longtime student of all things Yankees, remembers in telling detail a typical Lyle moment:

PAUL DOHERTY: *It's a hot summer night in the Bronx. Yankee manager Ralph Houk, head down, strides towards the pitcher's mound. On the way, he signals with his left hand to coach Jim Hegan in the right-field Yankee bullpen. A burly pitcher, his long brown hair flowing from under his Yankee cap, jumps up from the pen's bench, grabs his mitt and warm-up jacket, and heads to the waiting bullpen car, a 1972 pinstriped Datsun, "The Official Car of the New York Yankees."*

Grabbing a quick chaw of Red Man from a pouch in his jacket, he hops in the car and slams the door behind him. The car goes through the opened navy blue bullpen gate heading down the brown clay of the right-field track toward home.

Up in his tiny press box booth, Toby Wright, Yankee Stadium organist from 1971 to 1977, picks up the ringing phone. He shuffles through his sheet music and begins playing "Pomp and Circumstance" on his mighty Hammond. Each bar is greeted in the Stadium with louder cheers.

The Yankees' PR department created a tradition of bullpen entrance music. Somehow they decided "Pomp and Circumstance" was the appropriate music for Sparky foreshadowing the end of a game. It was a mirroring of composer Edward Elgar's march played at so many graduation endings, signifying the conclusion of academic studies.

PAUL DOHERTY: *Just before the Datsun comes to a complete stop in front of the Yankees' dugout, the pitcher jumps out, tosses his jacket into a waiting batboy's arms, puts his glove on his right hand, makes sure that chaw of Red Man is behind his right-hand cheek and jogs with confidence to the mound, where manager Houk and a couple of infielders wait.*

Bob Sheppard, poised in the press box in the loge above third base, glances up from the Chesterton poems he'd been immersed in and clicks on his gray Electrovos microphone. His cultured baritone interrupts the ponderous organ.

A prankster, a player with a prominent potbelly, a guy who was his own man, Sparky Lyle was all business on the pitcher's mound. Loose as a goose, primed and ready, in his seven Yankee seasons he racked up 141 saves and 1.41 ERA. His efforts helped the Yankees get into three World Series.

A three-time All-Star, Lyle never started a Major League game in a 16-year career. Unfortunately, it all ended badly for Lyle. At age 34, a key cog for the Yanks as closer from the early 1970s, he had thrown almost 260 innings for manager Billy Martin over the past two seasons. George Steinbrenner had signed relief pitchers "Goose" Gossage and Rawley Eastwick.

Now considered redundant, on November 10, 1978, Albert Walter Lyle was shipped off to the Rangers in a 10-player trade. And in the words of Graig Nettles, "Lyle went from Cy Young to Sayonara."

LARRY MACPHAIL

"There is a thin line between genius and insanity, and in Larry's case it was sometimes so thin you could see him drifting back and forth." —Leo Durocher

"The Rambunctious Redhead is not, after all, defiling Yankee history. He's writing it." —Fortune Magazine, July 1946

There are very few baseball general managers enshrined in the Hall of Fame. There have been very few general managers who have been at the level of Col. Leland Stanford MacPhail. He was with the Cincinnati Reds from 1933 to 1936, the Brooklyn Dodgers from 1937 to 1942, the New York Yankees from 1945 to 1947. As general manager plus much more he was all things to all these teams.

The red-haired native of Michigan's resume featured a law degree from Georgetown University, military service in the First World War as an artillery captain, and a decade's accomplishments in law and business. At Cincinnati, he pioneered night baseball and commercial air travel. At Brooklyn, he brought in Branch Rickey in 1938 and saw the franchise make money in its first year since 1920. Then it was on to the Yankees, where his brief tenure would leave an enduring mark.

In early 1943 MacPhail was working for the War Department and desirous of another baseball opportunity. His grandson Andy recalled: "Even though he didn't have a penny, really. As he often did, he went to '21' for a drink to try to figure out what to do. He met Dan Topping, his tenant, when Topping owned the Brooklyn Tigers football team and my grandfather owned the Dodgers and Ebbets Field. Topping, a sportsman and a playboy, was always interested in buying a baseball team with MacPhail. Later, Bing Crosby recommended as a third partner builder Del Webb," a

Larry MacPhail: As a Yankee owner, he was inventive, irascible and ingenious.

Season box seats were put in place as was individualized dining and increased seating for corporate patronage and business. These innovations would be standard throughout baseball. A new Stadium Club with luxurious seating was created. That move brought in $500,000 before the 1946 season even started. It became a place for box seat holders, a place where the privileged mingled with those who wanted to be seen with the privileged. The Club would hold the record for having the biggest bar in all of New York State.

PAUL DOHERTY: *Nat Cohen, who ran the Stadium Club, wouldn't let you pass through the club to get to the elevator and brought you to the media area unless you were wearing a jacket. There was a "jackets only" policy at the Stadium Club, whether you were a guest or a Yankee employee.*

MacPhail created a brand new clubhouse for the Yankees, a smaller new one for the visiting team, and a new and more utilitarian press box for media. He transferred the Yankee offices to Fifth Avenue. Old-Timers' Days had existed from the first Lou Gehrig Day on July 7, 1939, but MacPhail made the event an annual affair.

The imaginative MacPhail set in motion Yankee travel by air on a regular basis. He arranged the first Major League TV contract in a time when there were but 500 television sets in the New York area. He installed women ushers and a women's lounge at the Stadium. His promotions included free nylon stockings for women, foot races and an archery skills competition.

construction and real estate magnate from Arizona.

On January 25, 1945, the MacPhail-Topping-Webb trio purchased the Yankee franchise for $2.9 million from the estate of Col. Jacob Ruppert. Included in the transaction were 400 players, 266 of them in military service, Yankee Stadium, ballparks in Newark and Kansas City and leases on other minor league ballparks.

MacPhail was put in charge as president. Topping, Webb and George Weiss were elected vice presidents. The longtime and highly successful Yankee executive, now 75 years old, Ed Barrow was made chairman of the board. It was an empty title with no duties. MacPhail would become the new Ed Barrow and more. The longtime power of the Yankees, Barrow had contempt for MacPhail and had said: "Only over my dead body will MacPhail buy the Yankees."

Not only did he and his partners build the Yankees, but they also moved the franchise into another era of greatness making the right decisions. A case in point: The Giants had offered $50,000 for Yogi Berra. Owner Larry MacPhail passed in one of the smartest decisions he ever made.

"So I waited for my first look at the prize package," MacPhail told the story. "The instant I saw him my heart sank and I wondered why I had been so foolish to refuse to sell him. In busted a stocky little guy in a sailor suit. He had no neck and his muscles were virtually busting the buttons off his uniform. He was one of the unpresupposing fellows I ever set eyes on in my life. And the sailor suit accentuated every defect."

In 1946, boisterous and driven, MacPhail got to work allocating $600,000 worth of improvements at Yankee Stadium. He removed a number of flagpoles that stuck out from the stadium roof, and in their place had six large steel structures built and positioned to hold hundreds of electric lights for night baseball. The press release declared that "arc lights would equal the illumination of 5,000 full moons."

Dugout locations were switched. The third base side went to the visiting team and the Yankees taking over the dugout on the first base side of the infield. Reinstalling 15,000 seats, adding more promotional events, the new New York Yankees drew an all-time record 2,265,512 customers in 1946. Larry MacPhail was doing his thing and doing it well.

In 1945, with the world at war, with many first-string Yankee players still in the service, there was no real chance to re-shape the Yankees. In spite of a host of star players returning from military service, including Joe DiMaggio, the 1946 Yankees won only 87 games.

Much of MacPhail's energy was instead directed toward the day-to-day activities of the team, which ticked off Joe McCarthy, who had won seven World Series as the Yankees manager. McCarthy had always been a drinker, but during the almost serene times working with Ed Barrow he had kept his habit in check. In 1945, his alcohol consumption increased. He left the club on July 20, returning to his home in Buffalo. The word was spread that Joe McCarthy was struggling with poor health. He wanted to resign; MacPhail prevailed on him to come back and manage and he did.

Joe McCarthy left the club for "health" reasons again. He did not return. Bill Dickey as manager lasted from May to September. Realizing MacPhail had no plans to extend him to 1947, Dickey quit. Johnny Neun filled in the rest of the season. MacPhail then hired Bucky Harris, a managerial veteran of 20 seasons for 1947.

During the off-season of 1946 MacPhail sent star second baseman Joe Gordon to the Indians for pitcher Allie Reynolds. It would be hailed as an excellent move. In January of 1947 MacPhail signed veteran first baseman George McQuinn. That also turned out well for MacPhail. The 37-year-old had one good year left.

With Harris at the helm in 1947, the Yanks romped to 97 wins and the American League pennant. A dramatic World Series victory over the Dodgers in seven games made the good times roll again for the Yankees and their fans and their front office.

All season long, bad blood and much bickering had existed between MacPhail and Topping and Webb. MacPhail also did not get along with some of the players. There were times that season that he had threatened to resign. Then the shocker took place. An out-of-control Larry MacPhail in the Biltmore Hotel celebratory dinner, with a cigarette in one hand, a bottle of beer in the other, hurled insults, slugged a sportswriter. And then shocked everyone by resigning: "I'm through. I'm through. My heart just can't stand it anymore."

The next day Topping and Webb bought him out. Topping was elected president. George Weiss was named general manager. "MacPhail's connection with the Yankees is ended," said Topping.

Webb, Topping and Weiss would remain in place and in power for thirteen years with the Yankees. There would be ten pennants and seven World Series titles.

Larry MacPhail had turned his initial $250,000 investment in the New York Yankees into $2 million in less than three years. Baseball was his passion, his love. He would never work in the sport again.

Admitted into the Baseball Hall of Fame in 1978, the tempestuous MacPhail had passed three years before. He left behind a legacy; his son Bill a longtime TV sports executive and his other son Lee MacPhail was a Hall of Fame baseball executive, including a stint as Yankees GM and as President of the American League. His grandson, Andy MacPhail, is currently the president of the Philadelphia Phillies.

His son Bill said of him: "Unfortunately, a person with Dad's talent comes along only once every 50 years. I've never thought of imitating him. I inherited neither his genius nor his temper. I'm just an ordinary person."

MICKEY MANTLE

"He was a real country boy, all shy and embarrassed. He arrived with a straw suitcase and two pairs of slacks and one blue sports jacket that probably cost about eight dollars." —Whitey Ford

"I always thought he was the fastest human being I ever saw, and I saw Olympic sprinters." —Bobby Brown

Super scout Tom Greenwade was a quiet-spoken, straw-hat kind of guy. His basic equipment was a stopwatch and a notebook. What thoughts went through his mind in 1949 watching the semipro Baxter Springs, Oklahoma, Whiz Kids and seeing the 18-year-old shortstop named Mickey Mantle, named after the Hall of Fame catcher Mickey Cochrane. "I now know how scout Krichell must have felt the first time he saw Lou Gehrig," Greenwade said later. "Mickey possessed tremendous power from both sides of the plate, had blinding speed and a great arm."

The young Mantle grew up in Commerce, Oklahoma, excelling in baseball and football. His father Mutt and his grandfather Charlie helped him become what he became, the greatest switch-hitter in the history of baseball. Mutt helped him develop, pitching to his son right-handed.

Tom Greenwade and Mutt Mantle, Mickey's dad, sat in the Yankee scout's 1947 Oldsmobile in a parking lot and talked contract. The deal for the young Mantle was a signing bonus of $1,150 and a salary of $140 a month. Greenwade deliberately low-balled Mantle's arm, batting and fielding ability to get as economical a signing as possible. It didn't take much to downgrade Mickey's defense at shortstop, which was a work in progress.

In two minor league seasons, the "Commerce Comet" made 102 errors. But he batted .313 in 1949. In 1950, his average was .383. He smashed 26 homers and drove in 136 runs. He was also clocked running from home to first base in 3.1 seconds.

In spring training 1951, former Yankee outfield star Tommy Henrich was assigned to mentor the young and talented prospect. After a while the former star Yankee outfielder said, "There isn't any more that I can teach him."

That first spring, Casey Stengel switched Mantle to the outfield and said: "I never saw a player who had greater promise. That young fellow has me terribly confused. He should have a year in Triple A Ball but with his combination of speed and power he should win the triple batting crown every year. In fact, he should do anything he wants to do."

Later, Casey who had seen it all, added: "There've been a lot of fast men but none as big and strong as Mantle. He's gonna be around a long time, if he can stay well, that fella of mine."

The 19-year-old Mickey Charles Mantle made his debut for the New York Yankees on April 17, 1951. That season he would play in 96 games in right field alongside aging center fielder superstar Joe DiMaggio.

About that first game, he commented: "It was the worst day of my life. I don't think I slept a wink the night before. And I was trembling all over from the moment I reached Yankee Stadium. I was so scared." About Yankee Stadium, he said, "There was a great, dark mystery

when I first came here. Now I think this is about the prettiest ballpark I ever saw."

The teenager went through an emotional roller coaster in his rookie season. It was a time of excitement but also struggle adjusting to Major League pitchers. Reluctantly, Casey Stengel made the tough decision and sent him down on July 15th to the Yankee Kansas City farm team. A struggling Mantle considered quitting.

"I thought I raised a ballplayer," his father Mutt told him. "You're nothing but a coward and a quitter." Then Mutt Mantle began to pack his son's bags. Mantle changed his mind.

Facts show that after that father-son face-off, in the very next game Mantle broke out of his slump and after 40 games and 50 RBIs with Kansas City, Mantle made it back with the Yankees. His rookie numbers were not gaudy as they would be, but respectable: .267, 13 home runs and 65 RBIs.

The 1951 World Series was the battle of New York Yankees versus Giants. In the second game, Willie Mays sent the ball on a fly to short center. Instincts on fire, Mantle took off for the ball. DiMaggio called him off. Slowing down, pulling up, seeing that the ball would be caught by the Yankee Clipper, Mantle's spikes got caught in a drainpipe covering. His right knee was torn up. The mishap foreshadowed the tough luck and injury bug that would haunt Mantle through the 2,401 games he played in his 18-year Yankee career.

At one time there were doubts there would be a career for him at all. Mantle was kicked in the shin competing in youth football. His leg was infected with osteomyelitis. The fallout from the disease lasted his lifetime and might have triggered other injuries that sapped some of his speed.

In 1952, with DiMag retired, Mantle took over as center fielder. One legend left and another legend

was poised to prevail. The Yankees became Mantle's team—he became the centerpiece on the most successful team in history. Able to run like the wind, able to thrill to the joy of competing, the roar of the crowd, the center of the stage, "the Mick" was unlike any other player in baseball history.

He blasted tape-measure home runs. He hit for average. He had blinding speed and could take the extra base. He was the first power-hitting switch-hitter, the greatest switch-hitter of all time. He hit in the clutch, thrived on pressure, could carry the team on his back.

"He was fairly amazin' in several respects," Casey Stengel noted.

In ten seasons Mantle collected more than 100 walks, nine straight seasons he scored 100 or more runs, four times he won the American League home run and slugging titles. He collected 2,415 career hits, batted .300 or more ten times, won three MVP awards and was on an astounding 20 All-Star teams. He scored more runs than he drove in (1,677 to 1,509), a rarity among power hitters. He pounded 536 career homers.

So many home runs had been whacked in "The House That Ruth Built." But over the years dead center field at Yankee Stadium had been known as "Death Valley," too tough an area for most home runs to reach.

But "The Mick" put one into the ninth row, dead center, 486 feet from home plate in 1964. His signature slams were long and high and like cannon shots. Mantle would be the American League home run king in 1955, and again in 1956, 1958 and 1960.

"He hit balls over buildings," said Stengel.

There was the 565-foot blast he hit off southpaw Chuck Stobbs in Washington in 1953, the first of the "tape-measure" homers. In 1954, he slugged a ball that missed by 18 inches of being the first one to go out of Yankee

Hall of Famer Mickey Mantle played 2,401 games in his 18-year Yankee career.

Stadium. His shot off right-hander Pedro Ramos smashed into the top of the right field upper-deck facade and stayed in the park.

"In my whole career, I never looked up once at a home run. You don't want to embarrass the pitcher," Mantle said. "But on the ball I nearly hit over the roof at Yankee Stadium, I just had to look up. Pedro Ramos was pitching, and he threw me a perfect, hard fastball, right over the middle of the plate. I swung as hard as I've ever swung, and as soon as it left the bat, I knew it was fair and I also knew it was the longest ball I'd ever hit. So I looked up to see how far it would go. It

kept going up, and I thought it would go over the roof, but it hit the facade about two feet from the top and bounced back. When it hit, I put my head down and continued by trot. I never hit a ball that hard again."

In 1956, the "Mick" won the Triple Crown. His output was so great that he led both leagues in 1956, hitting .353 with 52 home runs and 130 runs batted in. He was also voted American League MVP that year, and again in 1957 and again in 1962.

Mickey Mantle was a favorite of Billy Crystal. He even had a couple of not so funny lines about the "Commerce

Comet." "I used to limp around my neighborhood imitating him" (a reference to the limp that Mantle developed in later years running the bases. And "I did my Bar Mitzvah with an Oklahoma drawl."

Sadly, after so many years of brilliance, Mantle's career was not what it had been. Physical injuries were just of the sad package. By 1967, he was forced to move to first base. The next season would be his last.

In his last years (1965–68), Mantle batted .255, .288, .245 and .237. "Falling under .300," Mantle said, "was the biggest disappointment of my career."

"Sometimes," Mantle said in retirement, "I sit in my den at home and read stories about myself. Kids used to save whole scrapbooks on me. They get tired of them and mail them to me. I'll go in there and read them, and you know what? They might as well be about Musial or DiMaggio. It's like reading about somebody else."

"When I retired," Mantle said, "I was probably an alcoholic but didn't know it. God gave me a body and the ability to play baseball and I just wasted it. I keep having these dreams. I go to the ballpark late, jump out of a cab, and I hear 'em calling my name on the public address system. I try and get in and all the gates are locked. Then I see a hole under the fence and I can see Casey looking for me, and Yogi and Billy Martin and Whitey Ford. I try to crawl through the hole and I get stuck at the hips. And that's when I wake up, sweating."

And there was the realization by

The "M&M Boys," Mickey Mantle and Roger Maris, for a time were in a battle to break Ruth's record.

Mickey Mantle: "I figure I got all the breaks. Otherwise, I'd have been in the mines."

Hall of Fame admission came in 1974.

On August 13, 1995, in Dallas, Mickey Mantle died of liver cancer. He was 63 years old.

ROGER MARIS

"You ask Maris a question, and he stares at you for a week before he answers."
—Casey Stengel

"Now they talk on the radio about the record set by Ruth, and DiMaggio and Henry Aaron. But they rarely mention mine. Do you know what I have to show for the sixty-one home runs? Nothing, exactly nothing."   —Roger Maris

He was born Roger Eugene Maras on September 10, 1934, in Hibbing, Minnesota. His parents were first-generation Croatian Americans. When he was five, his family settled in North Dakota. In high school, the young Maras was a standout in track, basketball and football. He starred in American Legion Baseball because his high school had no baseball team.

In 1955, he legally changed his surname to Maris. Hearing the taunts of "Mar-Ass" in his growing-up years spurred the change. At around that time he turned down a scholarship to the University of Oklahoma and signed with the Cleveland Indians. First stop—Fargo-Moorhead of the Northern League. In 1957, he made the big leagues with the Indians who traded him in June 1958 to Kansas City.

In December 1959 Roger Maris became a Yankee. Part of a big trade that sent Yankees Hank Bauer and Don Larsen to Kansas City, the 25-year-old, 6-foot-tall, 197-pound outfielder was never fully embraced by fans of the Yankees.

On Opening Day, April 19, 1960, at Fenway Park he came to play in his first

game as a Yankee. Blasting two home runs, going 4-for-5 with four RBIs, he was on his way.

That "rookie" Yankee Roger Maris slugged one less homer than the league leader Mickey Mantle's 40. His 112 RBIs paced the league. His slugging percentage of .581 led the league. He won his only Gold Glove and the first of two straight MVP awards.

The 1961 season for Number 9 began slowly. Then he caught fire and also caught a great deal of flak from those opposed to his challenging the season home run record of George Herman Ruth.

Hall of Famer Rogers Hornsby echoed the anti-Maris sentiment: "It would be a shame if Ruth's record is broken by a .270 hitter." But by season's end, Maris had broken Babe Ruth's single season home run record by smashing 61 four-baggers. He paid a price for being the unlikely one to break the record of a legend. He reacted with criticism to those who he felt disrespected him: "I never wanted all this hoopla. I was born surly, and I'm going to stay that way. Everything in life is tough."

"People just remember the 61 home runs," said his Yankee teammate Bill Skowron. "They forget that Roger was a superb right fielder. He was the best defensive right fielder in the majors. He was an all-around ball player, a humble guy, a real team player. History never gave him his due."

Named to the All-Star team for the fourth straight year in 1962, the next year, with injuries limiting him to just 90 games, Maris managed just 23 homers. But he helped the Yanks take a fourth straight pennant.

His last two Yankee seasons, 1965 and 1966 saw playing time reduced because of a hand injury. In December of 1966, the Yankees traded him to the Cardinals who he helped win two pennants.

Angry at being traded off, Roger Maris stayed away from a number of Yankee Old-Timers' games. Finally, in 1978, he returned to Yankee Stadium. The reception was very positive. "It's like obituaries," Maris said. "When you die, they give you good reviews."

Lymphatic cancer was the cause of death for Roger Maris on December 14, 1985. He was only 51 years old.

BILLY MARTIN

"I may not have been the greatest Yankee to put on the uniform, but I am the proudest." —Billy Martin

"He put fannies in the seats." —George Steinbrenner

"Billy Martin was a winner," recalled Dave Righetti. "I enjoyed playing for him, especially those early years. You knew he was going to be aggressive. He gave me the ball and let me pitch. He had confidence in me and when a manager of that stature feels confidence in you, you feel it more yourself."

"Billy Martin is not an intellectual," said Reggie Jackson. "But there is a cunningness to him that is something to behold."

Billy Martin had five up and down stints as Yankee manager with one World Series title. He had a remarkable .333 batting average in 28 career World Series games that included 99 at bats. He saved Game 7 of the 1952 World Series with a stunning catch. He set a World Series record in 1953 for most hits, 12, in a six-game Series, tying a record for highest batting average, .500.

Casey Stengel loved him. The New York City tabloids couldn't get enough of him. It seemed he was a Yankee forever, yet he only played seven seasons for the Bombers.

Alfred Manuel Martin was born May 16, 1928, in Berkeley, California.

Called Belli, Italian for "pretty" by his grandmother, Billy grew up fighting. A bit runt-like, smallish, with a chip on his shoulder, he carried that with him all his life.

When he was just a child, Alfred Manuel (Billy) Pesano's mother told him: "Don't take nothing from nobody. If you can't hit 'em, bite 'em." He never forgot what she said.

"I didn't like to fight," he once explained, "but I didn't have a choice. If you walked through the park, a couple kids would come after you. When you were small, someone was always chasing you."

In his adult years there were fights with Clint Courtney, a catcher for the St. Louis Browns, in 1952 and 1953. He broke the jaw of Jim Brewer in 1960. The Chicago pitcher won $10,000 in a lawsuit. In 1969, as a manager, he kayoed Dave Boswell, one of his players who was battling with another player. Six years later he battled with his own player Ed Whitson in a Baltimore hotel. Martin's arm was broken.

Billy Martin's Yankee debut was April 18, 1950. He showed up after two successful seasons playing in the Pacific Coast League for Oakland, managed by Casey Stengel. For the childless Casey Stengel, Martin was the son he never had. He was called "Casey's boy" and "Billy the Kid" for good reason.

Stengel said of him: "If liking a kid who never let you down in the clutch is favoritism, then I plead guilty."

Undersized, highly combative, bereft of even a touch of elegance, Billy Martin was not one who fit the typical Yankee image. Yet, in many ways he was the motor of those remarkable Yankee teams of the 1950s.

Only the "Ol' Perfessor" could get away with a line like this about Billy Martin: "Now you take Ernie Lombardi who's a big man and has a big nose and you

take (Billy) Martin who's a little man and has a bigger nose. How do you figure it?"

In 1957, it was reported in newspapers that the catalyst in the slugfest at Manhattan's Copacabana nightclub was Billy Martin. The Yankees garnered a lot of bad press that especially angered George Weiss. Never really a fan of Martin, Weiss shipped him off to Kansas City, the first of a half-dozen teams he would finish his playing career with. Martin thought it was his manager who traded him away. It took years for the Stengel-Martin relationship to return to what it had been.

BRAD TURNOW: *It was true Martin felt betrayed by Stengel after the trade and the two did not speak for years. Martin felt Stengel could have prevented the trade, not so much that it was Stengel who traded him.*

Martin had stints as manager of Minnesota, Detroit and Texas. The Rangers let him go on July 20, 1975. Thirteen days later he linked up with the Yankees again, taking over as manager.

His homecoming had true Yankees of New York touches. After 18 years of exile, a favorite son returned on Old-Timers' Day 1975. He put on the pinstriped uniform and got to work.

"Billy Ball" they called it—and the fans loved it, loved especially the pennant in 1976, another pennant in 1977 and a World Series win. Daring was in. Unpredictability was in. Billy Martin was king of the hill.

BOBBY MURCER: *A lot of managers were afraid to make certain unorthodox moves. They were afraid of the second-guessers. Billy was not.*

On July 25, 1978, the King of the Hill was no more. George Steinbrenner fired Billy Martin. Four days later, ironically at Old-Timers' Day, it was announced that Martin would return as skipper in 1980. Actually, he returned earlier. On July 19, 1979, the hyper Martin replaced Bob Lemon who had taken his place as manager.

In his second stint, Martin guided the Yankees to fourth place in the American League East. Key injuries, subpar performances by Catfish Hunter, Thurman Munson's passing—all contributed to the lackluster Yankees. An October 1979 marshmallow salesman fight in a Minnesota hotel eased Martin out of the manager's job. He was fired for the second time.

Billy Martin bounced back again for the 1983 season. It was not a very good time. Incidents made the back pages of the New York tabloids—kicking dirt on one umpire, suspension for a couple of games for calling another umpire "a stone liar." The door to the manager's office would be closed. And Martin

Collectible baseball card of Billy Martin, whose record as Yankee manager was 556 wins, 385 defeats.

stayed inside plotting, drinking, smoking his pipe. Drinking more and more, the hyperactive pilot grew nastier, abrasive and alienating. He made appointments with media people and failed to keep them.

Your scribe showed up for a long-scheduled appointment with Billy Martin only to be told in a nasty voice, "You got the day wrong. You better learn how to do your job. The appointment was for tomorrow."

Tomorrow came. I showed. "This is not the day and time we agreed on." Martin began.

I didn't dignify his madness with a response. I walked out.

It seemed those who knew him well were not too fond of him.

Coach Don Zimmer, players like Steve Kemp, Ken Griffey and Goose Gossage, went on record: If Billy returned in 1984, they would not. On December l6, 1983, it was "HELLO, YOGI BERRA. GOODBYE, BILLY MARTIN!"

The 1985 Yankees added speedster Ricky Henderson to their powerful lineup that included Don Mattingly, Dave Winfield and Don Baylor. The Yankees won six of their first sixteen games. George Steinbrenner's trigger finger grew itchy again. On April 25, 1985, headlines declared: "YOGI'S OUT, BILLY'S BACK."

The crazy managerial carousel continued. On October 27, 1985, Martin was canned for the fourth time by Steinbrenner. On October 19, 1987, Billy Martin returned as manager for the fifth time. On June 23, 1988, Billy Martin was out as manager.

Five times in the 1980s, Billy Martin managed the Yankees. In but three seasons—1976, 1977 and 1983— did he manage for the entire schedule of games. In 16 years as skipper with five different franchises, Billy Martin

managed 2,267 games, winning 1,253, losing 1,013. But the team he really belonged to in his heart of hearts was the New York Yankees where he was Number One. His record as manager was 556 wins, 385 losses, two American League titles and the one world championship.

On Christmas Day 1989, Billy Martin, 61, was killed in an automobile accident. "We used to tease each other about whose liver would go first. I never thought it would end for him this way," said Mickey Mantle.

GEORGE STEINBRENNER'S "SEVEN COMMANDMENTS" FOR JUDGING BILLY MARTIN

1. Does he win?
2. Does he work hard enough?
3. Is he emotionally equipped to lead the men?
4. Is he organized?
5. Is he prepared?
6. Does he understand human nature?
7. Is he honorable?

HIDEKI MATSUI

"Matsui is one of my favorite players. He's one of my favorite teammates. He comes ready to play every day. He's a professional hitter. All he wants to do is win."
—Derek Jeter

Born June 12, 1974, in Kanazawa, Ishikawa, Japan, Hideki Matsui was 28 years old when he made his debut with the New York Yankees.

"I'm aware the fans in the U.S. can be less forgiving," the nine-time All-Star in Japan said. "I'll just have to do my best to please them."

And did he ever. He was a big ticket free agent who showed up at the Stadium, a mighty weapon for the Bombers for 2003. Matsui signed for three years and $21 million.

Opening Day 2003 at Yankee Stadium was delayed by 24 hours because of the threat of a big snowstorm. The game was finally played on April 8th. Showing the power that earned him the nickname "Godzilla" in Japan, Matsui became the first Yankee to smash a grand slammer in his first game at the Stadium. It was also a terrific foreshadowing of his left-handed stroke—one tailor-made for the ballpark.

He was all the Yankees hoped he would be—finishing second in Rookie of the Year voting, Matsui batted .287 with 16 home runs and 106 RBIs. He was also an All-Star.

"He was a clutch player ever since I've known him," said Yankees manager Joe Girardi of the southpaw slugger, who took over for Joe Torre in 2008.

In his second season for the team from the Bronx, the 6-foot-2, 210-pounder at age 30 had what would be his best year as a big leaguer. He batted .298 and had career highs in slugging percentage and homers.

From 2003 to 2005, Matsui led the big leagues annually in games played. Mainly a left fielder, he also played other outfield positions and was a DH, too. Matsui was a clutch hitter, a constant, controlled performer for the Yankees no matter the game circumstance, the team's position in the standings.

There are still those who recall the song "Godzilla" by Blue Oyster Cult being played for him as he came up and headed for the left-handed batter's box.

He was the first player to win both a Japan Series Most Valuable Player Award (2000) and a World Series Most Valuable Player Award. Matsui's record-tying six RBIs in his final game as a Yankee in the 2009 World Series, powered the Yankees to the world championship.

In Game 3 in 2004, ALCS, Matsui had another notable achievement. He became the first player ever to have at least 5 runs scored and 5 RBIs in the same postseason game.

In 916 games with New York from 2003 to 2009, the always restrained slugger hit 140 home runs and finished with a career batting average of .282. Matsui's six RBI Game 6 (his final game as a Yankee) 2009 World Series at Yankee Stadium powered the Yankees to the world championship. That was some exclamation point to his time in pinstripes.

Slowed by injuries, the slugger moved on to play for the Angels, Athletics and Rays.

Then on July 28, 2013, Matsui signed a one-day minor league contract with the New York Yankees in order to officially retire as a member of the team.

DON MATTINGLY

"I don't believe any player on the New York Yankees was ever as great as Don Mattingly in every way during my years as an owner. He was a great athlete and a great player. Some great athletes are not great human beings and vice versa. This man combined all of that." —*George Steinbrenner*

A nine-time winner of the Gold Glove Award, a six-time All-Star, Don Mattingly's Number 23 was retired in 1997. In his rookie season he was paid $33,500. In his last season he earned $4,420,000.

And that is just part of his glowing Yankee profile.

Donald Arthur Mattingly out of Evansville, Indiana, was 21 years old when he made his Major League baseball debut September 8, 1982. In his first full season, 1984, he captured the American League batting title with a .343 average over teammate and expensive free agent Dave Winfield. The player they called "Donnie Baseball" was also the league leader in hits and doubles. And for good measure, making just five errors, Mattingly led all first basemen in fielding.

"The Hitman" continued his splendid work in 1985, winning the

"Donnie Baseball," Donald Arthur Mattingly hammered a record six grand slams.

MVP award, batting .324, smashing 35 home runs and driving in 145 runs. In 1986, he batted .352, led the league with 238 hits and 53 doubles. Tying a Major League record by hitting a home run in eight consecutive games in 1987, Mattingly also hammered a record six grand slams.

Mattingly would spend a half hour each day just hitting balls off a kid's batting tee. He would take indoor batting practice and outdoor batting practice. For him those practices were very serious work. He was a player always ready, always honed in, not dependent on luck. He always prided himself as being the "man," the one to produce when producing was paramount.

"He has that look that few hitters have," noted Dwight Gooden. "I don't know if it's his stance, his eyes, or what. But you can tell he means business."

His first six full seasons were remarkable. The eighties were Mattingly's time. The image lingers—cap set low on his head, bill down, thick lampblack under his eyes. A sweet swinger, from 1984 to 1989, he batted .300 or better each year. Problems with his back in the late 1980s into the 1990s negatively impacted his performance.

"Donnie Baseball" was the tenth player in Yankee history to be named captain. He is rated the greatest Yankee to never play in a World Series. The quiet Don Mattingly posted a lifetime .307 average, 2,153 hits and 222 home runs. He was a top-line first baseman with only 64 errors in 1,634 career games at that position.

"He was a great hitter and a great ballplayer," Yogi Berra said. "It's just a shame his career had to end so soon. I guess in the end that back just got too bad."

JOE McCARTHY

"Never a day went by, when you didn't learn something from McCarthy."
—*Joe DiMaggio*

He played in the minor leagues for 15 seasons, never played in the Major Leagues. After the untimely death of Miller Huggins in 1929, Yankee owner Jake Ruppert finally hired Joe McCarthy, late of the Chicago Cubs, to take over the 1931 Yankees. During an early press conference, McCarthy mangled Jake Ruppert's name. And the aristocratic Yankee owner half-joked: "Maybe McCarthy will stay around long enough to learn my name."

One more time the beer baron had picked another winner. Not only did McCarthy learn Ruppert's name, but he made him proud, made him lots of money. In his 16 years as pilot in pinstripes, McCarthy's teams won 1,460 wins, lost just 867 and compiled an amazing .627 winning percentage.

The new pilot was a no-nonsense type. The team he inherited had some bad habits, had not been what it could be. "Marse Joe" as some called him, pushed the pride button hard for his players. He taught them how to dress, how to tip in restaurants, how to act in a hotel lobby and how to be gentlemen. They looked like champions; they began

Hall of Famer "Marse Joe," Joe McCarthy, a great manager of the Yankees from 1931–1946.

again to play like champions.

No hot dogs or peanuts were allowed in the Yankee dugout. All players except for the starting pitcher had to appear before 8:30 a.m. for breakfast in jackets and ties. Players were told to shave before they came to the ballpark. "This is your job. Shave before you come to work," he told them.

For McCarthy, his only focus was the game. He permitted himself no diversions, no hobbies and no distractions. "A ballplayer has only two hours of concentrated work every day with occasional days off," the square-jawed taskmaster said. "If he cannot attend to business with the high pay and the working hours so pleasant, something is wrong with him and he ought to move on."

"Marse Joe" had his own Ten Commandments of Baseball. He even had the team's caps and uniforms cut larger so his Yankees would appear bigger

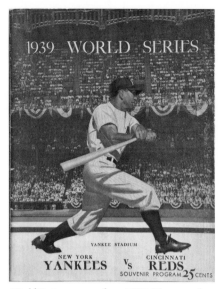

World Series program from 1927. That year the team featured many top-drawer players—Lou Gehrig, Pat Collins, Tony Lazzeri, Mark Koenig, Bob Meusel, Earl Combs and Wilcy Moore.

and stronger. The brilliant McCarthy held sway over all things from his seat in the dugout. "I never roamed the dugout," he said. "I was there seated in the middle, the command post." In McCarthy's first 13 seasons with the Yankees, his teams finished in first or second place in every season but one.

McCarthy was the first manager to separate a pitching staff into starters and relievers. In 1932, McCarthy became the first manager to win pennants in both leagues when his Yankees beat his former team, the Cubs, in the World Series. Afterwards, there was a string of second-place finishes. Writers unkindly and unfairly called him "Second-Place Joe."

Featuring power baseball, McCarthy piloted the Yankees from 1936 to 1939 to four straight world championships. There were pennants in 1941, 1942 and 1943. But the Yanks dropped to third place in 1944 and fourth place in 1945. Those two years the team was especially depleted of talent. McCarthy was drinking more than ever.

Then on May 24, 1946, 35 games into the season, Joseph Vincent McCarthy quit. "He was drinking too

much," Joe DiMaggio told reporters. "He wasn't eating right and he was worried about the team because it was playing so lousy."

His relationship with new Yankee owners—Dan Topping, Del Webb and Larry MacPhail—was strained, and so was he. There was a return to baseball by McCarthy in 1948 as manager of the Boston Red Sox and some fierce battles with the Yankees. Hall of Fame enshrinement for the hard-nosed Irishman Joseph Vincent McCarthy was well deserved.

He passed away in 1978 at age 90.

JOE MCCARTHY'S TEN COMMANDMENTS FOR SUCCESS IN THE MAJOR LEAGUES

1. Nobody can become a ballplayer by walking after a ball.
2. You will never become a .300 hitter unless you take the bat off your shoulder.
3. An outfielder who throws after a runner is locking the barn door after the house is stolen.
4. Keep your head up, and you may not have to keep it down.
5. When you start to slide, slide. He who changes his mind may have to change a good leg for a bad one.
6. Do not alibi on bad hops. Anybody can field the good ones.
7. Always run them out. You can never tell.
8. Do not quit.
9. Do not fight too much with the umpires. You cannot expect them to be as perfect as you.
10. A pitcher who hasn't control, hasn't anything.

BOB MEUSEL

"He had lightnin' on the ball."
—Casey Stengel

He played his career with the Yankees in the shadow of Babe Ruth and Lou

Gehrig. He also had a brother who played quite well in the National League, Irish Meusel. Nevertheless, Robert William Meusel out of San Jose, California made a name for himself. In ten seasons of playing Yankee baseball he batted a career .311.

The real rap against him by a lot of his teammates and, from those who played against him, from manager Miller Huggins was his indifferent attitude, his aloofness for which he earned the appellation "Silent Bob." That was putting it mildly. Meusel could be morose, moody, menacing. A heavy drinker, a scowler, a grunter, he was one of the bad guys in baseball. In 1924, the Yankee outfielder, bat in hand, raced out to the mound ready to lay it on a Tiger pitcher. The incident set off one of the worst riots in modern baseball history.

Rated the player with baseball's best arm, Meusel played left field in Yankee Stadium. Babe Ruth admitted: "I never saw a better thrower." On September 5, 1921, the Yankee outfield recorded five assists. Incredibly, four of those assists came from Bob Meusel, who would lead the American League in that category in 1921 and 1922.

When the Yankees were on the road, Meusel played in right field, switching places with Ruth. "Silent Bob" had it all going for him—power, speed, the ability to hit for average. His 24 stolen bases in 1927 was second best in the American League. But on the move in the outfield he was a talented and graceful and supremely competent performer.

From 1920 to 1929, Babe Ruth was the only Yankee to have more RBIs than Meusel. Five times Meusel led the league in stolen bases. He is up there in all-time Yankee rankings for doubles, triples, RBIs and batting average. Indeed "Long Bob" had it all including a sour disposition and more than a touch of arrogance. In his last years in pinstripes, he softened just a bit. It was too late.

"He's learning to say hello when it's time to say goodbye," writer Frank Graham Jr. said of him.

BRADFORD H. TURNOW: *After retiring from baseball, Meusel served as a security guard for the US Navy for 15 years. He also appeared in the movies* The Pride of the Yankees *in 1942 and* The Babe Ruth Story *in 1948, playing himself in both films. He died at age 81 in 1977.*

THURMAN MUNSON

"I never did use that bat again. I gave it to Diana."   *—Bobby Murcer*

In 11 seasons, Munson was a Rookie of the Year, seven times an All-Star, three times a Gold Glove winner, two times a world champion and once an MVP. He was the first Yankee since Lou Gehrig to be named captain. His time was the era of the Bronx Zoo, a time he was the engine of Yankee clubs who copped three American League pennants (1976–1978) and two world championships.

Driven, dogged, he admitted his flaws: "I'm a little too belligerent. I cuss and swear at people." In a Yankee uniform, the catcher was a throwback to the talented and winning players who had worn the pinstripes. A superb handler of pitchers, a top notch defensive catcher, with a bat he was lethal.

Tragedy struck Munson on August 2, 1979. His Cessna Citation jet crash-landed just short of the runway at Akron-Canton (Ohio) Regional Airport. He was killed. He was only 32 years old. At his wife Diana's urging, the Yankees played baseball the next night before 51,000 plus. A ten-minute standing ovation for Thurman Munson was one of the saddest moments in franchise history. Many tears were shed by players and fans.

Three days later was his funeral. That night it was Yankees vs. Orioles.

Outfielder Bobby Murcer, one of his close friends, batted in all the runs to account for the Yankee victory.

On September 20, 1980, the Yankees retired Thurman Munson's Number 15 and placed a bronze plaque in his honor in the Stadium. There are many who believe he should be in the Baseball Hall of Fame. He is not. However, a re-creation of his locker, including spikes, glove and jersey, are displayed in Cooperstown.

BOBBY MURCER

"Bobby was one of the finest human beings I've ever met."   *—Michael Kay*

There were all the comparisons to Mickey Mantle and all the regrets that he came along after the dynasty years of 1949 to 1964 when the Yankees ruled baseball. Nevertheless, Bobby Murcer's pleasing presence and all-around athletic skills were high points in down times for fans of the team from the Bronx.

The only Yankee to play with both Mickey Mantle and Don Mattingly, Murcer and "the Mick" hailed from the same state and were signed by Tom Greenwade, the same scout.

Military service during the Vietnam War postponed Murcer's first full year as a Yankee until 1969. He showed fans he was worth waiting for. Smashing 26 homers, and driving in 82 runs, he flashed power potential even if he was not to be the next Mickey Mantle. The lefty slugger in 1971 batted a career best .331 and finished second in the pursuit of the batting title in the American League. Part of the reason for the elevated average was his enhanced bunting skills. Yankee brass were impressed. In 1973, Murcer was signed to a $120,000 contract. He became the highest salaried player in Yankee history to that point. Only DiMaggio and Mantle had earned more.

Murcer remembered that George

Steinbrenner became "the Boss" of the Yankees in 1973: "He told me that I was a big part of the Yankee tradition, and always would be." "Always would be" ended on October 21, 1974. Murcer was traded to the San Francisco Giants for Bobby Bonds, Barry's dad. That was where I entered the story. The summer of 1975 I was traveling about with the Philadelphia Phillies (the Mets had informed the League Office that they could not host me), writing my first book, *A Baseball Century: The First Hundred Years of the National League*. It was a very interesting experience going from city to city and interviewing. I used a big boom box tape recorder and an even bigger briefcase to store my tapes, credentials and media guide. I truly was a "beginning author."

At San Francisco's Candlestick Park, I had marvelous and detailed interviews with quite a few baseball figures including the longtime owner of the Giants, Horace Stoneham, his longtime publicist, Garry Schumacher, and other Giants. Then I came upon Bobby Murcer. He was not a part of the National League story, but I had always admired the way he could tell stories. Affable, smiling, a bit out of uniform in the garb of the Giants, Murcer was a pleasure to be with.

I thanked him for his time and continued on in my relentless pace of interviewing. Somehow my big bag with tape recorder and tapes disappeared. Weeks of work, nowhere to be found. Panic. I asked everyone; no one could help. Out on the windy Candlestick Park field, I spied Bobby Murcer. He said something about never letting things important to you out of your sight. He suggested we go back into the locker room to look.

He reached up and into his locker. "Here they are," he smiled. "Someone must have put them there," he continued in that distinctive Oklahoma drawl. "Let me autograph a couple of baseballs for you to make your day a little better."

I always suspected that Bobby Murcer was the "someone."

Named to five All-Star teams, from 1971 to 1974 while with the Yankees and in 1975 with the San Francisco Giants, Murcer played 17 years in the big leagues, 13 of them with the Yankees. Back with the Yanks for a long run as a broadcaster after his playing career ended, Murcer won three Emmy Awards.

He passed away in July 2008 in Oklahoma City, where he was born in 1946. The cause of death was a cancerous brain tumor.

"Bobby was one of the finest human beings I've ever met," said Michael Kay, his colleague at the YES Network. "He handled his battle with a grace and class that was hard to fathom. For me personally, it's an incredible loss. He was my idol growing up. I was lucky to work with him as a broadcaster, and it showed me that I had great taste."

At the induction ceremony for the Oklahoma Sports Hall of Fame in August 1993, Mickey Mantle, according to the Saturday Oklahoman, said: "the first time I ever heard of Bobby Murcer they said a kid from Oklahoma was gonna be the next Mickey Mantle. They were right. Sure enough, he couldn't play shortstop either."

JOHNNY MURPHY

"In those last years, I could go, maybe, six innings, and then my arm would stiffen up, and I just couldn't go anymore. It was always nice to see Murphy coming in to save me. A very special relationship. Murphy listed me as a dependent on his income tax." —Lefty Gomez

"How many games will you win this season?" —Reporter

"Ask Murphy." —Lefty Gomez

John Joseph Murphy was born July 14, 1908. A New Yorker through and through and a lover of baseball, he pitched at Fordham Prep in the Bronx. Yankee legendary scout Paul Krichell kept tabs on the youngster all the way through his time at Fordham University. Murphy signed a Yankee contract just before his final college baseball game.

By 1934, he was a solid part of Yankee pitching. That year he posted a 14–10 record. Manager Joe McCarthy moved the big right-hander to the bullpen in 1935—the first real instance of a winning pitcher being placed there. Ten times he would lead the Yankees in saves. "Fireman" and "Fordham Johnny" were a couple of his nicknames. But "Grandma" was also in play. It was claimed that his rocking motion on the mound was the reason for the name. Others made the point that he was called "Grandma" by Yankee teammate Pat Malone, annoyed at Murphy's complaints about lodgings and meals on the road. An orderly, dignified, fastidious person on the baseball field and off it, Murphy was an anomaly among the rough and ready players of his time. More sophisticated, he appreciated upscale attractions such as fine French cooking and wine.

The native New Yorker was an All-Star from 1937 to 1939. His postseason numbers were a 2–0 record, 1.10 ERA, and four saves in eight games. In five separate World Series, Murphy allowed no runs. His best season was 1941 where he posted an 8–3 mark, 1.98 ERA, and 15 saves.

A control pitcher with a big breaking curveball, Murphy's 107 saves and 73 wins in relief held up as records until the 1960s. He had losing records in only two seasons, and led the majors in saves in four seasons. His best save year was 1939; he had 19.

The first "Fireman," fifth all-time still on the Yankee save list with 104, sixth in games pitched, 13th in winning

percentage and 17th in wins, Murphy won 93 games and lost 53 in a dozen Bronx seasons.

In 1944, "Grandma" opted out of baseball for employment in a special defense project. On March 7, 1946, fans read the curveball was reupping with Joe McCarthy and crew. The *Washington Post* reported, "Baseball's Bronx Bombers will have an atomic specialist in their ranks this year . . . Johnny Murphy had come to terms . . . on the retired list the past two seasons while he worked on the atomic bomb project at Oak Ridge, Tennessee."

Intelligent, ambitious, well connected throughout baseball, Johnny Murphy held several top positions throughout the sport once his playing career was concluded. His most important accomplishment was as General Manager of the New York Mets during their magical world championship season of 1969. He surely did contribute much to New York City baseball. He passed away from a heart attack at age 61 on January 14, 1970, in New York City.

GRAIG NETTLES

"When I was a little boy, I wanted to be a baseball player and join the circus. With the Yankees I have accomplished both."
—Graig Nettles

The story of Graig Nettles is amazingly puzzling. This was a player who spent half his career in pinstripes, was arguably the top third baseman in Yankee history, whose Number 9 was retired, not for him but for Roger Maris, who never was given a plaque in Monument Park, who never got close to even getting into the Baseball Hall of Fame.

His Major League debut was on September 6, 1967, with Minnesota. He went on to have a 22-year career—from 1973 to 1983 in pinstripes. The best all-around third baseman of the 1970s, probably the best defensive one ever, Graig Nettles had pop in his bat and even more in his mouth.

The remarkable thing about the Nettles trade is that a lot of the then-media were down on the transaction because Yankees surrendered a lot of "youth" for Nettles. Of course, none of that youth turned out to amount to much of anything.

Pounding out 20 or more home runs in eight of his seasons with the Yankees, in 1976, he led the American League in home runs helping the Bronx Bombers to win their first pennant in a dozen years.

Maybe it was that he was sarcastic, caustic, moody, at home with denigrating and sometimes cruel one-liners, like:

"What the Yankees need is a second base coach."

Criticized and fined for missing a luncheon, he snapped: "If this club wants somebody to play third base, they've got me. If they want somebody to go to luncheons, they should hire George Jessel."

"It's a good thing Babe Ruth isn't here. If he was, George Steinbrenner would have him bat seventh and say he's overweight."

"Since it's a two-team town, to keep my sanity I preferred to think that many of those who were booing me were Mets fans."

The left-handed power hitter had a career year in 1977 when he hit 37 homers, drove in 107 runs, scored 99 runs and led the Yankees to the first of back-to-back World Series victories over the Dodgers.

A two-time Gold Glover, a five time Yankee All-Star, Nettles was named captain of the team in 1982. It was a brief honor. Spring training 1984, the Yankees traded the outspoken Nettles away to San Diego.

PAUL O'NEILL

"Paul was unique. I have to tell you I had as much fun being his teammate as anyone I've ever played with." —Joe Girardi

The 29th plaque on August 9, 2014, added by the Yankees to Monument Park, honored Paul O'Neill as "an intense competitor." He was all of that and more. "When I look at this plaque and I think about what the Yankees mean to the sports world, basically, they are the best," O'Neill said. "That's just the way it is."

The left-handed hitting Paul O'Neill became a Yankee before the 1993 season, since he was acquired late in November 1992 in a trade for Roberto Kelly and minor leaguer Joe DeBerry. Others who came to the Yankees that season included Jimmy Key and Wade Boggs. All added talent and desire to the Bombers that put an end to four straight losing seasons.

I went over to him. "What's going on?"

Paul had a tear in his eye and he said, "I just cannot believe that I am going to get to play right field in Yankee Stadium.

Paul O'Neill, born in Columbus, Ohio, a relative of Mark Twain, was comfortable playing for his "hometown" team and was stunned by the trade. Some said devastated. His father, however, saw the future, telling his son: "This will turn out to be the best thing that happened to you."

The 1993 Yankees were a mediocre club. That was one of the negatives. Another for the highly emotional O'Neill was that his car was stolen twice that first season. With the Reds, he had been a dead pull hitter. That was another adjustment to be made, and he made the most of it. Hitting in Yankee Stadium he worked away on becoming a professional batsman. His second season with the Yankees, adjusted, comfortable, O'Neill batted over .400 the first two months and wound up winning the batting title with a .359 average.

An instant fan favorite, in his first six seasons, the intense O'Neill batted .300 or better. His batting skills for some obscured his fielding talents, which were considerable. Perhaps most remarkable of all his ball-playing traits was his ability to get things done under pressure, in the clutch.

In 1995, the Yanks wound up in postseason play for the first time in fourteen years. Number 21, O'Neill, called "the Warrior" by George Steinbrenner, was one of the main reasons why. The tall, talented, honed-in O'Neill was the anchor of Yankee baseball in the 1990s. The "heart and soul of the Yankees" was how manager Joe Torre referred to him. He was the man with the vicious swing, the man who opposing pitchers did not like to face with the game on the line.

In 2001, O'Neill announced that he would be playing in his final year. Nevertheless, he still managed to become the oldest player to steal 20 bases and hit 20 homers in the same season. His final game at Yankee Stadium was Game 5 of the 2001 World Series. Fans screamed out his name, made him shed some tears.

At age 38, with an injured left foot and other aches and pains, Number 21 called it a career. And what a career it was—a batting title, four All-Star appearances, a big factor in four Yankee World Series victories in five years, 1996 to 2000.

The fan chants of "Paul-ie, Paul-ie" now belong to memory. But the rock group Scandal's 1980's classic, "Warrior," is played during a video montage of Paul O'Neill baseball highlights at some Yankees home games. The one time "Cincinnati kid" has also been a broadcaster for the YES network's telecasts of Yankees games. He was one of a kind.

I was privileged to have him write the introduction for my book *A Yankee Century*. Just part of that introduction declares: "I hit the jackpot. I came here at the right time. I played with the right people. I was a little part of the right team. You expect to win but not the way we won. I had the honor to play right field—the same position that had been held down by such greats as Babe Ruth, Tommy Henrich, Hank Bauer, Roger Maris, Reggie Jackson and Dave Winfield."

JOE PAGE

"The way you live, you're letting yourself down and the whole team down."
—Joe DiMaggio

Joseph Francis Page was born on October 28, 1917. He grew up in Springdale, Pennsylvania, a coal-mining section near Pittsburgh. As a youth he rose before dawn to work as a breaker boy with older and handicapped miners. By hand, the young Page extracted impurities from chunks of coal.

A major focus of his leisure time activity was spent firing a baseball from the pitcher's mound for a local league baseball team. Word about Page reached Paul Krichell, Yankee scouting kingpin who agreed to the signing of Page in 1940. With the Butler Yankees in the Class D Pennsylvania State Association, the strapping southpaw went 11–3. There were two years with the Newark Bears, the top Yankee farm team. In 1943, Page won 14 of 19 games, led the Bears in strikeouts and walks. He was good, but he was still a work in progress.

The demands of World War Two saw the Yankees without major talents like Joe DiMaggio, Joe Gordon, Charlie Keller and Spud Chandler, who were in the Armed Forces. A bad leg kept Page out of military service and brought him to the Major Leagues in 1944. His time as a rookie was a mixed success. Part of the "mixed" was his fondness for drinking and carousing. In July, manager Joe McCarthy, sent Page back to Newark for the rest of the season.

"I hated his guts," Page said. "But there never was a better manager. A day never went by when you didn't learn something from McCarthy."

In 1945, Page returned to the "Big Show." At 6-foot-3 and 200 pounds and packed with muscle, he had the goods to be very good. His fastball was excellent as was an occasional spitball. Finishing the season winning five of six starts, posting an ERA of 2.82, the promise of the former "breaker boy" was evident. Yet, he was still a work in progress, walking as many batters as struck out that season.

New manager Bucky Harris in 1947 proved to be a Joe Page career saver. He shifted the erratic Page to the bullpen where he flourished. In the '47 World Series, he saved Game One, won the final game by holding the Dodgers to one hit in five scoreless innings, earned the first World Series Most Valuable Player award.

In 1948, Page was the league leader with 55 appearances and was picked as an All-Star for the third time. Casey Stengel took over as Yankee skipper in 1949 and had a significant influence on the hurler many were calling the "Gay Reliever" because of his night owl activity. The "Ol' Perfessor" tinkered with all kinds of pitching matchups for his Yankees—the one he seemed to like the most was late innings, enter Joe Page, do your thing.

Did he ever! The "Fireman" won 13 games, saved 27 games and posted a 2.59 ERA. That winter, the Yankees raised Page's salary to $35,000. It was the biggest contract ever given a relief pitcher. There had been other top relief pitchers up to that point in time, but Joe Page was more colorful than most of them and better paid. He added a glamour and a glitz to the role of the closer. In 1949, he became the first recipient of the Babe Ruth Award given for player post-season excellence.

When Joe DiMaggio married Marilyn Monroe, he was asked what it was like. His response: "It's got to be better than rooming with Joe Page."

No one would room on the road with Joe Page after 1950, his seventh and final Yankee season. Perhaps it was the heavy workload through the years, perhaps it was that Page could have taken better care of himself, whatever it was, the brawny kid out of the Pennsylvania mines had an abbreviated Yankee tenure. He did a great deal in his time in pinstripes. He could have done much more.

After baseball retirement, Joe Page ran a tavern in Latrobe, Pennsylvania, home of Rolling Rock Beer. He died of throat cancer in April, 1980. He was 62 years old.

GABE PAUL

"He was the man who took George's money and made the 76, 77, 78 teams."
—Paul Doherty

Gabriel Howard Paul was born in Rochester, the son of a tailor. At age 10, in 1920, he was the batboy for his hometown Red Wings of the International League. Paul stayed in the game of baseball for the next fifty years, realizing heights and honors he never dreamed of attaining.

Cautious, controlled, confident, Gabe Paul was instrumental in arranging for George Steinbrenner to buy the Yankees. Even more important, in five years on the job as the first president of the team for "the Boss," he built their championship teams of the late 1970s through a series of brilliant trades and free agent signings.

George Steinbrenner gave him the money to spend and the freedom to make his own decisions. Just some of the "right" moves made by Paul included: trading for Willie Randolph, Chris Chambliss, Bucky Dent, Mickey Rivers, Oscar Gamble, Dick Tidrow, Ed Figueroa, Ken Brett, Dock Ellis and Bucky Dent. Paul was able to sign stars like Catfish Hunter, Reggie Jackson and Don Gullett.

The irrepressible Steinbrenner, full throttle into winning, had a good counter-balance in the restrained Gabe Paul, whose motto was: "You can't look at the hole in the doughnut. You've got to look at the whole doughnut."

Dubbed the "Smiling Cobra" for his expertise in the universe of baseball transactions, Gabe Paul in his long career sold and traded more than 500 players.

The Gabe Paul Yankee years were a glorious time for fans of the team in the Bronx. Exciting players, momentous moments of the field of play—all this after a period of down times made "happy days are here again" the Yankee theme song. There was a pennant in 1976 and world championships in 1977 and 1978.

It was back to Cleveland at the start of the 1978 seasons for Gabe Paul as the new "head man" for the Indians. He retired in 1984. Fourteen years later in Tampa, Gabe Paul passed away at age 88.

He had spent 60 years in baseball with the most dramatic and productive time being with the New York Yankees. Inducted into the Rochester Jewish Sports Hall of Fame, the Ohio Baseball Hall of Fame, a two-time winner of the Executive of the Year award, there are those who say for all he accomplished, he belongs in the National Baseball Hall of Fame.

HERB PENNOCK

"The greatest left-hander in the history of baseball."
—Miller Huggins

He came to the Yankees in a trade with the Red Sox in 1923. Fifty thousand dollars and three forgettable players was the price. Another in the long line of "steals" from the team from Boston, he was in a class by himself. Given a new life in pinstripes, Pennock led the American League in winning percentage (.760) the first of four seasons over .700. He topped that "rookie" Yankee season with two victories in the 1923 Series against the Giants.

The lanky Pennock started that way and continued to amaze. In 1924, he became the first Yankee southpaw to enter the 20-win club. In 1926, he won twenty-three games. His nickname was the "Squire of Kennett Square." It was a reference to Herbert Jefferis Pennock's country home near Kennett Square, Pennsylvania, where he bred red silver foxes. The classy hurler was a graduate of top prep schools, was a horticulturist and one of the more refined personages in the baseball of the time. It showed, too.

On the pitcher's mound he was a thinker, a master of different arm angles, grace and style personified with a flowing pitching motion. Not overpowering, Pennock let batters make contact. He gave up more than a hit an inning in his career. Nevertheless, he also recorded 35 lifetime shutouts.

His manager Joe McCarthy said of him: "I'm going to pitch Pennock in spots this season—the tough ones."

In 11 Yankee seasons, 1923 to 1933, Pennock posted a record of 162–90 for a .643 winning percentage. The man who never lost a World Series game, Herb Pennock was elected to the Baseball Hall of Fame in 1948, the year he died.

HERB PENNOCK'S TEN COMMANDMENTS FOR PITCHERS

1. Develop your faculty of observation.
2. Conserve your energy.
3. Make contact with players, especially catchers and infielders, and listen to what they have to say.
4. Work everlastingly for control.
5. When you are on the field, always have a baseball in your hand and don't slouch around. Run for a ball.
6. Keep studying the hitters for their weak and strong points. Keep talking with your catchers.
7. Watch your physical condition and your mode of living.
8. Always pitch to the catcher and not the hitter. Keep your eye on that catcher and make him your target before letting the ball go.
9. Find your easiest way to pitch, your most comfortable delivery—and stick to it.
10. Work for what is called a rag arm. A loose arm can pitch overhanded, side-arm, three-quarter, underhanded, any old way—to suit the situation at hand.

Yankee star hurler Herbert Jefferis Pennock was a staple on the Yankees from 1923 to 1933.

ANDY PETTITTE

"Roger Clemens taught me that better shape you're in, the better you'll throw the ball."
—*Andy Pettitte*

On August 23, 2015, a Sunday, the New York Yankees dedicated a plaque in Monument Park at the Stadium to Andy Pettitte and retired his Number 46.

"Wow, thank y'all so much," Pettitte said. "You know, 20 years ago, I sat in the old Yankee Stadium bullpen. We were playing the Texas Rangers and it was a beautiful day. I had made the team out of Spring Training as a left-handed reliever and I sat there, looked around, and said, 'Wow. This is absolutely amazing.' A dream of mine as a child had come true."

A lot happened to the stylish southpaw Pettitte since that day in 1995. He would go on to be a big part of the franchise for 15 seasons and wind up as the Yankees all-time strikeout leader, a three-time American League All-Star and the only pitcher drafted by the Yankees to win 200 games.

BRADFORD TURNOW: *Pettitte, a five-time World Series Champion, featured an arsenal of pitches. Along with his four-seam fastball, he had a cut fastball that fooled most hitters. Those along with a slider, changeup and wicked slider gave Pettitte the pitches he needed to dominate for years.*

Pettitte also had one of the best pick-off moves in the history of the game. He picked off more than 100 "would be" base-stealers during his career. His move to first base was so awkward for runners that many players and managers thought his delivery to first was a "semi-balk." Umpires disagreed and base runners were always aware when Andy was on the mound.

Pettitte spent a three-year break with Houston, after which he returned to the Bronx and gave the Yanks solid production for six more years.

PAUL DOHERTY: *Had Pettitte stayed with the Yanks and not gone to Houston for three seasons, and won the same number of games with the Yankees as he did with the Astros, he would have exceeded Whitey Ford's all-time 236 wins for the Yankees by 19. He then would have been the winningest Yankees pitcher of all time and not third on the list.*

A member of the Core Four—with Derek Jeter, Mariano Rivera and Jorge Posada, all of whom were signed in the amateur draft in the early 1990s—Pettitte was the first of that group to retire.

An ace among aces during his time in the big leagues, Pettitte is first all-time in postseason wins, 19. He is first in strikeouts and third in wins all-time among Yankee pitchers. A two-time 20-game winner, Pettitte never had a losing season as a pitcher.

With all the stars and superstars that have been part of the Yankee universe, Andrew Eugene "Andy" Pettitte, the kid of Italian and Cajun descent born in Baton Rouge, Louisiana, has to rank right up there with the best of them.

LOU PINIELLA

"I liked Lou. He was a very tempestuous, highly volatile ballplayer, and a tempestuous and highly volatile manager."
—*Bob Sheppard*

He was traded from Kansas City to the New York Yankees in 1973 for past-his-prime Lindy McDaniel. That was one of the better deals the franchise ever pulled off. He played in 1,037 games for the Yankees over 11 seasons. He batted .300 or more five times for the Yankees and was a major factor for the in two World Series for the franchise recording a .319 average.

LOU PINIELLA: *In 1978, my most exciting season, we were the defending world champions, and we were determined to repeat. After we lost the first two to the Dodgers, we came back to win the next four in a row and that had never been done before.*

A Major Leaguer at 21, Piniella bounced around with several teams and finally found a home with the Yankees for 11 seasons as a player and more years as a scout, batting coach, manager, broadcaster and executive.

His professionalism, his fire in the belly, made him a perfect fit for the Yankee teams he played on. Thurman Munson, Bobby Murcer and others on the club bonded with him. With the native of Tampa, Florida, making things happen, the 1974 Yankees finished two games out in the AL East.

The right-handed hitting Piniella quickly became a fan favorite. He gave the fans their money's worth and they knew it and loved to roar out: "Loooou, Loooou!"

A true, professional "hitter," Lou would pose in front of his hotel room mirror, the better to analyze and dissect his swing and stance. "Sweet Lou" he was for many. Terrible temper Lou he was for others.

Piniella was part of a platoon for a time with Bobby Murcer and Oscar Gamble because he was a more effective batter against lefties than righties. It did not bother him. "I'd rather be a swing man on a championship team than a regular on another team." After retirement in 1984, "Sweet Lou" remained with the Yankees organization. At first Piniella was a scout and batting coach. He was truly a student of hitting and helped out a young Don Mattingly.

In 1986, Lou Piniella became the Yankee manager after Billy Martin had been fired for the fourth time. George Steinbrenner said: "Lou was my kind of player—I think he'll be my kind of manager."

Steinbrenner's "kind of manager" lasted through 417 games. Then "the Boss" promoted him to General Manager. Billy Martin was put in to replace him as Yankee pilot. Midway into the 1988 season, Martin was fired. Piniella returned as interim manager.

"Sweet Lou" had quite a run.

My daughter, a teenager at the time, was a big fan of his. In the Yankee locker room on one of my various book or article adventures, I was in conversation with Piniella. Somehow, I mentioned that he had a major fan in my daughter.

"What's her name?" he asked

"Jennifer," I said.

He reached into his locker, took out a brand new baseball and signed it for her. That was such a nice gesture. She still has the ball. I still have the memory of Louis Victor Piniella, a guy who is a real mensch.

JORGE POSADA

"Today, I must say, I want to thank the Good Lord for making me a Yankee."
—*Jorge Posada*

"I can't believe I'm standing up here right now," Jorge Posada said, on the day his No. 20 jersey was retired and he was honored with a plaque in Monument Park. "And I can tell you," he continued, "I've never been nervous on a baseball field . . . being here seems surreal, I can honestly tell you, this is one of the happiest days of my life."

His life began on August 17, 1971, in Santurce, Puerto Rico. He was drafted by the Yankees in the 24th round 1990 amateur draft. He made his debut at age 24 on September 4, 1995. Signed by the organization as a second baseman, converted to catcher, despite playing in just one game in the regular season of 1995, he was placed on the postseason roster.

All of Jorge Posada's 17 seasons in the big leagues were spent with the Yankees: 1,829 games, 275 home runs, 1,065 RBIs. A five-time All-Star, Posada was on five Yankee World Series teams.

Dubbed "Hip-Hip" Jorge, the switch-hitting backstop made a habit of touching the Thurman Munson monument before every game at the Stadium. It was said that he was not that approachable, that all the fiery catcher seemed to care about was playing winning baseball games and being a great teammate. And if that meant offering being critical of pitchers he caught for or of other players on the roster, that was the way it had to be for the least publicized member of the "Core Four" of Derek Jeter, Mariano Rivera and Andy Pettitte.

Playing most of the time in his long career at the catcher's position, the most physically taxing position on the diamond, Posada put up pretty satisfactory offensive numbers, hitting

.273 for his career with 275 homers, the same as Roger Maris.

Posada hit the first home run at the new Yankee Stadium. "It's going to set in a little later," Posada said. "I'm going to remember the home run, no question about it. I'm going to remember—it's a great thing. I'm happy about it."

His last game was September 28, 2011. He was 40 years old. Someone asked him what that moment meant to him. He teared up, broke down, walked away and joined Bill Dickey, Yogi Berra, Elston Howard and Thurman Munson as one of the five greatest Yankees catchers of all time.

WILLIE RANDOLPH

"I was there playing with guys I had grown up idolizing." —*Willie Randolph*

He broke into the big league with the Pirates on July 29, 1975. That season he was traded to the Yankees along with Ken Brett and Dock Ellis. The soft-spoken Randolph was the regular second baseman from 1976 to 1988, playing more games at the position than anyone else in franchise history.

He was there through the wild and wacky Bronx Zoo years, a steady presence with good range and defense, patience at the plate, speed that contributed to the offense of his teams. A winner, reliable, Randolph was "Mr. Consistency" as the Yankees went through 32 different shortstops in his time.

Born in South Carolina, the slight and serious Randolph grew up in Brooklyn. His Yankee resume includes: four times an All-Star, helping five teams get into postseason play, being twice a key member of two world championship teams, 1977 and 1978.

From March 4, 1986, to October 2, 1988, Randolph was Yankee co-captain along with Ron Guidry. He also spent 11 seasons as third base coach from 1994 to 2003 and bench coach in 2004. That earned him four additional World Series rings (1996, 1998, 1999 and 2000).

In July 2015, Randolph was honored with a plaque in Monument Park at Yankee Stadium. "The kid from Brownsville in Brooklyn had come a very long way," he said. He was emotional as he spoke to the crowd: "Got a chance to sit on the bench on the greatest stage in sports and do it in his hometown. . . . You guys have made me feel like Yankee royalty. Thank you very much."

VIC RASCHI
"Springfield Rifle"

He started late but made up for it. Victor John Angelo Raschi out of Springfield, Massachusetts, was 27 years old when settled into his role as one of the anchors of the great Yankee pitching staff in 1948. He would be called "the Springfield Rifle," "Big Game Pitcher" and less positive things by hitters who so many times were over-matched coming up against his moving fastball. He also sported an effective slider and change-up.

A four-time All-Star, winner of 21 games for the Yankees for three straight seasons, posting a record of 120 wins and just 50 defeats during his eight-year tenure with the team, Raschi started eight World Series games and went 5–3 with a 2.4 ERA.

Mel Allen is given the credit for Raschi's nickname, "the Springfield Rifle," a reference to the pitcher's place of birth and his power arm.

There are still those who remember Vic Raschi's five o'clock shadow, his scowl on the mound, the popping fastball and a drive that made him the middle man of the "Big Three" of Reynolds, Raschi and Lopat in the Yankee dynasty years of the 1950s. He passed away in 1988, a year after he was elected to the National Italian American Sports Hall of Fame.

ALLIE REYNOLDS

"He was a dominating pitcher. He was as good as any pitcher who pitched during his time."

—Bobby Brown

If not for injuries and perhaps over-work, the sky was the limit for the man they called the "Chief" and "Super chief" because of his one-quarter Creek Indian background. And in his time as a Yankee power pitcher, he sure accomplished a lot.

A no-hitter against Cleveland on July 12, 1951. A no-hitter against Boston on September 28, 1951. Six selections to the American League All-Star team. His major role on six Yankee championship teams with a 7–2 record, four saves, a 2.79 ERA, 62 strikeouts in 77 World Series innings. Allie Pierce Reynolds in eight Yankee seasons won 131 games and saved 40.

A Yankee as a result of a 1946 trade that saw star second baseman Joe Gordon go to the Indians, the powerful right-hander in his first years as a Yankee, was more a thrower than a pitcher. The claim was that he was bull-headed. Joe DiMaggio had second thoughts about his campaigning for the Reynolds trade and became so exasperated at his pitching that in one game he physically challenged the big pitcher.

Change, fortunately, was on the way. In 1949, Casey Stengel took over as manager. Eddie Lopat became Reynolds's roommate. "Steady Eddie" helped Reynolds with control, with concentration. Stengel provided counsel. And Stengel's pitching coach Jim Turner worked his magic. The power-armed right-hander started lighting things up.

With Casey Stengel calling the shots as manager, Allie Reynolds started some games, relieved in other games. The Ol' Perfessor loved the luxury of being able to bring in Number 22 from the bullpen.

"Reynolds is two ways great," said Casey Stengel, "which is starting and relieving, which no one can do like him. He has guts and his courage is simply tremendous."

By 1952, Reynolds, the son of a preacher, was at the top of his game going 20–8, leading the league in strikeouts, ERA, shutouts and, for good measure, saving six games. Omnipresent in the 1952 World Series, he notched a shutout victory in Game Four, a save in Game Six and in relief in Game Seven he recorded the win over the Brooklyn Dodgers to clinch the Yankee championship.

"All the relief work I did was really a career shortener," Reynolds said. "But to me teamwork was more important than some kind of honor."

A freak accident during the 1954 season in Philadelphia—the Yankee team bus crashing into an overpass—brought the pitching career of Allie Reynolds to a premature ending. A severe back injury made it impossible for the Yankee star to continue pitching.

A fan favorite, part of the "Big Three" of Reynolds, Raschi and Lopat, Yogi Berra made the point: "We don't win those five straight championships without him. I think he's gotten overlooked a lot."

BOBBY RICHARDSON

"Look at him [Bobby Richardson]—he doesn't drink, he doesn't smoke, he doesn't chew, he doesn't stay out late, and he still can't hit .250."   —Casey Stengel

Richardson was born Monday, August 19, 1935, in Sumter, South Carolina. At age ten, he was already turning heads playing on a Salvation Army YMCA kids' team. At age 17, he starred for the state championship Sumter American Legion team in 1952.

BOBBY RICHARDSON: *When I was 14 years old playing American Legion baseball they took our team to see Pride of the Yankees. And at that time, I thought, man, what a great organization.*

The first few years under Casey Stengel, I'm not sure he ever learned my name. He said 'kid, do this' or 'kid, do that' and I listened. But they were wonderful years. I played at the right time. The only thing I hated was going into the Stadium or walking out of it—there were always so many young kids there. But you couldn't stop because if you did, there was no way you could sign for all of them.

Several colleges offered the talented second baseman scholarships. A dozen big league baseball teams showed interest. Enter Yankee scout Bill Harris. Richardson graduated from high school and the day after signed with the team from New York. With $85 in coins— money collected from family, friends and the fans, the 17-year-old boarded the bus to Norfolk, Virginia, to play for the Yankee farm team. He batted just .211, but he would get a lot better.

Richardson's Yankee debut was August 5, 1955. He was 19. Gil McDougald had been banged up by a line drive. The youngster was his replacement. The replacement stayed around playing in more than 1,412 regular season games, a time the Yankees copped nine pennants in his first ten years with the team. The one-time kid from Sumter seven times was an All-Star, five times a Gold Glove winner, the most by a Yankee second baseman. He also struck out only 243 times during his entire career.

An infielder with great range, highly skilled turning the double play, Richardson linked up with shortstop Tony Kubek as a dazzling duo. They led the league four times in double plays.

World Series time was Bobby Richardson shine time. In the 1960 Fall Classic he batted .367 with 11 hits, a grand slam and eight runs scored. He was the series MVP, the only player from a losing team to win that award.

In 1961, Richardson tied records for a five-game Series with nine hits and 23 at bats, for a .391 average. In 1962, he made "the Catch" of a Willie McCovey line drive that gave the Yankees another world championship. "I think the fact that I caught the ball," Richardson explained, "meant a lot to Ralph Terry. Talk about a redemption, to come back after two years after allowing the World Series–winning homer to Bill Mazeroski in 1960 in Game 7."

In 1964, in his final World Series appearance, he batted .406.

Bobby Richardson Day was staged at Yankee Stadium on September 17, 1966. After a dozen Yankee years, the soft-spoken, religious Richardson retired at age 31. He went on to be very active in Christian fellowship and a highly successful college baseball coach.

Although he played a big role on Yankee teams, he also played in the shadow of great stars. That being said, Bobby Richardson remains one of the best of the best people in Yankee lore. He had game.

DAVE RIGHETTI

"Rags"

Over 11 Yankee seasons, Dave Righetti pitched in 522 games, breaking Whitey Ford's career games record of 498 career appearances. He also finished as the Yanks' career saves record-holder with 224, a record since shattered by Mariano Rivera.

The handsome lefty out of San Jose, California, age 20, came to the Yankees in November of 1978 in a ten-player trade with the Texas Rangers. That was the deal that shocked lots of people for it shipped away the irrepressible and talented reliever Sparky Lyle. Righetti was one of several young players the Rangers dealt around that time.

"Being traded, that was a disappointment," remembered Righetti. "I was kind of a proud Texas Ranger farmhand. It was like, 'Oh, my God, I'll never see the big leagues.' The Yankees kept buying older pitchers. They had just gone to three out of four World Series, so it was going to be a lot tougher to get up there."

Righetti was not ready for prime time despite the excitement he stirred in manager Billy Martin in 1979 when he broke in wearing Jim Bouton's old number, 56, later becoming famous wearing Number 19.

"I was lockered at the start," Righetti said, "between Ron Guidry and Dick Tidrow. Luis Tiant's running around, Jim Kaat, Tommy John. Ed Figueroa. All these guys that either won 200 games or were close. I wondered, 'Jeez, when's my time going to come?'"

His time came in 1981, the strike-shortened season. "Rags," as he was being called, was ready. Copping 8 of 12 decisions, posting an ERA just over 2, Righetti won the Rookie of the Year award and was chosen MVP of the 1981 ALDS. Against the Brewers, Righetti won two games and had an ERA of 1.00.

In 1983, Rags posted a 14–8 record that included a no-hitter at the Stadium against the Red Sox on the Fourth of July, George Steinbrenner's birthday.

Having just signed Phil Niekro, who would turn 45 during the 1984 season, flush with what the powers-that-be who thought was a surfeit of starting pitching, Righetti was made the closer by manager Yogi Berra. "Goose" Gossage had moved on.

"Rags" saved 31 games in 1984 and 29 in 1985. An All-Star for the second time in 1987, Righetti was in the tradition of Allie Reynolds—both a reliever and a starter. For more than a decade, Righetti was a two-way fixture on the Yankee pitching staff.

His career year was 1986. Converting 29 of his final 30 save opportunities, including both ends of a season-ending doubleheader against the Red Sox, Righetti wound up with 46 saves.

After the 1990 season David Alan Righetti opted out of the Yankee world and signed as a free agent pitcher with San Francisco. He still is with the Giants, a franchise favorite, having been the Giant's pitching coach since 2000.

BRADFORD TURNOW: *"Rags" was one of the bright spots and a fan favorite for a decade of Yankee baseball that many wanted to forget.*

MARIANO RIVERA

"Without question we're talking about the best reliever in the history of baseball. This guy has become branded with the Yankee logo. People are going to remember this man for so long for what he's done."
　　　　　　　　　　　　—Brian Cashman

Talk about coming out of nowhere, from humble beginnings. Out of Panama City, Panama, Mariano Rivera was a skinny kid who used a milk carton for a glove, tree limbs and broom sticks for bats, fishing nets that were balled up and wrapped in electrical tape for balls.

Never in his wildest imagination did he dream he would play 19 years for the New York Yankees and become the greatest relief pitcher, the all-time gold standard for relief pitchers.

He spoke no English. He was a teenage shortstop, a converted pitcher who couldn't hit much. He didn't even begin pitching until he was 19. Taking a flyer, the Yankees signed him for $3,000.

Talk about coincidence. Rivera's first pitching coach with the Gulf Coast League Yankees was Hoyt Wilhelm, the first relief pitcher ever elected to the Hall of Fame and first official all-time saves leader.

At Single-A ball in Greensboro, North Carolina, Rivera pitched and no one thought he was going anywhere. He was not even protected by the Yanks in the '92 expansion draft. Rivera, however, knew what it was like to grind, to endure.

After five-plus seasons in the minors, on May 23, 1995, the slim and serious 25-year-old made his Yankee debut as a starter against the California Angels. The quiet Panamanian wore jersey Number 42. It was handed to him by a clubhouse attendant. The number had no special significance for the rookie. Never did he even have the thought that he would be last to wear that number in the majors, with Jackie Robinson's number retired by Major League Baseball. It soon became evident that the smooth-throwing right-hander was better suited to working out of the bullpen. He proved that point in a setup role in 1996, going 8–3, setting a Yankee reliever record with 130 strikeouts.

John Wetteland left the Yankees and signed as a free agent with Texas after the 1996 season. Rivera was given the closer role. It was one of the smartest moves manager Joe Torre ever made.

"He's the best I've ever been around," Torre said. "Not only the ability to pitch and perform under pressure, but the calm he puts over the clubhouse. He's very important for us because he's a special person."

"Mo" made terrorizing batters and shattering pitching marks part of his method of operations. Averaging 41 saves and a 1.86 ERA from 1997 through 1999, he was as dominant as any stopper had ever been. He was the 1997 and 1999 Fireman of the Year.

In 1999, the Yankee scoreboard staff tried out different songs to use to introduce Rivera coming in from the bullpen at home games. Finally, Metallica's "Enter Sandman" was settled on. The image of Rivera jogging across the grass of the outfield in a straight line to the pitcher's mound, the blaring of the opening cords of the song, is a Yankee ritual that will never be forgotten. It is now part of the legend and lore of the franchise. "Mo" becoming "Sandman."

Mariano Rivera was arguably the nuts and bolts of Yankee success in the World Series from 1996 to 2000 and also 2009—the seven pennants, the 11 AL East wins.

In 2001, Mariano Rivera became the best paid relief pitcher ever. He signed a $39.99 million, four-year contract. And George Steinbrenner donated $100,000 to Rivera's church in Panama as well.

"I think the good Lord is a Yankee," Rivera said.

What hitters said about the modest Rivera was something else. Facing him, they knew what was coming—the cut fastball that moved as much as 8 or 9 inches and shattered bats, the devastating pitch that made him, more times than not, unhittable.

The great Mariano Rivera at his final game in 2013 acknowledges fans.

"He's the most mentally tough person I've ever played with," said Derek Jeter.

"He's as automatic as anybody ever has been," said Mike Stanton.

The stats for the one-time kid from Panama who played with a cardboard glove are mind-boggling: He never allowed a run to be scored against him in nine All-Star game appearances. He was the first pitcher ever to make 1,000 appearances for one team. His 652 saves record with one team is a stat that probably will never be broken. He saved 23 postseason games in a row, and in 19 of those games he pitched more than one inning. A member of four World Championship teams, Rivera was on the mound as the Yankees closed out titles in 1998, 1999 and 2000. He is just the third reliever to be named World Series MVP (1999).

A quiet, religious and charitable man, a competitor like no one else, Mariano Rivera had a plaque in August 2016 honoring him put up in the Stadium's Monument Park. Deservedly, admission to the Baseball Hall of Fame is part of the future for the closer of all closers.

PHIL RIZZUTO

"He's the greatest shortstop I've ever seen. Honus Wagner was a better hitter, but I've seen this kid make plays Wagner never did."
—*Casey Stengel*

Back in the late 1980s I was working with the legendary former coach of the New York Knicks, Red Holzman, on his autobiography, *Red on Red*. He mentioned that during WWII he had become friends with Phil Rizzuto. They both were athletes, both originally from Brooklyn. And he told me this story about the time he and his wife Selma were invited to dinner with Phil and his wife Cora.

Red has his usual scotch or two to start things off. Then he asked about the menu and learned that it would be tomato juice, tomato soup, pasta with tomato sauce.

"And for dessert—tomato pie," Red smiled.

"No," Phil said, "huckleberry pie, you huckleberry!"

Under ordinary circumstances Red Holzman, lover of food that he was, might have left the room. But he dearly loved Phil Rizzuto. "That little guy," Red told me, "was one of my favorites. Just a lovely and decent man."

Then there was a time I was at Yankee Stadium, hungry, with my tray of food in the press room restaurant, if one can call it that. Full house. Phil Rizzuto was there. He gestured that I come over and arranged for another chair at his table so that I could sit and eat. Kindness to a guy he barely knew.

There was so much to like about Phil Rizzuto. There is so much to praise about his work on a baseball field and as a Yankee broadcaster.

"The Scooter" played 13 seasons for the Bombers, missing three years of his prime because of WWII. A superb defensive shortstop with great base-running skills, his career batting average was only .273. However, he copped the 1950 AL MVP after batting .324, was also the 1951 World Series MVP after batting .320 and was a winner in seven of the nine World Series he played in.

Philip Francis Rizzuto was born in Brooklyn, New York, on September 25, 1917, to Fiore and Rose (Angotti) Rizzuto. "The Italians of my time were laborers," the animated shortstop said. "They built homes, they built sidewalks, they built garages in New York City and out in Long Island. That is how a lot of them began."

The kid from Brooklyn had higher hopes—maybe getting a chance to play big league baseball. At a generously listed five-foot-six, 150-pounds, while attending Richmond Hill High School, 16-year-old Phil Rizzuto tried out with the New York Giants. An insensitive coach told him he was too small for the Majors. He tried out for the Dodgers, but the manager, Casey Stengel, also told him he was too small. "Go get a shoeshine box," he was told.

Top Yankee scout Paul Krichell not only saw potential but was very impressed seeing him work out and recommended the Yanks sign him. And Yankee boss man Ed Barrow bragged: "His signing cost me fifteen cents, ten cents for postage and five cents for a cup of coffee we gave him the day he worked out at the Stadium."

In 1937, the young and ambitious Phil Rizzuto was sent to the Bassett (Virginia) Furnituremakers, Class D Bi-State League. The next season he batted .336 at Norfolk in the Piedmont League. In 1939, he was moved up to Kansas City of the American Association. That was where his nickname "Scooter" reportedly came to be. His teammate Billy Hitchcock called him that, acknowledging Rizzuto's quick feet. His minor league best of times was 1940: 201 hits, a .347 batting average, MVP of the American Association, named by the *Sporting News* as Minor League Player of the Year.

Yankee fixture Frank Crosetti, the starter at shortstop since 1932, was fading near the end of a splendid career and had batted just .194 in 1940. Rizzuto was slated to be the Yankees' starting shortstop in 1941. Some Yankees were against the young, hotshot rookie and managed for a time to keep him out of the batting cage during spring training. That did not last long. Joe DiMaggio was very forceful in demanding that the twenty-three-

year-old rookie be given a chance. "The Scooter" made the most of it and took Crosetti's spot in the starting lineup as the 1941 season got underway.

"The first game that I played was one of my great thrills," recalled Rizzuto. "I saw my first real, live president. It was Franklin Delano Roosevelt. He threw out the first ball when we played in Washington, D.C. Joe DiMaggio told me don't try to get the ball because when he throws it everyone dives for it. People have gotten spiked and broken hands. I didn't come close to getting it, but I saw the president and that was a big thrill."

It was a thrill for Yankee fans seeing their new shortstop in action. What had largely always been part of the Yankee way—one generation helping another—came into play. "If it hadn't been for Crosetti," Rizzuto recalled, "I'd have looked like a bum. He made me look great."

And great he was that rookie season. His batting average was .307. Only the great DiMaggio at .357 had a higher average on the team. In 1942, he hit .284, was a member of the All-Star team

Collectible baseball card of Phil Rizzuto, who was thrilled to see President Franklin Roosevelt throw out the ball at his very first game with the Yankees.

and paced all league shortstops in double plays and putouts. He hit .381 in the Yankees' five-game World Series loss to the St. Louis Cardinals.

Like quite a few other Major Leaguers, Rizzuto was in the service for three years during World War II. He began playing baseball in 1943 at the Naval Training Station in Norfolk, Virginia. At that time, he also married Cora Esselborn. Sent to New Guinea the next year, he was appointed to lead a gun crew on a ship. That never developed. Malaria, continuing seasickness and other non-pleasantries made the Navy re-assign Rizzuto to organize sports programs in Australia and the Philippines.

Back with the Yankees, military service concluded, Philip Francis Rizzuto went on to be durable, driven, the glue on the teams he played on for 13 years that won nine pennants and seven World Series.

"I knew," the Scooter said, "every nook and cranny at Yankee Stadium, and we had the fans behind us. Being from New York, it meant a lot for me to play in my hometown."

JOE CARRIERRI: *Phil Rizzuto was my favorite player. At one point I became his secretary. He would get hundreds of letters every day. He would ask me to answer them so I would take them home and send a postcard with his signature engraved on it just so the good will public relations kept going.*

Casey Stengel assumed command as manager of the Yankees in 1949. "I reminded him of how he told me I would be better off shining shoes," Rizzuto recalled. "But he pretended he didn't remember. By '49, I didn't need a shoebox, anyway. The clubhouse boy at the Stadium shined my Yankee spikes every day."

In 1949, Rizzuto batted .275, scored 110 runs and finished second to Ted Williams in the MVP vote. He followed that performance with his single best season, with career highs in hits, average, slugging percentage, runs, doubles and walks. At one point, he handled 238 consecutive errorless chances at shortstop. Beginning in 1950, Rizzuto was named to four consecutive All-Star teams, starting at shortstop in 1950 and 1952.

"You played for the love of the game," Rizzuto said, "and for just enough money so that you might not have to work in the winter. I was lucky because with the Yankees we'd be in the World Series almost every year. There were two years when I made more money from World Series cuts than I did from my salary for the whole year."

Rizzuto liked to tell this story about what happened on September 6, 1950. "I got a letter threatening me, Hank Bauer, Yogi Berra and Johnny Mize. It said if I showed up in uniform against the Red Sox I'd be shot. I turned the letter over to the FBI and told my manager Casey Stengel about it. You know what [he] did? He gave me a different uniform and gave mine to Billy Martin. Can you imagine that! Guess Casey [Stengel] thought it'd be better if Billy [Martin] got shot."

The little and lovable Rizzuto was one of the most popular players of his time, beloved by fans and teammates. Fearless on the ballfield, he was fearful, obsessively so, of all things that creeped and crawled. That fear made him a playful target.

JERRY COLEMAN: *He didn't have a great arm, but he had a great pair of hands and he never made a mistake. . . . The only other shortstops I'd put in his class were Ozzie Smith and Luis Aparicio.*

They were always playing tricks on him. Once [outfielder] Johnny Lindell put a dead mouse in his glove [when infielders still left their gloves on the outfield grass between innings]. He put the glove on, then threw it in the air and ran into center field screaming.

The good times as a ballplayer for little Phil started to come to an end in 1954. Rizzuto batted just .195. The next season as a 37-year-old he got into only seventy-nine games at shortstop. Then came August 25, 1956. General Manager George Weiss gave him the bad news: Rizzuto was being cut to enable veteran Enos "Country" Slaughter to be on the Yankee roster.

It "was like the end of the world," Rizzuto said.

The end of one world became the beginning of another world. From 1957 to 1996, with a voice that showcased Brooklynese, as a Yankee broadcaster, the former shortstop spun tales of Yankee baseball. At the start Rizzuto was paired with a couple of Hall of Fame broadcasters to be—Mel Allen and Red Barber.

DON CARNEY (WPIX-TV DIRECTOR): *He used to drive me crazy. His talking about people's birthdays, Italian food or some restaurant or who got married. Once he announced a funeral. He used to take off the 8th and 9th innings, saying he had to go to the bathroom. And that was it. Gone. One of the greatest turnarounds in the history of baseball was when Rizzuto turned around on the George Washington Bridge and came back to the Stadium to do extra innings. He was afraid of lightning. I used to record giant lightning flashes, and before a storm, I'd get out those tapes and scare him half to death.*

PAUL DOHERTY: *What Carney said, for the most part, didn't happen [save for Phil at times cutting out a little early] until after the late 1970s. During Rizzuto's first six seasons as a broadcaster [1957–1962] he worked as hard as Mel Allen. In fact, back then Red Barber did not make the road trips, so it was only Mel and Phil broadcasting from the road and during an era when WPIX telecast practically every game [all of the games were covered on radio]. Phil couldn't leave! As for the birthdays and other non-baseball acknowledgments, it was Phil's longtime broadcast partner Frank Messer who told me that started one spring [probably 1978 or 1979] when Frank asked Phil about a friend of his birthday. Phil made mention of the birthday on air. It turned out to be Phil's gardener who gave him free service after that. Well, Phil made the most of the quid pro quo school of broadcasting from then on in.*

When the topic was Phil Rizzuto, everybody seemed to get into the act, some unkindly. David Letterman got a laugh at Rizzuto's expense: "I heard doctors revived a man who had been dead for 4½ minutes. When they asked him what it was like being dead, he said it was like listening to Yankees announcer Phil Rizzuto during a rain delay."

The enthusiastic and highly knowledgeable Rizzuto was a crowd pleaser as a player and perhaps even more so as a broadcaster. Your Aunt Tillie's birthday, his trademark "Holy Cow." His wife Cora was "my bride." There were always reports about his golf game, a new Italian dish. If a player's name caused him difficulty pronouncing, he'd just call him "Huckleberry." He scored games. He also came up with the symbol "WW." That was his code for "wasn't watching."

Another Rizzuto idiosyncrasy was the first names of his broadcast partners

in the booth. He never used the first names of his partners at WPIX-TV. "Coleman," "Murcer," "Messer," "Seaver" or "Cerone." Bill White was "White."

The princely Bill White had his say: "How would you like to work 18 years with a guy who still doesn't know your first name?"

PAUL DOHERTY: *This is a nice story but it's simply not true, especially White's statement. It's true in that Phil became an all-out character eventually, but not until after 1983 or so. The "Hey White!" "Hey Murcer" exchanges didn't really get going until Phil no longer did the radiocasts of the Yankees from 1985 through 1996. He never called Jerry Coleman [Yankees broadcaster from 1963 to 1969] only by his last name. Phil was simply not that comically abrupt until much later in his broadcast career. He was unique and brought a personal touch to his narrative, but it was very well-balanced before the later years.*

I asked Frank Messer [Phil's broadcasting colleague from 1968 to 1985] who he felt was the best in the well-known Yankees broadcast trio [1971–1985] of Rizzuto-Messer-White. He said flat out it was Rizzuto. In fact he took it a step further and told me, "Phil was not only the best of the three of us, he was among the best ever. In the years before he sidetracked his play-by-play with acknowledgements for freebies and other streams-of-conscious he was THE most observant broadcaster. He didn't miss a thing on that field when he was calling a game. Nothing!! Mel and Red really made him pay attention in his early years and he learned well. Had he not become clownish later on he would have gotten BBHOF Frick Award as a broadcaster. It's a shame he's not remembered more as a great broadcaster, rather than simply as a character."

His New York Yankees tenure was fifty-three years of service—more almost than anyone else in the fabled history of the franchise.

In 1985, the Yankees retired Rizzuto's Number 10. He got a plaque in Yankee Stadium's Monument Park. It was Phil Rizzuto Day on the fourth of August. The Yankees presented him with a cow. The cow knocked Rizzuto over and, of course, he shouted, "Holy cow!"

Passed over for the Baseball Hall of Fame after 28 years of eligibility, 15 times by the writers and 11 times by the Veteran's Committee, Rizzuto half-joked: "I'll even go in as a batboy."

A powerful speech by Ted Williams paved the way for Rizzuto to be admitted in 1994. The BoSox legend, a member of the Veterans Committee, made the point that Rizzuto was the difference between the Yankees and his Red Sox. "If we'd had Rizzuto in Boston," Williams argued, "we'd have won all those pennants instead of New York."

When he first began with Red Barber and Mel Allen, then–radio sportscaster Howard Cosell told him: "You'll never last. You look like George Burns and you sound like Groucho Marx." In 1996, Rizzuto, 79, finally retired from broadcasting.

The little man with the biggest heart, the guts and glue of the Yankee dynasty, a most listened to and popular broadcaster, the one-time kid from Brooklyn passed away on August 13, 2007.

"I guess heaven must have needed a shortstop," George Steinbrenner declared in a statement. "He epitomized the Yankee spirit—gritty and hard charging—and he wore the pinstripes proudly."

ALEX RODRIGUEZ
"The great thing is that he's always looking to improve. How good can he be? Well, we're talking about a guy who is Hall of Fame caliber." —Lou Piniella

The story of A-Rod and the New York Yankees began on February 16, 2004. The cash-strapped Texas Rangers were most anxious to move him and his $25-million-a-year salary. Enter the team from the Bronx. Second baseman Alfonso Soriano went to Texas. Rodriguez came to New York with the agreement that two-thirds of what was owed on his contract would be paid by the Yankees.

In 2007, the Yankees and Rodriguez made baseball history as he signed for the top salary to that point in time—for ten more years, $275 million.

Despite controversy, charges and counter-charges, bad press, Alexander Emmanuel Rodriguez and the New York Yankees has been on balance a match good for everyone involved.

In his first four years with the franchise, Rodriguez picked up two of his three career MVP awards. He posted a career year in 2007: 54 homers, 156 RBIs and 143 runs scored. In 2009, he led the Yankees to his first World Series championship. In the postseason, Rodriguez batted .365 with 6 homers and 18 RBIs.

The 6-foot-3, 230-pound A-Rod was drafted by Seattle as the first pick in the 1993 amateur draft. At age 18 on July 8, 1994, he made his Major League debut. He announced his retirement at the end of 2016, his 22nd season, at the age of 41.

Locked in at 695 career home runs, fourth on the all-time list as of June 20, 2016, a three-time American League MVP, a member of the 3,000-hit-club, a 14-time All-Star, the all-time grand slam home run leader, the youngest player in Major League baseball history to hit 400, then 500 career home runs, the list goes on and on.

His accomplishments are glittering. But the down side despite his initial denial that he did not use "steroids, human growth hormone or any other performance-enhancing substances" clouded his image, damaged his reputation.

Sarcastically labeled "A-Roid" in the tabloids of New York City, his back-walking, back-talking of what he did or did not do did not serve him well. There is also the 211-game Major League Baseball suspension that he served.

Alex Rodriguez will probably never be a Hall of Fame inductee. There are even doubts about his number being retired by the Yankees. Still, in the history of the franchise on the field of play, he got the job done most of the time at a very high level.

RED ROLFE

"They talk about all the other fellas on the Yankees, but I notice the man that hurts us is that third baseman." —Connie Mack

Robert Abial Rolfe was called "The "Pride of Penacook," New Hampshire, a reference to where he was born in 1908. A southpaw swinger, a gifted defensive player, he wore Number 2 when he joined the Yankees in 1931 for one game. He did not get an at bat. He would not return to the Yanks until 1934.

The bright and lively Rolfe was a star shortstop at Dartmouth College. After graduating in 1931 with a degree in English, Rolfe was signed to a $5,000 bonus by Yankee scout "White Ties" McCann.

"The luckiest thing I ever did was sign with the Yankees," Rolfe said. "When you're with really great players they pull you along."

In 1934, his time in pinstripes began. He had seven years as a regular, a time of six Yankee pennants and five world championships. He struck out just 9 times in 116 World Series at bats. Four times Rolfe hit .300 or better. He scored at least 100 runs every year he was a regular.

Legendary manager Connie Mack, who scouted Rolfe in college, noted: "There is a real team player. You might get him out three times, but then he'll come up where it means the ball game, and sure as anything, he's going to knock in those runs. Or, if the Yankees need that one big play in the field, they usually get it at third base."

Mel Allen called him the best third baseman he'd ever seen.

Medical issues made it impossible for him to keep playing professional baseball. He retired after the 1942 season when he was 34 years old. "Sick or well," his manager Joe McCarthy said, "Rolfe was a real ballplayer."

There were stints as manager of the Detroit Tigers, baseball coach at Yale, and then as respected Director of Athletics at Dartmouth from 1954 to 1967.

Famed sports columnist Red Smith said of Red Rolfe after he died at age 60 of colon cancer in 1969: "Even when he was the best third baseman in the business, he was a sick man. Nobody will ever know how great he might have been if he had had his health."

Great he was. His time as Yankee overlapped Babe Ruth and Lou Gehrig at the start and Joe DiMaggio at the end. In 1969, he was named the all-time best Yankee third baseman for the first century of baseball. He was arguably the top third baseman in Yankee history until Graig Nettles came along. Red Rolfe Field at Biondi Park in Hanover, New Hampshire, bears his name.

RED RUFFING

"If I were asked to choose the best pitcher I've ever caught, I would have to say Ruffing." —Bill Dickey

A Hall of Famer, winner of 20 games each year from 1936 to 1939, a time span when the Yankees copped four consecutive world champions, going 231–124 with the franchise, Charles Herbert Ruffing was truly a Yankee Doodle Dandy.

Nothing seemed to slow the solidly

built right-hander down, not even the loss of four toes on his left foot from a mine accident. He was born May 3, 1905, in Granville, Illinois. He pitched for the Nokomis mining company team when he was 15 years old. It was managed by his father. At age 19, Ruffing was pitching for the Red Sox without much success.

Enter the Yankees. They sent Cedric Durst and $50,000 to Boston. They got Red Ruffing, who became one of their all-time greats. He won 15 games his first season in pinstripes. He finished with 231 career wins, most for the franchise for a right-handed pitcher, and career record for completed games (261).

Ruffing ranks among the top fielding and hitting pitchers in Yankee history. Eight times he batted over .300. He managed more than 200 career pinch-hit at bats and was the all-time Yankee pitching leader in home runs and RBIs.

An odd biographical feature for Ruffing is his induction into the U.S. Army Air Corps in 1942 despite the handicap of missing four toes on one foot. Red Ruffing was an inspirational figure in many ways.

Hall of Famer Charles Herbert "Red" Ruffing was a Yankee star pitcher from 1930 to 1946.

BABE RUTH

"No one hit home runs the way Babe did. They were something special. They were like homing pigeons. The ball would leave the bat, pause briefly, suddenly gain its bearings and then take off for the stands."
—Lefty Gomez

"The greatest name in American sports history is Babe Ruth." —Ted Williams

Bigger than life, a giant of a man for his time, 6-foot-2 and over 200 pounds when the average American male was just 5-foot-6 or 5-foot-7 and about 140 pounds, George Herman Ruth was baseball.

Mythic, magical, marvelous, he had the world on a string and the world loved him for it. He homered once every 11.8 at bats. His home run to hit ratio was 1 to 4.02. He won 12 home run titles in a 14-year span, 12 slugging titles in 13 seasons, slugged .847 in 1920, .846 in 1921.

"He had such a beautiful swing," Yankee teammate Mark Koenig said of him. "He even looked good striking out."

"He hits a ball harder and further than any man I ever saw," noted Bill Dickey.

Casey Stengel observed: "He was very brave at the plate. You rarely saw him fall away from a pitch. He stayed right in there. No one drove him out."

Babe Ruth's swing was graceful, corkscrew-like. The pulling power came from his twisting his skinny ankles. His home runs usually took a longer time to get out and had more air under them, creating high rising home runs. "I use a golfing swing," Ruth explained, "loose and easy with a slight upward movement,"

His body was not one with many bragging rights—spindly legs, a potbelly, oversized hands and arms. Oh, did he have strength and power which made swinging his 44-ounce bat—heaviest in the majors—no problem at all.

Writers, opponents, teammates and fans all overreached with the nicknames they pinned on him: "Sultan of Swat," "The Big Bam," "Jovial Giant," "the Colossus of Clout," "the Behemoth of Bust," "the Wizard of Whack" and "Jidge."

Everything about him was over-the-top. His frame filled out to a top-playing weight of 254 pounds; he had appetites for food, drink, fun and women—all consumed in abundance.

"I don't room with Ruth, I room with his suitcase," was a reference to the big guy's late-night activities. Outfielder Ping Bodie, his first Yankee roommate, said the line, and second baseman Jimmie Reese, who roomed with Ruth a decade later, repeated it.

A flair for the dramatic, a zest for life, Babe Ruth had both of these as well as a quality of celebrity his era had never seen before. He smashed more home runs than most teams hit. War heroes and movie stars and politicians went out of their way to meet him. Like a pied piper, he attracted crowds wherever he went. Throngs appeared at railroad crossings just to catch a glimpse of him as his train went by.

"I've seen them," Waite Hoyt, his friend and Yankee teammate said, "kids, men, women, worshippers all, hoping to get his name on a torn, dirty piece of paper, or hoping for a grunt of recognition when they said, 'Hi-ya, Babe.' He never let them down not once. He was the greatest crowd pleaser of them all."

George Herman Ruth was born on February 6, 1895, in Baltimore, the second son of George Herman Ruth Sr. and Katherine Scanberg. As he grew into boyhood, his parents could not control him. They placed him in St. Mary's Industrial School for Boys for his "incorrigible" behavior: stealing, truancy, chewing tobacco and drinking whiskey. Going to St. Mary's changed his life. It was there that his incredible talent for baseball was developed.

Credit goes to big brother Matthias who turned the youngster into a pitcher around 1912. About two years later, Orioles' owner-manager Jack Dunn signed the ambitious Ruth on Valentine's Day for $600 to pitch for the Orioles. So smitten was Dunn with Ruth that he also signed court papers becoming his legal guardian.

Ruth was sent to spring training in Fayetteville, North Carolina. One of the older players looked at the young Ruth, shook his head and said, "Poor kid! You're just a babe in the woods." Another version was that he was referred to in a local paper as "Jack's Newest Babe." From there on, he was known as "Babe."

He was also known as someone destined for big league stardom. He was just 19 years old when his time came on July 9, 1914. Jack Dunn had sent him along with Ernie Shire and Ben Eagan to the Boston Red Sox. Ruth would win 89 games over six seasons. Paid poorly, young and restless, always at odds with Boston owner Harry Frazee, the Babe knew he could be in a better place. Frazee knew he could get a good price for the young and talented player. He sold him to the Yankees on December 26, 1919, for $100,000 and a $300,000 loan secured by a mortgage on Fenway Park.

"You ought to know," manager Ed Barrow told Frazee, "that you're making a mistake."

So pleased were Yankee owners Ruppert and Huston to have Babe Ruth, they tore up his contract and gave him one for two years at $20,000 a season. In his first season, 1920, with the Yankees who shared the Polo Grounds with the New York Giants, the Babe smashed an amazing 54 home runs. That total was more than that of any other team in the Major Leagues aside from the Phillies. Ruth's .847 slugging percentage that 1920 season was the all-time best until 2001 and Barry Bonds came along.

That was how the "Sultan of Swat" started on his way to becoming the star of stars in the Big Apple and all of baseball.

It was Ed Barrow of the Red Sox, who would be reunited with the "Bammer" in New York, who understood the hitting potential of the southpaw hurler and converted him into a sometimes southpaw slugger by having him hit as often as possible on off days from pitching.

In the war-shortened season of 1918, Ruth showed his power potential rapping out 11 home runs to tie Tilly Walker of the Athletics for most Major League homers.

With Babe Ruth a fixture in their lineup, the Yankees drew 1,289,244 fans to the Polo Grounds in 1920. He was not only changing attendance stats; the "Big Bam" was also revolutionizing the game—changing it from a pitcher-dominated, scratch-out-a-run contest to a home run hitting power game.

"I could have had a lifetime .600 average," he said. "But I would have had to hit them singles. The people were paying to see me hit home runs."

The 25-year-old Ruth batted .376 with 54 home runs. He pulled a record 1.3 million fans in and remarked: "They're coming out in droves to see me."

Later his manager Miller Huggins would comment: "They all flock to Babe Ruth because the American fan likes the fellow who carries the wallop."

Ruth's Yankees were a magnet, drawing more than a million each season from 1920 to 1922. The Yankee owners rewarded "Jidge" for his efforts by voluntarily raising his salary to $30,000 for 1921. They knew what they had and what they were doing.

What he did is just amazing to review: Thirteen times he had more than 100 RBIs. Eleven times he was the league leader in walks. Six times he led the league in runs batted in. There were

A thoughtful Babe Ruth, looking skyward.

16 seasons of more than 20 home runs, 13 seasons of more than 30, 11 times he had more than 40 or more home runs and four times he hammered 50 or more home runs.

The Yankees captured seven pennants and four Series with Ruth doing his thing. Ruth has the tenth-best batting average, the third-most runs scored, second-most RBIs, highest slugging percentage and second-highest on-base percentage (.483). His third in career walks with 2,056, one every fourth at bat.

In 1923, the Yankees spent a shocking $2.4 million on a new stadium. Sportswriters dubbed it "the House that Ruth Built." His home runs also had his specialty touch on them and were called "Ruthian clouts" by the writers of his time.

When the 1923 season opened, the Sultan of Swat already had 197 career home runs—25 percent of his lifetime total of 714. He bashed 41 home runs in 1923, a low total for him, but he also batted an astounding .393, his highest career average and best in the league then. The 1924 season was probably Ruth's career year. His incredible numbers were a .378 batting average, 46 home runs and 121 RBIs.

Babe Ruth is safe at third base in a 1925 game against the Senators, though the Yankees later lost 8–1.

In 1927, the "Bammer" bashed 60 home runs. It was a mark that stood until another Yankee broke the mark in 1961. For nearly 40 years, the Bambino's 714 career home run record went unbroken. Then Hank Aaron came along to pass the Babe. It took Aaron about 500 more games played to get there.

September 24, 1934, was the Babe's last game as a player in "the House That Ruth Built." Twenty-four thousand were there, including many youngsters in the stands in the area named for him, "Ruthville." He went hitless in three at bats.

Babe Ruth developed throat cancer in 1946. His wife and doctors kept the horrific diagnosis from him; however, he knew something bad was happening to him.

On June 13, 1948, the "Sultan of Swat" appeared for the last time at Yankee Stadium. It was a time commemorating the 25th Anniversary of Yankee Stadium, a time for Babe Ruth's uniform Number 3 to be retired.

One of his best friends on the Yankees, Joe Dugan had said, "To understand him you had to understand this: He wasn't human."

MARIO CUOMO (FORMER NEW YORK STATE GOVERNOR): *I once saw Babe Ruth, believe it or not, face Walter Johnson. It was a World War II bond rally game, and Babe Ruth made an appearance. He was quite sick. He fouled off a couple, and then damned if he didn't hit one into the right field stands. They started cheering and demanding that he run; he didn't want to run. And they kept hollering. And so he pulled his cap down the way he would, and did that little short jog he did with his belly hanging out in front of him.*

"Game called by darkness—let the curtain fall. No more remembered thunder sweeps the field. No more the ancient echoes hear the call to one who wore so well sword and shield. The 'Big Guy's' left us with the night to face, and there is no one who can take his place," wrote Grantland Rice on Babe Ruth's passing.

GEORGE SELKIRK

"He was one of my favorite players, taking over Ruth's spot at bat and in right field. George was under heavy pressure that first year but he came through brilliantly. No player ever had a tougher assignment."
—*Joe McCarthy*

He probably had the most unpopular role in all of baseball—replacing Babe Ruth as the Yankees' right fielder in 1935, taking Ruth's Number 3. But after eight minor league seasons, the Canadian-born George Selkirk learned to take the criticism and boos in stride.

The very muscular outfielder was a skilled wrestler, a match even for the likes of Lou Gehrig. Selkirk batted .300 or more five of his first six seasons. He was an important member of six Yankee pennant winners and five world champions from 1936 through 1942. Spending his entire Major League career with the Yankees, Selkirk was a two-time All-Star.

In 1936, he was one-third of an all-.300 Yankee outfield that included Joe DiMaggio and Jake Powell. The man they called "Twinkletoes" for the way he seemed to run on his toes had a sharp eye at the plate. Four times he drew two walks in an inning; in 1939 he walked 103 times.

His career year was 1939 when he drove in 101 runs and hit 21 home runs. That season Selkirk hit five home runs in four consecutive games. Ironically, the special season of '39 was Selkirk's last as

a regular. Tommy Henrich came along in 1940—and playing time wound down for Selkirk.

In 1942, he called it a career after 846 games. George Alexander Selkirk, one of the best baseball players to ever come out of Canada, averaged nearly a hit a game and recorded a .290 lifetime batting average. Not bad for a guy who heard a lot of boos when he first started.

BOB SHAWKEY
"Sailor Bob"

In 1923, he pitched the first game at Yankee Stadium. He hit the second home run there—Babe Ruth crushed the first. In 1976, he threw out the first ball at the newly refurbished Yankee Stadium. All eye-catching résumé items for Bob Shawkey, and there are more.

For 13 seasons (1915–1927) Bob Shawkey pitched for New York; in eight of those campaigns he was about as good a pitcher as the Yankees had. The wiry right-hander out of Sigel, Pennsylvania, was a very unassuming, some would say, colorless type. But he did sport a red-sleeved undershirt when he pitched.

Shawkey became a Yankee in mid-season, 1915, coming over from Philadelphia for cash. By 1916, the Yankees knew they had a steal as Shawkey won 24 games. "Sailor Bob's" success enabled the 1916 Yankees to post their first winning season in six years.

In 1919, Shawkey struck out 15 Athletics, a franchise record that stood for 59 years. His seven 1–0 shutouts (he had 37 career shutouts) are also a franchise record.

Four times Shawkey posted 20 victory seasons as a Yankee. His last active season was 1927. When Miller Huggins died, Shawkey took over as manager for the rest of the 1929 season and piloted the Yanks to a third place finish in 1930.

Of note, he graced the baseball program at Dartmouth College, which made two former Yankees (the other one being Red Rolfe) with links to the Hanover, New Hampshire, institution.

PETE SHEEHY
"He was like a father to all the players."
—*Lou Piniella*

It all began for Pete Sheehy as a Clubhouse Boy for the Yankees in 1927 and would come to an end after 58 seasons as Clubhouse attendant, equipment manager, confidante, involved onlooker—the little man did it all.

It was never publicized that Sheehy was drafted in 1942 during Spring Training with the Yankees. A soldier in the Pacific, including Okinawa, he rarely spoke about that time to anyone.

RON SWOBODA: *He told me how Babe Ruth would come in and say: "Petey, give me a bi [bicarbonate of soda]."*

FRANK HOWARD: *I was a visiting player with the Washington Senators in the seventies and hooked up with Pete Sheehy who took me on a tour after the game into the original Yankees clubhouse on the third base side of the Stadium. He knew everything. It was a hair-raising experience for me. "There's where Babe Ruth lockered. There's where Lou Gehrig lockered." Around the horn he took me. The aura, magic of the place and the team . . .*

Willie Randolph called him "a second father." Dave Righetti said: "When you needed something, Pete had it there before you could ask. He knew your needs."

Catfish Hunter remarked: "You knew you could confide in Pete. And it would never go any further. For years,

A 1926 snapshot of the "Babe" at bat shows how the Sultan of Swat went about hitting the ball.

Babe Ruth's casket is carried into Yankee Stadium, August 17, 1948, amid grieving fans.

people tried to get him to write a book. He always told them that what the players said to him was golden to him so why should he tell everybody else. It was so amazing how he never forgot a name."

A familiar sight to so many, Sheehy sitting on a trunk, munching on ice cream or half a sandwich, the Yankee constant through all the decades—the great times, the sad times. He would talk about Lou Gehrig walking off the field for the last time, flipping his glove to him and saying, "I'm done, Pete." And he would recall his time in charge of uniforms, handing Mickey Mantle Number 7 after "the Mick" came back to the Yankees from a brief time in the minors. Mantle had worn Number 6

earlier in the season for the Yankees and Sheehy thought giving the youngster Number 7 would bring him luck.

When Yankee Stadium was renovated, the home clubhouse was named for him and a plaque was placed in the dugout that read: "Pete Sheehy, 1927–85, Keeper of the Pinstripes." The clubhouse was named for him in April 1976. The plaque was not put in until after 1985.

Witness and participant to 29 New York Yankee pennants and 21 world championships, Michael "Pete" Sheehy's time with the franchise started at age 17 and ended with his passing at age 75.

The New York Times obit for him carried this commentary by Billy Martin:

"All the young players always got high uniform numbers but when Pete gave you a low number, you knew you were gonna stay with the club. He gave me No. 12 at first, but when I went in the service he told me, 'I'm gonna give you something smaller when you come back because your back's not big enough for two numbers.' That's how I got No. 1." Billy also said "I remember my first thought when I met him was that I was awed. Here's the guy who took care of Babe Ruth and Lou Gehrig. But he treated all of us the same—like we were all Ruth and Gehrig."

BOB SHEPPARD

"Good evening, ladies and gentlemen, and welcome to Yankee Stadium."
—Bob Sheppard

"There are three things that are perfectly Yankee—the pinstripes, the logo and Bob Sheppard's voice. When I go to heaven, I want Bob Sheppard to announce me."
—Billy Crystal

It has been said: "Every kid growing up has dreamed of lining up at Yankee Stadium and having Bob Sheppard announce his name." The legendary New York Yankees public address announcer announced many names working more than 4,500 games.

It all began for the mid-mannered and professorial Sheppard on April 17, 1951, Opening Day. The Yankee lineup that day was:

- Jackie Jensen lf
- Phil Rizzuto ss
- Mickey Mantle rf
- Joe DiMaggio cf
- Yogi Berra c
- Johnny Mize 1b
- Billy Johnson 3b
- Jerry Coleman 2b
- Vic Raschi p

Incomparable Pete Sheehy, legendary Yankee Stadium clubhouse manager, was a constant through all the decades.

BOB SHEPPARD: *I thought Yankee Stadium had a cathedral-like quality. I had been in St. Patrick's Cathedral many, many times. But getting into Yankee Stadium I felt it was almost like St. Patrick's Cathedral. It had a kind of dignity, a quietude that many ballparks did not seem to have. I liked it. And I think it fit my style more than the Polo Grounds or Ebbets Field where I had worked as a PA announcer.*

At one time Bob Fishel [public relations director] said to me: I think it would be nice to recognize the boys and girls, the young people. That was when I began saying: "Ladies and gentlemen, boys and girls." But I did it under force for a short time and then returned to saying just "ladies and gentlemen."

From that moment on through 56 years, including 22 pennant-winning seasons and 13 World Series championships, Bob Sheppard did his thing. He was there for 121 consecutive postseason contests, 62 games in 22 World Series championships and six no-hitters that included three perfect games.

He was called the "Voice of God" by Reggie Jackson and the nickname fit

and stuck. Favorite Yankee moments for the former St. John's quarterback and first baseman included: Larsen's Perfect Game, Maris hitting 61 home runs, Reggie's three home runs against the Dodgers and Mantle's shot almost over the roof at Yankee Stadium and Chris Chambliss's homer in the ninth inning of Game 5 of the 1976 ALCS against Kansas City that gave the Yankees their first AL pennant in 12 years.

Joe DiMaggio and Mickey Mantle made Sheppard's all-time favorite list. "DiMaggio's name was symbolic of the early Yankees," Sheppard said, "and Mickey Mantle has a nice ring to it because the two 'Ms' made it alliterative. I just loved announcing his name. And one day, shortly before he died, we were both being interviewed on a television program. All of a sudden, he turned to me and said—right there on the air— that every time he heard me announce his name, he got goose bumps. And I felt the same way about announcing him."

Hundreds of eulogies were written and delivered by the "Voice of God."

PAUL DOHERTY: *Bob delivered a eulogy on Opening Day 1981 for Elston Howard who had died in December 1980. Bob was very friendly with him. It was an exceptional tribute.*

BROOKS ROBINSON: *Doing Baltimore's games on television from '78 to '93, I made a lot of trips to Yankee Stadium and got to know Bob Sheppard. "Bro oks Rob in son" is how he said my name.*

BOB SHEPPARD: *I knew every name and uniform number and worked diligently to pronounce each name correctly.*

For years and years, nobody knew my face and I could walk around the

stadium with 50,000 people and never be recognized. But after a few television shows and movies, such as Billy Crystal's 61, wherein my voice was heard, I became better known.*

My first meeting with the great Bob Sheppard was in the late 1980s on assignment for *Yankees Magazine*, a gig I held down for almost 18 years. I entered the tiny soundproofed public address booth high up and behind home plate at Yankee Stadium. My objective was to do an interview and write a profile of the best public address announcer of all.

A cordial and elegant man, tall, lean, with thinning white hair, he was a charmer right off the bat. Sheppard took both my hands in his and smiling told me to take a seat and we would talk. The game was in progress. He was at work. I was concerned that my questions would interfere with his game announcements.

"No problem," he said, "Go right ahead. I have been doing this for a while now."

When I began work on my book *Remembering Yankee Stadium* I thought of Bob Sheppard as the best one to write the foreword. Just a taste of what he wrote follows: "I wish to be remembered as an announcer who carried the dignity and the style of the Yankee organization and tradition of this magnificent Stadium through the spoken word. My clear-concise-correct point-of-view has never allowed me to be a barker, a rooter, a screamer or a cheerleader. I've always aspired to be in harmony with the Yankee gestalt. Not a bad aspiration and accomplishment for a professor of public speech who arrived at the Yankee Stadium as a New York baseball Giants' fan!"

Bob Sheppard was grace, intelligence, elegance. He was a very special part of the New York Yankees experience. He was one of a kind.

BILL SKOWRON

"I am first and foremost a Yankee."
—Bill Skowron

A hulking, powerfully built six-footer, William Joseph Skowron, known affectionately as "Moose," is sometimes overlooked in the ranking of players who contributed mightily to the Yankee glory seasons in the 1950s into the early 1960s. A native of Chicago, he was an able kicker for Purdue for a time. But baseball was his game. And when the Yankees came up with a $25,000 bonus offer, he left college and signed with them in 1951.

The next year he won the Minor League Player of The Year award. He thought he was more than ready for the Major Leagues; the Yankee brass disagreed. They wanted him to get a bit more experience. On April 13, 1954, Skowron made his Major League debut with the Yankees. He would remain in pinstripes until 1962.

William Joseph Skowron was named "Moose" by the older guys in the neighborhood after his grandfather gave him a haircut shaving off his hair. It was said that the youngster with the new haircut resembled the former Italian dictator Mussolini.

Five times as Yankee, the affable Skowron batted over .300 and was an All-Star six times. "Moose" drove in 80 or more runs in five different seasons. Dependable, clutch, always prepared, he helped the Yanks win seven pennants and four World Series.

BILL SKOWRON: *I don't always swing at strikes. I swing at the ball when it looks big.*

Many who saw him play still remember his one-hand slams of the ball that resulted in powerful opposite field home runs. Not the most graceful of men, Skowron was given a valuable lesson by Casey Stengel. "The only way you can play is to play first base, and the only way you can learn, is by going to dancing school," Casey Stengel told him. "I went to Arthur Murray Dance Studios, in St. Petersburg, Florida, to learn how to shift my legs, because I was no gazelle," Skowron admitted.

The "Moose" was no gazelle but he loved being a Yankee hero. "I am first," he was fond of saying, "and foremost a Yankee." Just a couple of moments that showcased his Yankee heroics: In 1956, he hammered a grand slam home run in the seventh inning of the seventh game of the World Series. That clinched the world championship for the Yankees over Brooklyn.

In 1958, against the Braves in the World Series he batted in the winning run in Game Six. His three-run homer in the eighth inning of Game 7 propelled the Yankees to another world championship.

Age the age of 81 in April 2012, the Yankee hero passed away from lung cancer.

"There weren't many better guys than Moose," said Yogi Berra at the time. "He was a dear friend and a great team man. A darn good ballplayer, too. I'm going to miss him."

GEORGE STEINBRENNER

"If things go right, they're his team. If things go wrong, they're your team. His favorite line is, 'I will never have a heart attack. I give them.'"
—Bob Watson, former Yankee GM

Since he would come to view himself as a Yankee Doodle Dandy, it was appropriate that he was born on the Fourth of July, 1930, in Rocky River, Ohio. The son of a shipping tycoon, George Michael Steinbrenner III had a life of privilege; sports were always his thing. At Culver Military Academy he played on several sports teams.

A graduate of Williams College, the young Steinbrenner was an English major. His senior thesis was the heroines in the novels of Thomas Hardy. After graduation from Williams in 1952, Steinbrenner served two years in the Air Force, coordinating the athletic program at Lockbourne Air Force Base in Ohio.

There were also stints as assistant football coach at Northwestern and Purdue universities. And in the world of business, he was owner and CEO of the American Shipbuilding Company, a Cleveland-based firm. It was in Cleveland that Steinbrenner met the veteran baseball executive Gabe Paul. Way led onto way and with 13 partners, Steinbrenner purchased the team from CBS for the bargain price of an estimated $10 million.

PAUL DOHERTY: *I believe the city paid $1.2 million for the Stadium parking garages. And the most interesting and ironic part of this deal was Steinbrenner's personal cost for his shares was [in 1973 dollars] $168,000 [in today's dollars, $905,000]. What a bargain! The sports deal of the decade if not the century!!*

When CBS had purchased the Yankees, the team had been to the World Series 14 of the previous 16 years. In eight seasons of CBS ownership, the Yankees finished second only once and below fourth place five times. In 1972, attendance at Yankee Stadium fell below 1 million for the first time since 1945.

On January 3, 1973, a rainy morning, the youthful industrialist George Steinbrenner was at Yankee Stadium's Stadium Club for the purchase announcement and press conference. He said he would be too busy with his shipyard business to be that involved

"The Boss," George M. Steinbrenner, purchased the team from CBS in 1973 for an estimated $10 million.

in the day-to-day affairs of running the team. "I've got enough headaches with my shipping company," he said. "We're not going to pretend we're something we aren't. I'll stick to building ships."

PAUL DOHERTY: *At the "21 Club" on January 10, 1973, Steinbrenner's limited partners were introduced. They were all there and presented to the media.*

Limited partner John McMullen would later say: "Nothing is more limited than being a limited partner of George's." How right McMullen was. George Steinbrenner was the Yankees, involved in every aspect of the franchise from facial hair to boardrooms to bathrooms. And he was fond of spouting homilies, maxims and mottos, such as:

"When you're a shipbuilder, nobody pays any attention to you," he said. "But when you own the New York Yankees . . . they do, and I love it."

"Give me a bastard with talent."

"I'm really 95 percent Mr. Rogers, and only 5 percent Oscar the Grouch."

"Show me a good loser and I'll show you a loser."

"Owning the Yankees is like owning the Mona Lisa."

"I'm not a good loser. I believe in what Ernest Hemingway said: 'The way you get to be a good loser is practice.' And I don't want to practice."

"You measure the value of a ballplayer by how many fannies he puts in the seats."

"Winning is the most important thing in my life, after breathing. Breathing first, winning next."

With a fondness for quoting military figures, the Yankee top man viewed games as an extension of war. In the tunnel leading from the Yankees' clubhouse to the field, he had a sign for a time posted with a statement from General Douglas MacArthur: "There is no substitute for victory."

PAUL DOHERTY: *Later on it was replaced by the DiMaggio quote: "I want to thank the good Lord for making me a Yankee."*

Famed sportscaster Howard Cosell called Steinbrenner "Patton in pinstripes." That pleased "the Boss" greatly.

George Steinbrenner was a driven, dedicated, determined owner through his stormy, controversial, highly productive and record tenure with the Yankee franchise. So involved was he that in his first 17 years Steinbrenner changed managers 17 times. He then upped that total to 21 managers and 11 General Managers moving in and out in his 37 years as Yankee owner. Incredibly, his on-again, off-again relationship with Billy Martin saw the hyper pilot get five

separate terms as manager of the Yankees.

Frank Sinatra was Steinbrenner's favorite singer. The Yankees began to play "New York, New York" in 1980 after home games ended.

PAUL DOHERTY: *Frank Sinatra had recorded Kander and Ebbs's "New York, New York" in 1979. At some point in 1980, after Sinatra's "Trilogy" album was released, the Yankees began playing the song after home wins. It soon became a tradition.*

Originally, the Yankees played Sinatra's version after victories. Liza Minnelli's recording of the tune was played after losses. Minnelli was not pleased. She sought a change. She got a change. The Yankees stopped playing her version. "The Boss" again did his thing.

There were all "the Boss's" overreaching and annoying deeds, comments and moments that sullied George Steinbrenner's image among fans, media people and players.

The 1981 World Series pitted the Yankees against the Dodgers, the third time the ancient rivals went at each in five years. A 9–2 win at Yankee Stadium in Game Six made LA world champions.

FRED CLAIRE: *Steinbrenner's apology came in the form of a release which he passed out after we won the series. I thought it was strange. The Yankees had given all they could to win. There was really no need to apologize for an all-out effort by your team.*

Nearly a decade later the Yankees hadn't been back to the playoffs. On July 30, 1990, "the Boss" surrendered control of the Yankees. He was banned from baseball for life (which turned out to be three years) by Baseball Commissioner Fay Vincent for alleged payments made to a gambler in New York City seeking to gain damaging information on outfielder Dave Winfield. That day at Yankee Stadium fans chanted: "No more George." That was low ebb time for the Yankee principal owner. Steinbrenner had previously been suspended in 1974 for illegal contributions made to President Richard Nixon's 1972 campaign fund.

"I am dead-set against free agency," Steinbrenner said. "It can ruin baseball." He said one thing and then said something else. In the first five years of the free agency, Steinbrenner signed 10 players for of $38 million, big money then. Catfish Hunter, Reggie Jackson, Dave Winfield and many others were signed as free agents. There were years when so many free agent superstars were on the Yankee roster, that managers had to juggle to find places for them in the lineup.

There was always the bad, the ugly, the good when the subject matter was George Steinbrenner and his place in Yankee ownership history. The good was restoring the Yankee brand, mystique, legend and success. In addition to the seven World Series titles, the Yankees won 11 American League pennants and 16 AL East titles under the watch of "the Boss."

Steinbrenner negotiated a landmark $486 million, 12-year cable television contract with the Madison Square Garden Network in 1988. In 2002, he was the driving force behind the creation of the Yankees' own YES Network.

What never received much publicity was his sending of money to injured high school athletes so they could go to college. He believed in keeping older friends and contacts from his football days on the payroll. He believed in giving "second chances"—see Darryl

Strawberry and Dwight Gooden. Partial to the military, Steinbrenner set a policy at Yankee Stadium—men and women in uniform were admitted for free.

I had two chance meetings with George Steinbrenner. Both were memorable. I was sitting in his office at Yankee Stadium with the late Robert Merrill, the great opera singer, who for many Yankee fans was better known as the man who sang the "Star Spangled Banner." I was interviewing Merrill for a profile. This was late 1980s. Steinbrenner charged in, military stance, bristly and in charge.

"What the hell are you doing here?" he snapped at me.

"I was invited in here by Mr. Merrill."

"What for?"

When I explained, the Yankee principal owner relaxed and told me to get myself a drink. I declined, saying I wanted to fully concentrate on my interviewing job at hand. Hearing that, Steinbrenner exited.

The second meeting was around the same era at Madison Square Garden at halftime in the VIP quarters where drinks flowed freely and most tried to show off their hoop IQs. Steinbrenner came by and exchanged pleasantries with the late Red Holzman, then the former and legendary coach of the New York Knicks, who I was with.

"The Boss" then turned to me. "And you are writing Red's autobiography?" How he knew what I was doing I never knew.

The two interactions with "the Boss" gave me insights into a man on the top of his game, making connections, taking charge. He was something else.

In the mid-2000s, the Yankees became the first American professional sports franchise whose worth was estimated as being over $1 billion. After the 2007 season Steinbrenner's

health was poor. He officially retired and handed control of the Yankees to his sons Hank and Hal Steinbrenner. In 2009, the estimated net worth of George Steinbrenner was estimated at $1.3 billion according to *Forbes* magazine.

On July 13, 2010, the bigger-than-life George Steinbrenner died after suffering a heart attack in his Tampa home. It was the day of the 81st All-Star Game. In his 37 years in charge of all things Yankees, his team won more games than any other team in baseball.

CASEY STENGEL

"Make 'em pay. Make 'em pay you a thousand dollars. Don't go help those people with their shows for coffee-and-cake money. You're the Yankees—the best. Make 'em pay you high."
　　　　　　　　　—Casey Stengel

Charles Dillon Stengel was born on July 30, 1890, in Kansas City, Missouri. He died on September 29, 1975, in Glendale, California.

"There comes a time in every man's life," Casey said, "and I've had plenty of them." The salty Stengel seemingly was a man who had been around baseball forever. And he always seemed to reincarnate himself. Back in 1912, he began in the big leagues playing 17 games for the Brooklyn Dodgers. His salary was $2100.

Fresh off piloting Oakland in the Pacific Coast League and the team of "nine old men" to the Pacific Coast League championship in 1948, Casey Stengel was introduced on October 12th at a press conference as the new manager of the New York Yankees. It was said that he was offered the job on the recommendation of dour and business-like General Manager George Weiss. Their friendship went back decades.

"I didn't get the job through friendship," he said in a serious tone. "The Yankees represent an investment of millions of dollars. Because I can make people laugh, some of you think I'm a damn fool. But as player, coach and manager I have been around baseball for some 35 years. [He'd played in or managed over 5,000 games.] I've watched some successful managers as John McGraw and Uncle Robbie work. I've learned a lot and picked up a few ideas of my own. They don't hand out jobs like this just because they like your company. I got the job because the people here think I can produce for them."

The new contract covered two years and was for a total of $70,000. At the start, there were doubters. There were also supporters.

EDDIE LOPAT: *It was a shock when Stengel was announced as the new manager. We thought we got us a clown. When spring training started in 1949, we just sat back and watched his reaction. He never said too much about anything to anyone. It was a treat for him to be with us after all the donkey clubs he had. He was something. He didn't need notes. He knew what every hitter or pinch hitter could do against certain pitchers. He could make the moves.*

The great sportswriter Grantland Rice wrote: "Stengel is a high-grade manager who knows his trade."

That first Stengel Yankee season was one that he had to cope with injuries. The famous Charlie Keller-Joe DiMaggio-Tommy Henrich outfield was never in place. Keller missed the entire season while DiMaggio's damaged heel kept him out until late June. Phil Rizzuto missed playing time. Coping, Stengel mixed and matched, patched in non-prime time performers, game by game the new manager managed and led the Yankees to the first of five straight world championships.

EDDIE LOPAT: *When we won the World Series in 1949 and came to spring training the next year, Stengel told us: "Last year is past history. We never look back. We gotta go back and beat 'em again this year." We had guys on the bench who could play as good as the starters. They hated to get on the bench because they knew they might not get back for three or four weeks, or ever. When we played the other teams, we never underestimated them or ourselves. Casey's attitude was our attitude. They would have to run us off the field, but not in the newspapers.*

Together with his wife Edna, Stengel lived with in Manhattan's upscale Essex House. Formerly a silent screen movie star, always fashionably

dressed, Edna selected Casey's clothes. Off season, the Stengels lived in a big house in Glendale, California. At times there were 50 to 75 children there even though Casey and Edna had no offspring of their own. Edna's nieces and nephews and the children of Yankee players and their wives were always around. "It was a real Yankee family back then," Yogi Berra said. "Casey and Edna were like a father and mother to us all."

The Yankee pipeline of talent flowed in the Stengel years: Jerry Coleman and Gene Woodling in 1949, Whitey Ford and Billy Martin in 1950, Tom Morgan, Gil McDougald, Bob Cerv and Mickey Mantle in 1951, Andy Carey and Ewell Blackwell in 1952, Bill Skowron, Enos Slaughter and Bob Grim in 1954, Johnny Kucks, Don Larsen, Bob Turley, Bobby Richardson, Elston Howard and Tom

Casey Stengel in the dugout, his home away from home.

Sturdivant in 1955. Ralph Terry came in 1956 and Tony Kubek came along in 1957. In 1958, Ryne Duren, Clete Boyer in 1959, Roger Maris in 1960.

Stengel induced ferocious competition for playing time. Organizational loyalty, Yankee pride, were the cornerstones of Stengel's way, his way.

Left-handed hitting Gene Woodling and right-handed hitting Hank Bauer often shared outfield duties. "We didn't like it," Bauer said. "But you couldn't complain too much—we walked into the bank every October."

Oh, how they were ready to play. The Stengel Yankees became so successful that the line "Rooting for the Yankees is like rooting for General Motors" became a back-handed put down.

JERRY COLEMAN: *Casey was a great, great manager, probably the greatest of all. He understood his players, what they could do and what they couldn't do. He understood the front office—what they wanted from him. He understood the media and that was vital in New York. He understood the fans—he was a great communicator.*

BILL SKOWRON: *Sure he wasn't that young, but he knew and we knew what we had to do. He'd leave us alone when we were winning. He'd holler "butcher boy" and "don't swing too hard at ground balls" and "don't beat yourselves." But when he saw us making mistakes, he'd get excited and do some yelling.*

Always with a way with words, with his players, with the media, Charles Dillon Stengel was nobody's fool and he knew every trick of the trade. He rode the "hot hand." Platooning players, odd deployment of pinch hitters, strange pitching match-ups, playing hunches— all were part of his managerial persona.

"Casey knew his baseball," Sparky Anderson, another top manager said. "He only made it look like he was fooling around. He knew every move that was ever invented."

The man who for decades had traveled through baseball's wilderness was generally the only one who knew what the next day's batting order would be, what the pitching rotation would look like.

The amazing streak of five straight pennants and world championships for the New York Yankees began in 1949, and Casey Stengel won the "Manager of the Year" award. "I want to thank all these players," he said in the clubhouse celebration, "for giving me the greatest thrill of my life. And to think they pay me for managing so great a bunch of boys."

By 1958, Stengel's New York Yankees were still top dog in baseball, winning the pennant by 10 games. The following year, however, they finished in third place—their lowest position in Stengel's tenure.

Nearing 70, impatient, he made moves in games that were questioned, that seemed strange even for a manager who had always made some unorthodox decisions. There was another Yankee pennant in 1960 but a loss in the World Series to the Pirates on Bill Mazeroski's walk off home run.

That ended it for the "Ol' Perfessor." Owners Topping and Del Webb, having been dissatisfied with Stengel for a few years, moved him out. The word was that he had been let go because of a mandatory retirement age of 65—just for him.

"I'm just sorry Casey isn't 50 years old—it's best for the future to make a change," Topping said.

STAN LOMAX: *There was no doubt that Casey was a newspaperman's best friend. He only used "Stengelese" [his own special version of double-talk] when he didn't want to say anything. He would talk about how he met the King of England when he and George Kelly made a 'round-the-world tour. Case would talk you 'round the world in his talks, but if you were honest with Case . . . Case would be honest with you.*

TONY KUBEK: *There was the Casey Stengel who could talk for hours on the long 36 hours of train trips to Kansas City. There was the sensitive Casey Stengel. There was the Casey Stengel of the Yankee pride.*

"I commenced winning pennants when I got here," Stengel told those gathered at a press conference, "But I didn't commence getting any younger. They told me that my services were no longer desired because they wanted to put in a youth movement as an advance way of keeping the club going. The trick is growing up without growing old. Most guys my age are dead at the present time anyway and you could look it up. I'll never make the mistake of being seventy years old again."

In Casey's time as leader of the New York Yankees there were 10 pennants and seven world championships, the greatest run by any manager ever. Only once in his dozen seasons did his teams win fewer than 90 games; his Yankee career managing record was 1,149–696, a winning percentage of .623.

Again the life in baseball continued for Charles Dillon Stengel. He was installed and allied again with George Weiss as manager of the New York Mets.

I met him for a brief interview in the dugout for one of my early books. I had a clipboard and a letter from a publisher: "Please extend all professional courtesies to Dr. Frommer."

"Oh," Casey got excited reading the letter. "Oh, doctor, I got a little pain here." He started to rub his right bicep.

"I am a PhD."

"I'll take whatever doctor I can get. Take a look," he smiled.

What a character, what a manager, what a man.

Inducted into the Baseball Hall of Fame in 1966, Casey Stengel was fittingly selected as "Baseball's Greatest Manager" during the sport's centennial. He passed away on September 29, 1975, in Glendale, California.

SELECT STENGELISMS

- *"If Yogi Berra fell in a sewer, he'd come out with a gold watch."*
- *"Don't cut my throat, I may want to do that later myself."*
- *"Anyone comes looking for me, tell 'em I'm being embalmed."*
- *"Good pitching will always stop good hitting and vice versa."*
- *"I came in here and a fella asked me to have a drink. I said I don't drink. Then another fella said, hear you and Joe DiMaggio aren't speaking, and I said I'll take that drink."*
- *"I couldna done it without my players."*
- *"I don't like them fellas who drive in two runs and let in three."*
- *"I got players with bad watches—they can't tell midnight from noon."*
- *"Kid [Phil Rizzuto], you're too small. You ought to go out and shine shoes."*
- *"The secret of managing is to keep the guys who hate you away from the guys who are undecided."*
- *"The Yankees don't pay me to win every day, just two out of three."*
- *"Son, we'd like to keep you around this season, but we're trying to win the pennant" [to a Yankee rookie].*

- *"Some of you fellers are getting 'Whiskey Slick.'"*
- *"These Old-Timers' games, they're like airplane landings; if you can walk away from them, they're successful."*
- *"About the autograph business—once somebody sent up a picture to me and I write: 'Do good in school.' I look up to see who was gettin' the picture. This guy is 78 years old."*
- *"What I learned from McGraw [whom he played for in the 1920s], I used with all of them. They are still using a round ball, a round bat and nine guys on a side."*
- *"What the hell is baseball but telling the umpire who's gonna play and then watching them play?"*
- *"All I ask is that you bust your heiny on that field."*
- *"Being with a woman all night never hurt no professional baseball player. It's staying up all night looking for a woman that does him in."*
- *"Don't drink in the hotel bar, that's where I do my drinking."*
- *"He [Mickey Mantle] has it in his body to be great."*
- *"Managing is getting paid for home runs someone else hits."*
- *"There comes a time in every man's life, and I've had plenty of them."*
- *"They say some of my stars drink whiskey, but I have found that ones who drink milkshakes don't win many ball games."*
- *"You have to have a catcher, otherwise you will have a lot of passed balls."*

MEL STOTTLEMYRE

"I can honestly say, that every time I put this uniform on—even though we weren't—I felt unbeatable."

—Mel Stottlemyre

In the 1960s, the New York Yankees had bragging rights to four 20-game winners: Ralph Terry in 1962; Jim Bouton in 1963; Whitey Ford in 1961 and 1963; and Mel Stottlemyre in 1965, 1968 and 1969.

Born on November 13, 1941, in Hazleton, Missouri, he made his pitching debut for the Yankees on August 12, 1964. He was sensational that rookie season, winning 9 of 12 decisions and posting a 2.06 ERA. In the only post-season he ever appeared in, he started two games against the Cardinals, besting St. Louis ace Bob Gibson in Game 2.

"The era that I played in was an era, for the most part," Stottlemyre said. "The Yankees have tried over the years to try to forget a little bit. We went to being in the World Series in 1964 to being sixth in 1965 to being dead last in 1966."

One of the most underrated hurlers in Yankees history, Stottlemyre pitched 11 seasons in pinstripes. In 1965, his first full year, he was a 20-game winner. Over the following nine years the New York Yankees gave their fans very little to cheer about. Nevertheless, he was a workhorse, a pitcher who took ball and his turn, did his job, and was always ready when the bell rang. On average, he pushed the needle to almost 300 innings a season. A weak offense doomed him to failure. Two times he led the league in losses including 20 in 1966.

All those innings, all that stress and strain, did him in. A rotator cuff injury forced Number 30 into retirement. He was done as a pitcher at age 32. He did, however, have the claim to fame of being the only pitcher who had two sons, Todd Stottlemyre and Mel Stottlemyre (Jr.), make it to the Majors as pitchers.

Stottlemyre returned to the Yankees as pitching coach in 1996 under manager Joe Torre. He remained in that position for a decade, winning four World Series rings. It was Number 30 whose guidance shaped Mariano Rivera, Andy Pettitte and other hurlers into the aces they became.

On June 20, 2015, Mel Stottlemyre, just one of three pitchers in Yankee history to have pitched forty or more career shutouts, was honored with a plaque in Monument Park.

Mel Stottlemyre: pitching was his game until a rotator cuff injury forced him into retirement at age 32.

Battling multiple myeloma, the blood cancer he was diagnosed with in 1999, a determined Stottlemyre reported in early 2016, "This is the best I've been in some time."

DAN TOPPING

"I'm going to buy the Yankees. I don't know what I'm going to pay for them, but I'm going to buy them." —Dan Topping

Born into wealth on June 11, 1912, in Greenwich, Connecticut, Daniel Reid Topping was a graduate of an expensive boarding school and the University of Pennsylvania. He loved the good life and developed into a top amateur golfer and an avid and active participant in the world of sports.

As a co-owner in the late 1930s of the Brooklyn Dodgers of the NFL who played at Ebbets Field, Topping became friendly with Larry MacPhail who ran the baseball Brooklyn Dodgers. When word that the New York Yankees franchise was for sale, the two put a plan in motion to make the purchase. They added mover and shaker Del Webb to their ownership group.

Topping, who had served for 42 months in the Marines during the Second World War, enjoyed his role as Yankee owner and was always looking to improve the team. As the story goes, he got together with Boston Red Sox owner Tom Yawkey at Toots Shor's in Manhattan, a watering hole and meeting place for the sporting crowd of New York City. That April night in 1947, one drink led to another. And the two owners agreed on a trade that would change the face of both their teams—Joe DiMaggio for Ted Williams.

The meeting was followed up with a phone conversation. Yawkey was still agreeable to the trade, but he insisted "the little Yankee left fielder" be included. Topping refused. No deal. The "the little Yankee left fielder" was Lawrence Peter Berra.

He was married six times, one of his unions was to skating star Sonja Henie, but despite his active matrimonial life, Topping was immersed through the years as Yankee co-owner and was extremely instrumental in the team's success.

He was also behind many momentous organizational decisions. When the Yankees were beaten by the underdog Pittsburgh Pirates in the 1960 World Series, Topping was the one who pulled the trigger on the firing of George Weiss and Casey Stengel. "A contract with Casey didn't mean anything," Topping said. "Casey was always talking about quitting. For a couple of months there in 1958 we didn't know whether we had a manager or not. We decided right then that we would never be put in that position again."

When the Yankees were sold in in 1964 to CBS, Topping stayed on as Yankee president for the next two years. Flamboyant, honed in, Daniel Reid Topping had his detractors, but he was a key component in one of the greatest winning runs in the history of the New York Yankees.

Dan Topping, prime-time Yankee owner, was a key component in one of the greatest winning runs in the history of the New York Yankees.

JOE TORRE

"The media was against it. He never won anywhere, they said. But he was a New Yorker, and mentally tough."
—George Steinbrenner

The New York Yankees and manager Buck Showalter ended their relationship as the word got out "under amicable terms" following the team's ALDS 1995 loss to the Mariners. A search for the new Yankee manager got underway.

Arthur Richman, whom I knew through his brother, Milton Richman, a world-class sports writer who tutored me when I worked the night shift at UPI as an undergraduate at New York University, gave me the inside scoop.

Discharged by the Mets in 1988, Arthur was part of the Yankees since May 1989, the team's vice president of media relations. George Steinbrenner had asked him for a list of candidates who he thought would be a good fit as the new Yankee manager.

"Prominent on the list," Arthur told me, "was Joe Torre." The Richman-Torre relationship extended back to the New

York Mets when Torre was their manager. "So I guess," Arthur continued, "I can claim the credit for the Yankees putting Joe Torre in as manager."

On November 2, 1995, the Yankees held a press conference to introduce Joseph Paul Torre, the 20th manager in the reign of George Steinbrenner. Out of Marine Park in Brooklyn, a heck of a player in his time, a nine-time All-Star, an MVP, now 55 years old, Torre was the outsider.

His career managerial record was 891 wins and 1,003 defeats. His resume as an MLB skipper included piloting the Mets (1977–1981), Braves (1982–1984) and Cardinals (1990–1995). One division title with the 1982 Braves and no postseason wins ever was also part of his record.

The New York media reacted with shock, puzzlement. Why Joe Torre? His hiring was considered an awful decision. "Clueless Joe" was the cruel back page New York Daily News headline.

"When I first got the job," Torre said, "I felt a little strange putting on the Yankee uniform because of all the tradition that went with being a part of this organization."

Torre's salary for the 1996 season was $500,000. He did not take the job for the money. He had earned more money as a broadcaster. "The Godfather" wanted the challenge. Never one to be intimidated, he knew he would not be bullied by George Steinbrenner, whose track record showed "the Boss" was no-holds-barred with his managers.

Incredibly, the Joe Torre 1996 Yankees posted a 92–70 record and a first place finish in the AL East. That season 22-year-old Derek Jeter, who had appeared in 15 games in 1995, was chosen by Torre to be the starting shortstop for the Yankees and would recieve the Rookie of the Year award. He was part of an infield that included Tino

Joe Torre was the 20th manager in the reign of George Steinbrenner and was awarded the Manager of the Year in 1998.

Martinez and Wade Boggs, an outfield that featured Bernie Williams, Gerald Williams and Paul O'Neill.

In the playoffs the Yankees defeated Texas and Baltimore. And then Torre's team bested Atlanta for the first Yankee world championship since 1978.

There was much drama associated with Torre's rookie season as manager including his brother Frank getting a new heart right in the middle of the World Series. Torre won American League Co-Manager of the Year.

The 1997 Yankees won 96 games and a Wild Card berth under Torre. Then there were three straight World Series titles from 1998 to 2000. They called 1998 "the perfect season" with a total of 114 regular season wins and a world championship. Torre was awarded the Manager of the Year.

In 2001, there was another pennant for the Bronx Bombers and another in 2003. Torre's Yankees were the toast of the Big Apple, appearing in the playoffs each year from 1996 to 2007. It was an incredible run with Joe Torre and his sidekick Don Zimmer as bench coach whispering away on the sidelines. There were twelve playoff appearances in twelve Yankee seasons under Torre.

"He's a great manager," said former Yankees third baseman Scott Brosius. "There is more to [managing] than who to pitch and play. It's managing people, the press . . . and Joe does that all great. Players follow the tone set by the manager, and Joe is the calming influence of this team."

The Yankees won four World Series titles in Torre's first five years as manager, and overall they won four championships, six pennants and 10 AL East titles in his 12 years with the team. They went 1,173–767 (.605) under his watch.

The team won 103 games in 2002, but an ALDS loss. In 2003 the Yanks won 101 games, the AL pennant thanks to a dramatic Aaron Boone homer, but lost in the World Series. The 2004 season was a heartbreaker. There were 101 wins in the regular season again. Then after being up 3–0 in the ALCS, Torre's guys lost the next four. The Yankees became the first big league team to flush away a 3–0 lead in a best of seven series.

The next three years for Joe Torre were filled with more frustration, high hopes dashed. The Yankees had not reached the World Series since 2003. Tension with the front office and especially with George Steinbrenner was now part of the new environment for Joe Torre.

After the 2007 season ended, Torre resigned, turning down a $5 million, one-year contract. It would have paid him $2.5 million less than he made that season.

"This has been a great 12 years," the articulate Torre said. "Whatever the hell happens from here on out, I'll look back on these 12 years with great, great pleasure. The 12 years just felt like they were 10 minutes long, to be honest with you."

His father had been a New York City policeman. Torre once thought of becoming a priest or a doctor. But he became the first Yankee manager to be born in the New York area, the sixth manager in franchise history to reach the 500-victory plateau.

In 2013, the one-time kid from Brooklyn was voted into the Hall of Fame. Even though he had an excellent playing career, he was inducted as a manager, especially for his accomplishments with the Yankees.

DEL WEBB
"Unless Webb has known you a long time, you'll get a 'yes,' 'no' or 'maybe' from him."
—Harold Rosenthal

Delbert Eugene Webb was born in Fresno, California, on May 17, 1899. His growing-up years were spent playing baseball. He grew to be 6-foot-3 and became a good but limited semi-pro first baseman.

Business was more his way. During the Depression and World War II, Del Webb secured highly profitable government contracts and was able to transform his construction company into a powerhouse.

But it was in Las Vegas where Webb made his real money. He built the Flamingo for mobster Bugsy Siegel, and then the Sahara, and bought a stake in the Mint. There was an FBI file on Webb with minimal data. The file had minimal impact because the word around the Bureau was: "Mr. Webb is known to the Director on a first-name basis."

At one point during the war years Webb had some interest in buying the Oakland Oaks of the Pacific Coast League. That did not pan out. A friendship with Dan Topping led to something bigger and better in baseball.

Both sportsmen, both always angling for new deals, Topping told Webb that the Yankees were for sale, and the wheels

were pushed into motion. The duo partnered up, adding Larry MacPhail and purchased the team from Jacob Ruppert's estate.

Baseball Commissioner Happy Chandler did not approve of the Webb "connections." No problem. Using some muscle, Webb convinced owners that Chandler should be out. Enter Ford Frick as new Commissioner.

The Webb-Topping ownership of the Yankees was equal after they bought out MacPhail's interest after the 1947 Yankee world championship. Both independent and strong-willed men, they were always questing for the "next great thing" for the Yankees. In general, Webb handled league matters; Topping watched over operations.

Del Webb, like George Steinbrenner decades later, was at first not interested in playing an active role as owner. That said, one thing led to another and Webb became the top power broker in the American League.

He made the cover of *Time* magazine on August 3, 1962. Oddly enough, just one paragraph of the article

Del Webb, another luminary who helped build the Yankee legend, owned the Yankees from 1945 until 1965.

was concerned with his ownership of the Yankees. At that point in time Del E. Webb Corporation had built and owned hotels in Las Vegas, shopping malls and office buildings in Phoenix and Tucson, large housing communities throughout the Southwest. Additionally, Webb's company had built military bases, missile silo complexes all over the country and major global construction projects. Webb left a legacy of introducing giant retirement communities, now staples all across the United States.

Delbert Eugene Webb's life was lived in the fast lane of sports and commerce. Perhaps best of all he was a mover and shaker who owned the Yankees during a golden era for the team.

Webb remarked when he became a Yankee owner—"Best deal I ever made." It probably was. The team that he and his partners took possession of in 1945 for $2.9 million sold twenty years later based on a valuation of $14 million.

GEORGE WEISS

"He didn't have a social relationship with anyone. They called him Lonesome George for good reason." —Jerry Coleman

As a student at Yale University, George Weiss was employed by a semi-pro team in New Haven. It outdrew the local professional Eastern League club in the same city. By 1919, the 24-year-old Weiss was the owner of the New Haven team. By 1929, he was burnishing his skills with Baltimore of the International League. Ed Barrow and Col. Jacob Ruppert soon took notice of the driven executive and hired him in 1932 as a Yankee executive.

The Yankee owner sought a farm system better than the one Branch Rickey put in place for the St. Louis Cardinals. Weiss got to work. Ruppert got his wish.

The great Yankees farm system at one point was composed of more than 20 teams. So much talent was on those clubs

of the late 1930s that it was claimed that their top farm team, the Newark Bears, winners of the league's pennant in 1937 by 25 games, could defeat a few Major League teams. This International League crown jewel sported talent that was a who's who of future New York Yankee stars.

So much of what the farm system was all about sprung from the machinations and maneuvers of George Weiss, the man who always minded the store for the Yankees.

JIM THOMSON: *Weiss was a quiet man who did not like to get into crowds. But how he could pay attention to details.*

In 1945, Dan Topping, Del Webb and Larry MacPhail purchased the Yankees. In 1947, at the party celebrating the Yankee World Series triumph, Larry MacPhail, a bit tipsy, announced he was quitting as a Yankee owner. He also fired his Farm Director George Weiss.

The next day, Topping and Webb bought out MacPhail's ownership share and "rehired" Weiss as general manager. A year later, Weiss brought Casey Stengel to New York to manage the Yankees. The two of them went back decades to Eastern League days and Stengel's time as a manager in Worcester, Massachusetts.

Together, the Weiss-Stengel team would rule baseball for a dozen years, winning 10 pennants and seven world championships. The Yankee roster was populated by superstars and stars, many of them there as a result of Weiss, who remained in the background with little personal contact with players.

"I don't think I ever met him," said Bobby Richardson. Weiss usually negotiated with just the top three or four players on the Yankee roster. He left the rest to assistants and others.

Focused, always prepared, George

Weiss held sway over the greatest sustained run of accomplishment and excellence in baseball history. He was a four-time winner of the Sporting News Executive of the Year. "There is no such thing as second place," Weiss was fond of saying. "You're first or you're nothing."

Cold and colorless, dour and humorless, sometimes shy, even nasty, always driven, all "Lonesome George" truly cared about was the New York Yankees, his wife and a small circle of old friends—in that order. He had deep disdain for sports writers: "To hell with newspapermen, you can buy them with a steak," Weiss said on more than one occasion.

JERRY COLEMAN: *He was thoroughly Yankee all the way. Very tough and cold, but brilliant. I worked in the front office for a couple of years. At five minutes to five the phone would ring. It was George—he wanted to make sure you were still working.*

Frugality was almost a religion with Weiss, who believed in making maximum profits at minimal cost. Taking a cue from his mentor Ed Barrow, he could be nasty in contract talks with players.

Weiss informed Mickey Mantle that he was cutting his pay $17,000 for the 1958 season. Mantle had batted 12 points higher than he did in 1956 but hadn't won the batting title or the Triple Crown as he had that year.

"Why the pay cut?" Mantle asked.

"It's what you're worth," Weiss responded.

Mantle took the cut.

Always at the ready to end things with players, Weiss spared no one who did not please him.

"You eat like a Yankee, but you don't perform like one on the field," he chastised a player he moved out for running up extra-large room service tabs.

He ended star pitcher Vic Raschi's Yankee career after a salary dispute.

He traded away Billy Martin after the much-publicized battle at the Copacabana nightclub involving the second baseman and other Yankees.

He removed Phil Rizzuto from the roster on Old-Timers' Day 1956.

Perhaps his worst failing as general manager of the Yankees and as a human being was his racism. A stubborn slowness to sign black players was a hallmark of Yankee corporate culture cultivated by Weiss. There were chances to sign Willie Mays and Ernie Banks. Nothing was done.

Pickets outside Yankee Stadium in the early 1950s charged the Yankees with racial discrimination. Weiss responded by signing a few black players to minor league contracts including Artie Wilson,

Ruben Gomez, Vic Power, Frank Barnes and Elston Howard. Gomez, Wilson and Barnes were traded away. And an annoyed and haughty Weiss reacted to charges of bigotry with the line: "The Yankees will bring up a Negro as soon as one that fits the high Yankee standards is found."

Vic Power, a talented, dark-skinned Puerto Rican first baseman, had much potential. He was sort of in line to become the first black Yankee. However, Power was considered too flashy and "uppity." And once it was revealed that Power dated white women, that was the end of any chance to wear pinstripes.

On December 16, 1953, Weiss orchestrated a massive 11-player trade that sent Vic Power and others to the Philadelphia Athletics. Power would play a dozen years in the big leagues with seven teams and be a five-time All-Star.

It was not until 1955 that the Yankee got their first black player— Elston Howard. He would be the only African-American during the Weiss years to come to the Yankees through their farm system.

"If Weiss had to have a Negro on the Yankees, he would have one. But only one, and he wasn't going to have an aggressive, crusading, loud mouthed Negro like Jackie Robinson or Vic Power," wrote Peter Golenbock in *Dynasty*. "He would be a Negro," Golenbock continued, "who would accept the conditions under which he had to play and not make trouble or headlines. He would live in segregated headquarters during spring training and in the southern cities and accept it, and he would be grateful just for the opportunity to play on the Yankees."

George Weiss led the Yankees to 10 AL pennants and 7 world titles in 13 seasons.

PAUL DOHERTY: *In all fairness, the Yankees weren't alone in being slow to sign blacks [there were nine other slowpoke teams as well out of the then sixteen teams in the majors]. And the Yankees in particular had exceptionally strong, almost permanent position players during the 50s. Given that Mantle-Berra-Rizzuto-Bauer-Skowron-McDougald-Kubek-Richardson et al. were bound to the Yankees forever [or until a trade] there genuinely wasn't much room for bringing on new all-star players, black or otherwise.*

And Weiss reported to Topping-Webb who didn't seem to be in a rush either to sign blacks.

In the end, the "color line" that operated against African-Americans and was overseen by George Weiss would hurt the franchise and cause it to miss out on incredible talent.

But while Weiss was minding the store, wheeling, dealing, tinkering with the roster, planning ahead with player and office personnel moves—pennants and world championships kept coming.

A few cases in point:

The price for Joe DiMaggio was $25,000 and five players. Other teams shied away, concerned not only about the price, but an injured knee. "Getting him," Weiss would say on many occasions, "was the greatest thing I ever did for the Yankees."

Even after the Yankees in 1954 finished in second place, Weiss traded for young pitchers Bob Turley and Don Larsen, who had unimpressive records that year. As Yankee pitchers, they blossomed. It was Weiss who traded before the 1960 season for Roger Maris, giving up Larsen and three others to Kansas City.

PAUL DOHERTY: *Weiss's cozy relationship with the Kansas City Athletics [owned by a friend of Topping-Webb] enabled him to make several high end deals with the Athletics which, more or less, made them the Yankees' own farm team in the same league. Weiss would trade someone and then get that someone back later. The Roger Maris trade at the end of 1959 was the peak of the "KC–NY shuttle" as it was called. Ralph Terry, Ryne Duren and Clete Boyer came out of KC, too. And Billy Martin, Don Larsen and Hank Bauer wound up there.*

In his 29 seasons as chief power broker for the New York Yankees, George Weiss had bragging rights to 19 pennants and 15 world championships. He was named Executive of the Year four times.

When he and Casey Stengel were cut loose by the Yankees after the 1960 season, Weiss set the stage for quite a lot of things to happen for the new team in Flushing, the New York Mets.

In 1971, a year before he died, George Weiss was inducted into the Baseball Hall of Fame. His plaque begins: "Master Builder of Championship Teams . . ." That he was.

BERNIE WILLIAMS

"He's got a calm about him that I trust, and he's electric at times. For me, he's in the upper echelon among switch-hitters all-time."
                              —Joe Torre

In his growing-up years playing baseball in Puerto Rico's Mickey Mantle League, Bernabe (Figueroa) Williams never dreamed that one day he would play center field for the Yankees and follow in the footsteps of the man his league was named for. Williams, a talented classical guitarist, even toyed with the idea of passing up a baseball career in favor of studying music.

Signed on his 17th birthday for $16,000 as a non-drafted free agent by the Yankees in 1985, a teenage track star, winning four gold medals in 1984 at the Central American and Caribbean Junior Championships, Williams mastered switch-hitting in the minor leagues.

In 1991, he joined "the Show" in the second half of the 1991 season. His rookie salary was $100,000. Graceful, professional, in control, by 1993 he was the regular center fielder for the Yankees following in the tradition of others who had held down that position with great distinction: Earle Combs, Joe DiMaggio and Mickey Mantle.

"Through my third to fourth year, I started to be aware of all the tradition that came just for being a Yankee," Williams said. "And the sort of responsibilities, if you will, were to me, to play in the same position that all those great players in the past played in Yankee Stadium, and to me it's an honor."

Many marker moments highlight the 16-year Yankee career of Bernie Williams:

In the 1996 ALCS, the Jeffrey Maier game, Williams slugged a walk-off homer off Randy Myers in the 11th inning.

In the 1996 World Series, his eighth inning, Game 3 homer was key in a crucial game after Atlanta had defeated the Yanks in the first two games.

In 1998, Williams won a batting title, a Gold Glove award and a World Series ring—the first player ever to win all three in one season. After he clinched the batting title on the last day of the season, he wore his shower slippers as he took a curtain call.

In the 2000 World Series, the soft-spoken Williams pulled in a fly ball by Mike Piazza of the Mets to account for the final out of the Fall Classic.

Bernie Williams played his career with the Yankees, and the franchise was all the better for it.

Controversy characterized Dave Winfield's tenure with the team, but he could play the game.

BRAD TURNOW: *Williams's guitar was his constant companion even on road trips. He played it much as he could. Many times before games or during rain delays, Bernie could be heard playing his guitar along with teammate Paul O'Neill keeping the beat on his set of drums. There were times that MVP closer John Wetteland joined in as well on guitar and added his hard rock sound to the trio.*

"While attending my first Yankee game, which also happened to be my first live baseball game ever," Paul McCartney recalled, "I was told that one of the team members Bernie was an excellent guitar player and composer. I was intrigued to hear his music. I heard him on a CD. I was blown away by his talent." Later on, it was McCartney's publishing company, MPL Communications, that signed Williams to his first major label. The *Journey Within* was released in 2003.

Williams was the last ex-player announced when the Yankees had their farewell to the Old Stadium at the last home game of the 2008 season. He had a .297 lifetime batting average. The first player in Major League history to homer from both sides of the plate in a post-season game, a switch-hitting cleanup hitter who drove in 100 runs five times, a five-time All-Star, a four-time Gold Glove winner, a force on four Yankee world championship teams. Bernie Williams was a Yankee thoroughbred.

BRAD TURNOW: *Bernie was honored with a plaque in Monument Park during the 2015 season. Along with his plaque, Bernie's number 51 was retired by the Yankees on May 24, 2015. A great honor for such a beloved Yankees player.*

DAVE WINFIELD

"For a guy to be successful, you have to be like a clock spring—wound but loose at the same time." —Dave Winfield

Born on October 3, 1951, in St. Paul, Minnesota, Dave Winfield was a gifted athlete all through his growing-up years. On a baseball scholarship at the University of Minnesota, the 6-foot-6, 220-pound Winfield strutted his stuff. He was a "natural" in most any sport he went out for.

Incredibly, he was drafted by four teams in three different sports. A starting power forward on Minnesota's Big Ten Championship team, he was selected by the NBA Hawks, the ABA Utah Stars, the NFL Vikings and the MLB Padres of San Diego, who he would be a star for during eight seasons.

In 1981, Dave Winfield and the New York Yankees made history. He signed a ten-year free agent contract and became the highest salaried player in baseball. A right-handed line-drive hitter, Winfield was an imposing figure with size and strength in the batter's box and also in the on-deck circle.

The first homer he smashed for the Yankees won a game. It also set a tone for Winfield's eight full seasons in pinstripes, a time he averaged over 25 home runs per season and was awarded four straight Gold Gloves.

Winfield got into 105 games in his Yankee rookie season because of the MLB strike but batted .294 with 13 home runs and 68 RBIs. In divisional play he performed admirably . . . but a sickly .045 batting average in the World Series that the Yankees lost to the Dodgers prompted George Steinbrenner to say, "When we have important games in October, I have 'Mr. May.'"

It was an undeserved nickname for a player who gave it all he had and that was quite a bit. The Steinbrenner jab was anger at Winfield's one hit in 22 at bats in the Series and a sarcastic reference to the big Yankee's red-hot May and sub-par performance in the Fall Classic. Winfield fired back: "There wouldn't be any important games in October if not for me."

Steinbrenner notwithstanding, Winfield drove in over 100 runs from 1982 through 1986, becoming the first Yankee since Joe DiMaggio to do so in five consecutive seasons.

David Mark Winfield's years as a Yankee from 1981 to 1990 were a roller coaster of controversy, missed signals, bruised egos. The "Seagull Incident" happened in 1983 when Winfield slammed a baseball into a bird. The next year as the "outsider" he battled "the favorite son" Don Mattingly for the '84 batting title and lost. There were lawsuits between George Steinbrenner and the Dave Winfield Foundation. Yet, through it all on the playing field, literally and figuratively, "Winnie" stood above it all.

In 1990, Winfield in 38 games was batting just .213 and had a back injury. On May 11th, the Yankees traded him to the Angels for Mike Witt. At first balking at the trade, the outspoken outfielder five days later reported to California.

Entering the National Baseball Hall of Fame on his first ballot, Dave Winfield chose to go in as a Padre rather than as a Yankee. But despite that and other controversies, in his almost decade in pinstripes, "Winnie" gave the fans their money's worth.

The "Mick's" milestone 500th dinger on May 14, 1967.

Three

EPIC MOMENTS, STREAKS AND FEATS

Yankee Stadium opens: April 18, 1923; DiMag, 56-game hitting streak, 1941; Reggie Jackson, three homers on three consecutive swings, October 16 to 18, 1977; and other great moments in Yankee history

Magical and dramatic moments have been a major part of the Yankee story from the very beginning. The legends and lore could fill an entire book. What follows are some of the most unique happenings on the field of play, more than a century's worth of Yankee baseball.

- Chesbro's Wild Pitch: October 10, 1904 ... 124
- George Mogridge No-Hitter: April 24, 1917 ... 124
- Yankee Stadium Opens: April 18, 1923 ... 124
- Sam Jones, No-Hitter: September 4, 1923 ... 125
- Tony Lazzeri, Babe Ruth, Botch 'Em Up: October 10, 1926 ... 125
- Babe Ruth, Home Run Number 60: September 30, 1927 ... 126
- Lou Gehrig, Four Homers: June 3, 1932 ... 127
- The Called Shot: October 1, 1932 ... 128
- First Stadium No-Hitter, Monte Pearson: August 27, 1938 ... 130
- Lou Gehrig Appreciation Day: July 4, 1939 ... 130
- All-Star Game Yankee Stadium: July 11, 1939 ... 132

- Joe Dimaggio, 56-Game Hitting Streak: 1941 ... 133
- Babe Ruth, Number Retired: June 13, 1948 ... 135
- Joe DiMaggio Appreciation Day: October 1, 1949 ... 136
- Allie Reynolds, Two No-Hitters: July 12 and September 28, 1951 ... 138
- Mickey Mantle, Tape Measure Homer: April 17, 1953 ... 139
- Don Larsen, the Perfect Game: October 8, 1956 ... 139
- Roger Maris, the 61st Home Run: October 1, 1961 ... 141
- Bobby Richardson, the Catch: October 16, 1962 ... 146
- The Mick's 500th Homer: May 14, 1967 ... 146
- Mickey Mantle Day: June 8, 1969 ... 147
- Ron Blomberg, First Designated Hitter to Bat: April 6, 1973 ... 147
- Chris Chambliss, Home Run: October 14, 1976 ... 147
- Reggie Jackson, Three Homers: October 18, 1977 ... 149
- Ron Guidry, 18 Ks, One Game: June 17, 1978 ... 150
- Bucky Dent Home Run: October 2, 1978 ... 150
- Dave Righetti, No-Hitter: July 4, 1983 ... 151

- Pine Tar Episode: July 24, 1983 ... 152
- Mattingly vs. Winfield, Batting Title: September 30, 1984 ... 153
- Andy Hawkins, No-Hitter?: July 1, 1990 ... 153
- Jim Abbott, No-Hitter: September 4, 1993 ... 154
- Dwight Gooden, No-Hitter: May 14, 1996 ... 154
- Derek Jeter, Jeffrey Maier: October 9, 1996 ... 155
- Jim Leyritz, World Series Comeback: October 23, 1996 ... 155
- David Wells, Perfect Game: May 17, 1998 ... 156
- David Cone, Perfect Game, Yogi Berra Day: July 18, 1999 ... 157
- Mike Mussina, Near Perfect Game: September 2, 2001 ... 158
- 2001 World Series, Bush Throws Out First Ball in Game 3: October 30, 2001 ... 158
- Derek Jeter Becomes "Mr. November": November 1, 2001 ... 159
- Rocket's Revenge: September 4, 2002 ... 159
- Boone Town: October 16, 17, 2003 ... 159
- Final Game at Original Yankee Stadium: September 21, 2008 ... 160
- Mariano Rivera Sets All-Time Save Record: September 19, 2011 ... 161
- Derek Jeter Day: September 7, 2014 ... 161

CHESBRO'S WILD PITCH: OCTOBER 10, 1904

The New York American League team maintained its hold on first place throughout most of the 1904 season. Down the stretch the team from Boston came on strong. On the final day of the season the Bostonians had a game and a half lead over the Highlanders.

Showdown time was at Hilltop Park. The hometown needed a doubleheader sweep over the Pilgrims to lock down the pennant. A rabid and partisan crowd of 25,584, the largest in the park's history, showed up. Fans were 10 and 20 deep in the outfield; some spectators spilled onto the field of play. The matchup was New York spitballer "Happy Jack" Chesbro, 41-game winner versus Boston's Bill Dineen, a 22-game winner that season.

No score after four innings. Both teams scored twice in the seventh. Ninth inning. Game tied 2–2. Boston catcher Lou Criger singled and was moved to second by a sacrifice, moved to third base by a ground ball.

Freddy Parent stepped in to face Chesbro. The count moved to a ball and two strikes. The next pitch was another spitter. It sailed over the head of catcher Jack "Red" Kleinow. Criger raced home. Boston nipped New York, 3–2 and the American League pennant was theirs.

There are claims that even though they were few in number at the game, the claim later was that the rabid, rowdy "Royal Rooters for Boston" triggered Chesbro's loss of control and the wild pitch.

Whatever, for Chesbro, it was a very unsatisfying finish to an incredible season. His 41 victories were best in the big leagues. He led the majors in wins, appearances, starts, complete games, batters faced. The game triggered a debate: Was his final pitch of that historic game a wild one or a passed ball?

GEORGE MOGRIDGE NO-HITTER: APRIL 24, 1917

It was the first no-hitter in Yankee history, the only Yankee regular season no-hitter.

A long and thin lefty, George Anthony Mogridge from Rochester, New York, was a Yankee from 1915 to 1920. He had been picked up by the Yankees from Minneapolis of the American Association in 1915. Mogridge was adept at getting a lot on the ball including resin, which the American League banned in 1920. Mogridge, it was reported, was able to put the powder under the bill of his cap. For him, it was an efficient and evasive move.

It all certainly worked that April day against the world champion Red Sox and their storied knuckleballer Dutch Leonard. Boston managed a run in the seventh putting together a couple of walks, an error and a sacrifice fly. But the New Englanders could not get a hit off Mogridge.

After the 1927 season, Mogridge called it a 15-year league career. He had won 398 games. However, the one most fans asked him about was the no-hitter he hurled on the 24th day of April in 1917 for the Yankees.

And that was the one he liked to talk about.

YANKEE STADIUM OPENS: APRIL 18, 1923

It was Opening Day at "The Yankee Stadium." That was what it was called at the start. The celebrity box was filled with such as Governor Al Smith, Mayor of New York City John Hylan and Yankee owner Colonel Jacob Ruppert. Baseball Commissioner Kenesaw Mountain Landis was there, too. He arrived by subway and was caught up in the mob of bodies outside the gates and had to be rescued by the police.

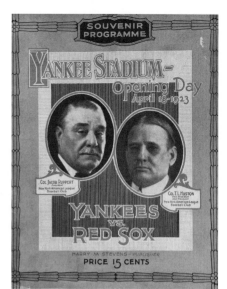

Yankee Stadium Grand Opening Day program, April 18, 1923.

Directed by the acclaimed John Phillip Sousa, the Seventh Regiment Band escorted both teams to the center field flagpole. The American flag and the 1922 pennant were raised.

Within minutes of each other, Babe Ruth was given a glass case enclosed oversized bat, New York State Governor Smith threw out the first ball to Yankee catcher Wally Schang, and home plate umpire Tommy Connolly shouted "Play ball!"

It was New York Yankees versus Boston Red Sox, a cold day with an announced game-time temperature of 49 degrees. A brisk wind blew dust and dirt from the road leading to the ballpark. Heeding the weather forecasts, many in the crowd of some 60,000 wore coats and hats. Some came in dinner jackets—dressed up for their best Bronx moment.

A crush of people and chaos intermingled outside the park. The Fire Department ordered the gates to the structure locked. Many tarried, braving the wind and the cold, resigned to partake of the atmosphere, the history, the roar of the crowd.

Frank Chance and Miller Huggins at the first Opening Day at Yankee Stadium, April 18, 1923.

Built at a cost of $2.5 million, a very economical $35,167,942.83 in today's dollars, a giant horseshoe shaped by triple-decked grandstands with huge wooden bleachers, the brand new ballpark in the Bronx was the first to be called a stadium—Yankee Stadium.

A Joe Dugan third inning single drove in the first Yankee run. Many in the festive crowd stood up as George Herman Ruth came to bat. Whitey Witt and Joe Dugan were on base.

"I'd give a year of my life if I can hit a home run in the first game in this new park," the Babe had said.

Home run—a booming drive into the right-field bleachers—the first homer in Yankee Stadium history. Rounding third base, coming home, the Sultan of Swat stepped on home plate. Then Ruth removed his cap and holding it at arm's length, he waved. The enthusiastic crowd was ecstatic.

"Sailor Bob" Shawkey's pitching iced the Yankees a 4–1 victory.

Yankee Stadium's day of days was now in the record books.

F. C. Lane, in a 1923 issue of *The Literary Digest*, called the new Yankee Stadium "the last word in ballparks."

SAM JONES, NO-HITTER: SEPTEMBER 4, 1923

His full name was Samuel Pond Jones. His nickname was "Sad Sam" or "Sad Sam the Cemetery Man" for the dour and down look he had on the field of play. Out of Woodsfield, Ohio, Jones played 22 seasons, started in 1914 with Cleveland and finished in 1935 with Chicago's White Sox. He won 229 games and lost 217.

A stylish right-hander, one of the first Major Leaguers to wear eyeglasses on the field, Jones had his ups and downs. Like most pitchers of his time, he relieved and started.

Jones won 67 games as a Yankee in five seasons. But no game was more dramatic for him than his September 4, 1923, no-hitter, a 2–0 gem against the Athletics. It capped his career year, a time he was the Yankee ace, hurling New York to its first World Championship.

TONY LAZZERI, BABE RUTH, BOTCH 'EM UP: OCTOBER 10, 1926

In the seventh inning of the seventh game of the World Series on October 10, 1926, at Yankee Stadium, Tony Lazzeri came to bat for the Yankees. The number six hitter in the potent Yankee lineup, the second baseman had banged out 18 home runs and driven in 117 runs that season. Bases loaded, two outs. His team down 3–2 to the St. Louis Cardinals.

The damp, dreary weather had held attendance down to 38,093, a small crowd for Yankee Stadium. Many had already exited the ballpark. The weather had gotten worse. Cardinal player/manager Rogers Hornsby called time. He went to the mound to talk to his ace pitcher. It was a brief talk. Jesse Haines was spent.

Hornsby waved to the bullpen. A ghost-like feeling pervaded the air as a mist had crept into the ballpark. In the bullpens under the bleachers, players were not aware of what was taking place on the field.

Grover Cleveland Alexander shuffled across the grass of the outfield onto the infield. "It's Alexander," the sound streamed through the crowd in the stands. "Alex the Great!" "Old Alex?"

"There was a telephone in the only real fancy, modern bullpen in baseball," Alexander later related. "Well, I was sitting around down there not doing much throwing. The phone rang and an excited voice said 'Send in Alexander.'"

"So I come out from under the bleachers," Alexander continued. "I see the bases full and two out and Lazzerri standing at the box. Tony is up there all alone with everyone in that Sunday crowd watching him. So I just said to myself, 'Take your time, Lazzerri isn't feeling any too good up there and let him stew.'"

"Poosh 'em up, Tony! Poosh 'em up, Tony!" the screams got louder. Alexander had won the game the day before. Lazzerri had gone 0 for 4 against him.

Alexander worked quickly, no wind-up.

First pitch, curve, a swinging strike.

Next pitch lined into the left-field seats. Foul ball.

Curveball, low and outside, Lazzeri swung and missed and struck out.

The game, however, was not over. It moved to the ninth. Alexander was still on the mound. He got two outs in the ninth. In Alexander's phrasing, "the big son of a bitch" Babe Ruth came to the plate. The fourth free pass of the game went to the "Big Bam." Dangerous Bob Meusel was next. On Alexander's first pitch to Meusel, Ruth rushed to second base. Cardinal catcher Bob O'Farrell put everything he had on the throw.

"There," Alexander said afterward, "was one of the grandest sights of my life. Hornsby, his foot anchored on the bag and his gloved hand outstretched, waiting for Ruth to come in."

The Yankees blew it. The Cardinals had their first world championship.

There were various sidebars to that game that experts still cannot agree on. As the story goes and the way it came to be understood was that "the Sultan of Swat" was not attempting to steal. At least that was what he claimed. It had simply been a hit and run play that got botched.

And the kid? Tony Lazzeri, was the "goat." He should not have struck out. He was too over-anxious. He cost the Yankees a world championship.

And 39-year-old Alexander, one of the greatest pitchers of all time, it was claimed by many that he was an alcoholic, had caroused the night before, came into the game loaded after sleeping it off in the bullpen. The public relations director of the National League, however, who would go on to be Commissioner of Baseball, Ford Frick, affirmed that he saw the St. Louis star awake and alert. Alexander asserted that he was on his game, awake and sober.

For years, Alexander said: "Less than a foot made the difference between a hero and a bum." One irony of that day and matchup was that both Alexander and Lazzeri were epileptics.

BABE RUTH, HOME RUN NUMBER 60: SEPTEMBER 30, 1927

Sports writer John Drebinger wired the *New York Times:* "The ball landed halfway up the right field bleacher, and though there were only 7,500 eye witnesses, the roar they sent up could hardly been drowned out had the spacious stands been packed to capacity. The crowd fairly rent the air with shrieks and whistles as the bulky monarch jogged majestically around the bases, doffed his hat, and shook hands with Lou Gehrig."

Those words described the moment when Babe Ruth smashed his 59th home run on September 29, 1927, at Yankee Stadium. The big man slammed two homers that day into "Ruthville," the right field bleachers. Both came off rookie Washington pitchers, Horace "Hod" Lisenbee who would be an 18-game winner in 1927, and Paul "Hoppy" Hopkins who had the tough luck of Babe Ruth being the first batter he ever faced in the majors.

"I guess I would have been nervous," Hopkins told the story, "if I knew who the next batter was. It was Babe Ruth. It was Babe Ruth with the bases loaded. I threw him a series of curveballs and he finally hit one into right field at least five rows in."

Game finally over, Yankees 15–4 victors. Hod Lisenbee, in street clothes, meandered into the Yankee clubhouse. In his hand was the ball Ruth had slugged for homer number 58. The Babe did not know who the visitor was, but he graciously signed the ball.

The next day, the last day of September, was the second-to-last game of the season. It was a weekday. In those times the top deck at the cavernous Stadium was not opened with a small crowd on hand. On this day only about 8,000 were in the house.

Bottom of the eighth, tied 2–2, one out. Mark Koenig had tripled and was on third base. A Quaker, Tom Zachary, was still on the mound for Washington. Babe Ruth had touched him that year for home runs number 22 and 36.

Zachary had announced: "I had made up my mind that I would not give Ruth a good pitch to hit, not give up Number 60."

Home run number 59 had been hammered with the bat the Ruth dubbed "Black Betsy." The ash blond "Big Bertha" and the reddish "Beautiful Bertha" were his other favorite bats. Zoned in, "the

Bammer" had singled and scored in his first two at bats. "Big Bertha" and "the Big Babe" were ready.

In a letter written in 1965, Tom Zachary finally had his say: "Tied 2–2 in 8th; 2 outs, one man on and a count of 3 and 2 strikes on Ruth. I threw him a curve, but I made a bad mistake. I should have thrown a fast one at his big fat head. Lost game, 4–2. It was a tremendous swat down right field foul line. At that time there were just bleacher seats in right field with foul pole. But since [at first] it went so high and far up in bleachers that it would be difficult to judge it accurately. I hollered 'foul ball' but I got no support, very little from my team mostly so it must have been a fair ball—but I always contended to Ruth that it was foul."

George Herman Ruth reached out for the ball. His mighty power went into the swing that pulled the ball and sent it into the first row of the bleachers near the right field foul pole, fair by about l0 feet.

A disgusted Zachary fired his glove to the ground and seemed to be mumbling to no one in particular. In no hurry going around the bases, Ruth doffed his cap several times to the fans

An early and most valuable Babe Ruth baseball card.

who cheered him as he carefully touched each base. His Yankee teammates celebrated his feat by banging bats and stamping feet on the floor of the dugout and forming a double line of greeting when he crossed home plate.

In "Ruthville" in right field his fans waved handkerchiefs, tossed hats and programs and cheered as he took his fielding position in the top of the ninth. Not giddy, but playful, G. H. Ruth gave back a series of exaggerated military salutes.

PETE SHEEHY: *It was matter of fact. There wasn't the excitement you'd imagine.*

There wasn't anything matter of fact about the "Babe's" reaction: "Sixty!" he screamed out at the top of his voice. "Let's see some son of a bitch try to top that one!"

"I don't think I would have established my home run record of 60," Ruth would reflect later in life. "If it hadn't been for Lou. He was really getting his beef behind the ball that season . . . Pitchers began pitching to me because if they passed me, they still had Lou to contend with."

The magnitude of what George Herman Ruth had accomplished viewed through the prism of time is astounding. A third of the 60 home runs were hit in his final 32 games of the 1927 season. After 123 games, Ruth had just 40 home runs. The 60 homers out-homered all Major League teams except the Cardinals, Cubs and Giants. The Babe slammed home runs in every park in the American League. More homers, 32, were hit on the road than at home, 28. All of what he accomplished—and he still managed to bat .356, score 158 runs, drive in 164 runs, draw 138 walks, steal

7 bases and manage 14 sacrifice bunts.

Paul Gallico, *New York Daily News* Sports Editor, wrote in his daily column: "They could no more have stopped Ruth from hitting that home run than you could have stopped a locomotive by sticking your foot in front of it. Once he had that 59, that Number 60 was as sure as the rising sun. A more determined athlete than George Herman Ruth never lived. . . . Succumb to the power and romance of this man. Feel the athletic marvel that this big, uncouth fellow has accomplished."

LOU GEHRIG, FOUR HOMERS: JUNE 3, 1932

It was Yankees versus Athletics at Shibe Park in Philadelphia. The "Iron Horse" had yet to fully hit his stride that season, managing but seven home runs in his first 42 games.

The game was played on a Friday afternoon before a less than full ballpark—just 7,300 in attendance. Facing the Yankees was top-flight hurler George Earnshaw, with bragging rights to having recorded three consecutive 20-game seasons.

Earnshaw did not have much to brag about his performance that day. Gehrig touched him for a home run in his first at bat, slashing the ball into the stands in left-center. The Iron Horse victimized Earnshaw again in the fourth inning with a four-bagger slugged over the right field wall. It was power personified by "Larrupin' Lou" in the fifth inning—his third homer of the day. Earnshaw was done.

In came Leroy Mahaffey to pitch. In the seventh inning the red-hot Gehrig ripped a shot over the right field wall. The home run was historic. It was the Yankee first baseman's fourth circuit blast, making him the first player in American League history to do that. He also tied Ty Cobb's American League

record for total bases in game—16.

Even the Athletics fans on this early summer day cheered Lou Gehrig on. Many stood up when he came to bat in the eighth inning, questing for his fifth home run of the day. He was retired on a ground out.

Ed Rommel was on the mound in the ninth inning as the Yankee superstar came up for his at bat. Putting all his beef into the swing, Gehrig whacked the ball into the deepest part of center field. It looked as if he had his fifth home run, but Al Simmons stayed with the drive, leaped at the wall and made a one-handed leaping catch. It was Gehrig's hardest shot of the game, missing going out by inches.

The game was completed in just under three hours, quick work considering the 20–13 score and the Yankee home runs by Earle Combs, Babe Ruth, Tony Lazzeri and the four by Gehrig.

As a special reward for what he had accomplished, Gehrig was given four boxes of chewing gum.

The *New York Times* sports page headline read: "Gehrig Ties All-Time Record with Four Straight Home Runs as Yankees Win."

And the AP story declared: "Lou Gehrig, long accustomed to play(ing) second fiddle to the one and only Babe Ruth, today has carved himself a place in baseball's permanent record the result of a home run spree never equaled by his illustrious teammate, or by any other batsman in the last 38 years."

After the game, Manager Joe McCarthy told him, "Well, Lou, nobody can take today away from you."

However, on that same day, John McGraw chose to announce his retirement after 30 years of managing the New York Giants. It was McGraw, not Gehrig, who dominated the headlines in the sports sections the next day.

THE CALLED SHOT: OCTOBER 1, 1932

It was Chicago Cubs versus New York Yankees in the 1932 World Series. The two teams did not have much love lost for each other. The Yanks were managed by Joe McCarthy, who had been fired as skipper of the "Windy City" team in 1930. "Marse Joe" could hold a grudge.

In August of '32, the former Yankee shortstop Mark Koenig signed with the Cubs and played in 33 games. He was voted a half World Series share by the Cubs. Koenig was angered by the half share. Several of his former Yankee teammates, most notably his friend Babe Ruth, were miffed at the reduced share. The "Bambino," never at a loss for words at the start of the Fall Classic called the Cubs "a bunch of cheapskates, nickel-nursers and misers." There were other choice words uttered that did not make their way into the newspapers.

That season of 1932, George Herman Ruth had more mileage on him, seemed a step slower on the field of play. Cub players referred to the 37-year-old as "grandpop." But he was still the star of stars. He was the driving force behind the Yankee pennant batting .341, smashing 41 homers and driving in 137 runs.

The first two games of the World Series were played at Yankee Stadium. The home team won both. Separate trains were used to bring Yankees and Cubs and their supporting casts to Chicago as the Series continued.

"I heard words that even I had never heard before," Ruth said later. "But what annoyed me most was their spitting and their bad aim."

As Ruth and his wife Claire arrived, they were spit at by women. "I've seen some nutty fans in my life, but never quite like those girls," the "Big Bam" remarked. The saliva ejections made Ruth salivate at the thought of defeating the Cubs and he let them know how he felt.

At batting practice at Wrigley Field, Ruth screamed at Chicago players: "Hey, you damn bum Cubs, you won't be seeing Yankee Stadium again. This is going to be all over Sunday."

Before 49,986 frenzied fans at Wrigley, the mood was decidedly anti-Yankee, anti-Ruth. All matter of things were thrown onto the playing field. From the dugout of the Cubs came curses. Most of the venom was directed at the Babe. The favored target just doffed his cap and smiled.

The portly looking Yankee star came to bat in the fifth inning. He had earlier in the game whacked a three-run home run deep into the right center field bleachers. There was one out, the game was tied, 4–4. The fans taunted and teased Ruth.

Chicago right-hander Charlie Root got a strike on Ruth, who raised a finger and yelled, "strike one!"

Another fastball strike. The Babe raised two fingers. "Strike two!" he yelled.

As the story goes, Ruth stepped out of the batter's box. Some claimed he pointed at Root. Others said he pointed at the Chicago bench. Others said he pointed at the center field bleachers.

The count was 2–2. The Babe got all of the next pitch. The Chicago center fielder Johnny Moore, backpedaled, stopped. The ball wound up 436 feet from home plate into the seats in center field. It was the 15th and final World Series home run for Babe Ruth, the longest homer in Wrigley Field in history.

Chicago fans cheered and applauded the Babe. Rounding the bases, he shouted a different curse for each of the Cub infielders. When he reached third base, the showman Ruth slowed, bowed toward the Cub dugout and then headed for home plate.

The Yankees were victorious that day and the next day won another game and another world championship.

"As I hit the ball," Ruth would say later, "every muscle in my system, every sense I had, told me that I had never hit a better one, that as long as I lived nothing would ever feel as good as this one. I didn't exactly point to any spot like the flagpole. I just sort of waved at the whole fence, but that was foolish enough. All I wanted to do was give the thing a ride . . . outta the park . . . anywhere.

"Every time I went to the bat the Cubs on the bench would yell 'Oogly googly.' It's all part of the game, but this particular inning when I went to bat there was a whole chorus of oogly googlies. The first pitch was a pretty good strike, and I didn't kick. But the second was outside and I turned around to beef about it. Their catcher Gabby Hartnett said 'Oogly googly.' That kinda burned me and I said, 'All right, you bums, I'm gonna knock this one a mile.' I guess I pointed, too."

"To tell the truth," Joe McCarthy said, "I didn't see him point anywhere at all. But maybe I turned my head for a moment."

Lou Gehrig, honest to a fault, was waiting in the on-deck circle for his turn to bat. "There was never any question that Ruth called the shot," he said.

Program for Babe Ruth's famous "called shot," 1932 World Series Game 3.

The "Windy City" team in 1930, the year Joe McCarthy was fired as skipper.

Other Yankees, Lefty Gomez, George Pipgras and Joe Sewell said Ruth called the shot. Cub player Guy Bush, one of the main antagonists to Babe Ruth, also affirmed that the Babe called the home run.

"The Babe pointed out to right field," said Yankee pitcher George Pipgras, who won that game, "and that's where he hit the ball."

In the press box, according to Ed Sherman in his book *Babe Ruth's Called Shot*, Davis J. Walsh, sports editor of the International News Service, "leaped to his feet and shouted, 'Hey, he hit it exactly where he had pointed.'"

In the *New York World-Telegram* that night Joe Williams wrote: "On the occasion of his second round-tripper [Ruth] even went so far as to call his shot." His editor took the phrase a step further, headlining the piece, "Ruth Calls Shot as He Puts Homer No. 2 in Side Pocket."

Later, still according to Sherman in his book, Williams wrote: "It was just as easy to believe Ruth had actually called the shot as not, and it made a wonderful story, so the press box went along with it."

Yankees Bill Dickey, Ben Chapman and Frank Crosetti all said Ruth, upon coming back to the dugout, claimed to have simply been giving Chicago pitcher

Root a hard time of it. Crosetti was emphatic, according to author Sherman, telling the Yankee infielder that Ruth said: "You know I didn't point, I know I didn't point, but if those bastards want to think I pointed to center field, let 'em."

And according to Sherman, early in the 1933 season, the Yankee icon responded to Chicago reporter Hal Totten query if he had pointed: "Hell no. Only a damn fool would have done a thing like that. There was a lot of pretty rough ribbing going on . . . there was that second strike, and they let me have it again. So I held up that finger . . . and I said I still have one left. Now, kid, you know damn well I wasn't pointing anywhere. If I had done that, Root would have stuck the ball in my ear. I never knew anybody who could tell you ahead of time where he was going to hit a baseball."

So like Rashomon, different perspectives provide different stories. The "Called Shot" belongs to history.

FIRST STADIUM NO-HITTER, MONTE PEARSON: AUGUST 27, 1938

Montgomery Marcellus Pearson, out of Oakland, California, a Yankee from 1936 to 1940, a two-time All-Star, Pearson went 63–27 with the team. His overall record was 100–61. He was especially on the top of his game in the World Series of 1936 to 1939 for the Bronx Bombers where he won four games including a two-hit shutout of the Reds in the 1939 Fall Classic.

Pearson was talented, but he battled control problems and various illnesses, real and imagined, throughout much of his career. No matter how much inducement there was, he was not one to take the mound unless he felt like it. There were those days when he just did not want to pitch, begging off because of one ailment or another.

But all of that was not the case on his day of days—August 27, 1938. Despite pitching on just two days' rest, "Hoot" Pearson threw the first innings perfectly, " " . . . like reeds before a high gale," a *New York Times* story noted the next day. And he continued his precision pitching all nine innings.

The powerful Yankee offense rolled to a 13–0 walk over Cleveland before 40,959, who witnessed the first no-hitter in Yankee Stadium's 15-year history. So excited were the fans that they stormed the field celebrating the no-hitter. Pearson was thrilled with accomplishment but annoyed that he lost his cap to a fan who pulled it off his head.

BRAD TURNOW: *"Hoot" allowed only two walks that day as he struck out seven. He also retired the last 18 batters in consecutive order. The no-hitter was his 10th consecutive win and 13th overall win for the season.*

LOU GEHRIG APPRECIATION DAY: JULY 4, 1939

On this hot and muggy day, Yankee Stadium was bunting bedecked and jam-packed. Eleanor Gehrig said there were 70,000 in attendance; author Richard Bak put the figure at 61,808; Author Ray Robinson who was there said 62,000. No matter, it was people on people, elbow to elbow. And they had come to pay their respects to the great legend—Henry Louis Gehrig.

So many puffed away on pipes, cigars and cigarettes that the smoke of burnt tobacco crept onto the field. The scheduled event was a Fourth of July doubleheader with the Washington Senators. However, most had shown up for the between-the-games activity—the honoring of one of the franchise's all-time greats, the pride of the Yankees.

MEL ALLEN: *Lou patted me on the thigh and said, "Kid, I never listened to the broadcasts when I was playing, but now they're what keep me going." I went down the dugout steps and bawled like a baby.*

Those in attendance that July day in the Bronx included Gehrig's mother and father and his wife, Eleanor Gehrig. They were in box seats along the third baseline. Technically, it was the first-ever Old-Timers' Day held by a Major League team. Many members of the 1927 Yankees were there, plus New York mayor Fiorello H. LaGuardia, U.S. Postmaster General James A. Farley and other dignitaries were in attendance.

Sid Mercer was the MC for the ceremony. Babe Ruth showed up late, as was his style. He and Gehrig once had been close. They had not spoken to each other in years. One could only wonder what thoughts went through the mind of the "Iron Horse."

A 27-year-old Mel Allen introduced Lou Gehrig.

A parade kicked off the 40-minute ceremony as the Seventh Regiment Band escorted '27 Yankee players to the center field flagpole where a banner was hoisted, saluting that team.

Gehrig had remained in the Yankee dugout throughout the first game. He knew when it ended the ceremony would begin at home plate and that his manager Joe McCarthy would make a short speech and then introduce him.

Workers scrambled, setting up microphones behind home plate. Past and present Yankee players lined up along the foul lines. Clad in a uniform that barely fit, pants bunched up at his waist, his jersey windblown, Lou Gehrig stepped onto the field. He was a shell of his once powerful self. His head was bowed, his arms dangled at his sides, he shuffled his feet as he moved forward and took up a position near the microphones.

Twisting his blue Yankee cap in his hands, the Iron Horse swayed a bit listening to a series of short speeches from a line of well-wishers from various occupations and stations. Gehrig stood nervously, humbled. He lowered his head and with his spikes made a small circle of impressions.

Speeches concluded, the presentation of gifts was next—a fishing rod, some silver plates, all manner of objects. Gehrig accepted them. He said nothing. The item that garnered the most attention was a silver trophy with all the Yankee players' signatures on it. Inscribed on the front was a poem the Yankees had asked *New York Times* writer John Kiernan to compose:

We've been to the wars together:
We took our foes as they came;
And always you were the leader,
And ever you played the game.
Idol of cheering millions;
Records are yours by sheaves;
Iron of frame they hailed you,
Decked you with laurel leaves.
But higher than that we hold you,
We who have known you best;
Knowing the way you came through
Every human test.
Let this be a silent token
Of lasting friendship's gleam
And all that we've left unspoken.
                    —*Your Pals on the Yankee Team*

Sid Mercer turned to Gehrig. He asked if he had anything to say. Gehrig shook his head, no. "Lou has asked me," Mercer said, "to thank all of you. He is too moved to speak."

Workers came out ready to roll up the wires and pull down the microphones. Cries of protest rang out. All the fans were on their feet. The chanting shook the grandstand: "We want Lou! We want Lou!"

The din of the crowd made the great Yankee reverse course and head back to the home plate area. A surprised manager Joe McCarthy accompanied him. Workers backed off for Gehrig to move into position to give the speech. He held up his hand requesting silence from the crowd. He began to speak without notes. It would be the most moving and famous baseball player retirement speech in history.

His speech, according to his wife Eleanor, was as follows:

"Fans, for the past two weeks you have been reading about a bad break I got. Yet today I consider myself the luckiest man on the face of the earth. I have been in ballparks for 17 years and have never received anything but kindness and encouragement from you fans.

"Look at these grand men. Which of you wouldn't consider it the highlight of his career just to associate with them for even one day?

"Sure, I'm lucky. Who wouldn't consider it an honor to have known Jacob Ruppert; also the builder of baseball's greatest empire, Ed Barrow; to have spent six years with that wonderful little fellow, Miller Huggins; then to have spent the next nine years with that outstanding leader, that smart student of psychology—the best manager in baseball today, Joe McCarthy?

"Sure, I'm lucky. When the New York Giants, a team you would give your right arm to beat, and vice versa, sends you a gift—that's something! When everybody down to the groundskeepers and those boys in white coats remember you with trophies—that's something.

"When you have a wonderful mother-in-law who takes sides with you in squabbles against her own daughter—that's something. When you have a father and mother who work all their lives so that you can have an education and build your body—it's a blessing. When you have a wife who has been a tower of strength and shown more courage than you dreamed existed—that's the finest I know.

"So I close in saying that I might have had a tough break; but I have an awful lot to live for. Thank you."

Booming and sustained applause from the Yankee Stadium crowd and the players from both teams continued for nearly two minutes. Backing away from the microphones, a tearful, shaken Gehrig reached for a handkerchief in his back pocket. He wiped tears away. Many in the vast arena cried as Babe Ruth came over to hug him.

John Kiernan wrote in the *New York Times*: "He was there every day at the ballpark bending his back and ready to break his neck ready to win for his side. He was there day after day and year after

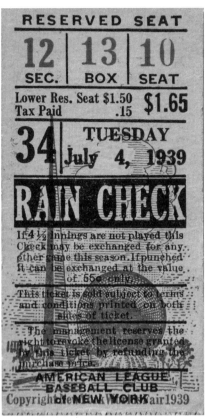

Lou Gehrig Appreciation Day ticket stub, July 4, 1939.

year. He never sulked or whined or went into a pout or a huff. He was the answer to a manager's dream."

Part of the *New York Times* news coverage the next day included this bit of eloquence: "The vast gathering, sitting in absolute silence for a longer period than perhaps any baseball crowd in history, heard Gehrig himself deliver as amazing a valedictory as ever came from a ball player."

Until season's end even as his health condition worsened and he had trouble lifting his arms, the great Gehrig was there with and for his team. He spent every day on the bench and traveled with the Yankees on road trips. He sat through all four of the 1939 World Series games.

On June 2, 1941, Gehrig passed away. He would have turned 38 years old on June 19.

Manager Joe McCarthy presenting the trophy to Lou Gehrig on his day.

GIFTS GIVEN TO LOU GEHRIG ON HIS APPRECIATION DAY

- Silver service set from the Yankees front office
- Fruit bowl and two candlesticks from the New York Giants
- Silver pitcher from the Harry M. Stevens Company and two silver platters from their employees
- Fishing rod and tackle from Yankee Stadium employees and ushers
- Silver, three-handled loving cup from the Yankees office staff
- A ring and a scroll from the Old-Timers Association of Denver
- A scroll from Washington fans
- A tobacco stand from the New York Chapter of the Baseball Writers' Association of America

ALL-STAR GAME YANKEE STADIUM: JULY 11, 1939

It was only the seventh All-Star Game ever played. Yankee Stadium was selected as the site in order for it to link in with the 1939 New York City World's Fair. A box seat ticket for the All-Star Game cost

Program for the 1939 All-Star game, which featured six Yankees starters—Red Rolfe, Bill Dickey, George Selkirk, Joe Gordon, Red Ruffing and Joe DiMaggio.

$2.20. Bleacher seats were 55 cents. One could buy a scorecard for a nickel. In today's dollars the costs would be $37.95, $9.49 and $0.86.

Just the week before, "Lou Gehrig Day" had been staged at the Stadium. Now the "Iron Horse" was on hand as an honorary member of the American League team.

"It was a beautiful day," Bob Feller remembered. "Not too hot, but warm enough. It was just a beautiful day at Yankee Stadium."

There were 62,892 crowded into the big ballpark. When the American League lineup was announced, a fan screamed out: "Make Joe McCarthy play an All-Star American League team. We can beat them, but we can't beat the Yankees."

Six starters were Yankees—Red Rolfe, Bill Dickey, George Selkirk, Joe Gordon, Red Ruffing and Joe DiMaggio. With manager Joe McCarthy, and non-starters Frank Crosetti, Lefty Gomez and Johnny Murphy, there were ten Yankees on the All-Star team. Eleven, if Lou Gehrig was counted.

The SRO crowd was especially charged up seeing Yankee favorite hurler Red Ruffing start the game and all position starters play the entire contest. Joe DiMaggio's home run highlighted the 3–1 American League triumph in a game that took just one hour and 55 minutes to play. Times sure have changed.

After the All-Star break, the Yanks went on a tear, winning 35 of 49 games. The "Yankee Clipper" finished first in batting average, second in RBIs and third in home runs. Bill Dickey, George Selkirk, Joe Gordon and Joe DiMaggio drove in more than 100 runs each. The Yankees led the American League in home runs, RBIs, slugging percentage, walks, runs and fielding percentage.

Allowing nearly 150 runs fewer than any other team in the league, the Yankees outscored their opponents by 411, a greater run differential than any other team in history. They took the pennant, finishing 17 games ahead of second-place Boston. No wonder they had so many players on that 1939 All-Star team.

JOE DIMAGGIO, 56-GAME HITTING STREAK: 1941

The star-studded 1941 Yankees would post 101 victories, and win the pennant and the world championship. At age 26, not even near his prime, only in his sixth big league season, Joe DiMaggio was the main man.

On May 15th, the Yankees were ripped, 13–1, by the White Sox and pushed six-and-a-half games behind the first-place Indians. That day Joe DiMaggio went one for four, a single off southpaw Eddie Smith.

On May 24th at the Stadium against the Red Sox, the Yankee center-fielder singled in two runs. He had a modest 10-game hitting streak.

On May 30th in the second game of a doubleheader in the fifth inning, DiMag flied to right. Red Sox outfielder Pete Fox lost the ball in the sun, and DiMaggio was credited with a hit. He now had hit safely in 16 straight games.

War news was everywhere that year of 1941. Newspaper images showed London pounded in deadly attacks by Nazi Luftwaffe bombers.

On June 1st, the streak reached 18. DiMaggio hit safely in both games of a doubleheader against the Indians. The American League record of hitting in 41 straight by George Sisler still seemed out of reach. However, radio programs and newspapers began to focus on what the Yankee superstar was doing.

On June 2nd, DiMaggio managed two hits off Cleveland great Bob Feller. "DiMaggio, incidentally, has hit safely in nineteen straight games," the New York Times reported the next day. It was claimed that mention was the first serious printed reference to the streak.

"That's when I became conscious of the streak," DiMaggio admitted. "But at that stage I didn't think too much about it."

Virtually all big league baseball games in that era were played in the afternoon. And radio announcers made it a practice to interrupt programs with the news of the Yankee Clipper's hitting progress. Day and night, radio disc jockeys played the Les Brown band recording:

Who started baseball's famous streak
That's got us all aglow?
He's just a man and not a freak,
Jolting Joe DiMaggio.
Joe . . . Joe . . . DiMaggio . . .
We want you on our side.
From Coast to Coast, that's all you hear
Of Joe the One-Man Show.
He's glorified the horsehide sphere,
Jolting Joe DiMaggio.
Joe . . . Joe . . . DiMaggio . . .
We want you on our side.
He'll live in baseball's Hall of Fame,
He got there blow-by-blow
Our kids will tell their kids his name,
Jolting Joe DiMaggio.
(Copyright 1941 by Alan Courtney)

PAUL DOHERTY: *But that information passed on through the years is not correct. The Les Brown/Betty Bonney song wasn't recorded until August 8, 1941, and didn't debut until November 10, 1941, after the season was over.*

On June 17, official scorer Dan Daniel of the New World-Telegram credited DiMaggio with a hit when his ground ball to Chicago's Luke Appling took a bounce and hit off his shoulder. Busting it all the way, DiMaggio beat the throw to first base. The streak stood at 30. DiMag was closing in on 41—the George Sisler American League record.

There were those who disagreed with Dan Daniel, a friend of DiMaggio, and other official scorers who seemed to make questionable calls as the streak moved forward. Nevertheless, the beat

A young Joe DiMaggio in 1941 kisses his bat.

went on. Now not only George Sisler's American League record but also "Wee Willie" Keeler's Major League record of 44 straight seemed within reach of the driven, determined DiMaggio.

On the 29th of June, it was Yankees versus Senators. A DiMaggio single off knuckle-baller Dutch Leonard in the first game of a doubleheader tied him with Sisler for the American League record. A seventh-inning single off Walt Masterson in the second game put the new AL record at 42.

Shy, some would say taciturn, Joseph Paul DiMaggio now was the most sought after, admired and adored athlete in the United States. He was pestered by the media, ogled by fans, adored by his Yankee teammates.

His quest for perfection, his streak was being played out against the drama and the devastation of the summer of '41, the tragedies and terrors of World War II. In some ways the context of the streak made what Joe DiMaggio was doing the good news, the best news, a way for people to take their minds off the news of war if only for a little while.

At Yankee Stadium, at Comiskey Park, at Briggs Stadium, at Fenway Park, at all the ballparks in the eight team American League he was so familiar with, the Yankee Clipper bore down, kept pushing.

"The streak is alive! The streak is alive!"

"Joltin' Joe DiMaggio got another hit!"

Many stayed up past bed times to receive news about how Joe was doing, had done. Many players around both leagues were keenly interested in how he was doing.

DOM DIMAGGIO: *Despite their own personal rivalry Ted Williams rooted for my brother Joe. They had great admiration for each other. As a great hitter Ted could appreciate what Joe was doing. It was Ted, playing left field for our team the Red Sox at Fenway Park, who would receive info from the scoreboard operator about the streak.*

And Ted would yell out to me in center "Joe's got another hit."

Joseph Paul DiMaggio played on in day games and night games, home games and away games, in Yankee triumphs and losses, single games, doubleheaders, meaningless games and games that meant a lot.

On July the first, a cloudy doubleheader day at Yankee Stadium, 53,832 were on hand to watch Yankees versus Red Sox and especially Joe DiMaggio.

Mike Ryba gave up two hits to DiMaggio in the first game. Controversy attached itself to the first hit. It was a grounder to third baseman Jim Tabor, who made a hurried and off-line throw to first base. DiMaggio wound up on second base. Dan Daniel, official scorer, raised his right arm—"hit." Bedlam prevailed. Fans stamped their feet.

Roars and loud applause punctuated the moment. The hometown crowd was into it. The second game was called because of rain after five innings. DiMaggio managed to stroke a first-inning single, tying Keeler's 44-year-old Major League mark of 44.

On July the second, it was one of those insufferable days in New York. The temperature was 95. The humidity was unbearable. The miserable weather was why only 8,682 showed at the Stadium. Cigar and cigarette smoke merged with the body odors of summer sweat; pigeons scurried for leftover food. Shouts of vendors trying to make a buck seemed louder with the small crowd.

Near the Yankee clubhouse before the game, Tom Connolly, head of American League umpires, chatted with DiMaggio. The amiable Irishman had admired "Wee Willie" Keeler. Nevertheless, Connolly said: "Joe, I hope you do it. If you do you will be breaking the record of the finest fellow who ever walked and who never said a mean thing about anyone in his life. Good luck to you."

Star hurler Lefty Grove was supposed to be the Red Sox game starter. He had made it clear that he was all in to stop the streak. The horrific heat made Boston plug in a different starter—a talented rookie, Heber (Dick) Newsome.

Hitless as he came up for the third time in the game, DiMaggio surveyed the playing field, one Yankee runner on base. The count moved to 2–1. The pitch. The swing. Home run—the 15th of the streak, into the seats in lower left field. Yankee Stadium rocked. Exultant fans shouted Joe's name. Applause erupted in what was supposedly a neutral press box.

Running the bases, tipping his cap to the fans, touching home plate, there was joy in Joe DiMaggio's step as he entered the Yankee dugout.

Teammates engulfed him, hugged him, congratulated him.

Joseph Paul DiMaggio had the all-time record—hitting in 45 straight baseball games.

Game over and Yankees victorious, the Yankee center fielder sat in front of his locker, a beer in one hand, smoking a cigarette. Sometimes moody, sometimes testy, now Joe DiMaggio was relaxed as reporters gathered around.

"I don't know how far I can go," DiMaggio said, "but I'm not going to worry about it now. I'm glad it's over. It got to be quite a strain over the last 10 days. Now I can go back to swinging at good balls. I was swinging at some bad pitches so I wouldn't be walked. The pressure has been as tough off the field as on it. It was a great tribute to me, and I appreciated it but it had its drawbacks, too. I got so much fan mail. There was some kind of good luck charm in every letter that I had to turn it over to the Yankee front office."

The 16th of July saw the Yankees in Cleveland for the start of a series with the Indians at League Park II that seated 30,000. At this game only 15,000 showed. Stroking a first-inning single off Al Milnar and two more hits later in the game, Joe Di moved the streak to 56. The sparse and partisan Cleveland crowd appreciated what he had done that 1941 season. They gave him a warm ovation.

The next game was at night, Thursday July 17th, at the 10-year-old Municipal Stadium. It was a commodious facility that could seat more than 78,000. DiMag and his good buddy Lefty Gomez, scheduled to start the game for the Yankees, took a taxi to the ballpark.

Stopping at a traffic light, the Cleveland cabby, who had recognized DiMaggio, turned around: "I've got a feeling that if you don't get a hit your first time up tonight, they're going to stop you."

An angry and enraged Gomez snapped: "Who the hell are you? What are you trying to do, jinx him?"

DiMaggio kept his thoughts to himself.

Outside the big ballpark there was hustle and bustle, hawking of souvenirs. Attendance would be announced as 67,463, largest ever for a night game. Forty thousand tickets had been purchased in advance. DiMaggio and his quest to keep his streak going was the big draw.

Walking the field earlier that day DiMaggio realized rain had left the ground wet. The run down to first base would be a bit slower.

The huge crowd applauded. Joe DiMaggio stepped into the batter's box for his first at bat of the game. There was one out, and Tommy Henrich was on second base. Veteran lefty Al Smith was on the mound.

DiMaggio took a high and away fastball and then jumped on the next pitch pounding the ball past third base. Positioned perfectly, Ken Keltner's throw nipped DiMaggio busting it down the line. His second time up the Yankee center fielder walked. Boos rang out.

Almost grim, very honed in, the Yankee Clipper stepped out of the on deck circle and came to bat in the seventh inning. Time was running out. The deafening din continued in the big ballpark. "C'mon, Joe!" "You can do it!"

Again another swing, another ball to Keltner at third. Backhanded, the throw to first. Out! Again no emotion, no reaction from the great Yankee.

In the eighth inning with one out and the Yankees leading, 4–1, a spent Smith walked Tommy Henrich. The bases were loaded. DiMaggio was next. Smith was done. Right-hander Jim Bagby, Jr. took over. He ran the count to two balls, one strike.

Some said DiMag swung at ball three, a low fastball. A grounder to

shortstop Lou Boudreau. It seemed to hit something in the grass and jumped up. Boudreau did not panic. Gloving the ball, he shuffled it to second baseman Ray Mack. The step on second, the throw to first. Double play. The graceful DiMaggio ran past first base and continued his run into shallow center field. In full stride, bending down, he lifted his glove off the grass and automatically assumed his fielding position. The game still had to be played out.

"I can't say I'm glad it's over," DiMaggio said after the game. "Of course, I wanted it to go on as long as I could."

Game over, Ken Keltner was given a police escort out of the ballpark for his own safety. Joe DiMaggio and Phil Rizzuto waited for the crowd to thin out. Then they walked through the mist back to the Cleveland Hotel. The Yankee shortstop headed to his room. The Yankee Clipper wound up in the bar.

The entire experience was remarkable. Joe DiMaggio stroked a hit every game for two months, from May 15 through July 16, 1941, in Yankee wins and defeats, in games played in the daytime and at night. Single games, doubleheaders, unimportant games and ones that counted—Joe DiMaggio was locked in for 56 straight. He batted .408, posted a slugging average of .717, faced four future Hall of Fame pitchers, even played in the 1941 All-Star Game and even hit in that game, going one-for-four.

The consecutive games hitting streak included 56 singles and runs scored. It covered 53 day games and three night games, 29 at Yankee Stadium and 27 road games. During that sensational run Joe DiMaggio had 91 hits, 22 multi-hit games, 5 three-hit games, 4 four-hit games, 15 home runs. He did not bunt even once for a hit.

It was reported that had the streak gone to 57, the Heinz Corporation had

promised to pay Joe DiMaggio $10,000 for endorsements of their Heinz 57 products.

With the streak over, DiMaggio began a new one. He hit safely in 16 consecutive games. That was a special feat hitting safely in 72 of 73 games that 1941 season.

A P.S. to that remarkable streak was a party staged for the great Yankee Clipper later that 1941 season. DiMaggio's roommate, Lefty Gomez, guided him to a surprise team party at a Washington, D.C. hotel during a road trip. His teammates presented DiMaggio with a sterling silver cigar humidor. Atop it was a statuette of DiMaggio in his classic swing. On one side was "56"; the other had "91" for his hit total during the streak. Below were his teammates' engraved autographs.

"It was," DiMaggio remembered, "Just a little party in a hotel room, but it was the biggest party I'll ever go to."

BABE RUTH, NUMBER RETIRED: JUNE 13, 1948

It was a time for commemorating the 25th Anniversary of Yankee Stadium, a time for Babe Ruth's uniform Number 3 to be retired.

PAUL DOHERTY: *He was the last to come into the original Yankees clubhouse [the clubhouse during the Babe's stadium seasons] located on the third base side of the stadium. The Yankees switched to the first base dugout and a new clubhouse in 1946.*

He had on a dark suit and an oyster white cap. He seemed to barely move his feet as he slow walked with a friend on either side of him. He paused when he recognized someone, smiled and stuck out his hand.

Babe Ruth, his Number 3 retired, June 13, 1948, at Yankee Stadium.

Babe Ruth steps out onto the field, June 13, 1948, using his bat as a cane.

The Babe began to undress. His friends helped him. They hung up his clothes. They helped him into his uniform. He sat down again to put on his spiked shoes. Photographers took pictures of him.

Famed *LIFE* photographer Ralph Morse was there that day: "It was moving being there in the locker room, knowing that Ruth's number was going to be retired, that it was never going to be worn again on another Yankees jersey. But another thing, purely from a photographer's point of view, is that the Yankees' lockers were a bright, bright red, which in my experience was unusual. The color gave that quiet scene a bit of excitement. I mean, here's this man—once an incredible athlete, but now literally gray, sick, trying to get his clothes on—with this great big number three on a bright red locker behind him. It was just such a striking scene."

They brought out a dozen baseballs and a pen. And Ruth signed slowly, carefully.

"All right," somebody in the locker room said. "They're ready now."

It was raining that day and someone put a camel's hair coat over his shoulders. One by one to booming cheers his old teammates were introduced. A policeman walked in front of him, another walked behind. He was led to the third-base dugout crowded with members of the Cleveland Indians and 1923 Yankees. He sat down on the bench.

Finally, announcer Mel Allen called him to home plate. "George Herman," Allen's voice said, "Babe Ruth!"

In front of him the Indians moved back. Babe could see clearly in front of him two dozen photographers. He stood up. The camel topcoat fell off his shoulders. Using a bat as a cane, the Babe walked out slowly to home plate. The ovation was deafening.

He knew the end for him was near. "The termites have got me," he told Connie Mack and others. Cancer surgery had harmed his larynx. His once powerful and lively voice was now just raspy. He struggled but got through his speech.

Ceremonies done, the press plus old-timers gathered together in the locker room. "Jumpin' Joe" Dugan, called that for being AWOL from his first big league club as a youngster, poured out a beer for the "Bam."

"So," Joe asked, "How are you?"

"Joe, I'm gone," the Babe said and then began to cry.

Back in the hospital after that marker day, the man who was baseball signed autographs, watched baseball on television, listened to his wife read him some of the hundreds of letters sent to him every day. Visitors came and went. The Babe tried to look upbeat.

At 8:01 p.m., on August 16, 1948, the Babe passed away. He was fifty-three years old. He lay in state in "the House That Ruth Built" for two days as more than 200,000 paid last respects. Grieving fathers held up their children for one last look.

Three days later the funeral was held at St. Patrick's Cathedral. Tens of thousands in the streets outside and tens of thousands more lined the funeral cortege route.

JOE DIMAGGIO APPRECIATION DAY: OCTOBER 1, 1949

It was "Joe DiMaggio Day" at Yankee Stadium. The word was that Yankee officials had wondered how much longer their great star would continue to play. There was concern that if he retired in the off-season they would miss out on the chance to honor him while he was still in uniform. Hence, it made sense to give the 34-year-old his "day" as he completed his 11th season with the Yankees.

The "Joe DiMaggio Special" came down from New Haven, nine cars transporting 700 fans. Dom DiMaggio was in center field for Boston. Mom Rosalie DiMaggio had flown in from California as well as brother Tom and Joe, Jr., Joe's son. The great Ethel Merman was there to sing.

A reporter asked Mrs. DiMaggio: "Which team and which center fielder do you favor?"

Dom DiMaggio cut him off. "Mom is impartial."

The Yankee Clipper sat for a bit in the dugout with his good friend Frank Sinatra. Then it was on to the field.

PAUL DOHERTY: *Not too ironic that Joe D sat with Sinatra. Thirteen years later Joe banned Frankie from Marilyn Monroe's funeral.*

The cheers and applause would have probably moved anyone. Joe Di was not anyone. He showed no emotion. Joe DiMag was gracious in accepting more than 100 presents. Among the gifts were a Dodge for him and a Cadillac for his mother. Others were a Chris-Craft boat, Longine Baro Thermo calendar watch, Waltham watch chain knife, a wallet with religious gifts, golf cuff links, gold belt buckle, 14-karat gold cufflinks and tie pin, 51-inch loving cup trophy, Admiral television set, Dumont television set, deer rifle, bronze plaque, $100 fedora hat, golf bag, General Electric blanket and radio, Thermos water jug set, 14-karat gold key chain autographed in links, silver loving cup, 25 volumes of Joe DiMaggio Capitol records for Yankee Juniors, set of Lionel trains for Joe Jr., driving and sun glasses for Yankee Juniors, Christmas candy and baseball and bat, 500 Joe DiMaggio shirts in Joe's name to Yankee Juniors, ship's clock, oil

painting of Joe DiMaggio, carpeting for his living room in Amsterdam, NY, a Westinghouse toaster, a 14-karat gold money clip, open house privileges at hotels Concourse Plaza in the Bronx and Martinique at Greenly Square in Manhattan. These hotels also provided a four-year college scholarship for a boy of Joe's selection.

And . . . the Il Progresso newspaper medal of honor, 300 quarts of Cardini ice cream for any institution designated by Joe, a statuette neckerchief and clip from the Boy Scouts of America, an air-foam mattress and box spring, Fond du Lac Wisconsin cheese, 14-karat gold watch with diamond numerals from the Italian Welfare Association of Elizabeth, New Jersey, a case of shoestring potatoes, a case of Ventura County oranges, a sack of walnuts, a case of lemonade and frozen lima beans, a hand-painted tie, a polished wood paperweight, a leather wallet, a metal good luck elephant, sterling silver rosary beads for Joe Jr., a portrait from Frank Paladino of Brooklyn, New York, a Sporting News plaque, a dozen gold balls, an ash tray, a Thermo tote bag, a Columbia bicycle for Joe Jr., fishing tackle, luggage, a cocker spaniel from the American Spaniel Club, a plaque from the Columbia Civic Club of Newark, New Jersey, a traveling bag, a certificate of recognition from the Italian Historical Society of America, Lux Clock Company traveling alarm clock, a sterling silver money clip, hand painted ties for Joe and Joe Jr., taxi service for 300 fans from Newark ("This ride is on Joe D.") from the Brown and White Cab Company of Newark, New Jersey.

Joe DiMaggio thanked his manager Casey Stengel, his friends and teammates, "the fightingest bunch that ever lived." He went into detail telling the story of his time as a youngster preparing to leave San Francisco for New York City. His minor league manager

and mentor Lefty O'Doul offered good advice. "Joe," he said, "don't let the big town scare you. New York is the most generous town in the world." This day proves that, the Yankee Clipper said.

He also spoke what would become his most famous line: "I want to thank the good Lord for making me a Yankee."

Yankees broadcaster Mel Allen was master of ceremonies. New York City Mayor William O'Dwyer was part of the ceremony. The next day the *New York Times* declared: "It was America on parade at its Sunday best at Yankee Stadium as baseball fans in sardine-packed thousands paid tribute to the brilliant outfield star."

"Engulfed in an avalanche of gifts and a wave of affection which rolled in from bleachers to boxes," was how the *Sporting News* described DiMaggio's day.

PHIL RIZZUTO: *We were behind 4–0. Casey had told Joe Page who came in for Allie Reynolds "Just hold them, Joe, just hold them."*

Page held them through six and one-third innings. An eighth inning home run by Johnny Lindell beat them and the Yankees walked away with a 5–4 win.

The elegant, graceful, stoic Joe DiMaggio, ill with pneumonia and sick in bed three days before the game, bed-ridden for almost two weeks, had his day at bat, too. He slashed two hits. He played flawlessly in the field. It was what everyone expected.

Pete Sheehy, longtime Yankee clubhouse manager had perhaps the best comment on the Yankee Clipper: "I can describe Joe in one word: class. He was the most perfect ballplayer I ever saw, but, he was a shy fellow. I'll tell you something else though. When Joe DiMaggio walks into the clubhouse, the lights flicker."

Allie Reynolds, Number 22, wraps up his second no-hitter in 1951 amid affection from his teammates.

ALLIE REYNOLDS, TWO NO-HITTERS: JULY 12 AND SEPTEMBER 28, 1951

Born on February 10, 1917, in Bathany, Oklahoma, close by Oklahoma City, the man they called "Superchief" was three-sixteenth Creek Indian and one tough pitcher. The 34-year-old was matched up on July 12 against another very tough pitcher—Bob Feller of the Cleveland Indians. Once roommates and friends, Reynolds had become a Yankee after the 1946 season. Future Hall of Famer Joe "Flash" Gordon was traded to get him. As reports indicated, the Indians had such high regard for Gordon they made available any of their pitchers except for Bob Feller.

Allegedly, Joe DiMaggio recommended that the Yanks grab Reynolds. "I'm a fastball hitter," the Yankee star said, "but he can buzz his hard one by me any time he has a mind to."

Through six innings that July day at Municipal Stadium before 39,195, neither hurler had allowed a hit. Feller had pitched a no-hitter just eleven days before.

With one out in the seventh, Yankee outfielder Gene Woodling blasted a high pitch nearly 365 feet over the right field fence. That shot shattered Feller's no hit attempt. Reynolds, however, kept on, setting down in order the last 17 batters he faced, fanning the last hitter he faced, Bobby Avila. The "Super Chief" recorded his fifth shutout of the season and his first no-hitter. The Yankees won the game, 1–0 victory.

A fan favorite, Reynolds was also a favorite of manager Casey Stengel. "He was two ways great, which is starting and relieving, which no one can do like him. He has guts and his courage is simply tremendous."

On September 28, before 40,000, Allie Reynolds faced off against the powerful Red Sox at Yankee Stadium in the second game of a doubleheader. A win would position the Yankees one game away from clinching the pennant.

Cruising inning after inning against the dangerous Boston lineup, the "Super Chief" was on his game. The no-hitter was never really in danger. Two outs in the ninth inning. Up came the greatest hitter in baseball—Ted Williams.

"I was very much aware of the no-hitter and the ninth inning," Reynolds said later.

Pinch hitter Charlie Maxwell led off for the Sox and fouled out. Reynolds had gotten stronger as the game moved along. Maxwell could not catch up to his heat.

Dom DiMaggio wiped his glasses, kicked at the dirt, stepped in to the batter's box. He was patient; Reynolds was impatient. Over-throwing, Reynolds walked Dom.

Next was Johnny Pesky. Reynolds got the little infielder for his ninth strikeout of the game.

"All I had to get out was Ted Williams," Reynolds recalled. "Most times I tried to walk the damn guy. In my opinion it was just stupid to let an outstanding hitter like him beat you."

A fastball strike on Williams. Another fastball. The ball popped up behind home plate. Catcher Yogi Berra under it, waiting. The ball bounced off Berra's glove. Berra then bounced off Reynolds, who was backing up the play.

Reynolds helped Berra to his feet. Anxious but not annoyed, Reynolds told Berra: "Don't worry Yogi, we'll get him next time."

Ted Williams complained to Berra. "You sons of bitches put me in a hell of a spot. You blew it, and now I've got to bear down even harder even though the game is decided and your man has a no-hitter going."

Same pitch to Williams, fastball. Same scenario. Pop up to Berra. He snared the baseball. Allie Reynolds had his second no-hitter and the Yankees had an 8–0 triumph.

The first American League pitcher to record two no-hitters in one season, the only Yankee to ever pitch two no-hitters, let alone two in one season, the big right-hander had it all going in his 17 victory, seven shutout season of 1951.

MICKEY MANTLE, TAPE MEASURE HOMER: APRIL 17, 1953

PEDRO RAMOS: *I used to listen in Cuba on the radio to the World Series. I knew that Yankee Stadium was history, and to me it became the wonder of the baseball world and the Yankees when I came to the majors especially with Mickey Mantle later, the team of teams.*

It was Yankees versus Senators in an early spring game at DC's Griffith Stadium, fifth inning. Mel Allen's call brings back the time: "Yogi Berra on first. Mickey at bat with the count of no strikes. Left-handed pitcher Chuck Stobbs on the mound. Mantle, a switch-hitter batting right-handed, digs in the plate. Here's the pitch . . . Mantle swings . . . there's a tremendous drive going into deep left field! It's going, going, it's over the bleachers and over the sign atop of the bleachers into the yards of houses across the street! It's got to be one of the longest home runs I've ever seen hit. How about that! . . .We have just learned that Yankee publicity director Red Patterson has gotten hold of a tape measure and he's going to go out there to see how far that ball actually did go."

"Look out!" Yankee third base coach Frank Crosetti yelled at Mantle, who ran the bases head down. Billy Martin stayed at third base and pretended to tag up. Mantle almost ran over Martin.

Washington outfielders never moved. A ball only twice before had been smashed over the Griffith 55-foot-high left-field wall. Joe DiMaggio and Jimmy Foxx claimed bragging rights. Their homers bounced in the seats before clearing the final barrier. Mantle's shot rocketed toward left center, where the base of the bleachers wall was 391 feet from home plate. From there it was 69 more feet to the back of the wall. The ball struck about five feet above the high wall, jumped off to the right and out of sight.

Scrambling over the fence, Donald Dunaway, ten, was the first to get to the ball. Yankee publicity director Arthur E. Patterson was on his heels.

The ball was eventually recovered in the backyard of a house across a major thoroughfare and four houses up a bisecting street, some 562 feet from home plate. Patterson made the trade of

his life. It was reported that Dunaway would wind up with a dollar and three new baseballs autographed by Yankee players. Patterson in return got the home run ball.

Chuck Stobbs was not happy. His pride was bruised. "Mickey didn't get a hit every time he faced me. I got him out a few times, too."

Yankees PR director Red Patterson was very happy. He had a place in the history books. He coined the phrase "tape measure home run" by measuring the distance with a tape measure of that monster shot.

Or did he?

According to Marty Appel, who was the Yankees' public relations man from the late 1960s through 1977, "Red never got hold of a tape measure. He walked it off with his size 11 shoes and estimated the distance."

What is a matter of record is that the monster home run was hit with the bat Mickey Mantle liked to use batting right-handed. It belonged to Loren Babe.

DON LARSEN, THE PERFECT GAME: OCTOBER 8, 1956

October in New York City in the fifties. New York Yankees versus Brooklyn Dodgers for the last time in the Fall Classic. For some, the memory stays.

Autumn's shadows. Smoke, tobacco smell, haze, humidity. World Series buntings on railings along the first and third baselines. The zeroes on the scoreboard for the Dodgers of Brooklyn mounting inning after inning.

The big Yankee right-hander casually tossing the ball from a no-stretch windup to Yogi Berra. Larsen struck out Junior Gilliam on a breaking ball to start the game. Another strikeout, on a full count to Pee Wee Reese.

The 6-foot-4, 240-pound hurler was economical. No more than 15 pitches in any one inning against the mighty

Don Larsen, the "imperfect man," pitches the perfect game to catcher Yogi Berra in the 1956 World Series.

him, 'Hey, Don, you've got a no-hitter going!' He laughed and blushed, and I think that maybe that broke the tension for him, it being that sudden and all."

The game moved to the ninth. A quietness settled over the Stadium. Carl Furillo fouled off four pitches. He then flied out to Hank Bauer in right. Billy Martin threw out Campanella. Left-handed batter Dale Mitchell came up as pinch hitter for pitcher Sal Maglite.

GAME CALL, BOB WOLFF: *"Count is one and one. And this crowd just straining forward on every pitch. Here it comes . . . a swing and a miss! Two strikes, ball one to Dale Mitchell. Listen to this crowd! I'll guarantee that nobody—but nobody—has left this ballpark. And if somebody did manage to leave early, man he's missing the greatest! Two strikes and a ball . . . Mitchell waiting, stands deep, feet close together. Larsen is ready, gets the sign. Two strikes, ball one, here comes the pitch. Strike three! A no-hitter! A perfect game for Don Larsen!"*

That final pitch—Larsen's 97th of the game was disputed.

"The third strike on Mitchell was absolutely positively a strike on the outside corner," Berra said. "No question about it. People say it was a ball and that I rushed the mound to hug Larsen to make the umpire think it was a strike. Nonsense. It was a perfect strike."

Casey Stengel was asked, "Was that the best game you've ever seen Larsen pitch?"

DON LARSEN: *I have been asked a million times about the perfect game. I never dreamed about something like that happening and everybody is entitled to a good day and mine came at the right time.*

Dodgers of Campanella, Reese, Hodges, Gilliam, Robinson, Snider and Furillo.

A second inning Jackie Robinson liner off the glove of Andy Carey at third was picked up by Gil McDougald. Out at first. A fifth inning liner by Gil Hodges was run down by Mickey Mantle. Backhand grab of the ball. Out. An eighth inning Hodges slam down the third baseline. Andy Carey up to the challenge. Another out. Sandy Amoros and Duke Snider pounded balls into the right field seats—foul, barely so.

HANK BAUER: *When I saw that Amoros ball heading for the right-field seats I was ready to concede the homer. But when it hooked foul by a couple inches, I was the happiest guy in the park.*

"You're never supposed to talk about a no-hitter to the pitcher," Mickey Mantle said. "But I didn't even realize he had one going. When we went out for the eighth, I saw the scoreboard with all those zeroes, and I just blurted out to

NEW YORK YANKEES
1961
AMERICAN LEAGUE CHAMPIONS

Home Of Champions

OFFICIAL PROGRAM AND SCORECARD   15 CENTS

Yankee Stadium program from 1961, known as the year of Mantle and Maris.

"So far," was the Yankee manager's response.

Don Larsen received all kinds of letters and notes and cards including this one:

Dear Mr. Larsen: It is a noteworthy event when anybody achieves perfection in anything. It has been so long since anyone pitched a perfect big league game that I have to go back to my generation of ballplayers to recall such a thing—and that is truly a long time ago.

This note brings you my very sincere congratulations on a memorable feat, one that will inspire pitchers for a long time to come. With best wishes,

Sincerely,
Dwight D. Eisenhower
President of the United States

ARTHUR RICHMAN: *I wrote for the* **New York Mirror** *then. Don Larsen and I were friends. That night we went to the Copacabana to celebrate. I had called up for a table and they said there was no room but when I told them I was bringing Don Larsen, they brought a table down front and set us up. We ate and drank and Joe E. Lewis, the great comic, introduced Don to the audience. When the check came, we ordered so much we didn't have the money to pay. But Joe E. Lewis picked up the tab. It was a perfect day and night for Don.*

ROGER MARIS, THE 61ST HOME RUN: OCTOBER 1, 1961

I was a Yankee fan as far back as I can remember although not really a Roger Maris fan. I was a Mickey Mantle fan and watched every Yankee game as I was growing up because of him.

SAL DURANTE: *I was with my girlfriend Rosemarie who became my wife later on and my cousin and his girl. We were hanging out in Coney Island doing nothing. So I made a suggestion that we go to the last game at Yankee Stadium. I knew that Maris was going after the 61st home run. I knew about the promised $5,000 reward for the guy who caught the ball. I had read all about it in the* **News.**

We asked the ticket guy for four seats in right field. I never expected there would be any. The guy thumbed through tickets like a deck of playing cards, "Yeah, I've got four seats."

I had no money. Rosemarie paid for the tickets. We were in Section 33, Box 163D, and the sixth row of the right field lower deck. In those days you had six seats to a box. I was sitting in the row below Rosemarie with John and his girl. Rose-marie was sitting by herself in Seat Four. I switched seats with her so she could talk to them. It was the smartest thing I did.

GAME CALL, PHIL RIZZUTO, WCBS RADIO: *They're standing, waiting to see if Maris is gonna hit number sixty-one. We've only got a handful of people sitting out in left field, but in right field, man, it's hogged out there. And they're standing up. Here's the windup, the pitch to Roger. Way outside, ball one . . . And the fans are starting to boo. Low, ball two. That one was in the dirt. And the boos get louder . . . Two balls, no strikes on Roger Maris. Here's the windup. Fastball, hit deep to right! This could be it! Way back there! Holy cow, he did it! Sixty-one for Maris."*

That 1961 season Roger Maris did not hit a home run in his first ten games. By the end of May he had hit a dozen dingers. By the end of June, he had hit 27 home runs. By the end of July, Maris had smashed 40 home runs. He was a half dozen ahead of the immortal Babe Ruth record total that had stood since 1927.

"My going off after the record started off such a dream," the Yankee outfielder said. "I was living a fairy tale for a while. I never thought I'd get a chance to break such a record."

Reporters lined up by the Maris locker in ballparks all over the American League:

"How does it feel to be hitting so many home runs? Do you ever think of what it means?"

"How the hell should I know," Maris, short-tempered, surly, shot back.

There were all kinds of commercial capitalizations. An enterprising stripper using the name "Mickey Maris" got some play. The sales of M&M candy skyrocketed—a tip of the cash register to the "M and M Boys" who had not endorsed the confection.

Maris breaks Babe Ruth's season home run record; Sal Durante snags the ball.

There were stories and charts in newspapers and magazines comparing Mantle and Maris, Maris and Ruth, Ruth and Mantle, and on and on. Over-reaching journalists invented stories that bickering and animosity existed between Mantle who earned $75,000 in 1961 and Maris, whose salary was $42,000. The stories were completely untrue.

"BIG" JULIE ISAACSON: *When Roger Maris was going for the home run record he would eat only bologna and eggs for breakfast. I was his friend and every morning we would have breakfast together at the Stage Deli. We had the same waitress, and I'd leave her the same five-dollar tip every time. After, I would drive Roger up to the Stadium.*

Against his former Kansas City teammates on August 26th in his 128th game of the '61 season, Maris smashed number 51, eight ahead of the Ruth pace. It was about then that Baseball Commissioner Ford Frick, a former ghostwriter for Babe Ruth, ruled that an asterisk would be placed next to Maris's name in the record books if he broke the record of the "Sultan of Swat." Frick argued Ruth's record was set in a 154-game season. Maris played in a 162-game schedule. There would be a need to differentiate the "records."

The battle to break Ruth's record for a time was between Mantle and Maris. But injuries and fatigue sapped the "Mick." He managed but one home run from September 10th on—number 54. The Yankees clinched their 26th pennant. Mickey Mantle was no longer a threat to break Ruth's record. The prize, the pressure, the prestige now were all part of the package for Roger Maris.

CASEY STENGEL: *"You'd ask him a question, and he'd just stare away."*

The Yankees arrived in Baltimore on the 18th of September for a four-game series. Maris had 58 home runs. For the brooding Yankee star to officially break Ruth's record according to the ruling by Ford Frick, he would have to do it in the first three games at Baltimore. Those games were within the Yankees' 1961 154-game schedule. After that date, the ruling read, any accomplishment would have an asterisk.

In games one and two, a two-night doubleheader, games 152 and 153, Maris failed to hit a home run. On September 20, a night game, Maris matched up against Baltimore's Milt Pappas. Media was there in force from all over; however, attendance was just 21,000 or so in the stands.

In the third inning, Maris got all of the ball and sent it almost 400 feet into the bleachers in right field—home run number 59! He had passed Jimmie Foxx and Hank Greenberg. Maris had three more chances that night to tie the Babe. It was not to be. He struck out, flied out and grounded out.

Roger Maris was still questing, longing to break the single season home run record five days later on September

26th in game number 158 for the Yankees.

Third inning. Jack Fisher of Baltimore throws a high curve ball. "The minute I threw the ball," Fisher moaned, "I said to myself, that does it. That's number 60."

The record-tying home run smashed onto the concrete steps of the sixth row in the third deck in Yankee Stadium. The ball bounced back onto the field and was picked up by Earl Robinson, the Oriole right fielder who tossed the ball to umpire Ed Hurley, who gave it to Yankee first base coach Wally Moses who rolled it into the Yankee dugout. The ball and Maris, running out the 60th home run, arrived in the dugout of the Bronx Bombers at about the same time.

Maris had the ball. He gave it a couple of glances. Cheering and joyous fans urged him to take a bow. Uncomfortable, Maris moved up to the top step of the Yankee dugout and waved his cap. Mrs. Claire Ruth, widow of the Babe, watched the drama play out.

There were now three days left in the 1961 season for Maris and the Yankees. Yankees versus Red Sox. Maris versus Ruth. The "Rajah" did not hit a home run in the first two games.

The date was October 1, 1961. There were 23,154 roaring fans at the "House That Ruth Built." A worn, weary, worried Roger Maris stepped into the batter's box to face Red Sox right-hander Tracy Stallard.

The 24-year-old retired Maris in his first at bat. In the fourth inning, it was again Roger versus Stallard. The Yankee slugger made contact. The ball traveled just 360 feet, went over outfielder Lu Clinton's head, slammed into box 163D of section 33 into the sixth row of the lower deck in right field. Scuffling, scrambling fans fought for the ball and the promised and well publicized $5,000 reward.

"He threw me a pitch outside and I just went with it," Maris would say later. "If I never hit another home run—this is the one they can never take away from me."

SAL DURANTE: *As soon as Maris hit the ball, I knew it was going to be a home run that would go over my head. I jumped up on my seat and reached as high as I could. The ball hit the palm of my hand. It didn't hurt. It was a thing from heaven that knocked me over into the next row.*

On top of the world, Roger Maris trotted out the home run that he had quested for, shaking the hand of third base coach Frank Crosetti, then Yogi Berra's hand at home plate. Then he shook hands with a batboy, a young man from the stands and another batboy. Maris was in the dugout briefly when he left its relative calm and went out on the field for three mini cap tips.

"I hated to see the record broken," Phil Rizzuto said. "But it was another Yankee that did it. When he hit the 61st home run I screamed so loud I had a headache for about a week."

ROGER MARIS: 61 HOME RUNS							
HR	GAME	DATE/BOX	PITCHER	TEAM	THROWS	WHERE	INNING
1	11	04-26-1961	Paul Foytack	Detroit	Right	Away	5th
2	17	05-03-1961	Pedro Ramos	Minnesota	Right	Away	7th
3	20	05-06-1961	Eli Grba	Los Angeles	Right	Away	5th
4	29	05-17-1961	Pete Burnside	Washington	Left	Home	8th
5	30	05-19-1961	Jim Perry	Cleveland	Right	Away	1st
6	31	05-20-1961	Gary Bell	Cleveland	Right	Away	3rd
7	32	05-21-1961	Chuck Estrada	Baltimore	Right	Home	1st
8	35	05-24-1961	Gene Conley	Boston	Right	Home	4th
9	38	05-28-1961	Cal McLish	Chicago	Right	Home	2nd
10	40	05-30-1961	Gene Conley	Boston	Right	Away	3rd
11	40	05-30-1961	Mike Fornieles	Boston	Right	Away	8th
12	41	05-31-1961	Billy Muffett	Boston	Right	Away	3rd
13	43	06-02-1961	Cal McLish	Chicago	Right	Away	3rd
14	44	06-03-1961	Bob Shaw	Chicago	Right	Away	8th
15	45	06-04-1961	Russ Kemmerer	Chicago	Right	Away	3rd
16	48	06-06-1961	Ed Palmquist	Minnesota	Right	Home	6th
17	49	06-07-1961	Pedro Ramos	Minnesota	Right	Home	3rd
18	52	06-09-1961	Ray Herbert	Kansas City	Right	Home	7th
19	55	06-11-1961	Eli Grba	Los Angeles	Right	Home	3rd
20	55	06-11-1961	Johnny James	Los Angeles	Right	Home	7th
21	57	06-13-1961	Jim Perry	Cleveland	Right	Away	6th
22	58	06-14-1961	Gary Bell	Cleveland	Right	Away	4th
23	61	06-17-1961	Don Mossi	Detroit	Left	Away	4th
24	62	06-18-1961	Jerry Casale	Detroit	Right	Away	8th
25	63	06-19-1961	Jim Archer	Kansas City	Left	Away	9th
26	64	06-20-1961	Joe Nuxhall	Kansas City	Left	Away	1st
27	66	06-22-1961	Norm Bass	Kansas City	Right	Away	2nd
28	74	07-01-1961	Dave Sisler	Washington	Right	Home	9th
29	75	07-02-1961	Pete Burnside	Washington	Left	Home	3rd
30	75	07-02-1961	Johnny Klippstein	Washington	Right	Home	7th

HR	GAME	DATE/BOX	PITCHER	TEAM	THROWS	WHERE	INNING
31	77	07-04-1961	Frank Lary	Detroit	Right	Home	8th
32	78	07-05-1961	Frank Funk	Cleveland	Right	Home	7th
33	82	07-09-1961	Bill Monbouquette	Boston	Right	Home	7th
34	84	07-13-1961	Early Wynn	Chicago	Right	Away	1st
35	86	07-15-1961	Ray Herbert	Chicago	Right	Away	3rd
36	92	07-21-1961	Bill Monbouquette	Boston	Right	Away	1st
37	95	07-25-1961	Frank Baumann	Chicago	Left	Home	4th
38	95	07-25-1961	Don Larsen	Chicago	Right	Home	8th
39	96	07-25-1961	Russ Kemmerer	Chicago	Right	Home	4th
40	96	07-25-1961	Warren Hacker	Chicago	Right	Home	6th
41	106	08-04-1961	Camilo Pascual	Minnesota	Right	Home	1st
42	114	08-11-1961	Pete Burnside	Washington	Left	Away	5th
43	115	08-12-1961	Dick Donovan	Washington	Right	Away	4th
44	116	08-13-1961	Bennie Daniels	Washington	Right	Away	4th
45	117	08-13-1961	Marty Kutyna	Washington	Right	Away	1st
46	118	08-15-1961	Juan Pizarro	Chicago	Left	Home	4th
47	119	08-16-1961	Billy Pierce	Chicago	Left	Home	1st
48	119	08-16-1961	Billy Pierce	Chicago	Left	Home	3rd
49	124	08-20-1961	Jim Perry	Cleveland	Right	Away	3rd
50	125	08-22-1961	Ken McBride	Los Angeles	Right	Away	6th
51	129	08-26-1961	Jerry Walker	Kansas City	Right	Away	6th
52	135	09-02-1961	Frank Lary	Detroit	Right	Home	6th
53	135	09-02-1961	Hank Aguirre	Detroit	Left	Home	8th
54	140	09-06-1961	Tom Cheney	Washington	Right	Home	4th
55	141	09-07-1961	Dick Stigman	Cleveland	Left	Home	3rd
56	143	09-09-1961	Mudcat Grant	Cleveland	Right	Home	7th
57	151	09-16-1961	Frank Lary	Detroit	Right	Away	3rd
58	152	09-17-1961	Terry Fox	Detroit	Right	Away	12th
59	155	09-20-1961	Milt Pappas	Baltimore	Right	Away	3rd
60	159	09-26-1961	Jack Fisher	Baltimore	Right	Home	3rd
61	163	10-01-1961	Tracy Stallard	Boston	Right	Home	4th

BOBBY RICHARDSON, THE CATCH: OCTOBER 16, 1962

It was Yankees against Giants at Candlestick Park in San Francisco. The ballpark had experienced three days of rain. Whipping, gusting wind was still a problem. Outfielders were careful of their footing. The park had not fully dried out.

It was winner-take-all Game Seven. Ralph Terry had never won a World Series game. The Yankees pinned their hopes on him. San Francisco started 24-game-winner Jack Sanford.

With two outs in the sixth inning, Terry was pitching a perfect game and the Yankees clung to a 1–0 lead. In the bullpen of the Giants was former Yankee, "Mr. Perfect Game," Don Larsen.

A single by pitcher Sanford snapped Terry's perfect game attempt. Heading into the bottom of the ninth, Terry had a two-hitter going, but he also had trouble brewing: Matty Alou was the Giant runner on third base. Willie Mays was leading off second base. San Francisco cleanup hitter Willie McCovey stepped into the batter's box. Behind him was slugger Orlando Cepeda.

Even though McCovey had tripled off Terry in his last at bat, Yankee Manager Ralph Houk allowed him to pitch to the lefty slugger. On a one and one count, "Stretch" ripped a liner past the pitcher's mound.

"I moved over," Bobby Richardson recalled, "just a little bit, and he hit the ball right to me. I jumped. It was one of those balls like Mantle used to hit, with a lot of over spin. It looked like a base hit going to the outfield, but it came down in a hurry. I caught it. He really hit it hard."

The Yankees had their second straight world championship.

"When McCovey hit the ball, it lifted me right out of my shoes," said Yogi Berra. "I never saw a last game of a World Series more exciting."

THE MICK'S 500TH HOMER: MAY 14, 1967

GAME CALL, JOE GARAGIOLA, WHN RADIO, NYC AND THE YANKEE RADIO NETWORK: *Three balls, two strikes. Mantle waits. Stu Miller is ready. Here's the payoff pitch by Miller to Mantle. Swung on! There she goes . . . Mickey Mantle has hit his 500th home run . . .*

It was Mother's Day, a Sunday, as always. It was Yankees against Orioles at Yankee Stadium. Stu Miller was on the mound for the visitors. Mickey Mantle had slammed home run #499 eleven days before. New York City sports pages were full of news and speculation about the Commerce Comet's clubbing number 500.

Banged up and hobbled, an echo of the terrific talent he had once been, "the Mick" played first base and batted third in the Yankee order in front of Elston Howard. Just 18,872 were in the house that day.

It was the bottom of the seventh inning with two outs. The Yankees were holding on to a 5–4 lead. Mickey had worked Stu Miller to a full count. The next pitch was launched deep into the right-field lower stands. It was Mickey Mantle's 500th home run, making him just the sixth player in baseball history to hit that mark. He became the first switch-hitter to accomplish that feat.

"It felt like when you win a World Series," Mantle said after the game. "A big load off your back. I wasn't really tense about hitting it, but about everybody writing about it. We weren't doing well and everywhere you'd see, 'When is Mantle going to hit 500' instead of about the team winning or losing. Now maybe we can get back to getting straightened out."

Mickey Mantle would hit 36 more career home runs before he retired with a total of 536.

The "Mick's" milestone 500th dinger on May 14, 1967.

MICKEY MANTLE DAY: JUNE 8, 1969

The day was one that so many of his fans wished never came. Even 18 seasons of "the Mick" was not enough.

The most memorable line of the day belonged to Mel Allen: "Ladies and gentlemen, a magnificent Yankee, the great number seven, Mickey Mantle."

Before 61,157, one of the greatest of all Yankees had his number retired. Only Numbers 3, 4 and 5 had been retired before for Ruth, Gehrig and DiMaggio, who was among the 61,157 at the Stadium. Only 19 years old, Mickey Mantle debuted with the Yankees on April 17, 1951 in the same outfield with Joe DiMaggio. Now they would exchange plaques that would later be placed on the center field wall.

The one-time kid from Oklahoma was driven around Yankee Stadium. "And the guy that was driving me," Mantle said later, "was Danny, one of the ground crew guys who came up at about the same time I did in '51. The last time around the park, that gave me goose pimples. But I didn't cry. I felt like it. Maybe tonight when I go to bed, I'll think about it. I wish that could happen to every man in America."

Kids moved about the grandstands. Although there were messages on poster paper, bedsheets seemed to be more prevalent.

And then the most talented player of his era prepared to speak: "When I walked into this stadium 18 years ago," Mantle said, "I felt much the same way I do right now. I don't have words to describe how I felt then or how I feel now, but I'll tell you one thing, baseball was real good to me, and playing 18 years in Yankee Stadium is the best thing that could ever happen to a ballplayer. I've often wondered how a man who knew he was going to die [Lou Gehrig] could stand here and say he was the luckiest man on the face of the earth, but now I think I know how Lou Gehrig felt."

RON BLOMBERG, FIRST DESIGNATED HITTER TO BAT: APRIL 6, 1973

Opening Day, 1973 season at Fenway Park. Yankee Ron Blomberg, a lifetime .293 hitter, was the first official "Designated Pinch Hitter," as the position was originally called.

The first pick in the 1967 free agent draft for the Yankees who had finished in last place the year before, Blomberg was very talented. His lifetime batting average would be just below .300. Injuries and assorted aches and pains had given him limited mobility. Just 24 in 1973, he appeared to be perfect for the new DH spot.

Before the game, he received tips from Yankee bench coach Elston Howard.

RON BLOMBERG: *He said, "The only thing you do is go take batting practice and just hit." When it was my time to hit, the bases were loaded. I was batting sixth in the Yankee order against Luis Tiant. I walked and forced in a run. I was left at first base. And I was going to stay there because normally that was my position. Elston said, "Come on back to the bench, you aren't supposed to stay out here." I went back and said, "What do I do?" He said, "You just sit here with me."*

Facing Luis Tiant that day, Blomberg managed just the one hit in three at bats. Orlando Cepeda, Boston DH, went 0-for-6.

After the game, Blomberg's bat was shipped off to the Baseball Hall of fame in Cooperstown.

My P.S. to the Ron Blomberg story was that he was one of my father-in-law's favorite players. I was in Cooperstown doing research for one of my books. Ron was there. Pleasant, lively, he signed a baseball for my father-in-law.

CHRIS CHAMBLISS, HOME RUN: OCTOBER 14, 1976

New York Yankees were sitting on top of the world in 1976. Their home attendance was over the two million mark for the first time since 1950. They won the AL East with a 97–62 record, 10½ games ahead of Baltimore.

The ALCS was a matchup of Royals-Yankees at the Stadium on the 14th of October. This was the deciding fifth game. Winner to go to the World Series. It was a misty and raw Thursday night.

PAUL DOHERTY: *In the top of the ninth, a very controversial call went against the Royals. The fans started throwing stuff between innings because they were nutty Yankee fans who started celebrating and causing trouble early knowing this was going to be a "sudden death" finish. They rattled the KC pitcher Mark Littell and forced Bob Sheppard to make a "Please do not litter the field" announcement.*

It was "Bronx is burning," "Yankee Fever" time.

Chris Chambliss came to bat for the Yanks. The score was tied. "I was just thinking about hitting the ball hard," he said later.

GAME CALLS, ABC-TV:
REGGIE JACKSON: *Chambliss is so hot he's got his shirt unbuttoned. He's in heat.*
KEITH JACKSON: *Mark Littell delivers… there's a high drive hit to right center field.*
HOWARD COSELL: *That's gone!*
KEITH JACKSON: *It isssss GONE!!*

BILL WHITE, WMCA RADIO: *Look at those fans out on the field . . . somebody picked up second base . . . somebody just knocked Chambliss down . . . he's making it to third . . . these fans are all over the field trying to let . . . and the cops are out trying to let Chambliss score. And Chambliss running through the crowd . . . HEY!! He did NOT touch home plate! Chambliss hasn't touched home plate yet! Fans are out on the field . . . Fans are all over the field. Chambliss had to work his way all the way around the field from second base after he touched first. Fans out on the field pulled second base up. Somebody pulled third base up. They're down there now trying to take up home plate. And Chambliss still has not touched home plate. And the ballgame, I think, is over.*

Fans mob Chris Chambliss after he hits a home run that captures the American League pennant for the Yankees.

The burly Chambliss went into a bit of a victory dance seeing the ball go over the right-center field fence. Then he started to run the bases. "The fans ran on the field," Chambliss said. "I was in the middle of a mass of people."

BOB SHEPPARD: *The game was over. The Yankees had won. Ten thousand people, as if they were shot out of a cannon, ran out on the field. I just folded my arms and let them do it.*

"Some people joke about that, that I never ran the bases," Chambliss recalled. "But after I reached second base and tripped, someone tried to grab my helmet. I looked at third base and there was a ton of people there. So I decided to head straight to the clubhouse."

Most reports state that hours later, in an empty ballpark, accompanied by two security guards, as the story goes, Chambliss finally touched home.

PAUL DOHERTY: *Actually security guards took Chambliss back to the plate about five minutes after he hit the home run.*

The elusive pennant the New York Yankees had sought for the past dozen years, their 30th, was now theirs.

It was Lee MacPhail, yes, that Lee MacPhail, President of the American League, former Yankee General Manager, son of former Yankee part-owner Larry MacPhail. He was at the game. He ruled the ball left the field of play. No one was on base for Chambliss to pass to nullify one or more bases. The home run stood. The Yankees won the game, 7–6.

"The Chambliss home run was the highlight of our season," said Willie Randolph. "We celebrated that night and flew all the way to Cincinnati for a game the next day."

REGGIE JACKSON, THREE HOMERS: OCTOBER 18, 1977

World Series game at Yankee Stadium. Game Six. Yankees versus Dodgers. The home team was in a battle to win its first world championship in 15 years.

It was chilly weather time in New York City. That did not seem to bother Reginald Martinez Jackson. In batting practice, Reggie had been all over the ball.

Willie Randolph joked: "Save some of those for the game."

"No problem," Jackson said. "There are more where those came from."

MIKE FERRARO: *There was zip in his bat, pitches high, low, strikes, balls, he was right on it with power.*

Reggie Jackson, three pitchers, three pitches, three home runs. Epic!

GAME	DATE	INNING	PITCHER	RESULT
REGGIE JACKSON'S THREE HOME RUNS ON FOUR CONSECUTIVE SWINGS				
6	October 18	4th	Burt Hooton	Home run
6	October 18	5th	Elias Sosa	Home run
6	October 18	8th	Charlie Hough	Home run

Knuckleballer Burt Hooton walked Jackson on four pitches his first time at bat. Second time up, fourth inning, Jackson did not wait. He smashed Hooton's first pitch into the area that had once been called "Ruthville," the lower bleacher seats in right field.

Again Jackson was first pitch swinging in the fifth inning off Elias Sosa. The ball made it in a hurry into the seats in right center field. It was the Yankee superstar's second two-run home run of the game. The Yankees led 7–3.

Yankee Stadium was bedlam. Stamping feet, whistling, clapping hands. Chanting: "Reggie, Reggie, Reggie." The noise level kept rising. Kept intensifying.

"All I had to do was show up at the plate," Jackson said later. "They were going to cheer me even if I struck out."

Eighth inning. Knuckleballer Charlie Hough was on the mound for the Dodgers. Again Reggie Jackson first pitch swinging. The home run ball went deep into the "black seats" in right center field.

GAME CALL, HOWARD COSELL, ABC-TV: *Oh, what a blow! What a way to top it off. Forget about who the Most Valuable Player is in the World Series! How this man has responded to pressure! Oh, what a beam on his face. How can you blame him? He's answered the whole WORLD! After all the furor, after all the hassling, it comes down to this!*

"I felt like Superman," said Reggie afterwards. "If they had tied it up and we played eight more extra innings, I'd have hit three more home runs on the first pitch that night. Nothing can top this. Who in hell's ever going to hit three home runs in a deciding World Series game? Babe Ruth, Hank Aaron, Joe DiMaggio . . . At least I was with them for one night."

With "Mr. October" doing his thing, the Yankees won their first world championship in 15 years.

Even Dodger Steve Garvey was impressed. "I must admit when Reggie hit his third home run and I was sure nobody was looking, I applauded in my glove."

Anyone who was witness to what Reggie Jackson accomplished—the swings, the dropping of the bat, the white ball disappearing into the inky blackness of the chilly Bronx night—will always remember it.

Reggie Jackson remembered. Years later he made this comment: "It is the happiest moment of my career. I had been on a ball and chain all year, at least in my mind. I had heard so many negatives about Reggie Jackson. I had been the villain. Couldn't do this. Couldn't do that. And now suddenly I didn't care what the manager or my teammates had said or what the media had written."

RON GUIDRY, 18 KS, ONE GAME: JUNE 17, 1978

Born Ronald Ames Guidry on August 28, 1950, in Lafayette, Louisiana, the slight southpaw had paid his dues in the minors. He was 24 years old when he made his Yankee debut.

The magical moment of many magical moments for the pitcher they called "Louisiana Lightning" came against the California Angels in mid-season when Yankee Stadium fans, about 33,000 of them, stood up clapping every time he got two strikes on a hitter. The "standing clapping" became a tradition throughout baseball.

Number 49 fanned 18 Angels to set a new franchise record. Nolan Ryan, no stranger to strikeouts, watched from the California dugout. "The entire bench was laughing, because we felt we were overmatched," said Ryan. "His ball was exploding."

It's 18 Ks for "Louisiana Lightning," Ron Guidry, setting a new franchise record.

"He was just like a buzz saw," Willie Randolph said. "He mowed through lineups like a man playing with boys. He was so dominating that it wasn't even funny. It was like he was cheating. He grunted on every pitch. He had that slider. I can still see Thurman putting down slider, slider, slider."

"It was one of those games where they were swinging and missing. I didn't know I had that many strikeouts," Guidry said. "I knew I had several, but I didn't think I was that high.

"When they start hollering and screaming, you just get pumped up that much higher and you try harder. I felt I disappointed them when a guy hit a ball with two strikes. I thought I made a mistake."

A career New York Yankee, from 1975 to 1988, the "Gator" was on top of his game with a sharp fastball and a slider that at times was unhittable. He struck out the side in the 3rd, 4th and 6th inning. He gave up just 4 hits in his 4–0 shutout.

The five-time Gold Glove winner won the Cy Young award that season, finishing with a 25–3 record, a 1.74 ERA and nine shutouts. His last victory of the year came in the Yankees' edging the Red Sox, 5–4, in the tie-breaking playoff to decide the AL East.

With all of that, it was what he did on June 17, 1978, the 18 strikeouts, that was a truly memorable moment in "Louisiana Lightning's" truly memorable career.

BUCKY DENT HOME RUN: OCTOBER 2, 1978

It was a one-game playoff game between the Yankees and Red Sox at Fenway Park before 32,925.

"When I hit the ball," Bucky Dent recalled, "I knew that I had hit it high enough to hit the wall. But there were shadows on the net behind the wall and I didn't see the ball land there. I didn't know I had hit a homer until I saw the umpire at first signaling home run with his hand. I couldn't believe it."

Neither could the Red Sox manager Don Zimmer, who now called the Yankee shortstop "Bucky F_____g Dent." Red Sox fans had even choicer phrases.

On July 19, the Bombers had trailed the Sox in the AL East by 14 games. Billy Martin, canned as manager, was replaced by Bob Lemon. The former star pitcher was fabulous, leading the Yankees to a 48–20 record. Boston stayed in the race with a late-season run. Victorious in their last eight games, the Sox caught up to the Yankees on the last day of the season.

At Fenway Park, New York's 24-game winner Ron Guidry opposed Mike Torrez, ex-Yankee hurler. The "Gator" held the Sox to two runs through six on a Carl

Shot heard 'round New England: the Bucky "F____g" Dent pop fly dinger.

Yastrzemski homer and a Jim Rice single that drove in the other run.

Graig Nettles flew out to start the top of the seventh inning, and Chris Chambliss and Roy White singled. Enter Earl Russell Dent out of Savannah, Georgia. His fielding skills were there, but he had trouble hitting. In his last 20 games, the handsome Dent had batted .140.

It was the 5-foot-9 Dent against the 6-foot-5 Red Sox pitcher. Dent fouled the second pitch off his foot. The count was one and one. The Yankees trainer tended to Dent. Mickey Rivers, waiting in the on-deck circle, pointed out a crack in Dent's bat. Bucky borrowed Rivers's bat. He stepped in with the bat and swung. The ball cleared the infield. It headed out to the left field wall.

"Deep to left," Bill White, Yankees broadcaster shouted, "Yastrzemski will not get it!"

Yaz backed up. He had been in this position before. The ball sailed into the 23-foot net above the Green Monster, the 37-foot wall in left field. The impossible had happened: three-run home run!

"I was so damn shocked," Torrez said. "I thought maybe it was going to be off the wall. Damn, I did not think it was going to go out."

Most do not recall that the Red Sox still had a chance to win the game in the bottom of the ninth. But Goose Gossage got Carl Yastrzemski to pop out with 2 on and 2 out. The game's winning pitcher was Ron Guidry, who finished the season, 25–3.

"I had a dream as a kid," the player who was born Russell Earl O'Dey said. "I dreamed someday I would hit a home run to win something."

WALTER MEARS: *Speaker of the House of Representative Tip O'Neill went to Rome that fall and saw the Pope. When he came back, he was at some function with Yaz and told him the Holy Father had spoken of him. Yaz wanted to know what the Pope had said. "Tip," he said, "How COULD Yastrzemski pop out in the last of the ninth with the tying run on third?"*

My postscript to the Bucky Dent fever was that about a year later he still had celebrity status and accompanied me on a book store signing event. Teenage girls were all into seeing and making contact with the affable Yankee. I sat at a table in the store and the line of people outside waiting to sign was significant. The power of Bucky Dent was on display. A few of the teenage girls told me not to sign the book.

He told them, "He wrote the book."

They told him, "We only want your autograph. Not his."

That was the way it was. Bucky was very nice. And as long as the books sold I was happy.

DAVE RIGHETTI, NO-HITTER: JULY 4, 1983

The Fourth of July crowd of 41,077 was in a Yankee mood at the Stadium. Many sported Yankee hats—the giveaway promotion for the game against the Boston Red Sox.

Dave Righetti had come to the Yankees in a multiple player deal that sent Sparky Lyle to Texas. His Major League debut was as an end of the season call up on September 16, 1979. But it was not until 1981 that he returned to the Yankees to stay.

American League Rookie of the Year that 1981 season (8–4, 2.06 ERA), the player they called "Rags" won twice against Milwaukee in divisional play and once over Oakland in the LCS.

On this warm and sunny day, the 24-year-old Dave Righetti would make history. He would pitch a no-hitter against the BoSox. The stylish hurler walked four and struck out nine men, including Wade Boggs for the final out. Boggs, hitting .357 at the time, went down swinging on a hard slider, Righetti's bread and butter pitch that day.

"Rags" Dave Righetti pitching in Fourth of July no-hitter against the Boston Red Sox.

Ironically, it would be Righetti's last season as a regular starting pitcher. The next year, he replaced Goose Gossage as the Yankees closer, and in 1986 went on to set the then–Major League single season save record of 46.

The Fourth of July no-hitter was the first by a left-hander in Yankee Stadium history, the first no-hitter by a Yankee pitcher since 1956, when Don Larsen tossed a perfect game. It was only the sixth regular-season no-hitter in Yankee history, the first since 1951.

PINE TAR EPISODE: JULY 24, 1983

It remains one of the strangest of moments in Yankee baseball history. On July 24, the team from the Bronx was hoped to take over first place, faced off against Kansas City at Yankee Stadium before 33,944 spectators.

The Yankees led 4–3 going into the top of the ninth. Goose Gossage was one out away from the wrap. There was one runner on base. Boom! Superstar George Brett slugged a shot into the right field stands that gave his team a 5–4 lead.

Seconds after he crossed the plate and went into his dugout, Brett saw an intense Yankee manager Billy Martin approach home plate rookie umpire Tim McClelland. "I was feeling pretty good about myself after hitting the homer," Brett later said. "I was sitting in the dugout. Somebody said they were checking the pine tar, and I said, 'If they call me out for using too much pine tar, I'm going to kill one of those SOBs.'"

There was a call by McClelland to the Royal dugout. He wanted to see Brett's bat. Then there was a conference on the field by all the umpires.

Billy Martin watched. He stood a few feet away from them. Brett stared out from the KC bench. McClelland thrust his arm into the air, signaling George Brett was out. The reason—excessive use of pine tar on his bat.

Rule 1.10(b): "A bat may not be covered by such a substance more than 18 inches from the tip of the handle." The umpire ruled that Brett's bat had "heavy pine tar" 19 to 20 inches from the tip of the handle and lighter pine tar for another 3 or 4 inches.

No Brett home run. Game over. Yankees 4–3 winners.

An enraged Brett ran out of his dugout to protest. At one point, umpire Joe Brinkman had Brett in a chokehold. The furious Brett was ejected from the game. He went wild. Others, including KC manager Dick Howser, joined in.

Gaylord Perry, Royals pitcher, grabbed Brett's bat from McClelland. He tossed it to Hal McRae who passed it to pitcher Steve Renko who made it halfway up the tunnel to the team clubhouse. Yankee Stadium security guards grabbed Renko and grabbed the bat, impounding it.

The Royals lodged a protest. The Yankees went to Texas and won three games, taking over first place for the first time that season

Eventually, American League president Lee McPhail overturned McClelland's decision. Acknowledging that Brett had pine tar too high on the bat, McPhail explained that it was the league's reasoning that "games should be won and lost on the playing field—not through technicalities of the rules."

Yankee owner George Steinbrenner was terribly ticked off. "I wouldn't want to be Lee MacPhail living in New York!" he let everyone know.

Brett's home run was reinstated, and the protest of the Royals was upheld. On August 18th, play was resumed for the last four outs of the game that had begun on July 24th. The Yankees announced they would charge regular admission for the game's continuation. Fan protests convinced the Yankees to give up on charging admission. It was too late. Just 1,200 fans showed up for the "continuation."

The entire environment was bizarre. Annoyed and frustrated, for the "continuation" the Yankees positioned pitcher Ron Guidry in center field and Don Mattingly (a left-hander) at second base for the final out of the top of the ninth inning. Guidry played center field because the team had traded away Jerry Mumphrey, who had been in the game for defensive purposes.

New York's George Frazier fanned Hal McRae for the third out. In the bottom of the ninth, Royals' reliever Dan Quisenberry set the Yankees down in order. And that ended that.

MATTINGLY VS. WINFIELD, BATTING TITLE: SEPTEMBER 30, 1984

"Donnie and I were at different points in our careers," explained Dave Winfield. "He was a young kid who had a lot of support from the public."

Throughout that 1984 season, twelve-year stalwart Dave Winfield and Don Mattingly, just in his second year, battled for the American league batting title and the adulation of Yankee fans.

On June 25th Winfield notched four singles, one double and four RBIs, capping a Yankee victory over the Tigers. He had three five-hit days in June. But he was the outsider, the high-priced free agent who had disappointed some, who was booed at Yankee Stadium. Don Mattingly was the home boy, the talent from the farm system, the favorite.

By September's end just three points separated the two. The race for the batting title was still up for grabs. New York opened a four-game series at the Stadium against the Tigers. All season, Mattingly and Winfield mostly batted third and fourth in the Yankee batting order. It was claimed that gave "Donnie Baseball" an edge. Hitting ahead of Winfield, it was claimed, Mattingly received more pitches to hit.

The veteran Winfield led Mattingly .3410 to .3395. Mattingly singled to right field in the first inning. Winfield grounded into a force out. Mattingly

now led, .3406 to .3404. Inning three, Mattingly doubled into the right field corner. Winfield worked out a walk. Then Mattingly smashed his 44th double of the season. Winfield barely stayed on pace by beating out an infield single to third base. Both were hitless in their next at bats.

The last at bats for both would determine the batting title winner. Detroit's ace reliever Willie Hernandez (who would win both the AL MVP and Cy Young) was on the mound.

A ground ball single off the glove of second baseman Scotty Earl gave Mattingly his league leading 207th hit.

With Mattingly on first, Winfield grounded into a force-out. Mattingly was retired. Wise and caring Yankee manager Yogi Berra sent a pinch runner in for Winfield. It made it so that both Mattingly and Winfield came off the field together. They got a standing ovation.

"Donnie Baseball," the only player in any sport to have a nickname with the actual name of his or her sport in it, won the batting title with a .343 average.

Dave Winfield finished second in the league at .340.

ANDY HAWKINS, NO-HITTER?: JULY 1, 1990

A depressed and dreadful Yankee team with the worst record in all of baseball, 16 games under .500, showed up for their final game at old Comiskey Park in Chicago.

Out of Waco, Texas, on the mound for the visitors with a 1–4 record and a 6.49 ERA in a dozen starts, was Melton Andrew Hawkins. Just a few weeks before, the Yankees had almost released him.

The windy city that day was especially windy at Comiskey. Broadcaster Phil Rizzuto acknowledged that by saying: "I want to tell you, every fly ball is an adventure out there."

The 30-year-old Hawkins had a no-hitter going into the eighth inning.

With two outs Sammy Sosa grounded sharply to Yankee third baseman Mike Blowers. The ball hit the glove and fell to the ground. "Hit" was the ruling. Everyone in the Yankee dugout was annoyed big time.

An "E-5" appeared on the scoreboard. The no-hitter was still alive. Hawkins loaded the bases, walking Ozzie Guillen and Lance Johnson. Robin Ventura was next.

Fly ball to left field. Leyritz kept going back. Leyritz fell. And the baseball bounced off his glove. Three runs scored. Right fielder Jesse Barfield dropped the next fly ball. The Yankees were now down, 4–0.

"Holy cow, wheels coming off here," the Scooter said. The Yankees did not score in their last licks. The game was over. Bill Connors, Yankee pitching coach, shook hands with Hawkins. He offered congratulations.

"It still counts?" Hawkins asked.

The AP headline the next day: "No Hitter, No Winner."

Hawkins got the defeat. He also was credited with pitching a no-hitter—for a time.

The next year a rule change required pitchers to work at least nine innings to be credited with a no-hitter. The White Sox never batted in the ninth inning and Hawkins lost the credit for what was once an official no-hitter.

A postscript to the wild and wacky moment in Yankee history was a statement made by Hawkins after the game. He claimed the no-hitter was something "that will never be taken away from me."

Unfortunately, it was.

JIM ABBOTT, NO-HITTER: SEPTEMBER 4, 1993

The Yankees traded for him on December 6, 1992. He was born without a right hand, but he persevered; more than persevered, he prevailed.

Jim Abbott, left, savoring the "perfect" moment of his no-hitter game, September 4, 1993.

The graduate of the University of Michigan, Jim Abbott carried the United States flag during the opening ceremonies at the 1987 Pan American Games in Indianapolis. He also pitched for the 1988 U.S. Olympic team.

The following year he went directly from the University of Michigan to the Angels' starting rotation. A solidly built southpaw, the intense Abbott won a dozen games and posted a 3.92 ERA in his rookie season. On the mound, he wore a right-hander's fielder's glove over the stump at the end of his right arm. Pitch delivered, in his follow-through, Abbott skillfully switched the glove to his left hand. He was now positioned to field balls batted back to him.

In 1991, the young left-hander won 18 games for the Angels. The Yankees traded their best prospect, first baseman J.T. Snow, and pitchers Russ Springer and Jerry Nielsen to California for Abbott who said he wanted to be like Nolan Ryan and not like Pete Gray, the one-handed outfielder.

With the Yankees, Abbott was so-so, going 20–22 in two seasons. Six days after he had been touched for ten hits and seven runs in only three and a third innings against Cleveland, he faced the team again.

He was performing in the pressure cooker of the pennant race. He pitched a 4–0 no-hitter.

"I remember," Jim Abbott said, "it was a cloudy day. A day game, the kind of game I like to throw. The no-hitter was the highlight of my career. The specialness of it, I didn't know how lasting it would be when it happened. Everywhere I go, people talk about that game, how exciting it was. That makes me very proud. I'm awfully happy that a ball didn't bloop in somewhere."

DWIGHT GOODEN, NO-HITTER: MAY 14, 1996

Once he was the great pride of New York City as a member of the Mets, but substance abuse had ruined his image, weakened his skills. The "Doc" had just completed his second suspension from the game he loved.

"The Boss" went out of his way, giving the former superstar another chance. Gooden was signed to a Yankee contract on October 16, 1995. Steinbrenner said that Gooden would win 15 games in 1996. That seemed unlikely. Sent to the bullpen with a record of no wins and three losses and an ERA of 11.48, the 32-year-old was a shell of his former self.

"I've just got to keep working on my mechanics," he said. "It's complete frustration more than anything else."

On the 27th of April, Gooden came out of the bullpen shadows and was put into the injury-depleted Bomber rotation. He put together some nifty pitching: six solid innings against Minnesota, shutout innings against Chicago, his first win since 1994—in a gem against Detroit, setting down the 20 batters in a row.

The stage was set for May 14, 1996. His father in a Tampa hospital awaiting double bypass surgery the next day, "Doc" faced off against the Mariners who boasted a lineup that included future

It was a mob scene for Dwight Gooden and his improbable no-hitter against the Mariners.

Hall of Famers Ken Griffey Jr., Alex Rodriguez (if not for the PED scandal) and Edgar Martinez.

Through eight innings Gooden had a no-hitter going. There were 20,786 fans in the Stadium (some of them merry Met fans) this Tuesday night. And they went up and down, cheering Dwight. Now most were on their feet. The fatigued, but going on grit Gooden had thrown more than a hundred pitches.

Manager Joe Torre would say later: "It was Dwight's game all the way."

Seattle had men on first and second. They moved to second and third on a wild pitch with Jay Buhner at the plate. One out. Gooden reached back for something extra. Buhner went down swinging. Two out.

The next batter was Paul Sorrento. Gooden looked in for the sign. Out of the stretch he served up his 134th pitch of the game. A swerving curve ball to the Seattle hitter, a high pop to Jeter. No-hitter!

Yankee Stadium rocked! It was like old times for Gooden.

PAUL DOHERTY: *Celebrity time at Yankee Stadium. Gooden was carried off the field on the shoulders of his Yankee teammates. "The Doctor is in the House" was the message on the center-field scoreboard. Outside, the Major Deegan Expressway signboard lit up in Neon. "Oh My Gooden-ness!"*

"This is the greatest feeling of my life," Gooden said. "I never thought I could do this, not in my wildest dreams. A year and a half ago I thought I had pitched my last game, so being able not only to make it back but to throw a no-hitter, that's been an incredible blessing for me."

DEREK JETER, JEFFREY MAIER: OCTOBER 9, 1996

With the Yankees trailing 4–3 at home in the eighth inning of the ALCS, Game 1 against Baltimore, up came Derek Jeter. Everything was coming up roses for the shortstop winding down a very splendid rookie season.

He got ahold of a pitch from Oriole reliever Armando Benitez and slugged it high and deep toward the right field stands. Outfielder Tony Tarasco, tracking the ball from the time it left Jeter's bat, went back to the wall, waiting to jump and make the catch.

Also waiting to make the catch, playing hooky that day from his school in New Jersey, was 12-year-old Jeffrey Maier. He reached out over the railing and caught the ball with his black baseball glove.

Right field umpire Rich Garcia ruled "no interference." A TV replay showed clearly there was interference. Tarasco yelled and pointed. And others on the Orioles screamed and protested to no avail. Jeter's big poke was ruled a home run. The game was tied, 4–4.

The Yankees went on to win the game on an eleventh inning homer by Bernie Williams off Randy Myers. Afterwards, umpire Richie Garcia admitted he made the wrong call.

Jeffrey Maier became an instant celebrity. His "catch" was shown over and over on TV. He made all the talk shows.

He summed up what happened: "I don't think there's any reason to be mad at me. "I'm just a 12½-year-old kid going for the ball."

The Derek Jeter–Jeffrey Maier "moment" was one link in the chain of events that led the Yankees into the 1996 World Series, and eventually the world championship.

JIM LEYRITZ, WORLD SERIES COMEBACK: OCTOBER 23, 1996

Neither the moment, nor the player nor the outcome was in anyone's crystal ball.

The game was played before 51,881 on a Wednesday night at Fulton County Stadium in Atlanta. The Braves were ahead 2–1 in the 1996 World Series.

The noise and the din and the tomahawk chop-chop were all annoying, especially if you were a Yankee fan.

Celebrating Jim Leyritz's "hero ball" home run that clinched the 1996 World Series for the Yankees and gave the team its momentum to go on to win four world championships in five years.

A jubilant David Wells celebrates his perfect game against the Minnesota Twins.

Through five innings Denny Neagle was shutting down New York. The home team led 6–0.

The Yankees chipped away and cut the Atlanta lead in half in the sixth inning. Number 14, muscular Jim Leyritz, came into the game as a defensive replacement for Joe Girardi. Most of his time during that game had been spent in the weight room. He was a 6-foot, 224-pounder with Popeye-like forearms.

Eighth inning. Mark Wohlers, who could hit 100 MPH and was sent in by Atlanta pilot Bobby Cox to close things down. There were two runners on base when Leyritz came to bat. Wohlers let loose two blazing fastballs. Leyritz could not catch up to them, but he managed to foul them off. The count was 2–2. Slider that hung. Leyritz lunged into it. Fly ball deep left field. Over the wall. Game tied, 6–6.

"I'm not thinking home run right there," Leyritz said. "I'm thinking I've got an opportunity to drive in one run if I get a base hit."

"I lost it," Wohlers said. "I blew it."

The historic postscript to that Leyritz moment was the Yankees won the game, won the World Series in six, triggered a run of four world championships in five years.

For the journeyman Leyritz, that dramatic and unexpected home run was his greatest moment in baseball. "Because it was in the World Series," he said, "it helped us get the momentum back and go on to win the World Series. And it really made my mark as far as being a Yankee."

In the tenth inning, game tied, 6–6, lefty Steve Avery who came in for Wohlers, set down the first two Yankees. Tim Raines drew a walk. Jeter got an infield single. Bernie Williams was intentionally walked. Torre put his last pinch hitter in to replace rookie Andy Fox. Boggs walked. Score 7–6 Yankees as a run was forced in. Then it was 8–6 Yankees.

After using seven hurlers—five pinch hitters, a reserve catcher, a pinch runner—everyone on the Yankee bench aside from pitchers—the Yankees were victorious.

And Jim Leyritz sparked the whole incredible turnaround.

DAVID WELLS, PERFECT GAME: MAY 17, 1998

There were those who admired him. There were those who avoided him. There were those who wished they could have been as talented a pitcher as he was.

The 1998 season was a roller coaster of spills and thrills for the burly flake Wells. He was a guy who liked to make up his own rules, liked to call attention to his outrageousness.

One game he came out to the mound wearing an actual Babe Ruth cap. Manager Joe Torre did not spare the words telling him to get a regular Yankee cap. There was a start in Texas when Torre removed him. Angered, Wells did not hand the ball to his manager; he flipped it.

Going into this game on May 17, 1998, David Lee Wells, out of Torrance, California, took the mound. His ERA was 5.23 ERA. He was three days shy of his 35th birthday. Against the Minnesota Twins on this Sunday, Wells was sublime from the start. Perhaps it was because between innings he sat next to David Cone, a calming influence.

The veteran Cone told him, "In the seventh inning, it is time to break out the knuckleball."

"I started getting really nervous," Wells recalled. "I knew what was going on, I was hoping the fans would kind of shush a little bit. They were making me nervous."

The crowd of 49,820 gave him a standing ovation when he took the mound to pitch the ninth inning. The Yankees led 4–0. "Boomer" Wells still had not given up a hit. He also had not walked anybody.

Rookie Jon Shave flew out to right. Javier Valentin struck out, the eleventh "K" for Wells. Pat Meares flew out to Paul O'Neill in right field.

Wells pumped his left fist twice at the ground after the final out. A swarm of teammates carried him off the field.

Billy Crystal, always a wise guy, walked into the clubhouse after the game, walked over to the ecstatic Wells and asked: "I got here late, what happened?"

DAVID CONE, PERFECT GAME, YOGI BERRA DAY: JULY 18, 1999

It was "Yogi Berra Day" at the Stadium. Don Larsen was there among the 41,930 in attendance. He was there to toss the first pitch to Berra who caught his "Perfect Game" in the 1956 World Series.

In 95-degree heat, Cone served up all kinds of pitches from different arm angles. Even a 33-minute rain delay in the third inning did not affect what he was able to accomplish that day. Pitching perfection.

In the eighth inning, Montreal's Jose Vidro slapped the ball sharply up the middle. A backhanded stop by second baseman Chuck Knoblauch, the throw, the out.

"When Knoblauch made the great play," Cone said, "I decided there was some kind of Yankee aura. Maybe this was my day."

Cone got a standing ovation as the top of the ninth inning started. The large crowd kept standing up. The final out—Orlando Cabrera popped the ball up. Cone grabbed the sides of his head, fell to his knees and was swiftly lifted by teammates onto their shoulders.

The Yankees had a 6–0 win. Cone had only the 14th perfect game in modern history, the second (remember David Wells) thrown by a Yankee pitcher in 14 months. He hadn't gone to a three-ball count all day. He threw 88

David Cone is carried off the field by his triumphant teammates after pitching a perfect game on July 18, 1999.

pitches, 68 strikes, getting thirteen fly outs, ten strikeouts and four grounders.

"You probably have a better chance of winning the lottery than this happening," he said. "The last three innings, that's when you really think about it. You can't help feel the emotion of the crowd. I felt my heart thumping through my uniform."

A press release from the Office of the Mayor read: "Today was a perfect day for New York and the New York Yankees. David Cone made baseball and Yankees history not only by pitching just the 16th perfect game ever and the third in the history of the Yankees, but also by doing it with Don Larsen and Yogi Berra present on Yogi Berra Day. David Cone is one of the greatest pitchers in baseball and he is also one of the finest gentlemen in the game."

Rabid Yankee fan and Mayor Rudolph W. Giuliani overreached some more on July 20, proclaiming that day "David Cone Day" in New York City.

MIKE MUSSINA, NEAR PERFECT GAME: SEPTEMBER 2, 2001

It was September baseball between the two age-old rivals. Right-hander Mike Mussina against right-hander David Cone. Yanks-Sox.

Through eight innings, no score. Mussina, no walks, no hits given up. As the man they called "Moose" took a perfect game into the eighth for the third time, the Yankees' dugout was quiet.

The inning started with a Tino Martinez single. Jorge Posada flied out. Paul O'Neill slapped a sharp grounder. Second baseman Lou Merloni made an error. Runners on first and third. Clay Bellinger pinch ran for Martinez. A hit by Enrique Wilson scored him and gave the Yanks a 1–0 lead.

In the ninth, Troy O'Leary, pinch hitting for Shea Hillenbrand, lined to Bellinger, playing first base. The dive for the ball, the toss to Mussina. One out.

"I thought maybe this time it was going to happen," said Mussina, "considering that I thought that ball was through for sure."

Lou Merloni struck out. Carl Everett was in the clubhouse hitting off a tee; he got the call to pinch-hit for Joe Oliver. The moody Everett, in a 3-for-32 slump, was 1-for-9 with seven strikeouts in his career against Mussina.

The switch-hitter fouled off the first pitch. He swung at strike two. Pitch number three was a ball. The next pitch was a high fastball. Everett fought it off, lofting a soft liner to left-center, between Chuck Knoblauch and Bernie Williams. It dropped—single.

Mussina knew immediately. "I thought it was a hit," he said. "I'm going to think about that pitch until I retire, but that was the pitch I threw." All Mussina could do was hang his head and give a little smile. "I've never been part of a no-hitter before as an opponent," Everett said. "It was very satisfying to get the hit. It was very satisfying to hit the high fastball."

The tense game came to an end when Mussina was able to get Trot Nixon to ground out to second baseman Alfonso Soriano. The Yankee pitcher then weakly pumped his fist as his teammates ran out onto the field.

Mussina finished with his fourth career one-hitter, striking out a season-high 13. His wide breaking ball had the Red Sox off balance all night.

And Mike Mussina: "It was just a phenomenal game. I was disappointed, I'm still disappointed. But the Perfect Game just wasn't meant to be."

2001 WORLD SERIES, BUSH THROWS OUT FIRST BALL IN GAME 3: OCTOBER 30, 2001

After the tragedy of 9/11, Major League Baseball suspended the season for one week. It led to Game 3 of the 2001 World Series at Yankee Stadium being played on October 30, 2001. The game began around 9 p.m. EST.

With the other presidents, there would always be a crowd: reporters, photographers, Secret Service agents. But this night, when Bob Sheppard said: "And please welcome the President of the United States," the president came out of the Yankee dugout all alone. He walked to the mound and threw the pitch from the top of the mound like he was a player. It was a strike. And Bob Sheppard said: "Thank you, Mr. President."

What an ovation! There was such a sense among the fans that night.

PAUL DOHERTY: *After Bush threw the first pitch the crowd segued from their loud cheering, Bob's "Thank you, Mr. President," and Eddie Layton's playing on the Stadium organ "The Yellow Rose of Texas," to the Stadium throng, united, chanting "U-S-A! U-S-A! U-S-A! U-S-A!"*

BRAD TURNOW: *Our Commander in Chief, bare-headed and wearing a light gray-blue NYFD jacket [apparently covering a bulletproof vest] had thrown a perfect pitch. He waved to the crowd. They roared and cheered as the F-15s flew overhead.*

There were 55,820 people at the Stadium that chilly night. You had the coats, the hats. People were bundled up. I wore my 1998 championship New York Yankees jacket and my Yankee cap.

We had come back from Arizona down two games to none in the World Series. Spirits were a little down.

The Yankees took the game, 2–1, as Roger Clemens and Mariano Rivera combined on a 3-hitter.

DEREK JETER BECOMES "MR. NOVEMBER": NOVEMBER 1, 2001

It was Orlando Hernandez for the Yankees against Curt Schilling for the Arizona. Odds seemed to favor the home team. But with eight innings completed the home team trailed 2–0 and had three outs left, or so it seemed.

The Yankees' apparent "last licks" in the last of the ninth saw Derek Jeter lead off bunting and be thrown out. One out. Paul O'Neill singled to left field. Bernie Williams fanned. Two outs. Tino Martinez was next and he was zoned in to drive the ball. He did. A two-run homer to left—Martinez got the pitch he wanted and hit it a long way to right-center. The 50,000 plus went crazy, gaga, wild. It was a frenzied time at Yankee Stadium.

Mariano Rivera retired the Diamondbacks in order in the top of the tenth. Top Arizona relief pitcher Byung-Hyun Kim seemed impervious to the noise and the situation in the bottom of the tenth. He got Brosius to fly out. He got Soriano to fly out. Derek Jeter came up to hit. The clock on the scoreboard now was at 12:00 midnight.

October 31 had ended. Halloween was over. It was now November 1. It was the first time a Major League game was played in November. The scoreboard message read: "Welcome to November Baseball."

Two quick strikes on Jeter by Byung-Hyun Kim. Then a ball. Jeter was just attempting to get his pitch. He fouled off a fastball, then another. Finally, the count was full. Jeter finally got his pitch and went to the opposite field. The ball went over the right field fence.

GAME CALL, MICHAEL KAY, CBS RADIO: *Swung on and drilled to right field, going back Sanders, on the track, at the wall . . . SEE YA! SEE YA! SEE YA! A home run for Derek Jeter! He is Mr. November! Oh what a home run by Derek Jeter!*

The time was 12:04 a.m.

Pumping his fist in the air, circling the bases, jumping with joy onto home plate, Jeter's jubilant teammates welcomed him with open arms.

"When I first hit it," the Yankee captain said later, "I had no idea whether it was going to go out, but once it goes out, it's a pretty special feeling. I've never hit a walk-off home run before, so it was a special experience."

Jeter had gone 1–11 in the series before he hammered the homer. But as Yogi Berra told him and others: "It's never over, 'til it's over."

"This was a game that the 25 guys in the locker room will remember for a long time," said Paul O'Neill.

The next day's headline in the *New York Daily News* read: "DEREK Dinger Real Stinger."

The Yankees of New York had prevailed through three of the most amazing games in franchise history.

And their beloved Derek Jeter had become "Mr. November."

ROCKET'S REVENGE: SEPTEMBER 4, 2002

The Yankees had lost three in a row. The last loss was to the Red Sox in the opening game of the series they were in. The Bombers still led Boston by 6½ games in the AL East standings. Yet, another defeat would bring the Hub team too close for comfort.

"I don't care how good your team is," Torre said. "There's always that little uneasy feeling when you lose a few games in a row."

The Yankee manager told his 40-year-old pitcher Roger Clemens, "We need you today."

"I heard him, loud and clear," Clemens said. "When the skipper says that . . . it's pretty nice when you can come through."

Like an old warhorse, against his old team, Clemens was more than up to

the challenge. After 7⅓ innings, he had struck out 10, given up but four hits. At this point Torre and trainer Gene Monahan took a trip to the mound. They were concerned about how much Clemens had left.

"He was bending over," Torre explained after the game. "We didn't know if it was his back, his legs. He said: 'I'm 40 years old. I'm just trying to catch my breath.'"

Later Clemens reported that some of his teammates were laughing. He told them: "Wait until you all turn 40."

The Yankee ace got Johnny Damon to hit a ground ball to Derek Jeter, whose throw was off-line. That ended the Rocket's game time as he exited in the eighth inning. The 47,318 fans gave him a standing ovation. The Yankees won the game, 4–2.

"He gave us everything he could have possibly given us," Torre said. "He's a horse. No question, he's a horse."

BOONE TOWN: OCTOBER 16, 17, 2003

It was a match up that all baseball fans looked forward to with so much on the line: Pedro Martinez versus Roger Clemens.

It was also at Yankee Stadium in 61-degree October temperature—Yankees against Red Sox. It was the American League Championship Series. All tied up—winner take all.

Unfortunately for Yankee fans, Roger Clemens was off his game and Pedro Martinez was on his. The Rocket fizzled yielding four runs in three plus innings. Joe Torre replaced him with Mike Mussina, in his first career relief appearance. It was some spot for the "Moose" to be in—no outs, runners standing on first and third.

Varitek struck out. And Johnny Damon hit into a double play ending the threat. Yankee faithful cheered. Mussina held the Sox scoreless the next two innings. He was followed on the mound by Felix Heredia, Jeff Nelson and David Wells.

Pedro Martinez had the powerful Yankees on his string, just cruising along even though he surrendered solo homers to Jason Giambi in the fifth inning and seventh innings.

In the top of the eighth, David Ortiz homered, giving the Sox a 5–2 lead. Red Sox pilot Grady Little decided to let Martinez start the bottom of the eighth inning even though the Dominican star's pitch count was high.

When Nick Johnson popped up, the Yankees were down to their last five outs. For the many Red Sox fans in the stands, it seemed their team was destined to "break" the curse and finally get into the World Series.

Not so fast.

A Derek Jeter double.

A Bernie Williams single. Jeter scored.

Hideki Matsui, who had doubled twice off Martinez in the series, was ready.

The tired ace got two strikes on Matsui. Red Sox Nation relaxed a bit. A fastball inside. Matsui pulled the ball down the right field line. It bounced into the stands—ground-rule double. Posada was ready in the batter's box. The tying runs were on base.

No move from the beleaguered BoSox manager who was aware that his ace had thrown 111 pitches, most under mounting pressure.

Later Little said: "He had enough left in his tank to finish off Posada."

On the top step of the dugout Derek Jeter shouted to Posada: "Stay back. Wait for your pitch."

The count was 2–2. The next pitch was an inside fastball that Posada lifted over second base. Both Williams and Matsui scored.

Score tied. Little removed Martinez. Alan Embree and then Mike Timlin held the Yankees back as the game moved deadlocked 5–5 to the 11th inning. Mario Rivera choked off the Red Sox in the ninth, tenth and 11th innings—the longest stint for the Yankee closer in seven seasons.

Knuckleballer Wakefield with two victories over the Yankees in the series, had hurled a scoreless tenth inning. He came in to pitch the 11th inning.

The Yankees had traded for Aaron Boone on July 31, 2003, with the plan of his holding down third base. Ineffective in the ALCS, Torre benched Boone. In his place was the less-experienced Enrique Wilson for Game 7. Boone had entered the game earlier as a pinch runner. Now he came to bat.

The time was 16 minutes past midnight, Friday morning

Wakefield's first pitch was inside, below Boone's hands. Boone swung. The ball jumped off his bat and went deep over the left-field wall.

There was so much stamping and movement that it seemed like the big Bronx ballpark shook.

"I knew it was out. I finally put a good swing on it," Boone said later. The 6–5 New York win gave New York its fifth pennant in six seasons, its 39th American League pennant.

"Damn Yankees!" was the Friday front-page headline in the *Boston Herald*.

The Daily News banner headline read "Boone Town!"

"I don't know about a curse, but I believe we have some ghosts in this stadium that have helped us out," Derek Jeter said. "We've just had some magical stuff that has happened to us tonight."

Like Derek told me, "The ghosts will show up eventually," Boone said.

"I'm thankful that it's me instead of one of my players' taking the blame," Little said afterward. "If we don't win the World Series, which is the definition of winning here, somebody's got to be that man and I'm just glad it's me instead."

Boston general manager Theo Epstein remarked: "You can dwell on what happened and wake up in the middle of the night screaming, 'Five more outs!' but I'm not going to do that."

FINAL GAME AT ORIGINAL YANKEE STADIUM: SEPTEMBER 21, 2008

It was one of those picture-perfect days in New York City. At Yankee Stadium, summery, resplendent green grass, honey-brown colored base paths, a mix of all kinds of people from all kinds of places. It was Yankees versus Orioles, but in many ways that was the undercard.

The old calliope a bit past Gate 6 played a cheerful tune. Ancient green turnstiles with their dulled chrome arms were ready for one last time. Spike Lee was there wearing his Yankee cap, posing for pictures. It seemed everyone had a camera or a cell phone or a story about the team at the ready.

Gates were opened seven hours early to allow fans to stroll on the warning track, to go for one last walk in the park. Then they were escorted back into the stands.

Bunting along the upper deck, the presence of the United States Army Field Band, the mix of past and present, the unveiling of the American League championship flag that had been raised on the first Yankee Stadium Opening Day in 1923, all and more helped create one singular sensation.

The 65-minute pregame ceremony began with a recorded introduction from the legendary Bob Sheppard. He promised to return next year to christen the new Yankee Stadium. Players from both teams in the jammed dugouts stood on the top steps or sat on the dugout roofs watching as past Yankee stars were introduced and took positions on the field dressed in off-white uniforms made of genuine wool and baseball flannel.

Yogi Berra was one of six Hall of Famers on the field. Family members stood in for the greats who had passed—Phil Rizzuto, Thurman Munson, Elston Howard, Roger Maris, Mickey Mantle. Willie Randolph slid into his position, second base, rubbed some dirt on his jersey, happy returning to his place of glory. Whitey Ford made believe he was trying to steal the pitcher's rubber.

There were loud chants, echoes of the past:

"Bob-by Mur-cer!"

"Ti-no! Ti-no!"

"Reg-gie!"

Many stars who were not present were shown on the video board, including Rickey Henderson, Sparky Lyle, Chuck Knoblauch and Orlando Hernández.

George Steinbrenner, 78, remained in Tampa with health issues and watched on television. But there were about 25 former Yankees present for the pregame ceremonies. Paul O'Neill was there in a pinstriped brown shirt and so was Reggie Jackson in mufti wearing a blue baseball cap, watching batting practice. Ron Guidry, still handsome, and gentlemanly Bernie Williams drew loud applause. Mike Mussina drew a lot of attention. Elston Howard's daughter Cheryl, Catfish Hunter's widow, Helen, Bobby Murcer's widow, Kay, and her son and daughter, attended. Whitey Ford, Goose Gossage, appeared for a time standing on the pitcher's mound. Escorted and holding the arm of Mariano Rivera, Cora Rizzuto walked out to the shortstop position.

Julia Ruth Stevens, 92-year-old daughter of the Babe, threw out the ceremonial first pitch to injured catcher Jorge Posada.

The Yanks won the game, 7–3. Mariano Rivera pitched a 1-2-3 final inning, was given the game ball and said: "Mr. George, he gave me the opportunity and he gave me the chance,

the least I can do is give the ball to him."

Horse-mounted police appeared on the field as the game ended. Some Yankees and Orioles scoop dirt as souvenirs off the mound.

Derek Jeter spoke to the crowd in a final speech: "And we are relying on you to take the memories from this stadium, add them to the new memories to come at the new Yankee Stadium, and continue to pass them on from generation to generation."

Then there was a lap around the field by the Yankees waving their caps to the fans as Frank Sinatra's "New York, New York" played one more time.

The Baseball Hall of Fame received items from that last series at Yankee Stadium including cleats Jose Molina wore when he smashed the final home run in the old Yankee Stadium, a game-used Derek Jeter bat, Johnny Damon's bat used to hit a three-run home run in the final game's third inning. Oddly, Jeter's bat that wound up in the Hall of Fame belonged to teammate Xavier Nady. His name was etched on the barrel.

MARIANO RIVERA SETS ALL-TIME SAVE RECORD: SEPTEMBER 19, 2011

It was a Monday game, Yankees versus Twins at the Stadium. The announced attendance was 40,045. Many of those who showed had come to see if Mariano Rivera would break the all-time saves record.

Manager Joe Girardi said: "To think that he really burst on the scene in 1996 and, you know, we're talking a lot of seasons later and he's still doing it at a high level. He's got over 40 saves this year. . . . That doesn't really happen very often when you're 42 years old."

"Mo" got his shot at the record in the ninth inning. His one-two-three method on operations was on display. The 12-time All-Star retired Trevor Plouffe on a grounder to second base. He took

care of Michael Cuddyer on a fly ball to right field to tie the all-time record. Then he struck out Chris Parmelee for number 602—the record save. It was also Rivera's 43rd save of 2011. The record save took place 15 years and 125 days after his first Major League save.

The gentlemanly and religious Number 42 hugged his catcher Russell Martin. His Yankee teammates swarmed him in front of the mound. Then Rivera tipped his cap as he looked into the stands and felt the love and heard the cheers from the crowd.

"I can't describe that feeling because it was priceless," Rivera said later of the way the fans reacted to the landmark save. "It was a moment that, I didn't know it could be like that."

MVP of the 1999 World Series, Rivera at this point had 42 postseason saves, but they did not count in the record.

"He wants the ball in big situations and (is) not afraid of anyone," Jeter said. "[He] has a lot of confidence in his ability, and it shows."

And Jorge Posada who caught so many games that Rivera pitched, said, "We don't get to the playoffs, we don't win championships, we don't do a lot of the things that we were able to do without this guy."

DEREK JETER DAY: SEPTEMBER 7, 2014

A sunny Sunday at Yankee Stadium. Three weeks left in the baseball season, 22 games remaining for the New York Yankees. Yet, oddly enough this was the day of days selected for Derek Jeter's official farewell.

The big ballpark was "Jeterized." All its flags were replaced for the day with Derek Jeter's final season logo, which was also painted on the field. The guest list featured baseball and Yankee elite, all mixed together to honor one of the greatest and most adored players in franchise history: Commissioner-Elect

Scoreboard showing Mariano Rivera's total career saves, an all-time record.

Rob Manfred, Reggie Jackson, Dave Winfield, Hideki Matsui, Tino Martinez, Paul O'Neill, Mariano Rivera, Jorge Posada, Joe Torre, Cal Ripken Jr., Michael Jordan and several of Jeter's family members.

The Yankee captain Jeter's résumé included such sparklers as: 14-time All-Star, sixth on the career hits list, AL Rookie of the Year award and helping Yanks to win world championship, named captain in 2003, 3,000 hits plus. He was key in three consecutive Yankee championships from 1998 to 2000 and a fifth world championship in 2009.

The 45-minute pregame show before the 48,100 at the stadium featured the obligatory presentation of gifts including: a massage machine, a crystal engraved with his final season logo and, presented by George Steinbrenner's grandchildren, a 10-day vacation to Tuscany.

"It's kind of hard to believe that 20 seasons has gone by so quickly," Jeter spoke into the microphone on the field. The 40-year-old appeared unmoved but appreciative of the 90-second ovation before he began to speak.

"You guys," he said, "have all watched me grow up over the last 20 years. I've watched you, too. Some of you guys getting old, too. But I want to thank you for helping me feel like a kid for the last 20 years. I've had the greatest job in the world; I've had the chance to be the shortstop for the New York Yankees—and there's only one of those. I always felt as though my job was to try to provide joy and entertainment for you guys. But it can't compare to what you've brought me, so for that, thank you very much. We've got a game to play."

Hall-of-Famer Babe Ruth collectible card.

Four

YANKEE MONIKERS AND NICKNAMES

Noms de plume, aliases, sobriquets, catchwords—nicknames, all time, all ways for Yankees

Through the decades, sporting scribes, fans, friends and relatives, opponents and teammates have outdone themselves pinning noms de plume, aliases, sobriquets, catchwords and nicknames on Yankee personnel and experiences. These have run the gamut from apt to asinine, from complimentary to crude, from hero-worshiping to hellacious, from amusing to amazing.

Babe Ruth leads the pack in the number of nicknames attached to him. He was called "Babe" by his teammates on the Baltimore Orioles, his first professional team because of his youth. Early on he was also called "Infant Swatagy." His Yankee teammates called him "Jidge," which was short for George in German. Opponents referred to him negatively as "The Big Monk" and "Monkey." He was also called "Two Head," a negative nickname used by opponents to describe the size of his head, which seemed very huge to some. They also called him a lot of unmentionables.

Sportswriters glamorizing the big guy came up with these monikers: "Home Run King," "The Bambino," "Bammer," "the Bam," "the Wali of Wallop," "the Rajah of Rap," "the Caliph of Clout," "the Wazir of Wham," "the Sultan of Swat," "The Colossus of Clout," "Maharajah of Mash," "The Behemoth of Bust," "Behemoth of Biff," "The King of Clout" and the "Goliath of Grand Slams."

He called most players "Kid" because he couldn't remember the names of even his closest friends.

During spring training 1927, Babe Ruth bet pitcher Wilcy Moore $100 that he would not get more than three hits all season. A notoriously weak hitter, Moore somehow managed six hits in 75 at bats. Ruth paid off his debt and Moore purchased two mules for his farm naming them "Babe" and "Ruth."

But enough of George Herman Ruth. Now onto the bon mots, aliases and expressions for all manner of Yankees. Herewith, a sampler.

A

- **A-Rod** Abbreviation for Alex Rodriguez.

- **"All-American Out"** What Babe Ruth called Leo Durocher because of his limited hitting ability.

- **"Almighty Tired Man"** Mickey Rivers, for his slouching demeanor.

- **"American Idle"** Carl Pavano was known as this because he could never stay on the field and stay healthy.

- **"An A-bomb from A-Rod"** Classic home run call, John Sterling. ("It is high, it is far. It is gone! The Yankees win. Thuuuuuuuuh Yankees win!" —Another classic home run call, John Sterling.)

B

- **"Babe Ruth's Legs"** Sammy Byrd, employed as pinch runner for Ruth and "Bam-Bam" for Hensley Meulens, able to speak about five languages, but had a challenging name for some to pronounce.

- **"Banty rooster"** Casey Stengel's nickname for Whitey Ford because of his style and attitude.

- **"Barrows"** Jacob Ruppert's corruption of Ed Barrow's name.

- **"Battle of the Biltmore"** 1947 World Series celebration in Manhattan's Biltmore Hotel was a time and place where Larry MacPhail drunkenly fought with everyone ending his Yankee ownership time.

- **"Billyball"** The aggressive style of play favored by Billy Martin.

- **"Biscuit Pants"** Lou Gehrig, reference to the way he filled out his trousers.

- **"Blind Ryne"** Ryne Duren's vision, uncorrected -20/70 and 20/200.

- **"Bloody Angel"** During 1923 season the space between the bleachers and right-field foul line at Yankee Stadium was very asymmetrical causing crazy bounces. It was eliminated in 1924.

- **"Bob the Gob"** Bob Shawkey in 1918 served in the Navy as a yeoman petty officer.

- **"Boomer"** David Wells, for his in-your-face personality.

- **"The Boss"** George Steinbrenner, and that he was. Reggie had actually labeled the owner "the big guy with the boats" long before he became the "The Boss."

- **"The Boston Massacre"** Red Sox collapse in 1978 and the Yankee sweep of a four game series in September.

- **"Broadway"** Shortstop Lyn Lary was married to Broadway star Mary Lawler.

- **"Bronx Bombers"** For the borough and home run power of Yankees.

- **"Bronx Zoo"** A derogatory reference to off-color Yankee behavior on and off the playing field through the years, especially in the 1970s.

- **"Brooklyn Schoolboy"** Waite Hoyt had starred at Brooklyn's Erasmus High School.

- **"Bruiser"** Hank Bauer, for his burly ways.

- **"Bulldog"** Jim Bouton was dogged.

- **"Bullet Bob"** Bob Turley, for the pop on his fastball.

- **"Bullet Joe"** Joe Bush, for the pop he also could put on his fastball.

- **"Bye-Bye"** Steve Balboni, the primary DH of the 1990 Yankees, 17 homers but .192 BA.

C

- **"The Captain"** Derek Jeter was such an icon that the Yankees have yet to name a new captain since his retirement.

- **"Captain Clutch"** Derek Jeter, and that he was.

- **"Carnesville Plowboy"** Spud Chandler, for his hometown of Carnesville.

- **"The CAT-a-lyst"** Mickey Rivers, given this name by Howard Cosell.

- **"Chairman of the Board"** Elston Howard coined it for Whitey Ford and his commanding and take-charge manner on the mound.

- **"The Colonel"** Jerry Coleman saw combat in both World War II and the Korean War. As a Marine Corps aviator, he flew 120 combat missions and earned two Distinguished Flying Crosses. It was also a nickname for pitching coach Jim Turner, who came from the south, and used by Jim Bouton in Ball Four in a derogatory fashion.

- **"Columbia Lou"** Lou Gehrig, for his collegiate roots.

- **"Commerce Comet"** Mickey Mantle, for his speed and being out of Commerce, Oklahoma.

- **"Core Four"** Andy Pettitte, Mariano Rivera, Derek Jeter and Jorge Posada were all drafted or signed as amateurs by the Yankees in the early 1990s. After playing in the minors together they made their debuts in 1995. With the four as a nucleus, the Yanks in the next 17 seasons missed the playoffs only twice, played in the World Series seven times and won five world championships.

- **"The Count"** Sparky Lyle, handlebar mustache and lordly ways.

- **"The Count"** John Montefusco, because his name reminded people of the Count of Monte Cristo.

- **"The Crow"** Frank Crosetti for his loud voice and chirpy ways.

- **"Curse of the Bambino"** Since 1920 and the selling of Babe Ruth to the Yankees by Boston owner Harry Frazee in 1920, the Yankees have won all those championships. The Red Sox have won a few.

D

- **"Daddy Longlegs"** Dave Winfield, for his size and long legs.

- **"Danish Viking"** George Pipgras, for his size and roots.

- **"Deacon"** Everett Scott, for his not too friendly look.

- **"Death Valley"** The old deep center field in Yankee Stadium.

- **"Dial-a-Deal"** Gabe Paul, for his telephone trading habits.

- **"Donnie Baseball"** Don Mattingly's nickname. Some say it was coined by Yankee broadcaster Michael Kay; others say it came from Kirby Puckett. Kay takes the credit; Mattingly gives the credit to Puckett.

E

- **"El Duquecito"** Adrian Hernandez because of a pitching style similar to Orlando "El Duque."

- **"Ellie"** Affectionate abbreviation of Elston Howard's first name.

F

- **"Father of the Emory Ball"** Rookie right-hander Russ Ford posted a 26–6 record with 8 shutouts, 1910, using that pitch.

Poised, polished, Joe "Flash" Gordon had the goods.

- **"Figgy"** Ed Figueroa, short for his surname, which was tough, for some, to pronounce.

- **"Fireman"** Johnny Murphy, the first to have this nickname was the first great relief pitcher. Joe Page picked up this nickname for his top relief work later on.

- **"Five O'clock Lightning"** At five o'clock the blowing of a whistle at a factory near Yankee Stadium signaled the end of the work day in the 1930s and also the power the Yankees were unleashing against opponents on the Yankee Stadium playing field.

- **"Flash"** Joe Gordon was fast, slick fielding and hit line drives.

- **"Flop Ears"** Julie Wera. Was dubbed that by Babe Ruth. A backup infielder, Wera earned $2,400, least on the '27 Yankees.

- **"Fordham Johnny"** For the college Johnny Murphy attended.

- **"Four hour manager"** Bucky Harris, who put his time in at the game and was finished.

- **"Friday Night Massacre"** April 26, 1974, Yankees Fritz Patterson, Steve Kline, Fred Beene, Tom Buskey and half the pitching staff were traded to Cleveland for Chris Chambliss, Dick Tidrow and Ceil Upshaw.

G

- **"Gator"** Ron Guidry, for his hailing from Louisiana alligator country.

- **"Gay Caballero"** Lefty Gomez, for his Mexican roots and fun-loving ways.

- **"Gay Reliever"** Joe Page, for his night owl activity.

- **"Gehrigville"** The old bleachers in right-center at Yankee Stadium.

- **"Georgia Catfish"** James Augustus Hunter was his real name but the world knew him as "Catfish," primarily because of Oakland A's owner Charles O. Finley. Hunter ran away from home when he was a child, returning with two catfish. His parents called him Catfish for a while. Finley decided that Jim Hunter was too bland a name for a star pitcher and revived Hunter's childhood nickname.

- **"The Godfather"** Joe Torre, for his Italian roots and his leadership skills on the baseball field.

- **"Godzilla"** Hideki Matsui, his power earned him the moniker after the power-packed film creature.

- **"Goofy"** or **"El Goofo"** Lefty Gomez, for his wild antics.

- **"Gooneybird"** Don Larsen, for his late-night behavior.

- **"Goose"** Richard Michael Gossage, for his loose and lively style.

- **"Grandma"** Johnny Murphy, for his pitching motion, rocking chair style. Another explanation is that fellow Yankee Pat Malone gave him the name because of his complaining nature especially as regards food and lodgings.

- **"The Great Agitator"** Billy Martin, self-explanatory.

- **"The Great Debater"** Tommy Henrich, for his sometimes loquacious and argumentative ways.

H

- **"Happy Jack"** Jack Chesbro, for his time as an attendant at the state mental hospital in Middletown, New York, where he pitched for the hospital team and showed off a very pleasant disposition.

- **"Holy Cow"** One of Phil Rizzuto's ways of expressing awe.

- **"Home Run Twins"** (also "M and M Boys") Mickey Mantle and Roger Maris, phrase coined in 1961.

- **"Horse Nose"** Pat Collins via Babe Ruth, a reference to a facial feature.

I

- **"Iron Horse"** Lou Gehrig, for his power and steadiness.

J

- **"Joltin' Joe"** Joe DiMaggio, for the jolting shots he hit.

- **"Jumping Joe"** Joe Dugan, for being AWOL from his first big league club as a youngster.

- **"Junk Man"** Eddie Lopat, for frustrating hitters and keeping them off stride with an assortment of slow breaking pitches thrown with cunning and accuracy.

K

- **"Kentucky Colonel"** Earl Combs, for his Kentucky roots.

- **"The King and the Crown Prince"** Babe Ruth and Lou Gehrig, self-evident.

- **"King Kong"** Charlie Keller, for his muscular body type and black, bushy brows. Keller hated the nickname. When Phil Rizzuto used it, Keller would pick him up in one hand and kiddingly stuff "the Scooter" into his locker.

- **"Knight of Kennett Square"** Herb Pennock, for his raising of thoroughbreds and hosting of fox hunts in his hometown of Kennett Square, Pennsylvania.

- **"Knucksie"** Phil Niekro, for his knuckleball.

L

- **"Larrupin' Lou"** Lou Gehrig, named by the press for his hitting, he also used the name for his barnstorming team he ran during the off-season.

- **"The Lip"** Leo Durocher, for his talkative and sometimes profane and excessive verbiage.

- **"Lonesome George"** George Weiss, for his aloof ways.

M

- **"Mail Carrier"** Earle Combs, for his speed and base stealing skills.

- **"Major"** Ralph Houk, for rank held in the Armed Forces and demeanor.

- **"Man Nobody Knows"** Bill Dickey, for his blandness.

- **"Man in the Iron Hat"** Captain Tillinghast L'Hommedieu Huston, for the same squashed derby hat he wore over and over again.

- **"Man of a Thousand Curves"** For Johnny Sain and his assortment of curve balls.

- **"Marse Joe"** Joe McCarthy, for his commanding style.

- **"Master Builder in Baseball"** Jacob Ruppert, and that he was.

- **"The Merry Mortician"** Waite Hoyt, for his cheery soul and off-season mortician work.

- **"The Mick"** Short for Mickey (Mantle).

- **"Mick the Quick"** Mickey Rivers, for his speed.

- **"Mickey Mouth"** For Mickey Rivers and his motor mouth.

- **"Mighty Mite"** Miller Huggins, for his size and power.

- **"Milkman"** Jim Turner, for an off-season job delivering milk.

- **"Mo"** Mariano Rivera, a shortening.

- **"Moose"** Bill Skowron's grandfather called him Mussolini because of a resemblance to Mussolini. As the story goes, the family shortened the nickname to "Moose."

- **"Mr. Automatic"** Mariano Rivera, for his virtually unflappable behavior and special skills as a Yankee stopper.

- **"Mr. May"** George Steinbrenner's sarcastic jibe at Dave Winfield because of his postseason struggles as compared to Reggie Jackson's successes and Mr. October nickname.

- **"Mister Consistent"** Roy White, and that he was.

- **"Mr. November"** Derek Jeter, for his World Series home run, the first of November, 2001.

- **"Mr. October"** In Game 5 of the 1977 ALCS Billy Martin benched Reggie Jackson. In a comeback win against Kansas City Jackson returned to slap a single. Thurman Munson sarcastically called Jackson "Mr. October."

- **"Murderer's Row"** Yankee lineup boasting powerful batters: standard version was the meat of the 1927 lineup of Tony Lazzeri, Lou Gehrig, Babe Ruth, Earl Combs and Bob Meusel. Runner-up version was the 1919 entry of Ping Bodie, Roger Peckinpaugh, Duffy Lewis and Home Run Baker.

- **"Muscles"** Many in the press referred to the Mick as "muscles" because of his huge arms.

- **"My writers"** Casey Stengel's phrase for journalists he was close to.

O

- **"Old Reliable"** Mel Allen gave Tommy Henrich that nickname after a train that made its way from Cincinnati through Allen's home state of Alabama and was always on time and could be depended on.

- **"Ol' Perfessor"** Casey Stengel, for the time in 1914 when he had a spring training baseball coaching stint at the University of Mississippi.

P

- **"The Peerless Leader"** Frank Chance, for his keen baseball mind.

- **"Thuuuhh pitch . . ."** John Sterling's elongated call of a pitch being delivered.

- **"Popeye!"** The 5-foot-9, 185-pound Don Zimmer was a power-hitting shortstop with bulging biceps, which once prompted his Dodger teammate Roy Campanella to exclaim: "Lookit him! He looks like . . ."

- **"Poosh 'em up, Tony"** Tony Lazzeri was a magnet for Italian fans at Yankee Stadium who would scream out this phrase urging him to hit home runs.

- **"Prince Hal"** Hal Chase, for his charismatic, elegant, royal quality.

- **"Prince of Pounders"** The team of Ruth and Gehrig.

- **"The Principal Owner"** George Steinbrenner, no doubt here.

- **"Puff"** Graig Nettles was known for his quotes, and for his habit of saying something witty or controversial or playing jokes on teammates then disappearing. The primary reason for the nickname for him was his habit of quickly disappearing after games.

- **"Push Button Manager"** Joe McCarthy, for his by-the-book ways.

R

- **"Robbie Cano, don't you know"** Another classic John Sterling home run call for Cano.

S

- **"Sandman"** Greatest relief pitcher of all time, Mariano Rivera, putting batters to sleep.

- **"Schoolboy"** and **"Schoolboy Wonder"** Waite Hoyt, for his Major League debut in 1918 when he was a teenager.

- **"Scooter"** Phil Rizzuto, quick feet and steady hands.

- **"Second Place Joe"** Joe McCarthy's three straight second-place finishes prompted this tag in the three seasons before the Yanks won four consecutive world championships, 1936 to 1939. The name was also used when he was manager of the Cubs and had some disappointing second place finishes.

- **"Silent Bob"** Bob Meusel, for his aloofness.

- **"Silent One"** Chris Chambliss, for his taciturn manner, name given by Howard Cosell.

Bob Meusel shows off his batting style; he led the league in stolen bases five times and was considered baseball's best arm.

- **"Slick"** Whitey Ford allegedly used a spitter to strike out Willie Mays in the 1964 All-Star Game. That was just one of the reasons for the Yankee star's nickname. He was slick.

- **"Slow"** Joe Doyle, for his time consuming pace.

- **"Smash"** Gil McDougald, for the verve of his personality.

- **"Solid citizens"** Name Joe McCarthy gave to players he relied on.

- **"Springfield Rifle"** Vic Raschi, after his arm and his birthplace in Springfield, Massachusetts.

- **"Spud"** Spurgeon Ferdinand Chandler was called by his nickname, for obvious reasons.

- **"Squire (or Knight) of Kennett Square"** Herb Pennock came from historic Kennett Square, Pennsylvania, an area of horsemen and fox hunters. Pennock himself was an expert rider and a master of hounds.

- **"Steady Eddie"** Eddie Lopat, for his consistency year after year as a Yankee pitcher. The nickname originated with Mel Allen.

- **"Stick"** Gene Michael, for his lean and long appearance.

- **"Superchief"** Allie Reynolds, for his one-quarter Creek Indian ancestry and winning ways on the mound.

- **"Supersub"** Johnny Blanchard, home run hitter as a pinch hitter, extraordinaire.

- **"Sweet Lou"** Lou Piniella, .291 MLB average, sweet swing

- **"The Switcher"** Mickey Mantle, for switch-hitting par excellence.

T

- **"The Tabasco Kid"** Norman Arthur Elberfeld, for his liking of the stuff and especially for his outrageous temper on and off the field. He was the second captain in Yankee history.

- **"Tanglefoot Lou"** For Lou Gehrig, early days and fielding trials as a player.

- **"Three Million Dollar Man"** Nickname placed on Catfish Hunter when he signed with the Yankees as a free agent for that sum in 1974.

- **"T.J."** Tommy John.

- **"Tugboat"** Thurman Munson was given the nickname as he was the real power and drive behind his Yankee teams.

- **"Twinkletoes"** George Selkirk, for his running with his weight on the balls of his feet.

U

- **"The Unholy Trio"** Billy Martin, Mickey Mantle and Whitey Ford, for their devilish ways.

V

- **"Voice of God"** Bob Sheppard was called that by Reggie Jackson and the nickname rightfully stuck.

W

- **"The Wall"** Thurman Munson because he almost never let a pitch get past him and his ability to block the plate.

- **"The Warrior"** Paul O'Neill, name pinned on him by George Steinbrenner for the outfielder's pugnacious ways.

- **"The Weatherman"** Mickey Rivers, for his knack for predicting the weather.

- **"Wee Willie"** Willie Keeler, about 5-foot-5 and 140 pounds, he was a package of talent.

- **"The White Gorilla"** Goose Gossage, for the way he looked.

- **"Whitey"** Whitey Ford, for the tow head blonde hair he sported as a '50s hurler.

- **"Window breakers"** Name given to the 1936 Yankees for their slugging power.

- **"Winny"** Dave Winfield, affectionate shortening of his name.

Y

- **"The Yankee Clipper"** For Joe DiMaggio for the way he glided about center field at Yankee Stadium. According to DiMaggio's official website, Yankee Stadium announcer Arch McDonald came up with the moniker for the "gracefulness of his play in the field."

- **"The Yankee Clipper"** A slap at George Steinbrenner, who longed to see his players clean-shaven.

- **"Yogi"** Lawrence Peter Berra, that he was and one of a kind.

Baseball fans waiting in line to buy tickets for the World Series, c. 1938.

NUMEROLOGY: YANKEES BY THE NUMBERS FROM 0 TO $3.4 BILLION

The numbers, stats and figures that are a staple of Major League Baseball

Numbers, stats and figures have always been a staple of baseball in the Major Leagues. And the Yankees, who have been around for so long and accomplished so much, are no slouches when it comes to "numerology." What follows is a compendium of "Yankees by the numbers."

YANKEE WORLD CHAMPIONSHIPS

1923, 1927, 1928, 1932, 1936, 1937, 1938, 1939, 1941, 1943, 1947, 1949, 1950, 1951, 1952, 1953, 1956, 1958, 1961, 1962, 1977, 1978, 1996, 1998, 1999, 2000 and 2009

ZERO

- The 1927 Yankees made no changes to their roster all season long. The team began with 10 pitchers, three catchers, seven infielders and five outfielders, and ended that way.
- Fewest passed balls in a season, 1931.
- In 283 innings in 1961, Whitey Ford did not allow a single stolen base.

- Number of days Dave Winfield spent in minor-league baseball before reaching the majors.
- With Derek Jeter's Number 2 now retired, the Yankees are the only team with no single-digit uniform numbers.
- The Yankees have never had player names on the back of any jersey, unlike most other MLB teams.

.00009

- Difference between the batting average of George "Snuffy" Stirnweiss: .30854 and White Sox Tony Cuccinello: .30845 in the closest batting race in Major League history, 1945.

0002

- After Allie Reynolds pitched his second no-hitter for the Yankees in 1951, the Hotel Edison, where he along with some teammates lived, changed his room number from 2019 to 0002.

1

- Pitcher Clark Griffith, 1903 to 1907, was the first Yankee captain.
- Number of times Babe Ruth was pinch-hit for (Bobby Veach on August 9, 1925).
- Joe DiMaggio was the only player to get at least one hit in All-Star Games at Yankee Stadium, the Polo Grounds and Ebbets Field.
- During Joe DiMaggio's record 56-game hit streak, he had just one hit in 34 of those games.
- Mickey Mantle hit for the cycle only one time in his career. He did it against Chicago at Yankee Stadium in 1957.
- Billy Martin's number retired August 10, 1986.
- Derek Jeter is the only Yankees shortstop to win the Gold Glove Award.
- Earle Combs was given uniform #1 and as a leadoff man could have become the first Yankee player to bat identified by a uniform number. However, the Yankees had a rain

Overhead shot of a packed Yankee Stadium with no sign of an empty seat in the "House That Ruth Built."

delay that day. Cleveland played its game before the Yankees and it's likely one of their players wore the #1 first in 1929. So Combs would have been the first Yankee but not Major Leaguer to wear a number.

1.10

- The Major League rule banning a sticky substance such as pine tar on a bat beyond 18 inches from the bottom. That rule led to the "pine tar affair," Yankees against Royals in 1983.

1¹/₂

- When George Steinbrenner purchased the Yankees in 1973, he officially made Robert Merrill the singing voice of the Yankees for as long as the baritone opera singer wanted. The team even gave him his own pinstriped uniform and number sewn on the back. For many years Merrill sang the national anthem at Yankee Stadium.

PAUL DOHERTY: *Others sang the anthem in person after Steinbrenner took over, although Merrill's recording was used primarily with Jerry Vale's, The Boston Pops [of all Orchestras!!] and at times The New York Philharmonic's.*

1.64

- Top ERA in a season, Spud Chandler, 1943.

1.95

- Career earned-run average of Herb Pennock in World Series competition.

2

- Shortstop Kid Elberfeld, second Yankee captain, 1907 to 1909.
- Babe Ruth, two days in a row, hit grand slam homers.
- Most grand slams in a game by a Yankee, Tony Lazzeri, May 24, 1936, at Philadelphia's Shibe Park.
- The number of managerial tours of duty of Bob Lemon, Gene Michael and Lou Piniella.

- Fewest times in a season grounded into a double play: Mickey Mantle, 1961, Mickey Rivers, 1977.
- Fewest shutouts by a Yankee pitching staff in a season, 1994.
- Derek Jeter's number retired, the last single-digit number for the Yankee franchise.
- Alex Rodriguez homered twice in the seventh inning at Yankee Stadium on September 5, 2007, against the Mariners, giving him 48 home runs for the season.

2.45

- Bob Shawkey's 1920 season league-leading ERA title was the first ever won by a Yankee pitcher.

$2.50

- "Prior to the Second World War, box seats were regular wooden chairs that went back about two or three rows from third to first base. They cost about $2.50." —Red Foley, *New York Daily News*

2.57

- Lowest earned run average by a Yankee pitching staff, 1904.

3

- First baseman Hal Chase was the third Yankee captain, 1909 to 1912.
- Shortstop Joe Sewell struck out only three times in 503 at bats in 1932.
- Babe Ruth and Bob Meusel are two of the players in history to hit for the cycle three times.
- Babe Ruth's uniform number, retired June 13, 1948, second Yankee number. While the great Yankee was the first to wear it, he was far from the last. Seven other Yankees wore Number 3. Outfielder Cliff Mapes wore it in 1948 when it was retired.

Mapes switched to Number 7 the next year. After he was traded to the Browns in mid-1951, Number 7 went to a rookie named Mickey Mantle.

- Joe DiMaggio, Mickey Mantle and Yogi Berra each won three MVP awards.
- Top number of perfect games by a franchise: Don Larsen, David Wells, David Cone.
- All three perfect games in Yankee Stadium history were seen by Joe Torre: Larsen's beauty as a 16-year-old fan, and the ones pitched by David Wells and David Cone from the dugout as Yankee manager. The Yankees have the most perfect games pitched by one club, all at Yankee Stadium.
- In September 1998, Yankees outfielder Shane Spencer tied a Major League record by hitting three grand slams in one month.
- Paul O'Neill is the only player to have been in right field for three perfect games: Tom Browning of the Reds (1988), David Wells (1998) and David Cone (1999).

3.1

- Record time in seconds Mickey Mantle was able to run from home plate to first base, fastest for any player in history.

4

- Most consecutive losing seasons for Yankees, 1912 to 1915 and 1989 to 1992.
- Shortstop Roger Peckinpaugh was the fourth Yankee captain, 1914 to 1921.
- In 1923, Babe Ruth hit for his highest single-season average: .393. He came within four hits of batting .400.

- Lou Gehrig's number, retired on July 4, 1939, first athlete in any sport. He is the only Yankee to have worn Number 4.
- Four straight Yankee MVP awards twice: Yogi Berra in 1954 and 1955, Mickey Mantle in 1956 and 1957. Then Mickey Mantle in 1960, Roger Maris in 1961, Mantle in 1962 and Elston Howard in 1963.
- July 15, 2008, is the setting for the fourth All-Star Game at Yankee Stadium.
- The Yankee Clipper is the only player to earn a ring for winning the World Series in each of his first four seasons, 1936 to 1939.
- All-time record for All-Star saves by Mariano Rivera.

4.02

- Lou Gehrig's career RBIs for at bats, second to only Babe Ruth.

4.88

- Highest ERA by Yankee pitching staff, 1930.

5

- Outfielder Babe Ruth was the fifth Yankee captain, May 20 to May 25, 1922.
- Lefty Gomez was a starter in five All-Star Games, winning three of them.
- Number of times Mickey Mantle hit a ball into the copper facade that hung from the old stadium's roof.
- Joe DiMaggio's uniform number, retired in 1952.
- Yanks won the World Series a record five straight seasons, from 1949 to 53.
- October 16, 2003: Aaron Boone was the fifth player—and second Yankee—to end a postseason series with a walk-off home run. His solo shot in the bottom of the 11th inning

capped a 6–5, Game 7 victory over Boston, giving the Yankees their 39th American League Pennant.

- No team in baseball history matches the Yankees for five catchers the quality of Bill Dickey, Yogi Berra, Elston Howard, Thurman Munson and Jorge Posada.

6

- Playing fields for franchise: Hilltop Park 1903 to 1912, Polo Grounds 1913 to 1922, Yankee Stadium (original) 1923 to 1973, Shea Stadium 1974 to 1975, Yankee Stadium (refurbished) 1976 to 2008, New Yankee Stadium 2009 to present.
- Shortstop Everett Scott was the sixth Yankee captain succeeding Babe Ruth, 1922 to 1925.
- On June 6, 1934, Yankee outfielder Myril Hoag tied an American League record with six singles in six at bats.
- Second baseman Joe Gordon, who played mostly in the 1940s, wore No. 6. He was inducted posthumously into Cooperstown in 2009.
- Number of Yankee starters: Bill Dickey, Joe DiMaggio, Joe Gordon, Red Rolfe, Red Ruffing and George Selkirk in the 1939 All-Star game at Yankee Stadium.
- Mickey Mantle's rookie uniform number, changed by equipment manager Pete Sheehy to Number 7 after Mantle was recalled from Kansas City.
- Number of times Billy Martin had a tour of duty as manager.
- Don Mattingly hits a grand slam off Boston's Bruce Hurst at Yankee Stadium on September 29, 1987, setting a Major League record with six grand slams in a season.
- Joe Torre's number retired by Yankees.

Opening Day at new Yankee Stadium, April 23, 1923, well protected, especially owner Jake Ruppert on the left and Governor Al Smith on the right with Smith's wife in between both men.

6.4

- The 1939 Yankees led by 24-year-old Joe DiMaggio averaged an amazing 6.4 runs per game as a team.

7

- Hall of Fame manager Leo Durocher, an infielder in 1929, was the first Yankee to wear Number 7.
- First baseman Lou Gehrig was the seventh Yankee captain, April 21, 1935, to June 2, 1941.
- Joe DiMaggio heads the list of players with a minimum of 20 home runs who recorded more home runs than strikeouts in seven different seasons.
- From 1939 to 1945, New York City mayor Fiorello LaGuardia threw out the first ball in the Yankees' home opener, the longest streak for the event in franchise history.
- Mickey Mantle's number, retired June 8, 1969. He wore it from 1951 on.
- Mel Allen was the first announcer to broadcast Major League Baseball games over seven decades. His tenure ran from Lou Gehrig to Don Mattingly.

- In 1982, Graig Nettles became the seventh captain in Yankee history.

8

- Record held by Lou Gehrig, most seasons leading league in games played.
- Only number to be retired twice by the same team is Number 8 of the Yankees. It was retired in 1972 for catchers Bill Dickey and Yogi Berra. Berra took Number 8 in 1948 after Dickey retired but before he was a coach. Dickey wore Number 10 in 1929, Number 8 thereafter.
- Catcher Thurman Munson was the eighth Yankee captain, April 17, 1976, to August 2, 1979.
- Dwight Gooden's no-hitter on May 14, 1996, was the eighth in Stadium history.

9

- Joe DiMaggio's rookie number.
- Third Baseman Graig Nettles was the ninth Yankee captain, January 28, 1982, to March 30, 1984.
- Roger Maris's number, retired July 22, 1984.
- The 1990 Yankees had but one starting pitcher who won more than seven games, nine-game winner Tim Leary; he also lost 19.
- Most hits in an inning given up by Roger Clemens, August 2, 2007.
- The most shutouts by a Yankee in a season: Ron Guidry, 1978.

10

- Of Babe Ruth's 714 career home runs, 10 were inside-the-parkers. Ruth hit 10 career home runs off the great Walter Johnson. No other player hit more than 5 against the star hurler. With the Yankees from 1920 to 1934, the "Colossus of Clout" won 10 home run titles.
- Casey Stengel managed in a record 10 World Series, winning seven of them.
- The Yanks used a record 10 pinch hitters on September 6, 1954, in a doubleheader against the Boston Red Sox. They won the opener 6–5, and the BoSox took the second game, 8–7.
- Wins by Whitey Ford in World Series.
- Yogi Berra leads all with 10 World Series rings. Joe DiMaggio was second with 9.
- Second baseman Willie Randolph was the tenth Yankee captain, January 29, 1982, to August 2, 1979.
- Phil Rizzuto's number, retired August 4, 1985.
- Alex Rodriguez in 2007 became the first player in Major League history with 10 straight seasons of at least 35 homers, 100 RBIs and 100 runs scored.

11

- Record set for most RBIs in consecutive games, Babe Ruth, 1931.
- Most walks in one inning, the third, Yankees versus Senators, September 11, 1949.
- Most at bats one game, Bobby Richardson, June 24, 1962, game against Detroit went 22 innings.
- Pitcher Ron Guidry was the eleventh Yankee captain from March 4, 1986, to July 12, 1989.

11.8

- Babe Ruth career home run rate per at bat.

12

- The number of ballparks Babe Ruth hit at least one home run in.
- The number of times Babe Ruth led the American League in homers.
- Billy Martin's rookie uniform number.
- First baseman Don Mattingly was the 12th Yankee captain from February 28, 1991, to October 8, 1995.

13

- Home plate was moved 13 feet forward in 1924, eliminating the "bloody angle" in the right field corner of Yankee Stadium.
- Bill Dickey holds record catching over 100 games 13 consecutive seasons.
- Lou Gehrig had 13 consecutive seasons where he scored over 100 runs, the first player in baseball history to reach that total.
- Number of seasons Joe DiMaggio played for the Yankees.
- The number of All-Star teams Mariano Rivera appeared in second all-time to Warren Spahn.
- Derek Jeter was the 13th captain in Yankee history from September 3, 2003, to season's end 2014.

14

- The number of players the Yankees lost in the 1918 season to military service.
- Team record for runs scored in an inning: fifth inning against Washington, July 6, 1920.
- Yogi Berra stayed away from Yankee Stadium for 14 years after George Steinbrenner fired him 16 games into 1985.

14%

- In 1927, Babe Ruth blasted 14 percent of all the home runs recorded in the American League.

15

- Babe Ruth three times homered 15 times in one month; DiMaggio and Maris accomplished that feat once.
- Lou Gehrig, career steals of home.
- The number of consecutive seasons Yogi Berra was a member of the American League All-Star team. He actually made 18 teams in all.
- July 18, 1999: David Cone's perfect game against the Montreal Expos was the 15th regular season perfect game.
- $15.00, Bob Sheppard's per-game earnings in 1951 when he began working for the Yankees. Allowing for inflation this is approximately $138 today.
- Thurman Munson's retired uniform number.
- Babe Ruth, total World Series home runs, second place all time.
- Most runs allowed by the Yankees in post-season competition, Game 6, 2001 World Series.

16

- In their first 16 years, the Highlanders/Yankees didn't win a single pennant and had 10 losing seasons.
- Number of career grand slams for Babe Ruth.

- Whitey Ford's Number retired in 1974. The slick southpaw wore Number 19 as a rookie. Returning from the army in 1953, he wore Number 16 for the rest of his career.
- Dallas Green, George Steinbrenner's 16th manager to be fired.

17

- Monthly home run best: Babe Ruth, September 1927.
- Number of career homers Babe Ruth's hit off Rube Walberg, most off any pitcher.
- Late in his career, Gehrig's hands were x-rayed and doctors spotted 17 fractures that had "healed" while he continued to play.
- Bill Dickey played his entire 17-season career as a Yankee.
- In 16 All-Star games Mickey Mantle struck out a record 17 times.
- Roy White, franchise record for sacrifice flies in a season, 1971.
- In his first 17 years, Steinbrenner changed managers 17 times.
- On his 17th birthday in 1985, Bernie Williams signed a contract to play professional baseball for the Yankees.
- Number of years Jorge Posada played for the Yankees.

18

- Since their first title in 1923, the Yankees have not gone longer than 18 years without a world championship.
- Most years with the Yankees: Yogi Berra (1946–1963) and Mickey Mantle (1951–1968).
- Most World Series home runs, Mickey Mantle.
- Joe DiMaggio's original uniform, number given to him by equipment manager Pete Sheehy and later changed to Number 5.
- Number of years Frank Messer and Bill White were Yankee announcers.

19

- Babe Ruth and Lou Gehrig in a decade of playing together homered in the same inning 19 times.
- The 1927 Yankees won the pennant by 19 games, using only twenty-five players. Not one roster change was made that season.
- Longest winning streak, 1947.
- Whitey Ford's rookie uniform number.
- Dave Righetti began with the Yankees with Jim Bouton's old number, 56, but he became famous wearing Number 19.
- Number of managerial changes Steinbrenner made in eighteen years, before Buck Showalter came along and lasted four years as manager.
- Derek Jeter set a five-game World Series record with 19 total bases in 2000.

20

- Jorge Posada's number retired.

20/20

- In 2001, Paul O'Neill at age 38 became the oldest player to have a 20/20 season.

21

- Babe Ruth hit 21 of his 60 homers in 1927 with the same bat. Whenever he homered, he'd carve a notch around the trademark.
- Yogi Berra had an incredible total of 21 World Series appearances as a player, coach or manager.
- Since Paul O'Neill's retirement after the 2001 World Series, no Yankee has worn that number. Although Latroy Hawkins actually briefly wore Number 21 to honor Roberto Clemente in 2008. Yankee fans were not happy.

22

- Allie Reynolds's number 22, not retired, but he earned a plaque out in Monument Park.
- Most hits recorded in a World Series sixth game, 2001.
- Yogi Berra on June 24, 1962, age 37, caught all 22 innings of a Yankees game with the Tigers in Detroit. The Yanks won, 9–7, in the seven-hour game.

23

- The 1909 Highlanders improved upon their previous season's win total by 23 games, largest such increase in franchise history.
- Lou Gehrig, MLB record for grand slams.
- Don Mattingly's number retired, August 31, 1997.

24

- In 1927, 24 of Lou Gehrig's 47 home runs were hit at the Stadium.
- Yankee record for most times hit by pitch in a season, Don Baylor, 1985.

25

- Gene Michael, 25th Yankee manager in history.
- Fewest total players used in a season, 1923, and 1927.
- Most consecutive games with a home run, 1941.
- Mel Allen spent 25 years in his first term as Yankee broadcaster (1939–1964).

26

- No Yankee pitcher has won 26 games in a regular season since Lefty Gomez in 1934.
- Only Joe DiMaggio and Mickey Mantle recorded more hits by age 26 than Derek Jeter.

27

- Number of general managers that worked during George Steinbrenner's tenure.

27.6

- Average age of what was arguably the best team of all time, the 1927 Yankees.

28

- Of the 60 record-setting home runs hit by Babe Ruth in 1927, 28 were at Yankee Stadium.

29

- Joe DiMaggio, most homers by a Yankee rookie, 1939.
- Mel Allen was a Yankee broadcaster for 29 seasons, television and radio.
- Whitey Ford over a 16-year career allowed but 29 bases to be stolen off him.
- Paul O'Neill was awarded the 29th plaque in Monument Park.

30

- Wee Willie Keeler's bat length, measured in inches, shortest ever.
- Yogi Berra, most home runs in a season by a Yankee catcher, 1952, and 1956.
- Eddie Lopat, Mel Stottlemyre and Willie Randolph all wore Number 30.
- Of Roger Maris's 61 home runs in 1961, 30 were hit at Yankee Stadium.

31

- Bobby Richardson retired from the Yankees at the age of 31 and became baseball coach at the University of South Carolina.

32

- Most passed balls as a team in a season, 1913.
- When Combs became a Yankee coach in 1936, he chose uniform #32.

- Uniform number of Elston Howard, retired July 21, 1984.
- Number of Yankee managers all time through Joe Girardi.

33

- Second longest hitting streak in franchise history, Hal Chase, 1907.
- Number worn by Bill Dickey as Yankee coach.

33¹/₃

- Mariano Rivera's longest post-season scoreless innings pitched.

34

- Pitcher Foster Edwards in 1930 was the first Yankee to wear this number.

35

- Outfielder Dixie Walker in 1931 was the first Yankee to wear this number.

36

- Frank Crosetti wore Yankees pinstripes for a record 36 years.
- Reggie Jackson was the 36th Yankee elected to the Hall of Fame.

37

- Of the 37 players who performed for the 1949 Yankees, only Yogi Berra still played for the team in 1960.
- Casey Stengel's number, retired 1970.

38

- The Yankees belted more than 100 home runs per season 38 times from 1920 to 1961.
- Number of career homers hit by Phil Rizzuto.

39

- Joe DiMaggio, number of attempted career steals.
- Most consecutive winning seasons, 1926 to 1964.
- Alfonso Soriano, most home runs by a second basemen, set in 2002.

40

- The original Yankee Stadium had 40 turnstiles that ticked like clocks, tallying up the gate.
- Number of pounds Babe Ruth lost to play his younger self in 1942's Pride of the Yankees.
- Phil Rizzuto spent parts of 40 seasons as a Yankee broadcaster.
- Mickey Mantle, most total RBIs in World Series play.

41

- In 1904, the record number of games won by Highlanders hurler Jack Chesbro.

42

- Willie Keeler, most sacrifice hits one season by a Yankee, 1905.
- Mariano Rivera, last player to wear Number 42, retired by Major League Baseball to honor of Jackie Robinson.

43

- 1994 Yankees lost 43 games in a strike-shortened season.
- Alfonso Soriano, 43 stolen bases, Yankee rookie record, 2001.

44

- 1927 Yankees, fewest franchise defeats in a full season.
- Reggie Jackson's number, retired in 1993.

45

- Forty-five different players wore the Yankee uniform in 1913, including seven catchers.

46

- Don Mattingly's rookie number.
- Mickey Mantle and Derek Jeter played their final home game on the same date, September 25, and the final game of their careers on the same date, September 28, in the same ballpark, Fenway Park, 46 years apart.

- Dave Righetti set a big league record in 1986 for saves, since surpassed.
- Andy Pettitte's number, retired.

47

- Most home losses by the Yankees, 1908, 1913.
- The 1979 Yankees had 47 batters, a franchise record.

48

- Jack Chesbro, most complete games in a season, 1904.

49

- Lou Gehrig, career high most homers in a season by a Yankee first baseman, 1934, 1936.
- Yogi Berra threw out 49 percent of would-be base stealers.
- Most players used in a season by a Yankee team, 1989.
- Ron Guidry's number, retired 2003.

50

- Fewest wins in a season by a Yankee team, 1912.
- The bat Babe Ruth slammed his 50th home run with in 1920 was auctioned off to raise money to help starving Armenians in Turkey.
- Number of games saved by Mariano Rivera in 2001, new team record, third-highest total in AL history.

51

- Number worn by Bernie Williams for sixteen Yankee seasons. He is one of 13 players to wear Number 51. His tenure was the longest, 1991 to 2006. Two future Hall of Famers who wore that number on other teams—Ichiro Suzuki and Randy Johnson—were given other numbers as Yankees. Williams was given Number 51 because an equipment manager thought he played like Willie McGee, the Cardinal great outfielder at the time who wore the number.

52

- The first Yankee to wear this number was Johnny Lucadello in 1947. C. C. Sabathia has worn the number since 2009.
- Doyle Alexander in 1976 played his only season with the Yankees and wore Number 52.

53

- Don Mattingly, most doubles in a season by a Yankee, 1986.
- Mariano Rivera saves in 2004, new team record, third-highest total in AL history.

54

- Most road wins in a season, 1939.
- Mickey Mantle, most home runs by switch-hitter, 54 in 1961.
- "Goose" Gossage and Aroldis Chapman, shared this number many years apart.

55

- Number worn by Hideki Matsui in tribute to Japan's legend Sadaharu Oh's record 55 home runs in a season.

56

- Joe DiMaggio's 56-game hitting streak included 56 singles and runs scored.
- Number assigned to Jim Bouton in spring training 1962. When it was obvious that the rookie was going to make the team, he was given Number 27. But Bouton wanted to keep Number 56 to "remind me of how close I was to not making the team."
- Dave Righetti's rookie number.

57

- The 1927 Yankees won 57 games at Yankee Stadium, tying an American League record.

58

- Mariano Rivera's original number.

58.4%

- Stolen base percentage of the 1927 Yankees, fifth in the league. With their power, base stealing was not a priority.

59

- Juan Rivera was the last Yankee to wear this number, 2002 to 2003.

60

- Babe Ruth's record setting home run total produced 100 RBIs.

61*

- The film 61* was shot in Detroit, not Yankee Stadium. Filmmaker Billy Crystal explained that the look of the ballpark there resembled the 1961 Yankee Stadium more closely than the current Yankee Stadium at the time of the film's shooting in 2000.

62

- Number of strikeouts Allie Reynolds recorded in 15 World Series games.

63

- During his 56-game hitting streak, Joe DiMaggio hit safely against 63 right-handed pitchers.
- On August 13, 1995, Mickey Mantle died of complications from liver cancer at the age of 63.
- Original number given to Bernade Figueroa "Bernie" Williams, 1991.

65

- The number of games Mickey Mantle played in 12 World Series.

66

- Yankee players who wore number 66: Steve Baboni, Jim DeShales, Juan Miranda, Andrew Brackman and J. R. Murphy

68

- Dione Navarro and Dellin Batances wore this number for the Yankees.

69

- Alan Mills in 1990 wore this number for the Yankees.

71

- Yogi Berra, most career hits in the World Series.

72

- Games won by the Highlanders in their first season.
- Babe Ruth set a Major League record by homering twice in a game 72 times.
- Mariano Rivera earned his first save on May 17, 1996, against the Angels at the Stadium. Andy Pettitte got the win. Rivera saved 72 of Pettitte's wins, a record for any starter/closer combination.

73

- Gary Sanchez wore this number in 2015.

74

- Franchise record for stolen bases set by Fritz Maisel in 1914, broken by Rickey Henderson in 1985.
- Derek Jeter wore Number 74 in his first spring training in 1994. The next year Yankees equipment manager Rob Cucuzza gave Jeter Number 2.

75

- Yogi Berra appeared in 75 World Series games, most in baseball history.

77

- Humberto Sanchez wore this number in 2008.

80

- A 10–5 triumph over Oakland on August 4, 1998, in the second game of a doubleheader gave the Yankees 80 wins in their 108th game, earliest in franchise history.

81

- No one ever wore this Yankee uniform number.

82

- Most times caught stealing in a season, 1920, a franchise record.

83

- Of 158 home runs hit by the 1927 Yankees, 83 were hit at Yankee Stadium.

88

- Number of pitches David Cone tossed in perfect game, July 19, 1999, with 68 strikes and 20 balls.

89

- The Yankees and the Orioles played to a 1–1 tie September 30, 2001, in 15 innings, the 89th tie in franchise history. It was Cal Ripken's last game at Yankee Stadium.

91

- The fewest errors in a season— Yankees, 1996.
- Number worn by Alfredo Aceves.

93

- Most stolen bases by a Yankee in a season, Rickey Henderson, 1988.

95

- Dave Righetti's no-hitter on July 4th, was pitched on a day temperature at the Stadium reached 95 degrees.

95.1%

- Although part of the first Hall of Fame inductee class, Babe Ruth was strangely not voted in unanimously. He received 95.1 percent of the votes.

96.88

- Dan Topping, Larry MacPhail and Del Webb purchased this percentage of the Yankees from Jacob Ruppert's estate in January of 1945.

97

- Don Larsen used this number of pitches to hurl his perfect game against the Dodgers at Yankee Stadium in the 1956 World Series.

99

- The highest uniform number ever issued by the New York Yankees went to Charlie Keller (1952) and Brian Bruney (2009).

100

- Only two Yankee clubs have lost more than 100 games in a season: 1912, with a record of 50–102, and 1908, with a record of 51–103.
- Babe Ruth on September 24, 1920, hit his 100th home run. It was off Washington's Jim Shaw.
- Derek Jeter became, along with Earl Combs and Ted Williams, the only one to score a 100 runs in each of their first seven seasons.

101

- Charlie Keller was the first ever Yankees player to strike out over 100 times in a single-season, when we whiffed 101 times in 1946.

104

- Bill Virdon, Manager of the Year award winner in 1974, was fired after 104 games in 1975.

112

- Top franchise base-stealing duo in one season, 1914, Fritz Maisel, 74, and Roger Peckinpaugh, 38.

114

- Most wins in a season by an AL franchise, 1998, until the 2001 Mariners won 116.

115

- Mantle and Maris clubbed a total of 115 homers, the most by teammates in one season.

117

- Yogi Berra caught both games of a doubleheader 117 times.

119

- In 1921, Babe Ruth collected the most extra base hits in one season: 44 doubles, 16 triples and 59 home runs.

120

- Number of pitches thrown in his perfect game on May 17, 1998, David Wells.

121

- The number of consecutive postseason games Bob Sheppard worked for the Yankees.

123

- Most games completed by a Yankee pitching staff, 1904.
- Babe Ruth stole 123 bases in his career. He was also caught stealing 117 times. In the postseason, he stole 4 and was caught 3 times.

126

- The number of games that Cal Ripken played at Yankee Stadium—more than any other opposing player (June 18, 1982–September 30, 2001).

129

- Jack Reed's only career home run in 129 at bats came in the 22nd inning on June 24, 1962, giving the Yankees a 9–7 victory over the Tigers.

134

- Number of home runs hit by the Highlanders/Yankees at Hilltop Park, 1903 to 1912.

135

- Number of pitches Doc Gooden threw in his no-hitter on May 14, 1996.

139

- On July 18, 1921, Ruth hit his 139th career homer, breaking Roger Connor's record. From that point on each homer the "Big Bam" hit extended his record.

146

- Mickey Mantle in 1957 received the most bases on balls to a switch-hitter during a single season in Major League history.

148

- May 12, 1959, Yogi Berra's errorless streak of 148 games came to an end when he committed an error on his 34th birthday.

154

- Career triples by Earle Combs, second in franchise history to Lou Gehrig.

156

- Danny Tartabull, 1993, most strikeouts in a season—he played in only 133 games.

158

- Record number of postseason games played in by Derek Jeter.

161

- During the regular season Mickey Mantle recorded 161 career home runs batting right-handed.

162

- Most games played in a season: Bobby Richardson (1961), Roy White (1970, 1973) Chris Chambliss (1978), Don Mattingly (1986) and Roberto Kelly (1990).

163

- Lou Gehrig, most career triples, a Major League record.
- In 2003, Hideki Matsui played in 163 games, set a new franchise record for games played in the regular season.

170

- Babe Ruth, most walks in a season, 1923.

173

- Lefty Gomez is second all-time Yankee leader in complete games.

174

- The number of pitches Doc Gooden threw in his no-hitter on May 14, 1996.

177

- Babe Ruth, most runs scored in a season.

179

- Babe Ruth was charged with 179 errors in his career.
- Most home runs allowed by a Yankee pitching staff, 1987.

.183

- Yankee team batting average in 2001 World Series, lowest for a team in a series that went 7 or 8 games.

184

- Lou Gehrig, most RBIs one season, American League record.

184

- Number of working days it took 500 workers to build the original Yankee Stadium. They beat by a day the amount of days Yankee owner Ruppert had demanded.

200

- Babe Ruth recorded his 200th home run on May 12, 1923, in Detroit off Herman Pilette.
- Only Babe Ruth and Lou Gehrig on the 1927 Yankees weighed more than 200 pounds.

201

- Backup catcher Charlie Silvera played in a total of 201 games from 1948 to 1956.

203

- Section or area where the Bleacher Creatures, rowdy and rabid fans of the Yankees, typically sit, chanting "Roll Call" and other things.

236

- Whitey Ford, career wins, team record.

238

- From 1913 to 1922, the Yankees hit 238 home runs at the Polo Grounds, their home field then.
- Don Mattingly, number of hits in 1986 season.

239

- Bill Dickey struck out just 289 times in 6,300 career at bats.

240

- Most team home runs in a season in franchise history, 1961.

.241

- The 1990 Yankees batted an American League low .241 as a team.

.245

- The fewest hits given up by a Yankee pitching staff, 1903.

248

- Hal Chase, career stolen bases with the franchise.
- Ron Guidry, most strikeouts in a season, 1978, team record.

251

- Number of home runs hit at Yankee Stadium by Lou Gehrig.

252

- The amount of bases stolen by the 1914 Yankees.

259

- Babe Ruth hammered 259 home runs at Yankee Stadium.
- Yogi Berra, most World Series career at bats, a Major League record.
- Wally Pipp ranks fourth in career triples with 259.

261

- Red Ruffing, most Yankee career complete games.

266

- Mickey Mantle hit an all-time record 266 homers at Yankee Stadium, 1951 to 1968.

275

- Number of career home runs hit by Roger Maris (not all with Yankees) and Jorge Posada.

Traded from the Red Sox in 1930, pitcher Red Ruffing winds up before a game.

276.2

- Andy Pettitte post-season records: innings 276.2, wins 19 and is second in strikeouts, 183.

289

- The most bases stolen in a season by a Yankee team, 1910.

300

- Babe Ruth hit his 300th homer on September 8, 1925, off Buster Ross of Boston.
- Roger Clemens becomes the 21st pitcher in Major League history to win his 300th game, June 13, 2003. He is the first Yankee to win it in front of the home fans.
- Number of quarts of ice cream presented to Joe DiMaggio on his day, 1949.

.309

- Highest Yankee team batting average for a season, 1930. Six Yankee regulars batted over .300.

321

- Number of wins Casey Stengel had with his Oakland Oaks team in PCL before he became Yankee manager.

326

- Franchise leading stolen base total, Rickey Henderson.

332

- Home run total for the Yankees at their home park the Polo Grounds, 1913 to 1922.

.349

- Highest career batting average, Babe Ruth, 1920 to 1934.

.361

- Lou Gehrig, lifetime batting average, 34 World Series games.

361

- Joe DiMaggio Yankee career number of home runs.

.362

- Bill Dickey batting average in 1936, tops ever for a catcher.

372

- Number of regular season homers Mickey Mantle hit batting left-handed.

382

- Most season errors, 1912 Yankees.

.393

- Highest season batting average, Babe Ruth, 1923.

394

- Yankee pitching staff, fewest runs allowed in a season, 1904.

400

- Babe Ruth recorded his 400th career home run, September 12, 1927, off Philadelphia's Rube Walberg.

$400

- Funds paid to Mickey Mantle in 1949 to finish out his minor league season.

407

- The record for most homers by a father and son team was held by Yogi Berra and Dale Berra. It was surpassed by Bobby Bonds and Barry Bonds.

.408

- Joe DiMaggio's average in his 56-game hitting streak.

413

- Smallest attendance for a game at Yankee Stadium, September 22, 1966.

420

- Fewest strikeouts in a season for a Yankee team, 1924.

.421

- Mickey Mantle's career on-base percentage, Major League record for highest on-base percentage by a switch-hitter.

438

- Whitey Ford and Andy Pettitte are tied for most career starts for the Yankees in the regular season.

454²/₃

- Number of innings Jack Chesbro pitched for the Highlanders, 1904.

457

- Babe Ruth's number of total bases in 1921, all time season record: 85 singles, 44 doubles, 16 triples, 59 home runs.
- Before Yankee Stadium's renovation in 1976, the left-center field alley at Yankee Stadium was some 457 feet from home-plate. The area around the flagpole had no name other than the "Monuments." It was in the field of play.

459

- Fewest runs scored in a season by a Yankee team, 1908.

.471

- Joe Torre's career winning percentage as a manager before he came to the Yankees in 1996.

493

- Most home runs in a career by a first baseman, Lou Gehrig.

.498

- The 1927 Yankees slugging percentage, all-time best.

500

- Babe Ruth slammed his 500th home run on August 11, 1929, at Cleveland.
- Alex Rodriguez hit his 500th home run August 4, 2007.
- A-Rod, Babe Ruth and Mickey Mantle are in the Yankee "500" homer club.

514

- Horace Clarke, most put-outs in a season, 1970.

518

- Number of consecutive games played in by Hideki Matsui at the start of his Yankee career to set a new Major League record.

.521

- In 1957, Mickey Mantle set the Major League record for highest on-base percentage by a switch-hitter in a single season.

522

- Number of games Dave Righetti appeared in as a pitcher, franchise record.

536

- Mickey Mantle hit 373 left-handed homeruns and 163 from the right side. His 536 homeruns are the most ever by a switch-hitter.

545

- Babe Ruth, 1923, record on-base percentage.

548

- Bobby Brown, American League president from 1984 to 1994, played in 548 games for the Yankees and on four world championship teams.

.557

- Mickey Mantle's career slugging average—the Major League record for highest slugging average by a switchhitter in a career.

565

- Total number of games Billy Martin won as Yankee manager; lost 385.

600

- On August 21, 1931, Babe Ruth recorded his 600th career home run in St. Louis.

602

- Mariano Rivera's total of career saves, all-time record.

.623

- Casey Stengel, second highest career winning percentage for a Yankees manager.

.627

- Joe McCarthy, highest career winning percentage for a Yankees manager.

659

- Number of home runs Babe Ruth stroked as a Yankee from 1920 to 1934.

692

- Bobby Richardson, most at bats one season, 1962.

700

- Babe Ruth slammed home run 700 at Detroit on July 13, 1934, off Tommy Bridges.

701

- In his career, George Herman Ruth played at least one game in each position in the batting order. Batting in the 3 or 4 spot, he hit 701 of his 714 homers.

.704

- The Yankees in 1998 won 111 and lost 48 for .704 winning percentage.

.705

- In 1956, Mickey Mantle posted a career high .705 slugging average—the Major League record for a switch-hitter in a single season.

714

- Babe Ruth's career total of home runs, a record that was broken later by Hank Aaron.

757

- Frank Crosetti, most at bats in a season, 1938.

766

- The 1932 Yankees drew the most walks in a season. Babe Ruth had 130. Lou Gehrig had 108.

783

- All-time record number of homers by teammates Babe Ruth, 434 and Lou Gehrig, 349.

.800

- The Yankees in 1939 went 44–11 in their first fifty-five games.

.862

- The Yankees established a record .862 winning percentage in July 1941, going 25–4.

.891

- The slugging percentage Reggie Jackson recorded as a Yankee in the World Series.

955

- Career wins for Casey Stengel as manager.

.988

- Yogi Berra's exceptional lifetime fielding average.

996

- The amount of hits for Derek Jeter (1996–2000) were the most of any Major Leaguer.

1,000

- Second baseman Joe Gordon played exactly 1,000 games with the Yankees and collected exactly 1,000 hits.
- On May 5, 2001, Alex Rodriguez recorded his 1,000th career hit, singling against the White Sox.

- The number of losses Joe Torre had in 1996 when he began as Yankee manager.

1,043

- Most strikeouts in a season by a Yankee team, 1967.

1,067

- Most runs scored in one season by a Yankee team, 1931.

1,115

- Number of career appearances by pitcher Mariano Rivera, fourth most in baseball history.

1,137

- Fewest hits by a team in one season, 1968.

1,149

- Number of victories for Casey Stengel in a dozen years managing the Yankees.

1,172

- Dave Winfield, number of games he played as a Yankee.

1,173

- Joe Torre's number of victories as Yankee manager.

1,245

- The continuation of the "Pine Tar Game" between the Yankees and Royals drew just 1,245 fans to witness what could have been just four outs of play. The continuation lasted for nine minutes and 41 seconds.

1,330

- Babe Ruth struck out 1,330 times.

1,460

- Joe McCarthy holds the franchise's all-time record for most wins by a manager.

1,507

- Most innings pitched by a Yankee staff, one season, 1984.

1,511

- In Joe Sewell's career at bats with the Yankees, he struck out only 15 times. He fanned just three times in 503 at bats in 1932.

1,658

- The number of games Willie Randolph played at second base, more than any other Yankee.

1,677

- Mickey Mantle is third in all-time runs scored behind Babe Ruth and Lou Gehrig.

1,683

- Most hits by a Yankee team in a season, 1930.

1,710

- Number of times Mickey Mantle struck out in his career.

1903

- In the late 1990s, the same clubhouse safe used by players on the 1903 Yankees, with names like Chesbro, Griffith and Keeler stitched on the side of the safe, was found.

1912

- Black pinstripes first appeared on the uniforms of the Highlanders/Yankees during their final season at Hilltop Park. Pinstripes were not present in 1913 and 1914, but were brought back for good in 1915.

- Newspapers were calling the New York Highlanders the Yankees more and more.

1921

- In the World Series of 1921, it was brother versus brother—Bob Meusel of the Yankees against Emil Meusel of the Giants. It was the first time in baseball history that the World Series was played at one stadium, the Polo Grounds, the last best-of-nine game World Series.
- The year the Baby Ruth candy bar was introduced, the manufacturer denied it had anything to do with the Sultan of Swat. The claim was that it was a tribute to Grover Cleveland's late daughter Ruth.
- On May 21, Col. Ruppert bought out Tillinghast Huston as Yankee owner. $1.5 million changed hands. Huston made a 650 percent profit for his seven-year ownership (allowing for inflation, that is $21 million in today's dollars).

1923

- "The Yankee Stadium" opens, the proudest moment in the history of the Bronx.

1927

- Six players and one manager from that fabled team, whose average team age was 27.6, became Hall of Famers: Babe Ruth, Lou Gehrig, Herb Pennock, Miller Huggins, Waite Hoyt, Earle Combs and Tony Lazzeri.
- Seating capacity that '27 season at the stadium was 62,000.
- Tony Lazzeri's contract for the season was $8,000 plus round trip train fare for him and his wife from San Francisco to New York City and back.

World Series program from 1927, the year Ruth and Gehrig combined to slug 107 home runs.

1929

- In 1929, the New York Yankees introduced identifying numbers sewn on the backs of player jerseys. The first time that uniform numbers were used on a full-time basis, the "original" ten numbers were: #1 Earle Combs, #2 Mark Koenig, #3 Babe Ruth, #4 Lou Gehrig, #5 Bob Meusel, #6 Tony Lazzeri, #7 Leo Durocher, #8 Johnny Grabowski, #9 Benny Bengough, #10 Bill Dickey.
- A stampede in the right field bleachers during a sudden thunderstorm at Yankee Stadium that killed two people and left 62 injured ended the practice of selling more tickets than existing seats.

1936

- George Selkirk became the first Yankee to hit a home run in his first World Series at bat.
- The first Baseball Hall of Fame was the class of 1936. Babe Ruth was inducted along with Ty Cobb, Honus Wagner, Walter Johnson and Christy Mathewson.

President Franklin D. Roosevelt throwing out the first ball in D.C. for the Yankees-Washington game, Opening Day, 1936.

1959

- Babe Ruth set the franchise record for most runs scored in a season, 1920.

1965

- The year the longest-running Yankee promotion, Bat Day, debuts.
- September 7, Roy White, age 21, made his debut with the Yankees.

1977

- The Yankees become the first team to serve as host of both the All-Star Game and the World Series in the same season.

1989

- John Sterling became the play-by-play radio voice of the Yankees in 1989. He has never missed a single game. ("I have not missed a game I was supposed to work," he said. "I am blessed with a good immune system.")

1939

- The Yankees were the first team to retire a number—that of the terminally ill Lou Gehrig.

1941

- Yankee president Ed Barrow offered Civil Defense the use of Yankee Stadium in 1941 as a bomb shelter in case of attack. His reasoning was the area under the stands could provide a safe haven. He was not taken up on his offer.

1946

- The Yankees became the first team to regularly travel by airplane.
- Year the Yankees played their first night game at Yankee Stadium. They had 14 scheduled night games.
- Year the Yankees logo with the "bat-in-the-hat" first debuted.

1953

- The Yankees won their fifth straight World Series.

- Jerry Coleman Day held to acknowledge his Korean War service is staged at Yankee Stadium on September 13. A crowd of 48,492 came out to pay tribute.

1956

- Amazing Mickey Mantle numbers that season: first in slugging percentage, runs scored, RBIs and home runs.

John Sterling in the announcer's booth, where he coined his trademark expression "Thuuuhh pitch . . ."

1990

- It was the first time in Steinbrenner's tenure that his team wound up in last place. Despite the failures, the Yankees drew over two million fans into the Stadium. The team's best player was Jesse Barfield, with a .246 average and 25 homers. He also fanned 150 times becoming the first Yankee to earn that dishonor.

1995

- Lou Gehrig, career franchise record for RBIs.
- The number of career RBIs posted by Lou Gehrig despite batting behind Babe Ruth.
- Four youngsters made their big-league debuts for the Yankees in the 1995 season: Andy Pettitte, Mariano Rivera, Derek Jeter and Jorge Posada. The Core Four.

1997

- "In the winter of 1997, there was digging down three feet for a new sewer line. We came upon flagstones. I knew what they were right away. They were the flagstones from the 1923 walkway that had led fans from the field at the stadium out into the street." —Bob Wilkinson, stadium superintendent

2007

- The Yankees ran their playoff streak to 13 consecutive seasons.

2008

- The Yankees total won-lost-tie record at the old Yankee Stadium before moving to the new one in 2009 was: 4,133 wins, 2,430 defeats and 17 ties.

2011

- This season saw the Yankees clinch their 16th postseason appearance in the past 17 years.

2012

- The Yankees clinched the American League East for the 13th time in the last 17 seasons.

2014

- On April 17th at Tampa Bay, the Yanks recorded their 24th triple play in franchise history.
- Racked by injuries, the Yankees called on the services of 58 different players this season setting a franchise record.

2,120

- The number of games Babe Ruth played in for Yankees, from 1920 to 1934.

2,130

- Number of consecutive games Lou Gehrig played in.

2,153

- The number of career hits posted by Don Mattingly.

2,267

- In 16 years as a manager with five different franchises, Billy Martin managed 2,267 games. He won 1,253, lost 1,013. The franchise that he truly belonged to was the New York Yankees.

2,385

- Number of backless seats spread over 27 rows behind the right-field fence in the bleachers at the original Yankee Stadium.

2,743

- Derek Jeter, most regular season games played in by a Yankee.

3,000

- Alex Rodriguez was the 29th player to record 3,000 hits, not all as a Yankee.

3,461

- Derek Jeter career hit total.

3,654

- Number of home runs the Yankees hit at old Yankee Stadium, from 1923 to 1973.

4,000 PLUS

- Bob Sheppard was the Yankee public address announcer for more than 4,000 games.

$5,000

- Reward promised to the person who caught the 61st home run ball of Roger Maris. Sal Durante collected the money.

5,705

- Most at bats in one season by a Yankee club, 1964.

$6,000

- Amount Don Larsen received for being on Bob Hope's TV show after he pitched his perfect game in 1956, almost $53,000 is today's dollars.

6,581

- Original Yankee Stadium through 86 years hosted 6,581 Yankees regular season home games.

$6,595.38

- Amount payable in 1927 in biweekly checks to Babe Ruth, about $91,000 in today's dollars.

$7,500

- Mickey Mantle's 1951 rookie salary, around $69,000 in today's dollars.

$8,500

- Joe DiMaggio's rookie season salary, 1936, around $147,000 in today's dollars.

The imposing edifice of Yankee Stadium, shaped along the lines of the Roman Coliseum.

8,001

- Lou Gehrig's career at bats.

10,000

- Claudel Washington's pinch-hit home run on April 20, 1988, at Minnesota off Jeff Reardon was the club's 10,000th home run.

$10,000

- Average 1927 Yankee salary was $10,000. It ranged from Julie Wera's $2,400 to Babe Ruth's $70,000.

10,622

- Hank Aaron broke Babe Ruth's career home run and RBI records. It took the Babe 10,622 plate appearances. Aaron needed 13,941.

15,000

- The Yankees played their 15,000th regular season game defeating Tampa Bay on July 22, 1999. Their all-time record to that point in time was 8,451–6,463 plus 86 tie games.

$18,000

- Amount spent to purchase the Baltimore franchise in 1903 and transfer it to New York City, $479,000 in today's dollars.

20,000

- Letters that Mickey Mantle never answered and were not bid on in the old Yankee Stadium fire sale in 1974.

23,154

- Attendance at Yankee Stadium when Roger Maris hit home run number 61 that season of 1961.

32,238

- Attendance at the final game at old Yankee Stadium, September 30, 1973.

$35,000

- Salary of Don Mattingly in 1983 that increased to $4,420,000 by 1995.

$50,000

- Amount offered by the New York Giants to the Yankees for Yogi Berra at the start of his career.

51,800

- Seating capacity of new Yankee when it opened April 2009.

56,717

- The biggest Opening Day crowd at the remodeled Yankee Stadium (1976–2008) was April 10, 1998, against Oakland. The Yankees won that game, 17–13. Despite the 30 runs and 32 hits combined, there was only one home run—a three-run shot by Tino Martinez.

64,519

- Attendance at Yankee Stadium the day in 1956 when Don Larsen pitched the perfect game.

$65,000

- Amount paid by Gillette and Ford to televise the 1947 World Series, shown only in New York City, about $700,000 in today's dollars.
- Highest salary reportedly paid to Phil Rizzuto, 1951. That is $600,000 in today's dollars.

83,533

- The largest crowd, doubleheader with Red Sox, May 30, 1938.

$100,000

- Liebmann Brewery offered this amount to televise the 1947 World Series. Baseball Commissioner Chandler passed on the offer deeming it inappropriate to have a series sponsor be a producer of alcoholic beverages, around $1,073,000 in today's dollars.

$109,000

- Derek Jeter's salary in 1995 as a Yankee.

$130,000

- Derek Jeter's earnings as a Yankee in 1996.

$230,000

- Til Huston impressed everyone by peeling off 230 thousand dollar bills—his share of the purchase price of the Yankees on January 11, 1915.

$250,000

- The estimated total payroll for the 1927 Yankees, about $3,455,930.47 in today's dollars.

$300,000

- Total proceeds from the 1973 "fire sale" of Yankee Stadium items.

$416,400

- Lou Gehrig, estimated career earnings as a Yankee.

$451,541

- Uniform Lou Gehrig wore during his Farewell speech in 1939 sold for this amount in 1999.

$600,000

- In 1946, Larry MacPhail supervised massive and costly improvements at Yankee Stadium, about $7,360,876.28 in today's dollars.

$1 MILLION

- When a group headed by George Steinbrenner III purchased the Yankees from CBS, for a true bargain price, the City of New York paid more than $1 million for a parking lot as part of the package.

1,007,066

- First-season attendance at Yankee Stadium, 1923.

1,230,000

- Attendance at the Polo Grounds in Babe Ruth's first season as a Yankee.

2,561,123

- Shea Stadium attendance for the Yankees, from 1974 to 1975.

$2.8 MILLION

- On January 25, 1945, price Dan Topping, Del Webb and Larry MacPhail paid to purchase the Yankees from the estate of Col. Jacob Ruppert.

3,451,542

- Attendance at Hilltop Park, from 1903 to 1912.

3,719,358

- Attendance in 2009, first year in the new Yankee Stadium.

4,090,696

- Paid attendance at Yankee Stadium in 2005.

4.3 MILLION

- Yankee 2008 home attendance is the highest in Major League history.

6,220,031

- Attendance at the Polo Grounds for the Yankees, from 1913 to 1922.

$10 MILLION

- The amount George Steinbrenner and his group paid to purchase the Yankees, Steinbrenner's personal contribution to the sale was an estimated $600,000 to $700,000.

$11.2 MILLION

- Amount Dan Topping and Del Webb sold the Yankees to CBS for in 1964, about $86,501,511.31 in today's dollars.

$12,357,143

- Salary of Bernie Williams in 2001, sum greater than that earned by playoff competition Oakland infield and two outfielders.

$15 MILLION

- Mariano Rivera's annual salary from 2008 to 2012, the highest single-season salary for a relief pitcher in Major League history.

$25 MILLION

- Highest salaried Yankee in the 2016 season, C. C. Sabathia.

$39.9 MILLION

- In 2001, Mariano Rivera signed a four-year contract and became the highest paid relief pitcher ever, it was a far cry from his $3,000 signing bonus when he first became a Yankee.

$39.95 MILLION

- Prior to the 2005 season, the Yankees signed Carl Pavano to a four-year free agent deal. What they got for their money from Pavano was nine wins, a 5.00 ERA and a total of 145⅔.

60,010,531

- Total attendance at Yankee Stadium, from 1976 to 2001.

64,188,862

- Total attendance at Yankee Stadium, from 1923 to 1973.

$189 MILLION

- The amount of Derek Jeter's 10-year deal signed in 2001.

$200 MILLION

- The Yankees were the first team with a $200 million payroll.

$216,529,349

- Yankee payroll in 2016, lowered a bit from $228,000,000 in 2013.

$1 BILLION

- The Yankees failed to win a World Series from 2001 to 2006 despite huge salary expenditures of a billion dollars.

$1.5 BILLION

- Estimated cost of building the new Yankee Stadium.

$3.4 BILLION

- *Forbes* in March 2016 estimated the value of the New York Yankees.

Pitcher Bud Daley (center) shows his appreciation for the sluggers whose home runs led to victory over the Washington Senators on July 3, 1961.
From left: Bill Skowron, Roger Maris, Daley, Elston Howard and Mickey Mantle.

YANKEE DOODLE DANDIES

Assortment of all things Yankee—talkin' Yankees, oddities, spring training, greatest and worst team, uniform and logo, monuments, "meet me at the bat," Old-Timers' Day, apocryphal, lists and factoids

A miscellaneous collection of a variety of takes on the Yankee experience, from the ordinary to the arcane, from the top to the bottom, from the apocryphal to the amazing, it is all Yankee Doodle Dandies.

FACTOIDS, TRIVIA, LISTS AND ODDITIES

Yankees

A reference with the name "Yankees" first appeared in print in the *Boston Herald* in 1904. It referred to the American League baseball team in New York City. Sportswriters Sam Crane of the *New York Journal* and Mark Roth of the *New York Globe* are credited with first using the name "Yankees" in their writing about the team.

Logo

The iconic "bat in the hat" logo was introduced in 1947. It has been the Yankees' primary logo ever since. The artwork was originally credited to Henry Alonzo Keller, a sports illustrator who worked in New York. However, the *New York Times* reported in 2009 that the logo could have other origins.

According to the family of Sam Friedman, an artist who worked at the "21" club in the 1940s and '50s, it was their ancestor who sketched the logo onto a bar napkin for Dan Topping, a regular "21" patron. The Yankee owner allegedly immediately decided that would be the new logo for his team. That Yankee logo is the oldest still in use in the Major Leagues.

Shame

Negro League teams who played at the Stadium when the Yankees were on the road were not allowed to use their dressing rooms. Instead they were obliged to use the visitors' dressing room.

Unlikely Friendship

Pitcher Herb Pennock was born to a wealthy Pennsylvania family and graduated from elite prep schools. Babe Ruth was raised in an orphanage. Pennock was refined, dignified, sophisticated. The great Ruth was the opposite of Pennock. Nevertheless, they were friends for almost three decades. The friendship began when both were young lefty hurlers for the Boston Red Sox in 1916. The unusual friendship continued when they were teammates on the Yankees in the 1920s and 1930s.

On the Radio

WJZ 770 (1939–1940), WOR 710 (1942), WINS 1010 (1944–1957), WMGM 1050 (1958–1960), WCBS 880 (1961–1966), WHN 1050 (1967–1970), WMCA 570 (1971–1977), WINS 1010 (1978–1980), WABC 770 (1981–2001), WCBS 880 (2002–2013), WFAN 660 AM and WFAN-FM 101.9 (2014–present).

The official fight song for the Yankees, "Here Come the Yankees," was written in 1967 by Bob Bundin and Lou Stallman. Not used too often now at Yankee Stadium, it is still frequently played in instrumental form, most times in radio broadcasts.

Monuments

The first monument honoring a Yankee legend was created in 1932 for Miller

Huggins. Monuments and plaques were located in center field in front of the fence as part of the playing field, about 450 feet or so from home plate. Outfielders always had to be wary running back for long fly balls. At one time, ticket holders exited through the center field gates, viewing monuments on their way out of the Stadium. The monuments were on the field, in front of the fence. Starting in 1976, the monuments and plaques were behind the fence in Monument Park.

Yank Newsletter

Created by Larry MacPhail, the *Yank* newsletter was first published in 1946 and had a long run. It was published about six times a year. Its final season was 1967, when it was published in a newspaper format.

Travel by Airplane

In 1946, the Yankees became the first team to regularly travel by airplane. The team leased a United Airlines plane nicknamed the "Yankee Mainliner." Despite the advantages of flying, four players, including Red Ruffing, still chose to take the train.

Mascot

The Yankees are one of four teams today lacking a mascot. From 1982 until 1985, the team mascot was Dandy, a pinstriped bird. That did not work out.

Hideki Matsui

Before becoming a Yankee, Hideki Matsui recorded the second-longest consecutive games played streak in Japanese baseball history—1,250 straight games.

Elaine's

George Steinbrenner liked to dine at Elaine's on Second Avenue in Manhattan. With his team at home, he would often partake of an early supper.

Mantle's Locker

Yankee outfielder and future broadcaster Bobby Murcer took over Mickey Mantle's locker after "the Mick" retired in 1968.

YOGI BERRA, MOSTS, A PARTIAL LIST

Most post-season games—Yogi Berra holds the record for appearing in the most postseason games—75. In his 19-year career, Berra and the New York Yankees went to the postseason 14 times. Since Berra played during the years before divisional play, all of the games he appeared in were World Series games, meaning he also holds the record for most World Series games appeared in. The great Yankee also holds the record for most World Series at bats with 259, and is third behind Mickey Mantle and Babe Ruth in World Series homeruns with 12.

Yogi Berra, Everywhere!

- Bill Bevens's no-hitter broken up by "Cookie" Lavagetto October 3, 1947; Yogi was there as the Yankees' catcher.
- Sandy Amoros catch October 4, 1955; Yogi was there as Yankee catcher and smacked the ball that Amoros caught down the left field line.
- Don Larsen's perfect game, October 8, 1956; Yogi was the catcher.
- Bill Mazeroski's home run, October 13, 1960; Yogi was there as the Yankees' left fielder.
- Home Run Number 61 by Roger Maris, October 1, 1961; Yogi was there as Yankees' left fielder for part of the game.
- Willie McCovey's line shot to Bobby Richardson, October 16, 1962; Yogi was there as a part-time player on the bench.
- Chris Chambliss's home run in ALCS, October 14, 1976; Yogi was there as Yankees coach.
- Reggie Jackson's three home runs, October 18, 1977; Yogi was there as Yankees coach.

- The Bucky Dent Home Run, October 2, 1978; Yogi was there as Yankees coach.
- George Brett battles Goose Gossage, October 10, 1980; Yogi was there as Yankees coach.
- Yogi Berra was there after the Yankees fired Billy Martin on December 16, 1983, and took over as Yankee manager.
- David Cone's perfect game, July 19, 1999; Yogi was being honored on "Yogi Berra Day."
- On the field, in the dugout, in the clubhouse, throwing out a first ball, Lawrence Peter Berra did his thing during the 2001 World Series.

MEET ME AT THE BAT!

BRAD TURNOW: *A traditional meeting place began outside Old Yankee Stadium in 1975. This bat-shaped "smokestack" was constructed in 1975 for the refurbished original Yankee Stadium. Over the decades, the famous meeting place was the 138-foot-high baseball bat with Babe Ruth's signature and the Louisville Slugger logo. The old stadium needed a cover for a boiler stack and the Ruth bat served that purpose. The vent was an actual exhaust pipe that released steam from the old stadium. The structure was sponsored by the Hillerich and Bradsby Company.*

As fans approached the stadium, they would seek out the famous knob with the unraveling tape at the handle and then look for the famous Ruth logo on the barrel. The bat, located outside of Gate 4 of the old stadium, quickly became a meeting spot for fans of both teams. The term "Meet Me at the Bat" became a one-liner for all fans meeting someone at the Stadium. Chances were, if you were meeting someone at the Old Stadium, you met them at the bat.

There was a push by fans to have the iconic bat moved next to the new stadium after it opened in 2009, but that effort failed. Today the bat still stands near the old parking garage on 153rd Street and the Metro North Station repainted in a plain tan color with no logo or signature on it. Though it is not used much as a meeting place anymore, it reminds fans of the historic past of Old Yankee Stadium.

BABE RUTH'S BIRTHDAY

When applying for a passport for a trip to Japan, a mistake in Ruth's birthday was discovered. His father had made a mistake listing it when the Babe was enrolled at St. Mary's school. "What the hell difference does it make?" said the great Yankee, referring to the date that he continued to acknowledge as his birthday—February 7. According to the official records in Baltimore, Maryland, Ruth was born on February 6, 1895.

RIVALRY

Back then, as the story goes, there was a get-together in the woods. A Red Sox fan, a Cub fan and a Pirate fan were there. They all wondered when their

As the "Sultan of Swat," the Babe transformed the Yankees into the first great dynasty in American sports.

team would make it to the World Series again and decided to call on God for advice.

The Cub fan asked first: "When will my team return to the World Series?"

And God replied: "Not in your lifetime."

The fan of the Pirates popped the same question.

And God replied: "Not in your children's lifetime."

The Red Sox fan, who had listened quietly, finally worked up the nerve to ask: "When will my beloved Red Sox return to the World Series?"

God thought for a moment and then answered: "Not in My lifetime."

But that answer was incorrect. As all of us know, the guys from Fenway broke the "Curse of the Bambino" in 2004.

For six straight seasons through 2003, the Sox finished second to the hated New York Yankees, a combined total of 58½ games behind. So it was a big deal for the BoSox to show up their rivals from the Big Apple.

Nowadays, the tables seem to have turned and favor the Sox in a bitter rivalry that goes back to the first time the teams met on May 7, 1903, at the Huntington Avenue Grounds in Boston.

They weren't the Yankees and Red Sox then. They had more geographically correct names: the Highlanders, who played on the heights of Manhattan; and the Pilgrims—a nod to their New England heritage.

The competition has always been much more than a baseball team representing Boston going against a baseball team representing New York. It is a match-up between the provincial capital of New England and the mega-municipality of New York competing.

The New York Yankees are the sizzle and the steak, the glamour and the glitz, the most successful franchise in baseball history, perhaps in all sports history.

Joe DiMaggio and the Red Sox: he was still charming despite the rivalry.

Through the years, winning has been as much a part of Yankee baseball as their monuments and plaques, as much as the pinstriped uniforms, the iconic intertwined "N" and "Y" on the baseball caps.

The rivalry is the Babe and Bucky and Butch and Boo. It is Carl Yastrzemski trotting out to left field at Fenway Park after failing at the plate against the Yankees, cotton sticking out of his ears to muffle the noise of Sox fans. The rivalry is Mickey Mantle slugging a 440-foot double at Yankee Stadium then tipping his cap to the Red Sox bench.

It is Carlton Fisk's headaches from the tension he felt coming into Yankee Stadium. The rivalry is Ted Williams spitting, Reggie Jackson jabbering, Luis Tiant hurling for New York and Boston and smoking those fat Cuban cigars. It is the Yankees' Mickey Rivers leaping away from an exploding firecracker thrown into the visitors' dugout at Fenway.

It is the Scooter, the Green Monster, and the Hawk, Yaz and the Commerce Comet, Mombo and King Kong. It is Joe Dee versus the Thumper. It is Roger

Maris hitting number 61 off Red Sox pitcher Tracy Stallard, breaking the Babe's record.

It's Ted Williams spitting, Reggie Jackson gesturing, Billy Martin punching, Roger Clemens throwing inside.

The rivalry has been characterized by some of baseball's craziest moments. Incidents, anger, rage, occasionally violence, all have been there through the long decades. Sometimes it has been triggered by personality clashes. At other times the trigger has simply been the "Blood Feud."

The Yankees of New York versus the Red Sox of Boston is the greatest, grandest, strongest, longest-lasting rivalry in baseball history—a competition of images, teams, cities, styles, ballparks, fans, media, culture, dreams and bragging rights.

What happened on January 9, 1920, "Harry Frazee's Crime," supercharged the rivalry and changed the course of baseball history. At a morning press conference, an elated Jake Ruppert announced: "Gentlemen, we have just bought Babe Ruth from Harry Frazee of the Boston Red Sox. I can't give exact figures, but it was a pretty check—six figures. No players are involved. It was strictly a cash deal."

Since that "cash deal," all sorts of Red Sox misfortunes followed. Just a few include: losing Game 7 of the World Series in 1946, 1967, 1975 and 1986 (the ball dribbling through Bill Buckner's legs in Game 6); being done in by the Aaron Boone eleventh-inning home run on October 17, 2003, that gave the Yankees a stunning 6–5 come-from-behind triumph over Boston just five outs away from winning the American League championship; the wind-blown homer that forever made the guy who hit it always remembered in New England as "Bucky F_____g Dent" and adding another pennant playoff loss to one

suffered through in 1948; Pedro Martinez and Don Zimmer, age 72, going at it and the Yankee coach tumbling end-over-end a few times, and more.

═══════════

MIKE STANLEY: *Regardless of where either team is in the standings, people mark off the Yankee–Red Sox playing dates on their calendars.*

═══════════

It's the Charles River versus the East River, Boston Common against Central Park, the Green Monster versus the Monuments, Red Sox Rule versus Yankees Suck, WFAN versus WEEI, the *New York Daily News* matched up against the *Boston Herald*.

It's "I LOVE NEW YORK, TOO—IT'S THE YANKEES I HATE" versus "BOSTON CHOKES. BOSTON SUCKS. BOSTON DOES IT IN STYLE."

Part of the rivalry is the glaring contrast in the images of the teams. The New York Yankees are the glitz and glitter that comes with being the most successful franchise in baseball history. The Bronx Bombers boast an "A" list legacy: Yogi Berra, Bill Dickey, Joe DiMaggio, Whitey Ford, Lou Gehrig, Goose Gossage, Ron Guidry, Reggie Jackson, Derek Jeter, Mickey Mantle, Roger Maris, Don Mattingly, Thurman Munson, Vic Raschi, Allie Reynolds, Mariano Rivera, Phil Rizzuto, Alex Rodriguez and Babe Ruth.

Through the years, winning has been as much a part of Yankee baseball as the monuments and plaques in deep center field, as much as the pinstriped uniforms, the iconic intertwined "N" and "Y" on the baseball caps.

The Sox have also had their share of stars like Cy Young, Joe Cronin, Ted Williams, Dom DiMaggio, Mel Parnell, Johnny Pesky, Carlton Fisk, Carl Yastrzemski, Dwight Evans, Jim Rice, Wade

Boggs (he also played for the Yankees) Babe Ruth (also a Yankee), Roger Clemens (same), Manny Ramirez, Pedro Martinez, Nomar Garciaparra and Big Papi.

═══════════

MEL PARNELL: *The Red Sox–Yankee rivalry was one of the most unique things in baseball history, especially in my time. We were criticized as being a country club ball club being pampered by Mr. Yawkey, our owner. The differences in our ball clubs, Yankees and Red Sox, were that we were probably a step slower than the Yankees. They also had more depth.*

═══════════

LOU PINIELLA: *I was always aware of the mix at Fenway Park. There was always a lot of excitement in that small park that made it special. You might have 20,000 Red Sox fans at Fenway and 15,000 Yankee fans. Their rivalry helped our rivalry. It excited the players who had to respond to it.*

═══════════

MICHAEL DUKAKIS (FORMER GOVERNOR OF MASSACHUSETTS AND 1988 PRESIDENTIAL NOMINEE): *The games between the Yankees and Red Sox are always intense. I get a sense that the players feel it too. No matter who they are, or where they come from, how long or little they've been with the team, there's something about those series.*

═══════════

SOUNDS AND SIGNS AT YANKEE STADIUM

Some still there, many linger in memory.

Pigeons fat from peanuts and popcorn taking flight and flapping their wings, Frank Sinatra singing "New York, New York" after the game ends, shout-outs from the right field bleacher creatures as Yankee players take the field, the Yankee grounds crew dancing and dragging the infield to the bouncy sound of "YMCA."

Banging a frying pan with a spoon. Freddy "Sez" Schuman—"Clank! Clank! Clank-clank-clank!" The sound of spoon striking pan, several dozen times a game at a minimum "clap-clap A-Rod! clap-clap, A-Rod!" Bob Sheppard, first live and then on tape, announcing "Numbah Two, Derek Jee-tuh" at bat.

And there are many more:
- "Reg-gie! Reg-gie!"
- John Sterling's "The Yankees win! Theeeeeee Yankees win!"
- Michael Kay's "See Ya!"
- Mel Allen's "How 'Bout That?"
- Phil Rizzuto's "Holy Cow!"
- The #4 train pulling into the 161st Street Station.
- The vendors' chants "Hot dogs!" "Hey, beer!" "Soda!!!" and "Hey, ice cream!" through the grandstands.
- The nostalgic sound of the Hammond organ installed in 1967 and performed on by Eddie Layton until he retired in 2003 and also played over the years by Toby Wright, Paul Cartier and Ed Alstrom.

And anything from Bob Sheppard:
- "Batting for . . ."
- "Welcome to Yankee Stadium."
- "Will you please rise."
- "Coming in to pitch for the Yankees . . ."
- The song "Here Come the Yankees!" used on WPIX and other outlets.
- WPIX's 1970s "Those Yankees Are Alive" commercial song.
- 2 Unlimited's "Get Ready For This," the song played as the team comes out.
- The moving "God Bless America" and Kate Smith's voice, a staple of the Yankees game experience since September 11, 2001.
- The grounds crew rocking out

"YMCA" while doing its thing on the infield mid-game.
- The first seconds of 2 Unlimited's "Workaholic" is played after every run scored by the team.

Entrance and/or walk-up songs like this sampling for some who played for the 2016 New York Yankees:
- Jacoby Ellsbury—"Gettin' It" by Too $hort
- Brett Gardner—"Huntin', Fishin', and Lovin' Everyday" by Luke Bryan
- Alex Rodriguez—"Run This Town" by Jay-Z, Rihanna and Kanye West
- Brian McCann—"Till I Collapse" by Eminem
- Mark Teixeira—"Black or White" by Michael Jackson
- Carlos Beltran—"Timbalero" by El Gran Combo de Puerto Rico
- Chase Headley—"Surrender" by Third Day
- Starlin Castro—"Calentate Girl" by Shelow Shaq
- Didi Gregorius—"Notorious B.I.G." by Notorious B.I.G.
- Andrew Miller—"God's Gonna Cut You Down" by Johnny Cash
- Masahiro Tanaka—"My Dear Fellow" by Japanese girl group Momoiro Clover Z

ADVERTISING SIGNS AT YANKEE PLAYING FIELD

(Year indicates when many signs were added; with thanks to Paul Doherty, Hilltop Park.)

1908: "Young's Hats, None Better Made, Stores on Broadway and Fifth Ave"

1908: "Coronet Dry Gin"

1912: "Ajax Tires, 5000 Miles"

Ramly cigarettes did a lot of advertising at Yankee Stadium.

1912: "Hunter Whiskey"

1912: "Bushmill's Irish Whiskey, 10 Years Old"

1913: "Helmar Cigarettes"

YANKEE STADIUM #1, 1922 TO 1967

1922: First billboard hung during the Stadium's construction: "Let White Build It of Concrete." This was placed on the construction shack on site and then on the edge of the brand new loge down the third base line.

1923: First billboards when the Stadium opened in April—on the right center and center field fences—"You're Safe! Gem Safety Razor $3 deluxe models Now $1-Gem Double Life" (Gem would advertise through the 1957 season!).

Behind the bleachers:

"Arrow Collars"

"Hotel Commodore—Indoor Connection with Grand Central Station in New York—2000 Rooms"

"Champee Mushroom Paste"

"Chesterfield Cigarettes"

"Van Heusen Shirts"

"Murad—The Turkish Cigarette"

"Insist on This Label-Made for the BVD Best Retail Trade, Next to Myself I Like BVD Best—Worn the World Over By Well Dressed Men"

"Boston Garter—How did your Garters look this morning?"

"Everybody's Wearing 'em Kaufman Hats—America's Largest Retailer of Hats"

"Harry and Mannie Featuring GGG Clothes—Uptown Store Broadway at 49th St—Downtown Store 64 Nassau St."

"Edison Portland Cement—Used Exclusively in the Construction of This Stadium"

Overhead shot of Yankee Stadium in 1929, the year Miller Huggins died and Shawkey took over as manager for the rest of the season.

1925: "Cool Off in a New Palm Beach Suit"

1928: Billboard on the street side of the bleachers: "Camels, made for folks who think for themselves."

1929: Billboard on the street side of the bleachers: "Camels: If you smoke for pleasure, Camels were made for you."

1931: "Westminster Hosiery-Spotlights of Style," "The Yankees Use Lifebuoy"

1932: Drake's Cakes, Mrs. Wagner's Pies

1933: "No Brush Burma Shave," "Old Gold Cigarettes," "Gem Micromatic Blades-Gem Micromatic Razor"

1936: In July, first billboards behind the brand new bleachers in left field:
- "Gem Blades"
- "Horton's Ice Cream"
- "Corn Exchange Bank"

- "Canada Dry"
- "Vat 69"
- "Philip Morris"
- "The Bronx Savings Bank"
- "Burma Shave"
- "Calvert"
- "Lifebuoy"

1937: "Gem Micromatic Razor" moved from outfield fence to behind the brand new right field concrete bleachers

"Coca-Cola—The Pause That Refreshes" was on the street side of the billboards.

1939: Right field "Gem Singledge Blades-5 of 25"

1940: Right field: "Gem New Clog-Proof V-Slots Razor"

1942: "Buy War Bonds" was added to the structure itself for the duration of World War Two.

1943: Street side of the billboards: "Drink Coca Cola—The Pause That Refreshes—'It's the real thing'"

1945: "You'll Enthuse—As You Use—Burma Shave"

1948: "Ballantine Ale and Beer" replaces in right field "Gem Blades" which moves to middle section of left field

1949: "Manhattan Shirts" added to first slot in left field

1950: "Con Edison" is in left field and "Uptown it's Alexanders" replaced "Gem" in left field. "Silver Star—The Razor Blade Your Face Can Feel" to right field in place of "Ballantine."

1950 "Stadium Favorite Ballantine Beer Ale" signage goes to the bottom of the brand new scoreboard. This sign is also illuminated at night, a first.

1951: "Gem Feather Weight Razor" returns to right field.

1951: Street side of the billboards: "Coca Cola—The Pause That Refreshes-Enjoy the Game"

1952: "Bon-Bon Ice Cream" added in left field

1952: Right field: "Gem-More Clean Shaves Than Any Other Blade-Duridium Process Blades"

1952: Left field: "Buy Tydol-Flying A Gasoline"

1954: Left field: "You'll Score in Manhattan Shirts"

1954: Right field: "Gem Blades-Gem Razors Avoid 5 O'clock Shadow"

1955: Right field: "Gem Razor-Shave Closer Without Irritation"

1957: New Coke billboard in left field: "Pause…Refresh Coca-Cola."

1957: In right field: "Gem—Shaves Closer Without Irritation" (the final Gem billboard, they were featured in the Stadium from 1923 to 1957).

1957: Featured the last "old fashioned"– looking billboards, right to left field (each board was complete unto itself … no consistent background).
- First airlines ad—"Fly National to Miami-Cuba"
- "Burma Shave Bomb .59 cents,"
- "Manhattan Shirts,"
- "Coke, Fast! Wow!"
- "Burma Shave Bomb"
- "National Airlines, Flying A"
- "Camel/Winston/Salem Cigarettes"
- "Manhattan Manstay Shirts"
- "Seagram's 7"
- "Mobil Gas"

"Ballantine [on scoreboard Ballantine now reading "It's a hit" Ballantine Beer and Ale"] and the final Gem board.

1958: Each panel now has the same teal color background matching the color of the Stadium with advertising over it resembling a more modern Madison Avenue look. "Gem" is gone. Reading from right to left field: "Yoo-hoo" (debut), "Coca-Cola," "Women Say Deodorant-Men Say Trig, Vitalis," "Mobil" (new logo), "Mansmooth," "Teacher's Scotch," "Brakes Adjusted Tilden #1," "Flying A Gasoline," "National Airlines," "Volvo" (automobile debut and a foreign one), "Mild El Producto"

1959: New scoreboard added and larger "Ballantine" sign placed under it. Same pitch started in 1958: "It's a hit!" This illuminated ad would remain through 1966.

1959: Panels added for "BOAC Airlines," "The Yellow Pages," "Big Gallon Cities Service-Quality alone Makes It Big," "Banker's Trust," "Martin's VVO," "Coca-Cola"—Be Really Refreshed and "Burma Shave" returns.

1960: Panel added in left field for "Horn and Hardart," "Man Tan-Tans Without Sun," "Milium" and "Mrs. Wagner's Pies"

1961: Added were "Milk," "Fly to Fort Lauderdale"

1962: Added "M and Ms," "A and P First in the New York Area By Far w/ Plaid Stamps," "Anacin for Headache Pain," "Johnny Walker Red Label," "Big Yank Clothing," "Look for Clothing With Kodel" and "Coca-Cola's Refreshing New Feeling"

1963: Featured:
- "Top Brass-Medicated Hair Dressing for Men"
- "Trunz Quality Meats"

- "Sans a Belt Clothing Sold by B Altman's"
- "Everybody Shops at the 249 Johns Bargain Stores"
- "Esso-Happy Motoring"
- "Be Sure It's Hebrew National— New Stuffed Cabbage in Jars—Now at Food Stores"
- On right and left field boards, "BOAC to Bermuda"

1964: Added "Helps Ease Leg Fatigue-Supp-Hose Socks," "BVD Shirts-Self Ironing Belfast $3.99," "Treat Snacks," "Econ-O-Car"

1965: Added "When It Comes to Your Car Do We Worry—Flying A," "Aqua Velva," "Schick," and "Yashica" (first Japanese camera)

1966: "Look Magazine," "For Home Building Products-Johns Manville," "Flying A—Play to Win-A-Check," "Enjoy White Owl Cigars," "Find It Fast-Let your Fingers Do the Walking—NY Yellow Pages"

1967: Stadium and billboards completely repainted. "Ballantine" leaves the Stadium scoreboard after December 1966. This space is painted black for the 1967 season. Billboards' backgrounds are now an off-white color. New ads include: "Dreyfuss Fund Inc," "Flying A—Discover America Best By Car," "Be Cigar Wise-Smoke White Own," "Coca-Cola-Coke Has the Taste You Never Get Tired Of," "Get Your Hands on a Toyota You'll Never Let Go for $1760" (first Japanese car ad)

And others through the years …

"Ask the man for Ballantine"

"Bronx Savings Bank, Tremont and park Aves," (sic)

"By [sic] War Stamps and Bonds"

Over the scoreboard clock "OFFICIAL TIME LONGINES"

"Nobody Beats the Wiz" was later changed to just "The Wiz"

THE LOGO AND UNIFORM

The world-famous interlocking "NY" logo was first designed by Tiffany and Co. as part of a Medal of Valor for John McDowell, an NYPD officer who was shot in the line of duty in 1877. Seven years later the New York Highlanders on their uniform jersey breast featured a separate "N" and "Y."

In 1905, the team went for an interlocking version of the logo. Letters intersected to their previous logo and the Medal of Valor. The club over the next three seasons went back to featuring their old logo.

In 1909, Highlanders part-owner Bill Devery, a former NYC police chief, decided to bring the interlocking logo back. It appeared on the left sleeve of the jersey and the cap. In 1912, the logo was moved to the left breast. (That home jersey also was the first to feature pinstripes.) The logo was removed from the jersey in 1917 and made for a pinstripes-only home look until 1936. Aside from a few minor changes, the overall jersey has stayed unchanged since then.

The Yankees went through several different cap designs, including two-tone caps and those with different combinations of pinstripes and interlocking "NY" logos in the franchise's early years. The current version of the cap—navy blue with the white interlocking "NY" logo—dates back to 1922.

The Yankees cap has bragging rights to being top sporting headwear. Among the celebrities who have been spotted wearing one: Justin Bieber, LeBron James, Nelson Mandela, Tom Brady and Jay Z (whose hit song "Empire State of Mind" features the line "I made the Yankee hat more famous than a Yankee can").

The block "New York" first appeared on the front of Yankee road uniforms in 1916; from 1927 to 1930, it was

The interlocking "N" and "Y," considered the most recognizable logo in sports, made its debut in 1909.

replaced by the team name. In 1931, "New York" returned to the road grays where it has remained. In 1973, the letters and the uniform number on the back of the jersey were trimmed in white.

OLD-TIMERS' DAY

The Yankees are the sole team with a continuous and full-fledged Old-Timers' Day. Its roots go back to "Lou Gehrig Day" on July 4, 1939. Technically, that was not an "Old-Timers' Day." Rather it was a day where some old time Yankees were assembled to honor the critically ill "Iron Horse."

It was Yankee owner Larry MacPhail and publicist Red Paterson who continued the "reunion" idea, mainly to honor Babe Ruth in 1947. It was called "Old-Timers' Day" then and continued with that name through the years.

George M. Steinbrenner came up with the idea to create the Alumni Association for the New York Yankees. In 1974, he appointed Jim Ogle Sr. as the head of the Alumni Association, gave him responsibilities for the Alumni Association newsletter, "Pinstripes" and "Old-Timers' Day."

Greats and current players shared the same locker room and connected with each other and the different Yankee eras at Old-Timers' Days through the

years until 2009 when the Yankees moved to the new stadium.

Now the Old-Timers dress in an auxiliary dressing room and then go out onto the field. Despite the protocol, many Old-Timers still find their way into the Yankees locker room to interact with present day players.

Invited Old-Timers are paid for their appearance by the Yankees. Invited guests traditionally have been given gifts that become more collectible and valuable through the years, a far cry from 1970 when each guest walked away with a Zenith cassette tape recorder, with the guests' name and the date.

Many special guests have been invited to the gathering of the clan annual event. These have included former players, Hall of Famers and wives of deceased players. "A List" guests have included Mrs. Babe Ruth, Mrs. Lou Gehrig, Mrs. Casey Stengel, Mrs. Thurman Munson and Mrs. Elston Howard.

What began in 1939 as an event honoring one player, Old-Timers' Day now honors many who thrill to the applause and attention of a generally packed Yankee Stadium.

WORST TEAM

Worst Team: 1908
Won 51, Lost 103, .331%

Despite all the accomplishments of the greatest franchise in baseball history, there have been some teams along the way that have been clunkers. Topping the list is the 1908 Yankee/Highlander squad. It won just 51 games and lost 103 and finished dead last, 39½ games out of first place.

The record of the team many were now calling "the Yankees," should have been and could have been even worse than that based on their runs scored, 460, and runs allowed, 713. Additionally, every single pitcher on that staff had an ERA that was worse than the league average.

A highlight of the season, not for the Highlanders but for Cy Young, took place on June 30. He pitched a no-hitter against the sorry team. June was not a good month for the team many were calling the Yankees as they won only seven of 28 games. July was nothing to brag about either as the mediocre squad won but six of the 30 games it played that month.

The star of the Highlander's dreadful offense was outfielder Charlie Hemphill. He led the team in nearly every statistical offensive category and that as someone said, "ain't saying much."

Hal Chase, arguably the best player on the team the past two seasons, batted .257 and managed just 36 RBIs. In September, the big first baseman was gone—he had been charged with throwing games.

Hall of Fame bound "Wee Willie" Keeler was in a part-time role in the outfield. He appeared in just 91 games, batting just .263.

The pitching was just plain bad. Al Orth, a 27-game winner two years before, posted a 2–13 record. Bill Hogg was 4–16. Rookie Joe Lake won nine games and led the league with 22 losses. Jack Chesbro, 34, who won a 20th-century record 41 games four years earlier, finished the season 14–20.

The miserable record of the team, whose average age was 28.2, experienced some twists and turns, further diluting its ability to perform. Respected manager Clark Griffith, who was with the franchise from the beginning, was let go after the Highlanders in their first 56 games posted a 24–32 record. Back-up infielder Kid Elberfeld took over and made things even worse. The team lost 71 of its last 98 games under "the Kid."

And September of 1908 was bragging time for superstar hurler Walter Johnson of Washington. "The Big Train" shut out the New York Highlanders in three consecutive games.

There was a 3–0 six-hitter on September the 4th. The next day Johnson followed up with a 6–0 four-hitter. On September 6th, there was no game. The blue laws in New York banned Sunday baseball. On Labor Day, Johnson continued his mastery and the Highlanders were a hapless loser in a 2–0 two-hitter. In three games, the New York American League team managed just 12 hits and no runs against Walter Johnson.

Quite a few were calling the downtrodden team "Yankees" then. In truth, nothing about that 1908 edition had anything about it that was "New York Yankees" yet. It would take time and then the other teams would have to watch out.

THE BEST ALL-TIME YANKEE TEAM: 1927

110–44 (.714)

"By game time the vast structure was packed solid," A *New York World* account described the April 12, 1927, Opening Day at Yankee Stadium. "Rows of men," the *World* account continued, "were standing in back of the seats and along the runways. Such a crowd had never seen a baseball game or any other kind of game in New York."

The Seventh Regiment Band played for the 72,000 in attendance, just part of the 1,164,015 who came out that season of 1927 to cheer on the Yankees. The home team won that day, 8–3, settling into first place where they would remain throughout the season without a single change in their roster that featured seven new players for 1927.

Center fielder Earle Combs and shortstop Mark Koenig served as table setters in the batting order. Combs would bat .356 and be the league leader in hits, singles and triples. In his third Yankee season, Koenig would bat .285 and be one of the toughest to strike out—just 21 times in 526 at bats in 1927.

The "Sultan of Swat" was the hammer in the third slot in the powerful batting order. Babe Ruth would hit .356 with 164 RBIs and post a league best .772 slugging percentage. Scoring the most runs, drawing the most walks, getting the most total bases, compiling the highest on base percentage, the "Bammer" by himself out-homered all Major League teams except for the Giants, Cubs and Cardinals.

Lou Gehrig followed the Babe in the batting order. The cleanup hitter of all cleanup hitters batted .373 (third in the American League, drove in a league best 175 runs and homered 47 times. His RBI and doubles total were best in the American League. His slugging percentage of .765 was runner-up only to Ruth. The Yankees were 33–7 (.825) when Gehrig homered. Almost one quarter of all American League homers that 1927 season were hit by the combo of Gehrig and Ruth.

Bob Meusel batted fifth in the order. A .337 batter in 1927, he had 103 RBIs and 24 stolen bases. Tony Lazzeri batted sixth and played second base. The quiet athlete finished third behind Ruth and Gehrig in home runs, notched a .309 average and 102 RBIs.

In seventh place in the batting order was "Jumping Joe" Dugan, Babe Ruth's buddy, a peerless third baseman. He complained: "It's always the same. Combs walks. Koenig singles. Ruth hits one out of the park. Gehrig doubles. Lazzeri triples. Then Dugan goes down on the dirt on his can."

Catching duties were shared by journeymen Johnny Grabowski and Pat Collins. The third string catcher was Benny Bengough.

"The secret of success as a pitcher lies in getting a job with the New York Yankees," was Waite Hoyt's famous line. The ace of the '27 team, Hoyt paced the league in wins, winning percentage and was second in ERA.

Wilcy Moore's side arm sinker ball helped him log a (19–7) record, 13–3 in relief, the lowest ERA. Urban Shocker won 18 of 24 decisions. Walter Henry "Dutch" Reuther, (13–6) was replaced in mid-season by the hard-throwing rookie George Pipgras (10–3, .769). The '27 Yankees had the three lowest earned-run averages in the league, with Moore (2.28), Hoyt (2.63) and Shocker (2.84). Half a dozen pitchers won at least ten games.

Manager Miller Huggins kept it all together. Mark Koenig said of him: "He was a good manager, although he was a nervous little guy who moved his feet a lot in the dugout. But he didn't have to be much of a strategist with that club. Lots of times, we'd be down five, six runs, and then have a big inning to win the game."

By May's end, the Yankees had won 28 of 42 games. By June 24, they had a 44–17 record. Heading into a Fourth of July doubleheader at Yankee Stadium, the Senators had won ten straight. No matter.

In Game One, the Yankees clubbed Washington, 12–1. The nightcap was a 21–1 laugher. Whacking competition was a trademark of the 1927 Yankees. Special victims were the St. Louis Browns, losers of 21 in a row to the New Yorkers.

"This isn't just a ball club!" sportswriter Arthur Robinson emoted. "This is Murderers' Row!"

"It was murder," Babe Ruth explained. "We never even worried five or six runs behind. Wham! Wham! Wham! And wham! No matter who was pitching."

"When we were challenged," Waite Hoyt said, "when we had to win, we stuck together and played with a fury and determination that could only come from team spirit. We had a pride in our

performance that was very real. It took on the form of snobbery. And I do believe we left a heritage that became a Yankee tradition."

"Just putting on a Yankee uniform gave me a little confidence," said Mark Koenig. "That club could carry you. You were better than you actually were."

There was a ritualist, superstitious, at times ghoulish quality to the Yankees of 1927. Waite Hoyt warmed up only with his starting catcher. After hitting a home run, the Babe put another notch on his bat. But when he hit his 21st home run that season, the new notch split his bat. That ended that ritual. Joe Dugan always scratched out a mark at third base. Wilcy Moore threw his first warm-up pitch only to Eddie Bennett, Yankee batboy and good luck charm. Manager Miller Huggins relied on Mike Gazella to deliver messages to the bullpen. One player was only able to sleep sitting up. He had a heart condition that he kept secret from his teammates. Another player, seemingly unfriendly, at times very quiet, was Tony Lazzeri. He was an epileptic. His health condition was never revealed by the press.

The five o'clock blowing of a factory whistle close by Yankee Stadium signaled work day's end. And all the Yankees enjoyed the sound of the whistle. It was music to their ears underscoring that now was their time to beat up teams. They called it "Five O'clock Lightning."

By the end of July, a month the Yankees posted a 24–7 record, the lead was 13½ games, Yankee winning percentage was a gaudy .730.

By August 31, they led the second place Athletics by 17 games. On September 13, the Yankees swept a doubleheader from Cleveland and clinched the pennant.

On September 29, at Yankee Stadium Ruth homered off two different

Washington pitchers in a 15–4 Yankee cakewalk, tying his record of 59.

Wrapping up the '27 season with a 110–44 record, winning the pennant by 19 games, pounding out 158 home runs, batting .307 as a team, recording the all-time best slugging percentage of .489, averaging 6.5 runs a game, scored almost a thousand runs, the Yankees held opponents to 599 runs.

Leading the league in every individual offensive category except for batting average, the Bronx Bombers had five regulars who batted .300 or better. Four of the eight American Leaguers who drove in 100 or more runs were Yankees.

The pitching staff led the league in shutouts. Its ERA was almost a run below the league average. The four best winning percentages in the league belonged to Yankee pitchers.

The '27 Yankees were so free of injury that six of the eight position players logged more than 500 at bats. Durability was a tremendous edge for the club and it covered up its weakness of a thin bench.

It was Yankees against Pittsburgh's Pirates in the World Series. "We won before it even got started," Babe Ruth said. "The first two games were scheduled for Forbes Field. Naturally, we showed up a day early and worked out in the strange park—and we won the Series during that workout. We really put on a show. Lou and I banged ball after ball into the right field stands, and I finally knocked one out of the park in right center. Bob Meusel and Tony Lazzeri kept hammering balls into the left field seats."

The Yanks rolled over the Bucs in four, becoming the first American League team to sweep a World Series. "It all meshed for us," Mark Koenig said, "the personalities, the manager, the luck, everything that 1927 season."

SPRING TRAINING: MINI TIMELINE

1905 to 1906: After spending two springs in Atlanta, manager Clark Griffith moved his team to Alabama in 1905–1906. That first year the Highlanders stayed in Montgomery at the Highland Oval. Players march to and from the team hotel, which was located two miles away, to the playing field. In 1906, the team camp was at the Birmingham Training Grounds.

1907 to 1912: The Yankees in Georgia during this time played in Atlanta, Macon, Athens and then Atlanta again.

1913: Seeking sanctuary from the cold and rain that had been present during previous spring trainings, the Yankees moved their camp outside of the country for the first and only time. On March 3, most of the team and support staff sailed to Hamilton, Bermuda. A converted cricket field was used as the practice facility.

1914: Houston, Texas, was the Yankees spring training site.

1915 to 1918: Under manager Bill Donovan, the Yankees returned to Georgia for a three-year stay in Macon, the team's longest stay at one location to that point in time.

1919 to 1920: The Yankees became part of a growing trend relocating its spring training to Florida in 1919. All three New York teams were there, the Giants in Gainesville, the Yankees and Dodgers in Jacksonville. "The clubs expect to benefit by the arrangement, for it will give each club the advantage of playing against Major League opposition from the very start of the training season," noted the *New York Times*.

Newly acquired Babe Ruth was part of the 1920 spring training environment.

At an exhibition game he went into the bleachers to mix it up with a taunting fan. When the fan showed off his knife, Ruth backed off and went back to the safety of the playing field. Had Ruth not held his temper, the whole course of Yankee history may have been different.

1921 to 1924: Louisiana was the spring training location for the Yankees. In 1921, they trained in Shreveport. From 1922 to 1924, the club trained in New Orleans.

1925 to 1942: St. Petersburg, Florida and the New York Yankees had a longstanding and highly successful relationship.

1943 to 1945: World War II precluded teams traveling very far from home for spring training. In 1943, the Yankees made use of a high school in Asbury Park, New Jersey. The final two years of the war saw them training in the 112th Field Artillery Armory and playing exhibition games at Bader Field in Atlantic City.

1946 to 1950: The Yankees returned to St. Petersburg, Florida when WWII was over. In 1947, they moved into a new stadium, Al Lang Field. It was a joint home for the Yankees and St. Louis Cardinals.

1951: Spring training was in Arizona, the first and only time for the Yankees. The one-year trade-off of training sites was a courtesy by the New York Giants to Yankees' co-owner and vice president Del Webb, who hailed from Phoenix.

1952 to 1961: It was back to St. Petersburg in 1952 for the Yankees. As the fifties moved on, New York was dissatisfied with what was perceived as favoritism toward the Cardinals with whom they shared the spring training

site. There was a Yankee disappointment with spring training proceeds that went to the city. The spring of 1961 was the last for the Yankees in St. Petersburg. Yankee co-owner Dan Topping said: "In St. Petersburg, we practice on one field and play on another. In Fort Lauderdale, we would have the town to ourselves."

1962 to 1995: The Yankees' brand-new $600,000 Ft. Lauderdale Stadium is ready for spring training. The ballpark broke new ground with seating for 8,000, air-conditioned clubhouses and on-site offices.

1996 to present: The Yankees moved to George Steinbrenner's adopted hometown, Tampa, Florida. Legends Field, a state-of-the-art $30 million facility with identical dimensions to Yankee Stadium, received rave reviews. Seating capacity was 10,200 and expanded to 11,026 in 2007. It was re-named George M. Steinbrenner Field in 2008.

APOCRYPHAL MOMENTS

A story or statement of doubtful authenticity, although widely circulated as being true.

"THE TRADE"

As the story goes, Sox owner Tom Yawkey and Yankee boss Dan Topping were at Toots Shor's one night bantering about how much more suited to hit at Yankee Stadium Ted Williams was and how much more suited to hit at Fenway Park Joe DiMaggio was. The evening allegedly concluded with the two owners exchanging a handshake and agreeing to make a DiMaggio for Williams trade.

It was reported that when Topping arrived home at 4:00 a.m. and realized what he had agreed to, he picked up the phone and in a panic called Yawkey. "Tom," he began, "I'm sorry but I can't go through with the deal."

"Thank God," was supposedly Yawkey's reply.

Another version of the purported DiMaggio-Williams deal has Tom Yawkey being the one who made the phone call.

"Dan, I know it's very, very late, and I still want to make that trade we discussed. However, if you still want to make it you'll have to throw in that left-handed hitting outfielder. You know who I mean, that little odd-looking rookie."

"I can't," Topping said. "We're thinking of making him a catcher. I guess we'll have to call off the deal."

So Joe DiMaggio remained a Yankee.

Ted Williams remained a member of the Red Sox.

And the little and awkward-looking rookie remained with the Yankees and became a catcher. His name—Lawrence Peter Berra.

"413"

The 1966 season and September 22nd proved to be a sorry story for the sorry state of affairs for the New York Yankees. The whole week had a light schedule.

===

PAUL DOHERTY: *The only Yankee games scheduled for the week were Tuesday the 20th of September, a night game, and Friday, September 23rd. The Yankees closed out their home season that Sunday the 25th.*

===

Those who had tickets would get rain checks first for Wednesday (no go, rain) and then the Thursday. In effect, they would only be able to go to a weekday game on the 22nd. Prior to this 9/22 makeup game the Yankees had lost 10 out of their previous 14 games. And Mickey Mantle was not playing either. There were probably a number of people who assumed this game would not be made up at all.

There was a strong possibility of rain on September 22. The entire metropolitan area was wet generally. The day before that game, 5.54 inches of rain fell on New York City—still a record for that day. So, maybe people just assumed that the field would be unplayable? The forecast for the day of the game had a chance of rain in it too.

On September 22, 1966, just 413 showed at the Stadium, the smallest home crowd in the Yankees' proud history. The last-place Yankees were downed, 4–1 by the White Sox. Broadcaster Red Barber ordered TV cameras to show the empty seats. As the story goes, that assertiveness by one of the greatest baseball announcers of all-time cost him his job with the Yankees.

"I don't know," Red Barber said, "what the paid attendance is today, but whatever it is, it is the smallest crowd in the history of Yankee Stadium . . . and this crowd is the story, not the game."

===

PAUL DOHERTY: *Making an issue of the 413 in the house was not the reason Barber was let go. Although Red still called a good game on radio, he was never a good TV announcer. By 1966 his vocal instrument wasn't as supple as it had been in his Brooklyn heyday. And Red was far too caught up in broadcast booth politics and egotism to function properly as the broadcast team's leader. His Yankee fate was sealed no matter what happened at the low-attended game. By the end of 1966 Garagiola and Rizzuto wouldn't work with Barber who just worked on-air with Jerry Coleman. Alas, at this stage of the game, Red was the haughty one. And it cost him his Yankee career. He never landed a regular play-by-play gig with a Major League team again.*

===

And something rarely brought up. The next day's game, Friday September 23, against Boston, day game: 1,440 was the attendance. This game must also be among the lowest attended games ever. It was a breezy day, around 70 degrees. And Yom Kippur started at sundown this day.

"YOGI BEAR"

Yogi Berra never was paid for the character Yogi Bear even though it was obviously named for him.

"MICKEY MANTLE'S TAPE MEASURE SHOT"

According to Marty Appel: "Red (Patterson) never got hold of a tape measure; he walked it off with his size 11 shoes and estimated the distance."

"CENTER FIELDERS: JOE DIMAGGIO, MICKEY MANTLE, BERNIE WILLIAMS"

The popular perception is that Joe DiMaggio was a Yankee center fielder for 13 seasons. His tenure was actually for 12.5 seasons. In 1936 the Yankee Clipper started 54 times in center field. After that he made at least 113 starts almost every year for the remainder of his playing career aside from 1949. Injuries limited him to just 76 games. Service in WWII from 1943 to 1945 cut into his playing career.

After DiMaggio retired, Mickey Mantle became the next longest-serving center fielder. However, "the Mick" was not exclusively a center fielder. In his rookie season of 1951 DiMaggio was still there. The Commerce Comet played 84 games in right field and three games in center field. From 1952 for the next 15 seasons the Mick was a fixture as the Yankee center fielder. In 1967, Mantle moved to first base for his final two seasons.

Bernie Williams was not the regular center fielder until 1993. He actually played in 1991 and 1992, but that was part-time. The graceful Williams manned center field through 2005. His 16th and final year as a Yankee in 2006, he was splitting time between left field, center field and designated hitter.

"WALLY PIPP AND THE ASPIRINS"

"I took the two most expensive aspirins in history" has gone down in history as one of baseball's most famous quotes. It is untrue.

Technically, Gehrig's streak began a day earlier when he pinch-hit. The next day he was positioned at first base and his long tenure began—2,129 straight games. Back in those days a mild headache would never keep a player out of a game. They played on through pain and injury. That, in fact, was what the Iron Horse had to do to set his record consecutive games played.

"THE BABY RUTH CANDY BAR"

Introduced in 1921, the Curtiss Candy Company claimed that it was named after Ruth Cleveland, the late daughter of ex-president Grover Cleveland. That "naming" claim was a legal ploy allowing Curtiss to name the candy the Babe without getting his permission. Diphtheria actually claimed Ruth Cleveland at age 12 in 1904, 17 years before the "Baby Ruth" candy bar was introduced and when the Sultan of Swat was in his prime time years. A P.S. to the confection is that it originally was named "Kandy Kake." The name was changed after George Herman Ruth became the star of stars.

JOE DI, THE BOSS AND MONUMENT PARK

The story was that Joe DiMaggio wanted a monument in his honor at Yankee Stadium, one to take its place near other immortals in Monument Park.

In the 1990s, George Steinbrenner approached the Yankee Clipper and told him of his plans for a monument to DiMag.

Joe said, "I'm still breathing, still alive, I'm not going into a memorial park."

He didn't want the honor until after his death. Joe DiMaggio died on March 8, 1999. His monument was unveiled April 25 of that year.

"CATFISH"

Jim Hunter's nickname was totally fabricated by A's owner Charlie Finley, who invented a story for the media about Hunter catching fish in the backwoods creeks of North Carolina and was dubbed "Catfish." Truth be told, the name was briefly applied to a very young Hunter when he caught a catfish.

"SHEPPARD AND JETER"

PAUL DOHERTY: *Bob Sheppard was the Yankees public address announcer from Tuesday April 17, 1951, through his last game in the Stadium on Wednesday, September 5, 2007, an unparalleled 57 seasons. Although Sheppard never returned to the Stadium after September 2007, starting in 2008 the Yankees played a recording of Bob introducing Derek Jeter, the well-known "Now batting for the Yankees, Number 2, Derek Jeter, Number 2." Hard as it may be to believe, this was the first time Bob ever introduced a batter by saying "Now batting." It was a true urban legend, used in countless Sheppard impressions for years, that Bob introduced batters with "Now batting." Well, until the pre-recorded Jeter announcement, Bob never uttered such a phrase. He announced pinch hitters with, "Batting for X" but never using "now." When a batter came to the plate for the first time in a game the intro was always the same, "Number. Name, Position. Number." For 57 seasons. When a batter came to the plate for subsequent at bats, Bob's introduction template was reduced to*

"Position. Name." Period. Supposedly when Bob was recording at his home the special Jeter intro he decided to add "Now batting" to it since this was a unique "one-of-a-kind" introduction that needed to fit a Jeter at bat whether he was playing shortstop or DH or he was pinch-hitting. But Bob never uttered that type of intro before . . . no matter who you heard impersonating Bob before the 2008 season, including Derek Jeter!

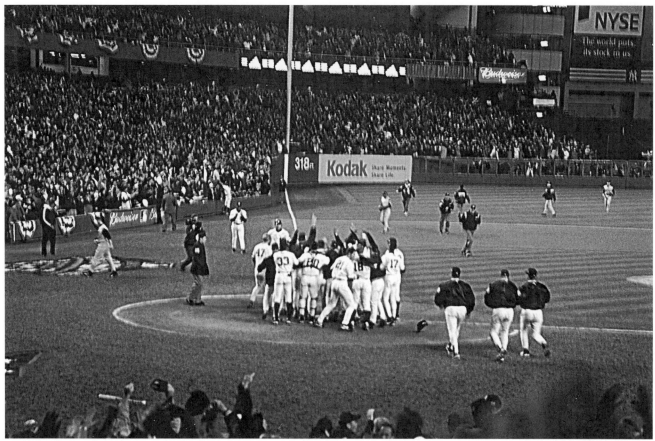

Derek Jeter homers the Yankees into the playoffs.

ULTIMATE YANKEE QUIZ

150 provocative questions and answers with some sure to be daunting even for the most extreme Yankee diehards

So you think you know all about the New York Yankees. Take the test that follows. Novices, learners and experts all are welcomed. There are lots of easy questions and some that are brainteasers. All are pinstriped pleasures. (Answers start on page 215.)

1. What player wore number 7 before Mickey Mantle did?

2. Whose number (and what was it) was retired by both the New York Mets and Yankees?

3. Who was the catcher behind the plate when Dave Righetti threw his no-hitter on July 4, 1983? The catcher wore #27 when he played for the Yankees from 1982 to 1986.

4. Name the four managers who have piloted both the Yankees and the Mets.

5. In 1977, who nicknamed Reggie Jackson "Mr. October"?
   A. Willie Randolph
   B. Thurman Munson
   C. Goose Gossage
   D. Mickey Rivers

6. Name the player Derek Jeter replaced in 1996 to become the regular shortstop.
   A. Andy Fox
   B. Pat Kelly
   C. Alvaro Espinoza
   D. Tony Fernandez

7. What former Yankee was the first pitching coach for the New York Mets in 1962?
   A. Joe Page
   B. Red Ruffing
   C. Vic Raschi
   D. Johnny Sain

8. Elston Howard was the first black player on the Yankees in 1955. Who was second?

9. Whom did George Steinbrenner buy the Yankees from?

10. Trick question: Which of the following was not a Babe Ruth nickname?
   A. "Bambino"
   B. "Wali of Wallop"
   C. "Rajah of Rap"
   D. "Caliph of Clout"

11. Name the National Football League coaching legend who played briefly for the Yankees.
   A. Tom Landry
   B. George Halas
   C. Jim Thorpe
   D. Curly Lambeau

12. What number did Mickey Mantle first wear when he came up to the Yankees?
   A. 7
   B. 6
   C. 5
   D. 47

13. Reggie Jackson hit three home runs in Game 6 of the 1977 World Series against the Los Angeles Dodgers— each off a different pitcher. What pitcher gave up Jackson's third home run?
   A. Burt Hooton
   B. Charlie Hough
   C. Elias Sosa
   D. Don Sutton

Rain check for Yankee Stadium field box dated 1941, the year DiMaggio had his 56-game hitting streak.

14. Reggie Jackson was inducted into the Hall of Fame as a member of what team?
  A. Oakland A's
  B. Baltimore Orioles
  C. New York Yankees
  D. Los Angeles Angels of Anaheim

15. What Yankee pitcher has the most World Series victories?
  A. David Cone
  B. Allie Reynolds
  C. Whitey Ford
  D. Lefty Gomez

16. In defeating the Oakland A's in the 2001 American League Division playoffs, what did the Yankees accomplish that no team ever had done before in a three-of-five-game series?
  A. Limited their opponents to a total of two runs
  B. Had a perfect fielding percentage
  C. Won three straight after losing two games at home
  D. Hit at least one home run in every game

17. What Yankees MVP appeared in the fewest games in the year in which he won the award?

18. Easy one: What was Yogi Berra's given name?

19. What uniform number was retired by the Yankees to honor a player who was never on the team?
  A. Jackie Robinson
  B. Bob Feller
  C. Dom DiMaggio
  D. Pee Wee Reese

20. Who remains the only Yankee to hit four home runs in one game?
  A. Lou Gehrig
  B. Reggie Jackson
  C. Babe Ruth
  D. Yogi Berra

21. Which Yankees pitcher once led the league in wins one year and saves the next?

22. Who was the last batter Don Larsen faced in the Perfect Game he pitched in the 1956 World Series for the Yankees?
  A. Roy Campanella
  B. Jackie Robinson
  C. Dale Mitchell
  D. Pee Wee Reese

23. What Yankee pitcher had the nickname "Rags"?
  A. Johnny Sain
  B. Joe Page
  C. Dave Righetti
  D. Don Larsen

24. What position did Wally Pipp play?
  A. First Base
  B. Center Field
  C. Catcher
  D. Third Base

25. What is the most games Mariano Rivera saved in a season?
  A. 61
  B. 47
  C. 53
  D. 51

26. "SEE YA! SEE YA! SEE YA!" is the signature call of?
  A. Suzyn Waldman
  B. John Sterling
  C. Michael Kay
  D. Mel Allen

27. Who was the only pitcher for the franchise to win 40 games in a season under modern rules?

28. What Major League team did Joe Girardi manage before the Yankees?
  A. Cubs
  B. Marlins
  C. Red Sox
  D. Indians

29. Who was the "Junk Man"?
  A. Ron Guidry
  B. Joe Page
  C. Eddie Lopat
  D. Don Larsen

30. What positions did Johnny Mize play for the Yankees and what other New York team did he play for? A bit of a trick question.

31. Who founded "Yankeeland Farm" in Frederick, Maryland after his playing career ended and had a successful career as a breeder?
    A. Charlie Keller
    B. Tom Tresh
    C. Elston Howard
    D. Bob Kuzava

32. Who was the central figure when the first Old-Timers' game was staged in a Major League park and the first uniform number retired?
    A. Babe Ruth
    B. Lou Gehrig
    C. Lefty Gomez
    D. Joe McCarthy

33. Who was the General Manager before Brian Cashman?
    A. Bob Watson
    B. Lou Piniella
    C. Bob Quinn
    D. Gene Michael

34. How many games did Ron Guidry win in his record Cy Young season of 1978?
    A. 19
    B. 20
    C. 23
    D. 25

35. Who was nicknamed "Chairman of the Board"?
    A. Whitey Ford
    B. Reggie Jackson
    C. Yogi Berra
    D. Frank Howard

36. Who was the last Yankee and Major Leaguer to wear Number 42?
    A. Billy Martin
    B. Mariano Rivera
    C. Carlos Beltran
    D. Johnny Blanchard

37. Who wore number 51 for sixteen Yankees seasons, from 1991 to 2006?
    A. Paul O'Neill
    B. Hideo Matsui
    C. Bernie Williams
    D. Jorge Posada

38. Who replaced Joe Torre as Yankee manager in 2008?

39. Who was called "Donnie Baseball"?

40. Who made the first error in the "House That Ruth Built?" And bonus question: Who made the first error in the new Yankee Stadium?
    A. Lou Gehrig
    B. Babe Ruth
    C. Tony Lazzeri
    D. Wally Pipp

41. What pitcher did Bucky Dent hit the go-ahead home run off at Fenway Park in the 1978 tie-breaker game?
    A. Mike Torrez
    B. Dennis Eckersley
    C. Bill Lee
    D. Bob Stanley

42. Mickey Mantle hit his final home run off a Red Sox pitcher. Who was it?
    A. Ray Culp
    B. Jim Lonborg
    C. Jose Santiago
    D. Sparky Lyle

43. Who has put in more consecutive years as the everyday play-by-play announcer than anyone else in Yankees history?
    A. Red Barber
    B. Mel Allen
    C. John Sterling
    D. Curt Gowdy

44. What was the smallest single-game Yankee Stadium crowd?
    A. 1,000
    B. 413
    C. 5,400
    D. 8,810

45. Who asked: "Where is Reggie Jackson? We need Mr. October or a Mr. September. Winfield is Mr. May."

46. How many times did George Steinbrenner change manager during his first twenty-three seasons?
    A. 10
    B. 15
    C. 18
    D. 20

47. Who made up the "Core Four"?

48. Who said "Yankee Stadium was a mistake, not mine, but the Giants."
    A. Yogi Berra
    B. Harry Frazee
    C. Jake Ruppert
    D. Babe Ruth

49. Very tough one: What is the significance of 3,465 to the Yankees?

50. When did the Yankees play at Shea Stadium when Yankee Stadium was being refurbished?

51. Who wore uniform Number 2 before Derek Jeter?

52. Who originally designed the intertwined Yankees logo, "NY"?
   A. Jake Ruppert
   B. NYC Police Department
   C. Louis C. Tiffany
   D. Til Huston

53. First-baseman Wally Pipp has gone down in history for being the player Lou Gehrig replaced. What other distinction belongs to Pipp?
   A. He was a manager.
   B. He came from the same neighborhood Gehrig grew up in.
   C. He was a home run champ.
   D. He made money endorsing aspirin.

54. Who was the first Major Leaguer to hit two grand slams in the same game?
   A. Babe Ruth
   B. Lou Gehrig
   C. Mickey Mantle
   D. Tony Lazzeri

55. Who played the most games for the Yankees?
   A. Mickey Mantle
   B. Yogi Berra
   C. Lou Gehrig
   D. Derek Jeter

56. Who was the first DH to bat? (He was a Yankee)
   A. Jerry Moses
   B. Ron Bloomberg
   C. Fred Stanley
   D. Johnny Callison

57. Who was the highest paid Yankee in 1973?
   A. Matty Alou
   B. Bobby Murcer
   C. Mel Stottlemyre
   D. Sparky Lyle

58. Which pitcher became the highest-paid player in history when he signed a $3.5 million contract for the Yankees in 1975?

59. What Yankee pitcher was nicknamed "Bulldog"?
   A. Jim Bouton
   B. Monte Pearson
   C. Joe Page
   D. Ron Guidry

60. The tradition of honoring legends at Yankee Stadium started on Memorial Day of 1932. Who was the first monument for?
   A. Babe Ruth
   B. Miller Huggins
   C. Lou Gehrig
   D. Jake Ruppert

61. How many games did Babe Ruth win as pitcher for the Yankees?
   A. None
   B. 10
   C. 5
   D. 7

62. Name the Yankees outfielder who won the 1962 AL Rookie of the Year Award when he batted .286 with 20 home runs and 93 RBI.

63. For seven consecutive years a New York Mayor threw out the first pitch for the home opener of the Yankees. Who was he?
   A. John Lindsay
   B. Abe Beame
   C. Fiorello LaGuardia
   D. Rudy Giuliani

64. What number did Earl Combs wear and why?
   A. 1
   B. 17
   C. 22
   D. None of these

65. What year did the Yankees begin playing Frank Sinatra's "New York, New York" at the Stadium?
   A. 1977
   B. 1978
   C. 1979
   D. 1980

66. Joe DiMaggio, Mickey Mantle, Bernie Williams each spent more than a decade playing center field for the Yankees. Who spent the most time?
   A. DiMaggio
   B. Mantle
   C. Williams
   D. Another player

67. What year did the first All-Star Game take place at Yankee Stadium?
   A. 1930
   B. 1935
   C. 1939
   D. 1947

68. Who was the first black player on the Yankees?
   A. Vic Power
   B. Elston Howard
   C. Satchel Paige
   D. Larry Doby

69. Who said: "I may not have been the greatest Yankee to put on the uniform, but I am the proudest."
   A. Lou Gehrig
   B. Joe Torre
   C. Dave Winfield
   D. Billy Martin

70. Who wrote "New York, New York," the song sung by Frank Sinatra at the stadium?
    A. Billy Joel
    B. Kander and Ebb
    C. George Gershwin
    D. None of these

71. What is the significance of William S. Devery and Frank J. Farrell in the history of the franchise?

72. How many times did George Steinbrenner hire and fire Billy Martin?
    A. 4
    B. 5
    C. 6
    D. 7

73. Who was the 20th manager in Steinbrenner's time?
    A. Billy Martin
    B. Stump Merrill
    C. Buck Showalter
    D. Joe Torre

74. Who pitched the first no-hitter against the Yankees?
    A. George Foster
    B. Cy Young
    C. Bob Feller
    D. Hoyt Wilhelm

75. Which former Yankees player went on to serve as president of the American League?

76. Mickey Mantle was a rookie in 1951 but a different Yankee won Rookie of the Year. Who was he?
    A. Gene Woodling
    B. Andy Carey
    C. Gil McDougald
    D. Hank Bauer

77. What Yankee in his first four years played on four world championship teams?
    A. Joe DiMaggio
    B. Derek Jeter
    C. Yogi Berra
    D. Lou Gehrig

78. Two Yankees came to the Major Leagues without having played one game in the minors. Who were they?

79. What Yankee was in the D-Day landing at Omaha Beach June 6, 1944?
    A. Ralph Houk
    B. Yogi Berra
    C. Jerry Coleman
    D. Hank Bauer

80. Bob Sheppard had the nickname "Voice of God." Who gave him the nickname?
    A. Red Barber
    B. Mel Allen
    C. George Steinbrenner
    D. Reggie Jackson

81. Who had the idea to create the Yankee "Stadium Club"?
    A. Casey Stengel
    B. Larry MacPhail
    C. Dan Topping
    D. Jake Ruppert

82. After Lou Gehrig, who became the next captain?
    A. Phil Rizzuto
    B. Lefty Gomez
    C. Mickey Mantle
    D. Thurman Munson

83. Which of the longest-standing Yankee managers has the highest winning percentage?
    A. Joe Torre
    B. Joe McCarthy
    C. Casey Stengel
    D. Buck Showalter

84. The Yankees have the distinction of being the first to train outside of the USA. Where did the training take place?
    A. Bermuda
    B. Jamaica
    C. Cuba
    D. Dominican Republic

85. All played for Yankees and Mets, aside from one. Who is he?
    A. Lee Mazzilli
    B. Gene Woodling
    C. Phil Linz
    D. Rusty Staub

86. What Yankee recorded the most steals of home?
    A. Mickey Mantle
    B. Willie Randolph
    C. Lou Gehrig
    D. Ricky Henderson

87. Easy one—Babe Ruth's uniform number?

88. Who hit the first home run in the new Yankee Stadium?

89. Another easy one: Who owned the Yankees before the Steinbrenners?

90. Joe DiMaggio played his entire career for the Yankees. What team did he coach for?
    A. Cardinals
    B. A's
    C. Padres
    D. Dodgers

91. When David Wells became a Yankee for the first time, what uniform number did he request and why?

92. How many Yankees were on the 1939 American League All-Star team that played at Yankee Stadium?
    A. 5
    B. 6
    C. 9
    D. 10

93. Which Yankee team is being referred to in the following quote? "This isn't just a ball club! This is Murderers' Row!"

94. Who said: "I won't be active in the day to day operations of the ball club at all."
    A. Jake Ruppert
    B. Casey Stengel
    C. George Steinbrenner
    D. Yogi Berra

95. Who said and why: "They told me my services were no longer desired because they wanted to put in a youth program as an advance way of keeping the club going. I'll never make the mistake of being seventy again."
    A. Casey Stengel
    B. Bucky Harris
    C. Miller Huggins
    D. None of these

96. Who struck out more times during their respective careers, Babe Ruth or Mickey Mantle?

97. Who loved the expression "That huckleberry"?
    A. Red Barber
    B. Phil Rizzuto
    C. Mel Allen
    D. Susan Waldman

98. Who was known as the "oh, say can you see" guy?
    A. Robert Merrill
    B. Whitey Ford
    C. Phil Linz
    D. None of these

99. Name two Yankees who were called "Moose."

100. Who was the only player on the Yankees to have played with both Mickey Mantle and Don Mattingly?
    A. Willie Randolph
    B. Bobby Murcer
    C. Yogi Berra
    D. Whitey Ford

101. Name the first season the Yankees drew over 3 million fans at Yankee Stadium? Attendance was 3,292,736.
    A. 1999
    B. 1969
    C. 2009
    D. 1989

102. Which Yankee Hall of Famer did Branch Rickey once predict would "never make anything more than a Triple-A ballplayer at best?"
    A. Mickey Mantle
    B. Ron Guidry
    C. Yogi Berra
    D. None of these

103. How many total Gold Glove Awards did "Donnie Baseball" win?
    A. 6
    B. 7
    C. 8
    D. 9

104. In 1933, Babe Ruth hit the first home run in All-Star Game history. In what park did he hit the historic home run?

105. Who was the first African-American pitcher to start a game for the Yankees? Hint—the year was 1961.

106. When Babe Ruth retired with 714 home runs, only one other player had more than 300 homers in his career. Who was he? Hint—he was a Yankee.

107. Which Yankees outfielder and future broadcaster took over Mickey Mantle's locker after Mantle retired in March 1969?

108. Which Yankees broadcaster introduced the home run call, "It's going, going, gone!"?
    A. Mel Allen
    B. Red Barber
    C. Phil Rizzuto
    D. John Sterling

109. Twice in their history the Yankees have had the #1 overall pick in the June amateur draft. Who did they take?

110. Name the first Yankee player to win both the Rookie of the Year Award and later the American League's Most Valuable Player Award?
    A. Tom Tresh
    B. Bobby Richardson
    C. Thurman Munson
    D. Babe Ruth

111. When was the last time the Yankees won the World Series?

112. Which Yankee number of the following is not retired?
    A. 2
    B. 3
    C. 4
    D. 8

113. This Yankee outfielder won the 1962 American League Rookie of the Year Award. He batted .286 with 20 homeruns and 93 RBI. Name him.

114. This pitcher became the highest-paid player in history when he signed a $3.5 million contract for the Yankees in 1975? Name him.

115. Who hit the first home run in the new Yankee Stadium?
    A. Derek Jeter
    B. Jorge Posada
    C. Brett Gardner
    D. Alex Rodriguez

116. Which key member of the Yankees 1996–2000 dynasty was not drafted until the 22nd round of the June 1990 amateur draft? Hint: He was a member of the Core Four.

117. What Yankee won the Rookie of the Year Award in 1951?
    A. Mickey Mantle
    B. Gil McDougald
    C. Andy Carey
    D. Jerry Coleman

118. Who was the last ex-player announced when the Yankees had their farewell to the Old Stadium at the last home game of the 2008 season?
    A. Don Larsen
    B. Willie Randolph
    C. Mariano Rivera
    D. Bernie Williams

119. How many games did Derek Jeter play as a Yankee, tops all-time?
    A. 2,000
    B. 2,743
    C. 2,913
    D. 2,998

120. Who is second in all-time games played for the Yankees?

121. What is Derek Jeter's middle name?

122. What Yankee pitcher was called "the Gay Reliever"?
    A. "Goose" Gossage
    B. Sparky Lyle
    C. Joe Page
    D. Dave Righetti

123. Who was the first World Series Most Valuable Player?
    A. Johnny Podres
    B. Johnny Murphy
    C. Johnny Sain
    D. Babe Ruth

124. What was the only year at Yankee Stadium that an opening day ceremonial first pitch was not thrown out?
    A. 1914
    B. 1941
    C. 1964
    D. 1978

125. Who was co-captain of the Yankees with Ron Guidry?
    A. Willie Randolph
    B. Reggie Jackson
    C. Thurman Munson
    D. None of these

126. Who played "Take Me Out to the Ballgame" at Fenway Park as a part of pregame ceremonies at Fenway for Derek Jeter's last game?

127. What Yankee executive was called "the silent Cobra?"

128. What position did Mickey Mantle mainly play in his rookie season?
    A. Shortstop
    B. Left Field
    C. Right Field
    D. Center Field

129. Mariano Rivera is first in Yankee history in saves. Who is second?

130. Only three pitchers in New York Yankees history recorded 40 or more career shutouts. Name them.

131. What Yankee set the record starting his career playing in the most consecutive games?
    A. Lou Gehrig
    B. Derek Jeter.
    C. Hideki Matsui
    D. Jorge Posada

132. How many consecutive games did that Yankee play in?
    A. 450
    B. 475
    C. 501
    D. 528

133. What Yankee outfielder was called "Twinkletoes"?
    A. Babe Ruth
    B. Cliff Mapes
    C. George Selkirk
    D. Bob Meusel

134. What was Babe Ruth's real name?
    A. Herman George Ruth
    B. George Harold Ruth
    C. George Herman Ruth
    D. Herbert George Ruth

135. Who was "Babe Ruth's Legs"?
    A. Sammy Byrd
    B. Bob Meusel
    C. Miller Huggins
    D. None of these

136. Who caught the ball Roger Maris hit for his 61st home run?

137. Who was the first captain of the Yankees?
    A. "Wee Willie" Keeler
    B. Jack Chesbro
    C. Clark Griffith
    D. Jack Kleinow

138. Which of the following was not a Yankee captain?
    A. Derek Jeter
    B. Whitey Ford
    C. Thurman Munson
    D. Everett Scott

139. Which Yankee broadcaster is known for the expression "Thuuuhh pitch . . ."?
    A. John Sterling
    B. Mel Allen
    C. Red Barber
    D. Michael Kay

140. What Yankee received the first monument?
    A. Babe Ruth
    B. Lou Gehrig
    C. Jake Ruppert
    D. Miller Huggins

141. Who was the last Yankee to wear Number 21?

142. What does the C.C. in Sabathia's name stand for?

143. Who of the following was not a 2016 Yankee All-Star?
    A. Carlos Beltran
    B. Dellin Betances
    C. Andrew Miller
    D. Alex Rodriguez

144. In Yankee history where was their first two years of spring training?
    A. Birmingham
    B. Miami
    C. Atlanta
    D. Bermuda

145. Which Yankee has the most career steals of home?
    A. Roy White
    B. Bob Meusel
    C. Mickey Mantle
    D. Lou Gehrig

146. All played for Mets and Yankees except one. Name him.
    A. Lee Mazzilli
    B. Rusty Staub
    C. Phil Linz
    D. David Cone

147. Who was the first Yankee World Series MVP?

148. Who took Lou Gehrig's place in the Yankee lineup?

149. Who was called "Whiskey Slick" by Casey Stengel?
    A. Whitey Ford
    B. Billy Martin
    C. Don Larsen
    D. Mickey Mantle

150. Which of the following Yankee books was not written by your loyal author?
    A. *New York City Baseball*
    B. *Bums*
    C. *Five O'Clock Lightning*
    D. *Remembering Yankee Stadium*

ANSWERS

1. Mickey Mantle was the last Yankee ever to don the number 7, wearing it from 1951 until he retired. Fourteen other Yankees wore the number in their career, the last two being Bob Cerv and Cliff Mapes. They wore the number at times during that first season.

2. Number 37—for Casey Stengel

3. Butch Wynegar

4. Yogi Berra, Casey Stengel, Joe Torre, Dallas Green

5. B. Thurman Munson

6. D. Tony Fernandez

7. B. Red Ruffing

8. Harry Simpson, 1957

9. CBS

10. Sorry about that. I said it was a trick question—all of the choices were nicknames for the Babe.

11. B. George "Papa Bear" Halas got into 12 games for the 1919 Yankees.

12. B. Uniform Number 6

13. B. Charlie Hough

14. C. New York Yankees

15. C. Whitey Ford, 10. He started 22 World Series games.

16. C. They won three straight after losing two games at home.

17. Pitcher Spud Chandler appeared in 30 games when he won the American League award in 1943.

18. Lawrence Peter

19. A. Jackie Robinson

20. A. Lou Gehrig

21. Waite Hoyt. In 1927 he had 22 wins. In 1928 he had 8 saves.

22. C. Dale Mitchell

23. C. Dave Righetti

24. A. First Base until Lou Gehrig came along.

25. C. 53

26. C. Michael Kay

27. The year was 1904. The pitcher was Jack Chesbro, who won 41 games.

28. B. Marlins

29. C. Eddie Lopat

30. He played for the St. Louis Cardinals and the New York Giants. He played exclusively first base for Yankees.

31. A. Charlie Keller

32. B. Lou Gehrig

33. A. Bob Watson

34. C. 23

35. A. Whitey Ford

36. B. Mariano Rivera

37. C. Bernie Williams

38. He is still there as of this writing—Joe Girardi

39. Don Mattingly

40. B. Babe Ruth; Bonus: Tony Graffanino, throw to first base, fifth inning

41. A. Mike Torrez

42. B. Jim Lonborg

43. C. John Sterling

44. B. 413

45. George Steinbrenner

46. D. 20 times

47. Derek Jeter, Jose Posada, Andy Pettitte, Mariano Rivera

48. C. Jake Ruppert

49. Derek Jeter's final hit total. Only five players in the history of baseball recorded more: Pete Rose, Ty Cobb, Hank Aaron, Stan Musial and Tris Speaker.

50. 1974 and 1975

51. A. Mike Gallego wore it in 1992, 1993 and 1994

52. C. The interlocking NY logo was originally designed by Louis C. Tiffany for the NYPD valor medal.

53. C. Pipp was an American League home run champion in 1916–1917.

54. D. Tony Lazzeri

55. D. Derek Jeter, 2,747

56. B. Ron Blomberg

57. B. Bobby Murcer made $100,000. Alou and Lyle made $70,000. Stottlemyre earned $78,000.

58. Jim "Catfish" Hunter

59. A. Jim Bouton, because of his overbearing nature

60. B. Miller Huggins

61. C. Five, and two were complete games.

62. Tom Tresh

63. C. Fiorello LaGuardia (1939–1945)

64. A. 1, because he batted first in a Yankee lineup that began the practice of wearing numbers.

65. D. 1980

66. B. Mantle, 15 years

67. C. 1939, to coincide with the World's Fair that year

68. B. April 14, 1955, the second game of the year, Elston Howard debuted.

69. D. Billy Martin

70. B. Kander and Ebb

71. They were owners of the Highlanders Yankees from 1903 to 1915.

72. The magic number—B. 5

73. C. Buck Showalter

74. B. Cy Young

75. Dr. Bobby Brown

76. C. Gil McDougald

77. A. Joe DiMaggio

78. Catfish Hunter, Dave Winfield

79. B. Yogi Berra

80. D. Reggie Jackson

81. B. Larry MacPhail

82. D. Thurman Munson

83. B. Joe McCarthy, .627

84. A. Bermuda, 1913

85. D. Rusty Staub

86. C. Lou Gehrig, 15

87. Three

88. Babe Ruth

89. CBS

90. B. A's

91. Three was the number he requested because it was the number worn by Babe Ruth, whom he admired. The number has long been retired.

92. D. 10. Six starters were Yankees: Red Rolfe, Bill Dickey, George Selkirk, Joe Gordon, Red Ruffing and Joe DiMaggio. Other Yankees on the AL squad included Frank Crosetti, Lefty Gomez and Johnny Murphy. Counting manager Joe McCarthy, there were ten Yankees on the All-Star team.

93. 1927 Yankees

94. C. George Steinbrenner after he purchased the Yankees from CBS.

95. A. Casey Stengel, when he was fired by the Yankees

96. Mantle 1,710 vs. Ruth 1,330

97. B. Phil Rizzuto

98. A. Robert Merrill, the famed opera singer who graced Yankee Stadium by singing the national anthem.

99. Bill Skowron, Mike Mussina

100. B. Bobby Murcer

101. A. 1999

102. C. Yogi Berra

103. D. 9

104. Comiskey Park, Chicago

105. Al Downing

106. Lou Gehrig. 378

107. Bobby Murcer

108. A. Mel Allen in 1948, his third year broadcasting Yankees games.

109. Ron Blomberg in 1967 and Brien Taylor in 1991

110. C. Thurman Munson

111. 2009

112. A. 2 (Derek Jeter)

113. Tom Tresh

114. Jim "Catfish" Hunter

115. B. Jorge Posada

116. Andy Pettitte

117. B. Gil McDougald

118. D. Bernie Williams

119. B. 2,743

120. Mickey Mantle

121. Full name Derek Sanderson Jeter

122. C. Joe Page

123. A. Johnny Podres

124. D. Mickey Mantle and Roger Maris raised the 1978 championship flag

125. A. Willie Randolph

126. Bernie Williams

127. Gabe Paul

128. C. Right Field

129. Dave Righetti

130. Mel Stottlemyre, Red Ruffing and Whitey Ford

131. C. Hideki Matsui

132. D. 528

133. C. George Selkirk

134. C. George Herman Ruth

135. A. Sammy Byrd who was employed as pinch runner for Ruth

136. Sal Durante, who bought tickets the day of the game at a less-than-sold-out Yankee Stadium.

137. C. Clark Griffith, 1903 to 1907

138. B. Whitey Ford

139. A. John Sterling

140. D. Miller Huggins

141. Paul O'Neill

142. Carsten Charles

143. D. Alex Rodriguez

144. D. Bermuda

145. D. Lou Gehrig, who stole home a surprising 15 times.

146. B. Rusty Staub.

147. Don Larsen, 1956, pitched the Perfect Game

148. Babe Dahlgren

149. A. Whitey Ford

150. B. Bums

Joe DiMaggio (far left) in the dugout during the first game of the 1937 World Series against the New York Giants.

Eight

MARCH OF YANKEE TIME

What follows is a year-by-year Yankee chronology dating from 1903 and going up to the present—highlights, low moments, record-setting events and dramatic, once-in-a lifetime occurences, the rhythm of Yankee baseball preserved.

1903

January 9: Frank Farrell and Bill Devery purchase the defunct American League Baltimore franchise for $18,000, worth $478,000 today. They move the team to Manhattan.

March 12: The new New York team's home field is an all-wood park at 168th Street and Broadway. The location prompted Manhattan's highest spots, giving birth to the team name "Highlanders" and home field "Hilltop Park."

April 22: The Highlanders play their first game before 11,950 in Washington, losing 3–1.

April 30: The Highlanders win their home opener at Hilltop Park, defeating Washington, 6–2.

July 14: Clark Griffith is the first Yankee pitcher to hit a home run.

December 20: In what would become a pattern for one-sided trades between the two franchises, the Highlanders trade southpaw pitcher Jesse Tannehill to Boston for right-handed hurler Tom Hughes.

1904

July 4: Jack Chesbro wins his 14th game in a row for the Highlanders.

August 24: Willie Keeler hits two inside-the-park home runs against the St. Louis Browns in a 9–1 win at New York.

October 7: Jack Chesbro pitches the Highlanders to a 3–2 win over Boston, his 41st victory. Chesbro's 41–12 record will top the American League in wins and percentage.

October 10: In the final day of the season, the Boston Pilgrims clinch the American League flag with a 3–2 victory over the Highlanders in the first game of a doubleheader. New York ace Jack Chesbro throws a wild pitch with a runner on third in the top of the ninth allowing the winning run to score.

1905

August 4: A unique battery works a game for the Highlanders. "Doc" Newton pitches and Mike "Doc" Powers catches. Powers is a physician.

August 5: First baseman Hal Chase has a record 38 putouts in a doubleheader against the Browns.

1906

May 7: Manager Clark Griffith is struck in the mouth by umpire Tim Hurst, who is suspended for five days.

September 1: The New York Highlanders win their sixth game in three days, sweeping their third consecutive doubleheader from Washington, an American League record.

September 4: The New Yorkers move into first place, sweeping Boston 7–0 and 1-0, their fifth doubleheader sweep in a row, a Major League record.

1907

May 31: Kid Elberfeld steals home twice against Boston.

June 28: A Highlander utility player named Branch Rickey has 13 bases stolen on him by the Senators. The young man, who will go on to greater moments in baseball, appears that season in 52 games and bats .182.

1908

June 30: At Hilltop Park, Boston's Cy Young hurls his third career no-hitter, an 8–0 gem against New York.

September 7: Washington's Walter Johnson pitches his third consecutive shutout in four days, a 4–0, two-hitter over the New York Highlanders.

1909

September 11: The Highlanders sell Jack Chesbro, the team's first star hurler, to the Red Sox.

1910

April 14: On Opening Day, the Yankees and Red Sox play to a 4–4, 14-inning tie at Hilltop Park in front of 25,000 fans.

1911

May 6: The Yankees record their first triple play, defeating Boston, 6–3 at Hilltop Park.

September 28: Topping the Browns, 18–12, the Highlanders rack up 29 hits in a game that features 20 walks, 12 errors and 15 stolen bases. The game has been called "the worst game ever played."

George Modridge, who threw the first no-hitter in Yankee history, on the mound and getting the sign.

1912

April 11: Opening Day at Hilltop Park sees the New York Highlanders wearing pinstripes for the first time. The Red Sox win the game 5–3.

April 20: Just a few days after the sinking of the Titanic, the Yankees and Red Sox match up in the first Major League game at Fenway Park. Boston Mayor John "Honey Fitz" Fitzgerald, the grandfather-to-be of John F. Kennedy, throws out the first ball. Boston ekes out a 7–6 win in 11 innings before 27,000.

April 21: A benefit exhibition game for the survivors of the Titanic disaster is staged at Hilltop Park. The Giants trounce the Highlanders, 11–2.

October 5: Highlanders play their last game in Hilltop Park. The facility will be demolished in 1914.

1913

April: After becoming tenants of the National League's New York Giants at the Polo Grounds, the Highlanders use the name "Yankees." Sportswriters complained that "Highlanders" was difficult to fit headlines. Sports Editor Jim Price of the *New York Press* started calling them "Yankees" back in the day of Hilltop Park, inspired by the flags in Hilltop Park. The name was not used officially until 1915.

1914

August 3: Les Nunamaker becomes the only catcher in the twentieth century to throw out three runners attempting to steal in one inning.

1915

January 7: Tigers waive Wally Pipp, and Yankees add him to roster. He will become a footnote to history as the man Lou Gehrig replaces at first base. Pipp was actually a very serviceable player from 1915 through 1925.

January 11: Col. Jacob Ruppert and Col. Tillinghast L'Hommedieu Huston purchase the Yankees for $460,000.

October 6: Boston sweeps a doubleheader from the Yankees, 2–0 and 4–2.

1916

September 29: Boston pitcher Babe Ruth defeats the Yankees, 3–0. It is the Babe's 23rd win, his ninth shutout.

1917

April 24: George Mogridge is the first Yankee in history to hurl a no-hitter, defeating Boston, 2–1, at Fenway.

1918

December 21: Boston ships pitchers Ernie Shore and Dutch Leonard and outfielder Duffy Lewis to the Yankees for four second-line players and cash.

1919

July 29: Boston pitching star Carl Mays is traded to the Yankees for pitchers Allan Russell and Bob McGraw and $40,000.

September 24: Boston's Babe Ruth breaks the single-season record with his 28th home run in a game against the New York Yankees at the Polo Grounds. The drive clears the right-field roof.

1920

January 5: The Red Sox sell Babe Ruth, 24, to the New York Yankees for $125,000. Red Sox owner Harry Frazee is also given a $350,000 mortgage on Fenway Park by Yankee owner Jacob Ruppert.

"The price was something enormous, but I do not care to name the figures. It was an amount the club could not afford to refuse." —Harry Frazee

"Frazee is not good enough to own any ball club, especially one in Boston." —Babe Ruth

May 1: Babe Ruth hits his first home run as a Yankee. Clearing the roof of the Polo Grounds, it torques a 6–0 Yankee victory over the Red Sox.

July 6: The Yankees set a team record for runs scored during an inning with fourteen in the fifth inning against the Washington Senators.

October 29: Ed Barrow, former Red Sox manager, is appointed general manager of the Yankees.

December 15: Boston trades pitchers Waite Hoyt and Harry Harper, infielder Mike McNally and catcher Wally Schang to the Yankees. The Sox receive outfielder Sam Vick, third baseman Derrill Pratt, pitcher Herb Thormahlen and catcher Muddy Ruel in addition to cash.

1921

February 6: The Yankees announce that 10 acres in the western Bronx, City Plot 2106, Lot 100, land from the estate of William Waldorf Astor, has been acquired for $675,000. In today's dollars that land would be worth $9,057,286.34.

May 29: Babe Ruth homers over the right field roof at the Polo Grounds in a 9–4 Yankees' win over Philadelphia.

July 18: The Sultan of Swat slams a home run that is estimated to go 575 feet.

September 5: New York's outfield makes a record five assists, four of them by outfielder Bob Meusel.

October 2: Babe Ruth slams his record 59th home run in the last game of the season as the Yankees nip the Red Sox, 7–6. Shortstop Everett Scott plays in a Yankee team record 832nd consecutive game.

December 20: Boston trades pitchers Joe Bush and Sam Jones and shortstop Everett Scott to the Yankees for three pitchers, shortstop Roger Peckinpaugh and cash.

1922

May 2: White Construction Company starts to build "The House that Ruth Built."

"Some thought it should be named Ruth Field, but Ruppert's name won out: Yankee Stadium." —Robert Creamer

May 20 to 25: Babe Ruth has one of the shortest tenures in the history of baseball captains.

May 21: Col. Ruppert buys out Col. Huston's share of the Yankees for $1,500,000. In today's dollars that would be $21,480,579.48.

September 10: An estimated overflow crowd of 40,000 shows up for the farewell home games of the Yankees at the Polo Grounds. More than 25,000 are turned away. The Yankees sweep a doubleheader from the A's.

September 30: Nipping the Red Sox at Fenway, 3–1, the Yankees clinch their second AL pennant.

1923

January 30: The Red Sox trade Herb Pennock to New York for infielder Norm McMillan, pitcher George Murray, outfielder Camp Skinner and $50,000.

April 18: Yankee Stadium opens before a reported crowd of 74,200 for the first game at Yankee Stadium. Babe Ruth hits the first home run, a three-run shot in the third inning, torqueing the 4–1 Yankee victory over the Red Sox.

Snapshot of a packed stadium at the 1926 World Series.

"The last word in ballparks."
—*F. C. Lane, The Literary Digest*

September 4: Sam Jones no-hits the Athletics 2–0.

September 28: Coasting to a 24–4 victory, the Yankees pound out thirty hits against Boston, the most in team history and the most hits in a nine-inning game in team history.

October 10: Yankee Stadium hosts its first World Series game, the first one heard on a nationwide radio network. Casey Stengel of the New York Giants hit the first homer at the Stadium, an inside-the-park shot.

October 15: The Yankees defeat the New York Giants to win their first World Championship in the first all New York World Series. The victory in the Fall Classic came in the franchise's 21st season in the Big Apple.

1924

May 4: Lou Gehrig and Babe Ruth switch positions to take pressure off the Babe's lame leg. Babe Ruth plays first base. It is Gehrig's last game as an outfielder. Ruth and Gehrig combine for five hits but the Yanks lose to Washington, 7–3.

May 24: It is Babe Ruth Day, and the Sultan of Swat receives his American League Most Valuable Player award for performance in 1923.

1925

June 1: Lou Gehrig begins his record streak of playing in 2,130 consecutive games in the eighth inning of a game against Washington at the Stadium. He pinch-hit for shortstop "Pee Wee" Wanninger.

June 2: Wally Pipp reportedly complains of a headache. Lou Gehrig replaces him at first base.

July 23: Lou Gehrig hits the first of what will be his Major League record of 23 grand-slam home runs in a Yankee 11–7 victory over the Washington Senators.

August 1: The contract of Tony Lazzeri is purchased for spring delivery from Salt Lake City of the Pacific Coast League.

September 8: Red Sox pitcher Buster Ross yields Babe Ruth's 300th career home run.

September 10: Babe Ruth and Lou Gehrig homer in the same game for the first time.

September 22: Ben Paschal of the New York Yankees hits two inside-the-park home runs at Yankee Stadium as the Yanks defeat the White Sox, 11–6.

1926

May 26: New York runs its winning streak to 16, nipping Boston at Fenway, 9–8, sweeping Boston, putting them ahead in the American League standings by 8½ games.

October 6: Blasting three home runs in a single World Series game in Game 4 at St. Louis, Babe Ruth is the first to accomplish that feat.

October 10: Grover Cleveland Alexander of the Cardinals exits the bullpen in the seventh inning and fans Tony Lazzeri with the bases loaded. The old veteran's two shutout innings gives St. Louis a 3–2 victory at the Stadium. Babe Ruth is thrown out in the ninth trying to steal second base.

1927

May 29: The Yankees rip the Red Sox, 15–7, in a game played at the Stadium. Scoring seven runs in the 8th inning, the Yankees coast to victory while Babe Ruth records his 13th homer.

At Yankee Stadium before a crowd of just 3,000, the Yanks defeat the BoSox, 13–6. New York wins its 5th straight; Boston loses its 12th straight.

August 16: Babe Ruth becomes the first player to hit a ball over Comiskey Park's roof.

September 6–7: Ruth hits five homers in two days against the Red Sox. He will wind up hitting 11 of his 60 homers against his old team in 1927.

September 13: Babe Ruth hits two home runs and the Yankees win a pair from Cleveland, clinching the AL pennant with a 98–41 record.

September 30: Babe Ruth breaks his own Major-League record with his 60th home run on the final day of the season. It is a record that will stand for 34 years.

1928

April 19: As a result of their losing the morning Patriots' Day game in Boston, 7–6, the Yankees are out of first for the first time since May 1926. But they come back to win the second game, 7–2.

April 20: The Yankees begin their sixth season at Yankee Stadium with the left field stands enlarged to three decks.

1929

April 16: The Yankees are the first team to make numbers a permanent part of the uniform.

April 18: At Yankee Stadium, corresponding to the batting order, leadoff hitter Earle Combs wears Number 1 in a 7–3 win on Opening Day over the Red Sox. The Yankees wear numbered uniforms for the first time in their history, two days after the Cleveland Indians permanently adopt them as well. (Numbers would become standard for all teams by 1932.) The Yankees come to Fenway as the first team to wear numbers on their road uniforms.

May 19: Babe Ruth and Lou Gehrig hit back-to-back homers off Boston's Jack Russell in the 3rd inning. Two innings later a cloudburst sends a standing-room-only crowd scurrying for the exits. A stampede in the right field bleachers leaves two dead and 62 injured. Jake Ruppert announces that never again will the Yankees sell more tickets than seats.

May 29: The Yankees rip the Red Sox, 15–7, scoring seven runs in the 8th inning. Babe Ruth records his 13th homer.

September 25: Yankee manager Miller Huggins dies of blood poisoning.

October 17: Former pitcher Bob Shawkey is signed as manager.

1930

March 8: Babe Ruth signs a two-year contract for $160,000, making him the highest paid player in baseball, a salary higher than the President of the United States. In today's dollars that would be $2,298,387.24. The Babe quips: "I had a better year than he did." Ed Barrow, Yankee GM, says, "No one will ever be paid more than Ruth."

May 6: Pitcher Red Ruffing becomes a Yankee when the Red Sox trade him for outfielder Cedric Durst. Boston also receives $50,000.

July 5: The New York Lincoln Giants and the Baltimore Black Sox split a doubleheader before 20,000 at Yankee Stadium. It is the first time Negro League teams play there.

August 23: Frank Crosetti's contract is purchased from the San Francisco Seals of the Pacific Coast league.

September 28: Babe Ruth returns to Fenway in a Yankee uniform and hurls a 9–3 complete game win over the Sox.

October 10: Joe McCarthy signs a four-year contract to manage the Yankees.

1931

February 15: The Yankee training site in St. Petersburg is renamed Miller Huggins Field, honoring the team's late manager.

April 12: Joe McCarthy debuts as Yankee manager.

1932

January 12: Jake Colonel Ruppert names George Weiss to head the Yankee Farm System.

May 30: In memory of former Yankee manager Miller Huggins, the first plaque attached to a monument in Yankee Stadium is dedicated.

June 3: In a 20–13 game with Philadelphia, Lou Gehrig becomes the first modern day player to hit four home runs.

June 5: The Yankees acquire Boston pitcher Dan MacFayden for pitchers Ivy Andrews and Hank Johnson and $50,000.

August 3: The Red Sox trade pitcher Wilcy Moore to the Yankees for pitcher Gordon Rhodes.

September 13: The Yankees clinch the American League pennant; Joe McCarthy is the first manager to win pennants in both leagues.

October 1: Babe Ruth homers into the center field bleachers in Game Three of the World Series off Chicago's Charlie Root. The home run will be known as the "called shot."

December 31: Col. Jacob Ruppert hires George Weiss to create and supervise the Yankee farm system.

1933

June 14: Lou Gehrig and his manager, Joe McCarthy, are ejected at Fenway Park for arguing that Boston's Rick Ferrell ran out of the baseline between first and second base. But Gehrig's consecutive-game streak is maintained at 1,249 as he goes 1-for-3 with a triple. The Red Sox romp, 13–5.

July 6: The first Major League All-Star Game is played at Comiskey Park, and Babe Ruth's two-run home run is the margin of victory in the American League's 4–2 win. Yankee pitcher Lefty Gomez gets the win.

August 17: Lou Gehrig plays in his 1,308th consecutive game breaking Everett Scott's Major League record.

September 23: The Yankees overcome five errors—three by Frank Crosetti—to beat the Red Sox, 16–12.

October 1: Attempting to draw fans to the final game of the season in the depths of the Great Depression, the Yankees give Ruth a pitching start. The thirty-eight-year-old Ruth hurls a complete game, nipping his old Boston team, 6–5. He also bats cleanup and goes 1-for-3 with a home run. It would be the last game he would ever pitch.

1934

June 2: The Yankees smash a record six solo home runs at Yankee Stadium to defeat Boston, 7–2.

June 3: Babe Ruth and Lou Gehrig homer in the same game for the last time.

June 6: Yankee outfielder Myril Hoag ties an American League record with six singles in six at bats. Hoag records just 67 hits that season.

July 13: Babe Ruth hits the 700th home run of his career. It comes off Detroit's Tommy Bridges as the Yankees win, 4–2.

August 12: Making his final appearance in Boston in a Yankee uniform, Ruth draws a Fenway Park record crowd of 47,766. More than 20,000 are turned away.

September 22: For the second straight year, Fenway's attendance record is broken in a Red Sox–Yankees doubleheader as 47,627 fans jam into the Fens. The Yankees win the first game, 6–4, and then slam seven ground-rule doubles into the roped-off crowd. After World War II, more stringent fire laws and league rule prevent the overcrowding that was allowed in the 1930s.

September 29: Babe Ruth hits his last home run as a Yankee in a doubleheader at Washington.

September 30: Babe Ruth plays his last game for the Bombers and goes hitless.

November 21: The New York Yankees acquire Joe DiMaggio from the San Francisco Seals of the Pacific Coast League for $50,000.

1935

February 26: The Yankees release Babe Ruth and he signs with the Boston Braves.

1936

March 17: Joe DiMaggio makes his debut in a spring training game and collects four hits.

May 3: Joe DiMaggio makes his Major League debut at Yankee Stadium before an estimated 25,000 Italian-Americans, many waving Italian flags. He raps out three hits.

May 24: Tony Lazzeri hits two grand slam home runs at Shibe Park against the Philadelphia Athletics, setting an American League record for single-game RBIs.

September 9: The Yankees clinch the pennant on the earliest date in history.

October 3: Game 3 of the World Series saw the debut of the stadium's brand-new electronic public address system, with announcer Jack Lenz at the microphone. Lenz joined the Yankees in 1913 at the Polo Grounds (sharing duties with George Levy) and moved with the Yankees to the stadium in 1923. From 1913 through most of 1936, Lenz used an old-fashioned megaphone to announce the batter's first at bat and subsequent line-up changes and other announcements. He sat in the stadium's Field Box 133 during the game, but moved around the stadium's track to announce the line-ups to each section prior to the game.

October 4: Lou Gehrig homers and doubles to place a 5–2 triumph in Game 4 of the World Series against the Giants. The Yanks take the series in six games.

1937

March 26: Joe DiMaggio accepts Ty Cobb's advice and replaces his 40-ounce bat with one that is 36 ounces.

April 20: The Yankee Stadium's 15th season opens with the right-field stands enlarged to three decks. The distance to center field is reduced from 490 to 461 feet.

PAUL DOHERTY: *The left-field bleachers made of wood were torn down. It took half of the season for them to be reconstructed. They seem to have been completed by July or August. Reconstruction then was started on the right field bleachers, which were completed in time for the World Series.*

July 5: Joe DiMaggio hits his first career grand slam home run. It comes off Boston pitcher Rube Walberg.

September 3: Stalling to avoid a loss as a Sunday baseball curfew looms, the Yankees anger Fenway fans, who shell the field with debris. The game is forfeited to the Yankees by umpire Cal Hubbard, who is overruled. AL President Will Harridge fines the Yankees for their tactics.

1938

April 29: The first Ladies' Day Game is played at Yankee Stadium. The Yanks nip the Red Sox, 6–4. Lou Gehrig singled twice and moved his consecutive-games played streak to 1,977.

May 30: A franchise record crowd of 83,533 watches a Yankee doubleheader sweep of the Boston Red Sox at Yankee Stadium. More than 6,000 fans are turned away; 511 are given refunds.

August 27: The first no-hitter is pitched at Yankee Stadium. Monte Pearson coasts to a 13–0 victory over Cleveland.

August 28: Joe DiMaggio ties a Major League record with three triples in a game against St. Louis.

1939

January 13: Colonel Jacob Ruppert dies at the age of 71. His estate takes over ownership of the ball club.

January 17: Ed Barrow is elected president succeeding Colonel Ruppert.

April 20: Prize Boston rookie Ted Williams racks the ball off the 407-foot sign in right-center field at Yankee Stadium for a double. The hit comes for Williams in the season opener in New York, which had been delayed two days because of rain. It will be the only game Williams will play against Lou Gehrig.

May 2: Lou Gehrig's 2,130 consecutive games played streak ends as Babe Dahlgren plays first base, then doubles and homers. The Bombers blast the Tigers, 22–2.

July 4: Lou Gehrig Appreciation Day is held at Yankee Stadium before 61,808. He makes his famous "luckiest man on the face of the earth" speech as his uniform number (4) is the first to be retired.

July 11: Before 62,892, the All-Star Game at Yankee Stadium selected to coincide with the World's Fair that year. Six starters were Yankees: Red Rolfe, Bill Dickey, George Selkirk, Joe Gordon, Red Ruffing and Joe DiMaggio. Other Yankees on the AL team included Frank Crosetti, Lefty Gomez and Johnny Murphy. Counting McCarthy, there were ten Yankees on the All-Star team. The six position starters played the entire game.

August 2: His back to home plate, Joe DiMaggio runs down slugger Hank Greenberg's drive, which winds up behind the flagpole in center. The Detroit superstar rounds second and stops in his tracks. The next day, newspapers call it the greatest catch in Yankee Stadium history.

October 24: Joe DiMaggio is voted the American League's Most Valuable Player.

December 8: Lou Gehrig is elected to the Baseball Hall of Fame by a special vote of the Baseball Writers Association at the organization's annual meeting in Cincinnati. The vote, by acclamation, was unanimous.

1940

April 16: A plaque in Jake Ruppert's memory is placed on the center-field wall close to the flagpole.

April 26: Yankee third baseman Red Rolfe has nine assists in a game against the Reds.

May 12: Red Ruffing's six-hit shutout trims Boston, 4–0, and halts New York's 8-game losing streak. The Red Sox, however, remain in first place in the American League while the Yankees are in last place.

September 8: Joe Gordon hits for the cycle.

1941

Yankee president Ed Barrow offered Civil Defense the use of Yankee Stadium as a bomb shelter in 1941 in case of attack. He thought the area under the stands could provide a safe haven.

May 12: Boston hurler Lefty Grove stops Lefty Gomez and the Yankees, 6–4, for his 20th straight win at Fenway Park. A Jimmie Foxx two-run homer is the margin of victory.

May 15: Joe DiMaggio's 56-game hitting streak starts with a single off Chicago's Edgar Smith at the Stadium.

May 25: Lefty Grove of Boston yields a single to Joe DiMaggio and becomes the first pitcher to take part in two of the greatest records in baseball history. The single locks Grove into DiMaggio's 56-game hitting streak. Fourteen years earlier, Grove had also given up one of the homers in Babe Ruth's 60–home run season.

May 30: The Red Sox and Yanks split a doubleheader. New York wins the opener, and Boston trounces New York in the second game, 13–0. The Sox cap it off with a triple steal. Ted Williams laces

six hits while Joe DiMaggio hits safely in both games, running his hitting streak to 16.

June 2: Lou Gehrig, 37, dies of amyotrophic lateral sclerosis exactly 16 years to the day that he replaced Wally Pipp at first base.

June 28: Joe DiMaggio reaches across the plate and singles off the A's Johnny Babich. The Yankee Clipper's hitting streak goes to 40 games. Babich attempted to walk DiMaggio in his previous at bats to end his hitting streak.

June 29: In a doubleheader against the Washington Senators, Joe DiMaggio ties and then breaks the American League record of hitting safely in 41 consecutive games.

July 1: Joe DiMaggio ties Wee Willie Keeler's 44-game hitting streak with a single (and the next day DiMag would break that record).

July 17: Joe DiMaggio's consecutive-game hitting streak ends at 56 when he goes 0-for-3 as the Yankees trim Cleveland, 4–3.

September 4: With 18 games remaining in the season, the Yankees record the earliest pennant-clinching date in history.

November 27: Joe DiMaggio edges out Ted Williams 291–254 for the American League Most Valuable Player award.

1942

August 14: The Yankees turn seven double plays against the Philadelphia Athletics.

September 27: Tex Hughson of Boston wins his 22nd game. The Red Sox edge the Yankees. A Fenway Park crowd of 26,166, including 4,293 youngsters who gained free admission by bringing 29,000 pounds of scrap metal to the Stadium, sees Hughson space 11 hits. Ted Williams, in his final appearance before entering WWII, finishes the season at .356.

1943

February 7: Joe DiMaggio enlists in the U.S. Army.

September 12: The first-place Yankees sweep a doubleheader from Boston, mathematically eliminating the Sox from pennant contention. The twin victory completes a five-game New York sweep of the Red Sox at Fenway.

October 11: Spud Chandler spins a 10-hit, 2–0 shutout of the St. Louis Cardinals as the Yankees win the World Series in five games.

1944

June 26: To raise funds for war bonds, the New York Giants, Brooklyn Dodgers and New York Yankees each play six innings against each other at the Polo Grounds.

1945

January 25: Dan Topping, Del Webb, and Larry MacPhail purchase the Yankees for $2.9 million from the estate of Col. Jacob Ruppert (in today's dollars $37,270,570.21).

1946

April 30: 54,826 fans are in attendance, a Yankee Stadium record for Opening Day.

May 2: Yankees' co-owner and general manager Larry MacPhail gave away 500 pairs of nylon stockings to ladies in attendance at a game with Cleveland. The promotional gimmick was a big success.

May 11: The Yankees end Boston's 15-game winning streak with a 2–0 victory. Tiny Bonham beats Tex Hughson and Boo Ferriss at Yankee Stadium.

May 24: Joe McCarthy resigns as Yankee manager; Bill Dickey replaces him.

May 28: The first night game is played at Yankee Stadium before 49,917 fans as the Washington Senators defeat the Yankees, 2–1.

1947

April 27: Babe Ruth Day is celebrated in every baseball park in the United States and Japan. Too frail and racked by cancer to wear his old uniform, the "Big Bam" appears at Yankee Stadium for the last time.

June 29 to July 17: Winning 19 straight games, the Yankees set a franchise record, outscoring the competition, 119–41.

October 2: Rookie Yogi Berra hits the first pinch-hit home run in World Series history in Game 3 against the Brooklyn Dodgers.

October 5: In the first nationally televised World Series, Dodger Al Gionfriddo makes "the Catch" in the sixth inning, denying Joe DiMaggio a home run that would have tied the 6th game.

October 7: Just moments after the final game of the 1947 World Series, Larry MacPhail resigns as Yankees general manager. Dan Topping and Del Webb then buy out MacPhail's one-third interest in the club for $2 million.

November 27: Joe DiMaggio wins his third American League MVP, edging out Ted Williams by a single point, setting off controversy.

1948

June 13: Babe Ruth's uniform (Number 3) is retired at "Babe Ruth Day" at Yankee Stadium before 49,641 fans. It is the 25th anniversary celebration of the Stadium and the Babe's final appearance there.

August 16: Babe Ruth dies in New York City at age 53 after a two-year struggle with throat cancer.

October 3: On the final day of the season, a 10–5 Boston win at Fenway enables the Sox to tie Cleveland for the pennant and move into the first single-game playoff in American League history. Joe DiMaggio collects four hits in the contest.

"We had nothing except satisfaction to play for. You might say there must have been a letdown in our play. It is never fun to lose, and besides, the league standings did not convince us that there were two better teams in the league."   —*Joe DiMaggio*

October 12: Casey Stengel replaces Bucky Harris as manager.

1949

February 7: Joe DiMaggio signs for $100,000, the first six-figure contract in baseball history, slightly over $1 million in today's dollars.

April 19: At the season opener, a granite monument to Babe Ruth is unveiled in center field.

May 13: Ed Barrow Day is staged at Yankee Stadium.

June 28 to 30: Joe DiMaggio returns after missing 65 games due to bone spur in foot. At Fenway Park, the Yankee Clipper batted .455 in the three games, hit four home runs and a single, and drove in nine runs.

"I don't think I was ever booed at Fenway. The fans there always respected clean competition and good baseball."
—Joe DiMaggio

July 19: The contracts of black players, catcher Elston Howard and pitcher Frank Barnes, are purchased from the Kansas City Monarchs. The players are assigned to Muskegon in the Central League.

September 11: The Washington Senators play the Yankees at the Stadium in game one of a doubleheader showcasing the wildest pitching staffs in the league. Walking 17 times, the Yanks win the game, 20–5.

September 25: Despite 71 injuries, the Yankees remain in first place all season. But a 4–1 victory by the Red Sox moves Boston into a tie for first.

October 1: It's Joe DiMaggio Day at Yankee Stadium, and the Red Sox need to win just one of the season's final two games to clinch the pennant. But they blow a 4–0 lead, losing 5–4 before 69,551 at the stadium.

October 2: The Yankees defeat Boston, 5–3, at Yankee Stadium in the final game of the season, giving New York the American League pennant.

"The first thing that comes to mind when I think of the Rivalry is the '49 Red Sox and Yankees and the weekend that DiMaggio had."
—Jim Kaat

October 5: Tommy Henrich breaks up a scoreless game with a bottom-of-the-ninth-inning homer, the second time a World Series game has a homer for its only run.

1950

April 18: Billy Martin becomes the first player to get two hits in one inning in his first Major League game. Martin's two hits are part of a nine-run Yankee eighth inning at Fenway Park on Opening Day.

July 1: At Fenway, rookie Whitey Ford gives up seven hits, six walks and five earned runs in his debut. Boston rookie Walt Dropo rips a grand slam homer in Boston's 13–4 route.

"I knew I was better than that."
—Whitey Ford

August 11: Batting .279, Joe DiMaggio is benched for the first time.

August 29: The first Yankee Stadium day game completed with lights.

September 17: "The highly touted Mickey Mantle, brilliant 18-year-old shortstop prospect, also will join the Yanks" on this road trip." —*New York Times*

"Nothing like giving these kids a first-hand demonstration of what it's like on a ball club shooting for a pennant."
—Casey Stengel

1951

March 26: Mickey Mantle blasts two monster home runs in an exhibition game played at Bovard Field at the University of Southern California.

April 7: Mickey Mantle is called up to the majors to play right field and is given Number 7.

April 17: It is Bob Sheppard's first Opening Day as Yankee Stadium public address announcer. He will remain on the scene for next 57 seasons. In the lineup for the Yankee 5–0 triumph over the Red Sox were Phil Rizzuto, Joe DiMaggio, Yogi Berra and 19-year-old Mickey Mantle who goes 1–4 in his Stadium debut, plays right field, bats third. In a Yankee Stadium opener against the Red Sox, steady rain holds attendance down to 13,923 as Mayor Fiorello LaGuardia throws out the first ball. New York scores seven runs in the 7th inning, clinching its 8–4 victory.

May 1: Mickey Mantle hits his first Major League home run. It comes off Randy Gumpert of the White Sox in Chicago at Comiskey Park. The ball travels nearly 500 feet.

May 16: Mickey Mantle hits his first Major League home run at Yankee Stadium.

June 19: Mickey Mantle homers in both games of a doubleheader for the first time.

"He's got more natural power from both sides, than anybody I ever saw."
—Casey Stengel

"The greatest prospect I can remember."
—Joe DiMaggio

July 8: A Yankee pitcher fails to complete a game for the 20th straight time at Fenway Park.

July 12: Allie Reynolds no-hits the Indians at Municipal Stadium in Cleveland.

July 13: Mickey Mantle strikes out three times in a game against the Indians.

Manager Casey Stengel decides to send him down to the Kansas City Blues in Triple-A.

September 8: Former Yankee manager Joe McCarthy is honored. Mickey Mantle homers into the last row of the right field bleachers. Eddie Lopat shuts out the Senators, 4–0.

September 28: In Game 1 of a doubleheader sweep against Boston at Yankee Stadium, Allie Reynolds tosses his second no-hitter of the season in an 8–0 victory over the Red Sox. In the second game, New York clinches its 18th pennant behind Vic Raschi, 11–3.

October 5: Mickey Mantle gets his first World Series hit but is seriously injured when his spikes get caught in a drain gate while he is chasing down a fly ball hit by Willie Mays.

October 9: Eddie Lopat is in command as the Yankees demolish the Giants, 13–1, in the fifth game of the World Series. Gil McDougald becomes the first rookie to record a grand slam homer in the World Series.

October 10: Mickey Mantle plays on his first world championship team as the Yankees beat the Giants in six games. It was to be the last World Series game Joe DiMaggio ever played in.

November 8: Yogi Berra wins the first of his three MVP awards.

December 11: Joe DiMaggio announces his retirement.

1952

May 10: New York's Hank Bauer goes 5-for-6 in an 18–3 thrashing of Boston at Yankee Stadium.

July 26: In Detroit, Mickey Mantle slams his first career grand slam. It lands in the upper deck in left-center field.

August 25: Virgil Trucks of the Detroit Tigers no-hits the Yankees, at the Stadium.

September 2: The Yankees shut out the Red Sox in both games of a doubleheader, 5–0 and 4–0.

1953

April 17: It is two years after his Yankee debut that Mickey Mantle slams a 565-foot homer off Chuck Stobbs at Washington's Griffith Stadium.

October 5: Billy Martin tied the record (since broken several times) for most hits in a World Series with 12.

1954

September 6: Ten Yankee pinch hitters are used by the Yankees against the Red Sox in a doubleheader.

September 21: The Yankees led the "will lead the league" in attendance with 1,475,171 in 1954, but only 1,912 fans show as rookie Bob Grim posts his 20th victory.

September 26: Casey Stengel's "power line-up" nips the Athletics, 8–6, in that franchise's final game in Philadelphia. Yogi Berra plays third base for the only time in his career. Mickey Mantle plays shortstop.

November 18: Don Larsen, Bob Turley and Billy Hunter are traded to the Yankees from the Orioles for Harry Byrd, Jim McDonald, Hal Smith, Gus Triandos, Gene Woodling and Willie Miranda.

December 1: The massive deal is concluded with Mike Blyzka, Darrell Johnson, Jim Fridley and Dick Kryhoski coming to New York for Bill Miller, Kal Segrist, Don Leppert and minor leaguer Ted Del Guercio. Seventeen players are involved in the largest trade in baseball history.

1955

January 26: Joe DiMaggio is elected to the Baseball Hall of Fame.

April 13: Mickey Mantle homers on Opening Day for the first time.

April 14: Elston Howard, the first black Yankee, singles in his first career at bat in a game against the Red Sox.

May 13: Mickey Mantle slugs three home runs, two batting left-handed and one from the right side. He goes 4-for-4 and drives in five runs pacing a Yankee win over the Tigers in New York.

June 6: Mickey Mantle hits the first home run to go over the center field screen at Briggs Stadium in Detroit. The next day the "Mick" smashes the first home run ever to go into the center field "black seats" at Yankee Stadium.

July 9: Mickey Mantle has his first five-hit game with one double and four singles.

September 28: In the first game of the World Series, Whitey Ford bests Brooklyn's Don Newcombe 6–5. In a controversial play, Jackie Robinson steals home in the eighth inning.

October 4: Brooklyn leftfielder Sandy Amoros makes a brilliant, running, one-hand catch of Yogi Berra's sixth-inning drive with the tying runs aboard. His throw triggers a double play. Brooklyn, finally after five straight defeats by the Yankees, wins its first world championship.

1956

April 17: Mickey Mantle slashes two long Opening Day homers against the Senators at Griffith Stadium. President Eisenhower cheers Mantle from his seat behind the Washington dugout.

May 5: Mickey Mantle homers, striking the facade at Yankee Stadium to beat the Kansas City A's 5–2.

"If not for the roof, it would have hit the subway across the street!"
—*KC Broadcaster Merle Harmon*

May 30: Batting against Pedro Ramos in Game 1 of a doubleheader vs. Washington, Mickey Mantle nearly hits a home run out of Yankee Stadium with the ball striking the upper deck frieze in right field.

August 25: Phil Rizzuto is given his unconditional release.

October 8: Don Larsen hurls the only perfect game in World Series history, a 2–0 gem over Brooklyn in Game Five at Yankee Stadium.

GAME CALL, BOB WOLFF, NBC-TV:
"Count is one and one. And this crowd just straining forward on every pitch. Here it comes . . . a swing and a miss! Two strikes, ball one to Dale Mitchell. Listen to this crowd! . . . Two strikes and a ball . . . Mitchell waiting, stands deep, feet close together. Larsen is ready, gets the sign . . . here comes the pitch. Strike three! A no-hitter! A perfect game for Don Larsen!"

September 30: Mickey Mantle nips Ted Williams for the batting title on the final day of the season to win the Triple Crown.

December 18: Former Yankee shortstop, Phil "Scooter" Rizzuto joins the broadcast team of Mel Allen and "Red" Barber as a color commentator. He will stay on for decades as a beloved figure.

1957

April 20: Moose Skowron homers out of Fenway Park, just one of only six balls to that time to ever hit out of the park.

May 16: Copa Incident. "Nobody did nothin' to nobody." —Yogi Berra
Mickey Mantle, Yogi Berra, Hank Bauer, Johnny Kucks, their wives and Billy Martin were at the Copacabana nightclub in Manhattan enjoying entertainment provided by Sammy Davis Jr. Two bowling teams came in to celebrate victories. Here is how Mickey Mantle remembered what happened: "They (the bowlers) kept calling him (Davis) Little Black Sambo and stuff like that. Billy and Hank kept telling them a couple of times to sit down. The next thing I knew was that the cloak room was filled with people swinging."

PAUL DOHERTY: *It was the Copa's bouncers who pounced on the bowlers, but the bowlers blamed Bauer, Martin.*

Billy Martin, after the episode, is traded to Kansas City and he and Casey Stengel did not speak for years afterward.

July 14: Moose Skowron hits a then–Major League record second pinch-hit grand slam of the season off Jim Wilson of the White Sox in the second game of a doubleheader.

July 23: Mickey Mantle hits for the cycle his first and only time. He goes 4-for-5, scoring two runs and driving in four.

November 22: Mickey Mantle is named American League Most Valuable Player angering Red Sox fans whose choice was Ted Williams. Boston owner Tom Yawkey called sportswriters "incompetent and unqualified."

1958

September 17: Mickey Mantle slams a home run over the roof and out of Tiger Stadium in Detroit.

September 20: Pitcher Hoyt Wilhelm of the Baltimore Orioles no-hits the Yankees.

1959

April 7: Opening day Yankees debut the major's first electronic message scoreboard.

May 20: The Yankees are stuck in last place for the first time since May 8, 1940.

December 11: Roger Maris is acquired in a seven-player trade that sends Don Larsen, Hank Bauer, Marv Throneberry and Norm Siebern to the Athletics.

1960

April 19: Roger Maris makes his Yankee debut on Opening Day, Patriot's Day at Fenway Park. He goes 4-for-5 with two home runs.

July 13: Yankee Stadium is the site of the second of two All-Star Games. The National League wins, 6–0. Seven Yankees are on the American League squad: Starters Whitey Ford, Yogi Berra, Mickey Mantle, Roger Maris and Bill Skowron. The Yankee reserves were Jim Coates and Elston Howard.

July 28: Cleveland center fielder Jimmy Piersall sits behind the monuments during a pitching change. Umpires ask that he go to his fielding position.

"I was having a conversation with The Babe. Sorry about that."
—*Jimmy Piersall*

August 13: Three days after his 86th birthday, Herbert Hoover throws out the first ball at the Old-Timers' Day game at Yankee Stadium.

September 10: Mickey Mantle slugs a tremendous home run over the right field roof at Tiger Stadium in Detroit. The ball crosses Trumbull Avenue and lands in a lumberyard. The Guinness Book of World Records lists it as the longest home run ever measured.

September 25: At Fenway Park, Casey Stengel clinches his 10th pennant in 12 years as Yankee manager. Ralph Terry pitches New York to a 4–3 win over the Red Sox.

September 28: Blasting his 39th and 40th home runs off Washington's Chuck Stobbs in a 6–3 Yankee win, Mickey Mantle clinches the 1960 home run title over teammate Roger Maris.

September 30: The Yankees win their 13th straight and set an American League record for home runs as they defeat the Red Sox 6–5.

October 8: Bobby Richardson drives in a record (to that point in time) six runs with a grand slam and a two-run single in a 10–0 Yankees World Series game 3 pounding of Pittsburgh.

October 13: A bottom of the ninth inning home run by Bill Mazeroski of the Pirates breaks a 9–9 tie, defeats the Yankees and gives Pittsburgh the world championship.

October 18: Casey Stengel is forced out as manager. Yankee co-owners Dan Topping and Del Webb institute a mandatory retirement age of 65.

October 20: Ralph Houk is given a two-year contract as manager.

1961

April 17: In freezing rain on Opening Day, just 1,947 spectators show up. Whitey Ford blanks Kansas City, 3–0.

October 1: Roger Maris hits his 61st home run in the season's final game off Boston's Tracy Stallard, breaking Babe Ruth's record of 60.

"He came into the dugout and they were all applauding. I mean, this is something that's only happened once in baseball, right? They wanted him to come back out. He wouldn't come out, so the players had to push him back out. They forced him to come out and take a bow. That's the kind of guy he was. He was great, and I really liked him."
—*Mickey Mantle*

October 8: Whitey Ford breaks Babe Ruth's World Series record of 29⅔ consecutive scoreless innings, running his streak to 32.

"When I was nine years old, I went to my first Yankee game and sat in the center field bleachers. Growing up in Astoria Queens, I'd be taken to Yankee Stadium by my father or my uncles. We'd sit in the bleachers. I wasn't even playing baseball. There were no baseball fields in Astoria. I never imagined I would be pitching one day on that mound."
—*Whitey Ford*

December 13: Mickey Mantle signs a contract for $82,000 for the 1962 season, the second highest ever for a Yankee.

1962

April 10: Mickey Mantle hits his last Opening Day home run. The ball lands some 425 feet from home plate into the right-center field bleachers at Yankee Stadium as the Yankees nip Baltimore, 7–6.

June 24: Jack Reed's 22nd-inning two-run home run ends the longest game in Yankee history, a 9–7 win at Detroit.

October 16: The Yankees win the World Series as second baseman Bobby Richardson snags Willie McCovey's two-on, two-out shot in the ninth inning of Game 7.

1963

February 27: Mickey Mantle signs his first $100,000 contract.

April 9: Joe Pepitone becomes the last Yankee to hit two home runs on Opening Day. There were five other times that a Yankee did as much in the history of the Yankees: Roger Maris in 1960, Mickey Mantle in 1956, Russ Derry in 1945 and Babe Ruth and Sammy Byrd on April 12, 1932.

May 22: In an 8–7, 11-inning win vs. the Kansas City A's, Mickey Mantle hits the upper deck frieze in right field for the second time in his career.

"The hardest ball I ever hit."
—*Mickey Mantle*

November 7: Elston Howard becomes the American League's first black Most Valuable Player.

1964

August 12: Mickey Mantle sets a switch-hitting record, homering for the 10th time in the same game from both sides of the plate.

October 3: Defeating Cleveland, 8–3, the Yankees clinch a fifth straight pennant.

October 10: Mickey Mantle's ninth-inning shot into the upper deck in right off Cardinals' knuckleballer Barney Schultz wins Game 3 of the World Series for the Yankees.

"It wasn't thrown, it was dangled like bait to a big fish. Plus it lingered in that area that was down, and Mickey was a lethal low-ball hitter left-handed. The pitch was so slow that it allowed him to turn on it and pull it." —*Bob Gibson*

October 15: In his final World Series game, Mickey Mantle hits his 18th and final World Series home run to set the all-time World Series home run record. The Yankees lose the World Series to the St. Louis Cardinals.

October 16: Manager Yogi Berra is fired.

November 2: CBS purchases 80 percent of Yankees for $11,200,000; that is $86,501,511.31 in today's dollars. The network later buys the remaining 20 percent.

1965

June 20: The first Bat Day is staged at Yankee Stadium and draws 71,245.

PAUL DOHERTY: *The 1965 season not only featured an organ but also the first of the Yankee promotional days (anything to draw some fans from the Mets at the brand-new Shea Stadium). The first was Bat Day June 20, when kids came to get bats and to see the Yankees dump both ends of a doubleheader to Minnesota.*

July 20: Yankees pitcher Mel Stottlemyre hits an inside-the-park grand slam, the first pitcher to do that in more than 50 years. The home run provides the margin of victory in the Yankees' 6–3 win over the Red Sox at Yankee Stadium.

September 18: Before a crowd of 50,180, including Joe DiMaggio and Bobby Kennedy, "Mickey Mantle Day" is staged. The "Mick" plays in his 2,000th game.

1966

May 7: With the Yankees losers of 16 of their last 20 games, General Manager Ralph Houk fires Johnny Keane and takes over as manager for the rest of the season.

July 25: Casey Stengel is inducted into the Baseball Hall of Fame.

September 17: Bobby Richardson Day is staged at the Stadium.

September 22: Just 413 show at the Stadium, the smallest crowd in its history. Broadcaster Red Barber orders TV cameras to show the empty seats. As the story goes, that was an action that lost the great announcer his job with the Yankees.

"I don't know what the paid attendance is today, but whatever it is, it is the smallest crowd in the history of Yankee Stadium . . . and this crowd is the story, not the game."
—*Red Barber*

December 8: Roger Maris is traded to the Cardinals for Charley Smith.

December 17: Mickey Mantle announces his willingness to move from the outfield to first base, if the move would help the team.

1967

April 14: Behind rookie pitcher Bill Rohr, Boston trims the Yankees, 3–0 at the Stadium. Elston Howard's single with two outs in the ninth inning breaks up Rohr's no-hitter bid.

May 14: Mickey Mantle becomes only the sixth player—and second Yankee—to reach the 500–home run plateau when he connects off Baltimore's Stu Miller in a 6–5 win at Yankee Stadium.

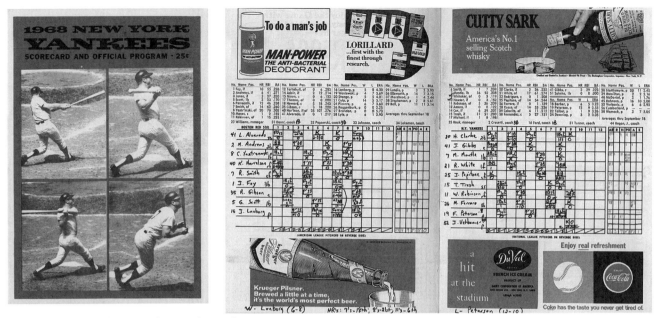

Scorecards from 1968, the year Mickey Mantle retired.

Three balls, two strikes. Mantle waits. Stu Miller is ready. Here's the pay-off by Miller to Mantle. Swung on! There she goes! . . . Mickey Mantle has hit his 500th home run!

May 30: After playing in just seven games in 1967, Whitey Ford retires.

June 7: Ron Blomberg is selected by the last place Yankees as the first pick in the free agent draft.

August 3: The Yankees trade catcher Elston Howard to the Red Sox.

August 29: The Red Sox lose a game that goes at least 18 innings to the Yankees for the second time. New York tops Boston, 4–3, in 20 innings in the second game of a doubleheader.

PAUL DOHERTY: *During the winter of 1967 Yankee Stadium was painted white by CBS and the seats a deep Yankee blue. Bleacher benches were replaced, new lights installed, a telephonic Hall of Fame was installed inside the Stadium. All ushers and vendors were given new uniforms. It was the biggest rehab to the Stadium since 1946.*

1968

September 20: Mickey Mantle hits his final home run, Number 536. It comes off Red Sox hurler Jim Lonborg at Yankee Stadium.

September 28: At Fenway Park, Mickey Mantle plays in his final game—number 2,401—the most ever for a Yankee to that time.

September 29: In the "Year of the Pitcher," Carl Yastrzemski goes 0-for-5 in the season finale against the Yankees, but he still wins the battle title with a .301 batting average—the lowest to ever lead the league. No one else hits .300 in the American League in 1968.

1969

June 8: "Mickey Mantle Day" is celebrated before a record crowd at Yankee Stadium. His uniform (Number 7) is retired. A crowd of 60,096 cheers and throws confetti as he tours the Stadium in a golf cart.

A plaque is dedicated in honor of Joe DiMaggio and attached to the outfield wall near the on-field monuments.

July 21: At the All-Star banquet in Washington, D.C., Joe DiMaggio is named the Greatest Living Player and Babe Ruth is selected as the Greatest All-Time Player.

1970

April 7: Mel Stottlemyre starts his fourth straight season-opener at Yankee Stadium. The Red Sox eke out a 4–3 win.

August 8: Casey Stengel's Number 37 is retired.

"Now that I've finally had my uniform retired, I think I'll die in it."
—Casey Stengel

August 29: Mickey Mantle becomes the Yankee first-base coach.

November 25: Thurman Munson is selected as American League Rookie of the Year.

1971

January 10: Bill White is hired by WPIX-TV to broadcast Yankee games. He becomes the first African-American play-by-play announcer in MLB.

1972

March 22: Sparky Lyle is acquired from the Red Sox for Danny Cater.

April 18: The first Opening Day night game is played at the Stadium. The Yankees defeat Milwaukee, 2–0.

April 22: Yankee third baseman Rich McKinney's errors contribute to the Red Sox scoring of nine runs and an 11–7 loss for the Bombers.

August 7: Lefty Gomez and Yogi Berra are inducted into the Hall of Fame.

"I thank everybody for making this day necessary."   —Yogi Berra

August 8: A 30-year lease is signed by the Yankees with the City of New York to play in 1976 in a remodeled Yankee Stadium.

1973

January 3: A limited partnership, headed by George M. Steinbrenner III as its managing general partner, purchases the Yankees from CBS.

March 5: Teammates Fritz Peterson and Mike Kekich swap wives, families and dogs.

April 6: Ron Blomberg bats as baseball's first designated hitter and draws a first-inning walk from Boston's Luis Tiant.

August 1: Red Sox catcher Carlton Fisk and Thurman Munson battle at Fenway Park after the Yankee catcher attempts to score from third base on a missed bunt attempt.

September 30: Completing their 50th anniversary season at the old Yankee Stadium, the Yankees play their final game before 32,238. The last home run is hit by Duke Sims in his seventh day as a Yankee. Ralph Houk resigns as manager triggering the string of 20 managerial changes George Steinbrenner would make through 1995.

1974

January 3: Bill Virdon becomes Yankee manager.

April 6: Playing their first home game outside of Yankee Stadium since 1922, the Yankees begin the first of two seasons at Shea Stadium when they defeat Cleveland, 6–1. The Yankees will go 90-69 at Shea over the two seasons of 1974 and 1975.

August 12: Whitey Ford and Mickey Mantle are inducted into the Baseball Hall of Fame.

November 27: George Steinbrenner is fined $15,000 by the courts and then suspended for two years by baseball commissioner Bowie Kuhn for illegal contributions to Richard Nixon's re-election campaign.

December 31: Free agent Catfish Hunter signs a five-year contract worth $3.75 million.

1975

July 27: In the not-so-friendly confines of Shea Stadium (Yankee Stadium is being refurbished) Red Sox outfielder Fred Lynn's running, stumbling catch enables Boston to win the first game of a doubleheader against the Yankees. The Red Sox victory ends Yankee pennant hopes and closes out Bill Virdon's future as manager.

August 1: Billy Martin replaces Bill Virdon as manager and begins the first of five tumultuous turns as Yankee pilot through 1988.

1976

March 1: George Steinbrenner's suspension is lifted after 15 months as a result of good behavior.

April 15: A remodeled Yankee Stadium opens; the Yankees defeat the Minnesota Twins, 11–4 before 52,613, the largest Opening Day crowd in 30 years. First home run hit by Dan Ford. First Yankee winning pitcher is Dick Tidrow.

April 17: Thurman Munson hits the first home run by a Yankee at the refurbished stadium. He is also named Yankee captain and will be in that role until August 2, 1979.

"Maybe they made me captain because I've been here so long. If I'm supposed to be captain by example, then I'll be a terrible captain." —Thurman Munson

May 20: In Yankee Stadium, Lou Piniella slams into Carlton Fisk at the plate. In the melee, Red Sox left-hander Bill Lee injures his left shoulder.

WHITEY FORD: *I hated it when we went to Shea and was so happy to come back. We all thought the refurbished Stadium was very nice. They cleaned the place up, did the dressing room over; there were mirrors and electric outlets in the lockers.*

June 15: A's owner Charlie Finley sells Vida Blue to the Yankees for $1.5 million.

June 18: Commissioner Bowie Kuhn orders the Yankees to return Vida Blue to the A's.

September 24: The Yankees win the American League East defeating the Tigers, 8–0.

October 12: First championship series game at Stadium, 5–3 win over Kansas City.

October 14: Chris Chambliss' ninth-inning home run off Mark Littell in Game Five of the ALCS against Kansas City gives the Yankees their 30th pennant, their first since 1964.

October 19: First night World Series game at Yankee Stadium, 6–2 loss to Cincinnati.

October 21: The Yankees, in the World Series for the first time since 1964, are swept by the Reds.

November 18: Don Gullett becomes the first free agent signed by the Yankees in the 1976 re-entry draft.

November 29: The Yankees sign Reggie Jackson to a five-year, $3-million free-agent contract.

1977

April 5: Shortstop Bucky Dent is acquired from the White Sox for outfielder Oscar Gamble, pitchers LaMarr Hoyt and Bob Polinsky, plus an estimated $200,000.

May 24: At Yankee Stadium, New York rallies to beat Boston, 6–5, thanks to back-to-back home runs by Carlos May and Graig Nettles.

June 18: Reggie Jackson is removed by Billy Martin from a game against the Red Sox in Fenway Park for "loafing" on a fly ball. The two men almost come to blows in the dugout as shown on national TV cameras.

July 19: The All-Star Game is played at Yankee Stadium. The National League wins, 7–5, at a managerial showdown of Billy Martin versus Sparky Anderson of Cincinnati before 56,683. Joe DiMaggio was the AL Honorary captain and Willie Mays had that role for the National League.

WILLIE RANDOLPH: *I was a young kid in that All-Star Game, in front of my hometown fans, my family, playing in the game with guys I had grown up idolizing like Reggie Jackson and Rod Carew.*

September 10: Expansion team Toronto rolls over the Yankees, 19–3, in one of the worst defeats in Stadium history for a Yankee team.

October 1: The Yankees win the AL East despite losing to the Tigers, 10–7.

October 9: The Yankees defeat the Royals, 5–3, to win the pennant.

October 18: Reggie Jackson hits three home runs in Game Six of the World Series against the Los Angeles Dodgers at Yankee Stadium. The Yankees win their 21st World Championship, their first since 1962.

GAME CALL, ROSS PORTER, CBS RADIO NETWORK: *Jackson, with four runs batted in, sends a fly ball to center field and deep! That's going to be way back! And that's going to be gone! Reggie Jackson has hit his third home run of the game!*

October 26: Sparky Lyle wins the American League Cy Young Award, becoming the first reliever to record that honor.

1978

January 13: Former Yankee great manager Joe McCarthy dies at age 90.

April 13: At the Yankee Stadium home opener, "Reggie Candy Bar Day," Reggie Jackson smashes a first-inning three-run homer. Fans throw candy bars out all over the field.

"The fans went crazy. It was his first at bat of the season after the three home runs in the World Series the year before. They threw all kinds of stuff on the field, including his candy bars. The game had to be delayed. Bob Sheppard had to tell people to stay off the field and conduct themselves properly." —Tony Ferraro, Yankee coach

"Ladies and gentleman," public address announcer Sheppard said, "we ask for your cooperation to avoid delay in this game or any games during the season. Please remember that the delay of the game is caused by the throwing of objects on the field, which necessitates the clearing of the field before the game can resume. We appreciate your cooperation."

April 14: Joe "Flash" Gordon dies.

June 17: Ron Guidry establishes a franchise record striking out 18 batters in a 4-hit, 4–0 shutout against the Angels at the stadium. His 11–0 mark is a record for American League left-handers. Yankees fans begin tradition of standing up and cheering each time the southpaw got two strikes on a batter.

July 24: Billy Martin resigns as Yankee manager.

July 25: Bob Lemon replaces Billy Martin as manager.

July 29: At Old-Timers' Day, the announcement is made that Billy Martin will return as manager in 1980 and Bob Lemon will be general manager.

September 7–9: The "new" Boston Massacre took place as the Yankees win all four games in a series pounding out 42 runs and 67 hits.

October 2: The Yankees, 14 games behind Boston at one point, defeat the Red Sox, 5–4, at Fenway Park in the second playoff game in AL history. Bucky Dent's homer over the Green Monster accentuates the comeback, clinching the pennant.

October 3: Reggie Jackson hits a 3-run home run, singles and doubles leading the Yankees to a 7–1 victory over the Royals in the opening game of the AL Championship Series.

October 7: The Yankees win the pennant by defeating the Royals, 2–1.

October 17: The Yankees win their 22nd world championship defeating the Dodgers, 7–2.

1979

August 2: Captain Thurman Munson dies while piloting his twin-engine jet at the Akron-Canton airport. The Yankees immediately retire his number.

"Thurman's death took everything out of the club." —Billy Martin

August 6: Thurman Munson's farewell night is held at Yankee Stadium. Yankees stand with heads bowed for nearly 10 minutes to honor Munson. No one occupies the catching spot behind the plate as the Yankees take the field. On the same day he delivers the eulogy for Thurman Munson, Bobby Murcer that night drove the Yankees to victory over Baltimore.

September 16: Jim "Catfish" Hunter is honored. Dave Righetti debuts as a Major League ballplayer.

October 28: Dick Howser replaces Billy Martin as manager.

1980

August 1: Reggie Jackson slams his 400th career home run on the same day in 1929 that Babe Ruth hit his 500th home run.

September 20: A bronze plaque is dedicated at Yankee Stadium in memory of Thurman Munson.

October 4: The Yankees win their fourth division title in five years defeating the Tigers, 5–2.

October 10: It was Yankees vs. Royals before more than 56,000 at the Stadium. It was Goose Gossage against George Brett, top of the seventh, Yanks ahead, 2–1, but down 2–1 in the best-of-five play-off series. Two outs. Two on for KC. Three run shot by Brett.

"Beating the Yankees had become the biggest obstacle in our lives. Walking up to home plate, I could hear the roar of the crowd, the anticipation. I knew I'd hit it good." —George Brett

"I was devastated." —Goose Gossage

November 21: Gene Michael is named manager after Dick Howser resigns.

December 15: The Yankees sign free agent outfielder Dave Winfield to a 10-year deal, making him the highest-paid player in baseball.

1981

April 21, 1981: George Steinbrenner, annoyed at Yankee yearbook images of him, orders 50,000 copies removed from Yankee Stadium concession stands.

September 6: Bob Lemon is named manager for the second time after the Yankees fire Gene Michael.

October 11: Home runs by Reggie Jackson, Oscar Gamble and Rick Cerone help the Yankees defeat the Brewers, 7–3, as the Bombers win their fifth division title in six years.

October 15: The Yankees win their 33rd American League pennant, shutting out the A's 4–0.

October 28: The Dodgers win their fifth World Series title by beating the Yankees, 9–2.

November 30: Dave Righetti is named Rookie of the Year in the American League.

December 23: Outfielder Dave Collins signs as a free agent.

1982

January 22: Reggie Jackson signs as a free agent with the California Angels.

January 29: Graig Nettles is named the sixth captain in Yankee history.

April 25: After Bob Lemon is fired, Gene Michael is named manager for the second time.

August 3: Continuing the managerial revolving door, Clyde King is named manager of the Yankees after Gene Michael is fired.

August 6: Bucky Dent is traded to the Texas Rangers for Lee Mazzilli.

December 1: Don Baylor signs a five-year, $5-million free-agent contract.

1983

January 11: Billy Martin takes over as manager for the third time in eight years.

May 31: AL President Lee MacPhail suspends Yankees owner George Steinbrenner for a week, citing "repeated problems" for publicly criticizing umpires. The Yankee owner is banned from attending games and for being in his Yankee Stadium office during his suspension.

July 4: Dave Righetti 24 'no-hits' the Red Sox 4-0 before 41,077 at Yankee Stadium.

GAME CALL, FRANK MESSER, WABC RADIO: *The Yankees lead, 4-0. Glenn Hoffman is at second base, two outs, in the top of the ninth inning. And Dave Righetti on the threshold of making history here at Yankee Stadium, sets the kick, and the pitch . . . HE STRUCK HIM OUT! RIGHETTI HAS PITCHED A NO-HITTER! DAVE RIGHETTI HAS PITCHED A NO-HITTER!*

July 24: The Yankees and Kansas City play the "Pine Tar" game at Yankee Stadium.

August 18: The "Pine Tar" game concludes with a 5–4 KC win.

December 16: Yogi Berra is named manager after the Yankees fire Billy Martin.

1984

January 5: Free agent Phil Niekro is signed to a two-year contract allowing Dave Righetti to move to the bullpen replacing Rich Gossage.

July 21: Plaques are unveiled in Monument Park honoring, in memory, Elston Howard, who had died, and also Roger Maris. Both had died at age 51. Howard's number 32 and Maris's number 9 were retired by the Yankees.

August 5: Lou Piniella Day is celebrated at the Stadium.

September 23: The Detroit Tigers defeat the New York Yankees, 4–1, making Sparky Anderson the first manager to win more than 100 games in each league.

September 30: On the final day of the season at Yankee Stadium, Don Mattingly edges teammate Dave Winfield to win the American League batting title with a .343 batting average. Mattingly notches four hits in five at bats; Winfield manages one hit in four tries.

December 5: Rickey Henderson is acquired in a trade with the A's.

1985

April 8: At Fenway Park, 46-year-old Yankees pitcher Phil Niekro becomes the second-oldest Opening Day starter in Yankees franchise history (as well as the third oldest all-time pitcher) to start an opening-day game.

April 28: Billy Martin is installed as manager for the fourth time, taking over for Yogi Berra.

August 3: White Sox catcher Carlton Fisk tags out two Yankees at home plate on the same play. With Bobby Meacham at first base and Dale Berra at second base, Rickey Henderson smashes a ball into the left-center gap. The relay cuts down both runners.

August 4: On Phil Rizzuto Day at Yankees Stadium. The "Scooter's" uniform number 10 is retired and a plaque is dedicated to honor him.

BILL GALLO: *It was a Daily News promotion. With the help of a cow trainer, I brought a cow from center field to home plate where Rizzuto, who had just been given a set of golf clubs. The cow stepped on his foot. And he went ass-up into the air. It was almost like a cartoon. And of course, he shouted, "Holy cow!"*

PHIL RIZZUTO: *That big thing stepped right on my shoe and pushed me backwards, like a karate move. That thing really hurt.*

August 14: The longest-serving Yankee, Equipment Manager Pete Sheehy, who had been a part of the scene from the time he was 17 years old, dies. The clubhouse at the Stadium is named for him.

September 13: On his seventeenth birthday, Bernie Williams signs with the Yankees.

September 15: George Steinbrenner calls Dave Winfield, "Mr. May," after the Yankees lose three key games to the Blue Jays. The Niekro brothers are re-united as the Yankees trade for 40-year-old Joe Niekro.

October 6: Phil Niekro wins his 300th game.

October 27: Billy Martin is fired for the fourth time. Lou Piniella is named manager.

November 20: Don Mattingly becomes the first player on a non-championship team to win the American League Most Valuable Player award since Jim Rice of the Red Sox in 1978.

December 14: Roger Maris dies at age 51 in Houston, Texas.

1986

March 28: Trading designated hitters, the Yankees send Don Baylor to the Red Sox for Mike Easler.

June 30: Ken Griffey is traded to the Braves for Claudell Washington and Paul Zuvella.

August 10: On Billy Martin Day, his uniform number is retired and a plaque appears in Monument Park with the inscription: "There has never been a greater competitor than Billy."

August 30: Tommy John, 43, and Joe Niekro, 41, are starters in a doubleheader for the Yanks against Seattle. They are the first age 40-plus teammates to start a doubleheader since 1922.

October 2: Breaking Earle Combs' team record set in 1927, Don Mattingly notches his 232nd hit of the season in a 6–1 win over the Red Sox.

October 4: Dave Righetti again makes history against the Red Sox, saving both games of a Yankees doubleheader sweep for a single-season Major League record 46 saves.

1987

January 14: Catfish Hunter is elected to the Baseball Hall of Fame.

July 18: Don Mattingly homers off Texas' Jose Guzman, tying Dale Long's Major-League record of hitting a home run in eight consecutive games. "Donnie Baseball" winds up with 10 homers in the eight games.

September 29: Don Mattingly's sixth grand slam of the season, a Major League record, comes off Boston's Bruce Hurst.

1988

January 6: Free agent Jack Clark signs with the Yankees.

June 23: Billy Martin is replaced as manager for the fifth and final time. Lou Piniella is named manager for the second time.

December 10: The Yankees sign a 12-year television contract worth $500 million with Madison Square Garden Network.

1989

Dallas Green is hired at the start of the season as manager.

April 28: For the 36th time, Rickey Henderson leads off a game with a home run.

August 18: In the 17th managing change of the George Steinbrenner ownership, Bucky Dent replaces Dallas Green as manager.

"We welcome Bucky, who has worked hard for this chance. I still consider Dallas to be a close friend." —George Steinbrenner

December 25: Billy Martin dies in an automobile accident at age 61.

1990

May 11: Dave Winfield cites a no-trade clause in his contract and refuses to report to the Angels after being traded. Five days later he changes his mind.

June 6: Bucky Dent is fired as manager with the Yankees in seventh place at 18–31. Carl "Stump" Merrill replaces him.

"Here we have a fellow who doesn't come with a whole lot of glamour. For the first five years I knew him I kept calling him 'Lump.' He was madder than hell."
—*George Steinbrenner*

July 1: With a no-hitter intact with two out in the bottom of the eighth at Comiskey Park, the Yankees make three errors behind starter Andy Hawkins, leading to four unearned runs as the Yankees go on to lose 4–0. While initially ruled a no-hitter, MLB removes the designation in 1991 after redefining a "no-hitter" as requiring pitchers to complete at least 9.0 innings.

July 30: Commissioner Fay Vincent permanently bans George Steinbrenner from the day-to-day operations of the Yankees because of the latter's dealings with a known gambler.

August 2: With ten home runs in 77 at bats, rookie Kevin Maas reaches that mark faster than any player ever.

August 20: George Steinbrenner resigns as managing general partner of the Yankees.

October 3: For the first time during the Steinbrenner era, the Yankees finish the season in last place.

1991

July 7: Bernie Williams made his Major League debut starting in center field and batting eighth. He was 1-for-3 with two RBIs. The Yankees lost 5–3 to Baltimore.

October 29: Buck Showalter is named manager of the Yankees, replacing Stump Merrill.

1992

June 1: The Yankees use their sixth pick in the amateur draft to select Derek Jeter.

December 6: The Yankees trade first baseman J. T. Snow and pitchers Jerry Nielsen and Russ Springer to the Angels for pitcher Jim Abbott.

December 10: Free agent Jimmy Key is signed to a four-year contract.

December 15: Wade Boggs signs a three-year free agent deal with the Yankees after 11 seasons with Boston.

1993

April 25: Mark Koenig is the last of the 1927 Yankees to die.

August 14: On Reggie Jackson Day, Jackson's uniform number 44 is retired.

September 4: Jim Abbott pitches a 4–0, no-hit win over the Indians at Yankee Stadium.

1994

February 25: Phil Rizzuto is elected to the Baseball Hall of Fame by the Veterans Committee.

"I'll go in even as a bat boy."
—*Phil Rizzuto*

April 4: Opening Day crowd of 56,706 is the largest in Yankee history.

1995

August 13: Mickey Mantle dies of cancer at age 63 in Dallas, Texas.

August 25: A monument to Mantle is dedicated, the first in 47 years. Its inscription reads, "A great teammate. A magnificent Yankee who left a legacy of unequaled courage."

September 6: Lou Gehrig's Major League record of 2,130 consecutive games played is broken. Baltimore's Cal Ripken Jr. plays in his 2,131st straight game.

November 2: Joe Torre is named manager of the Yankees after Buck Showalter resigns. He is the 31st manager and the first native New Yorker to manage the Bombers.

December 22: David Cone signs as a free-agent. He posts a 64–40 mark in his time with the team, helping the Yankees win four championships.

1996

April 2: Joe Torre achieves his first victory as manager of the Yankees, a 7–1 win over the Cleveland Indians at Jacobs Field.

April 9: Snowy weather at the home opener does not prevent the Yankees from defeating Kansas City 7–3, behind Andy Pettitte. Rookie Derek Jeter bats 9th in the New York lineup and goes 1–3.

May 14: Dwight Gooden hurls the only eighth regular-season no-hitter in Yankee history, a 2–0 blanking of Seattle at Yankee Stadium.

"The Doctor is in the House."
—*Message on the center-field scoreboard*

May 17: At Yankee Stadium against the Angels, Mariano Rivera recorded his first career save.

June 16: Mel Allen, legendary "Voice of the Yankees" from 1939 to 1964, dies at age 83.

MEL ALLEN: *Here I was, a guy supposed to practice law, broadcasting Yankee home games on radio from this mecca of baseball. This was the place, the number-one place in baseball. The stadium was like the Empire State Building or the Grand Canyon of baseball. Every time I stepped inside of it, I had to pinch myself!*

August 25: A monument in honor of Mickey Mantle is unveiled in Monument Park.

September 25: The Yankees win the AL East by defeating the Brewers, 19–2.

October 5: The Yankees defeat Texas, 6–4, and win the Division Series. Bernie Williams homers from each side of the plate.

October 9: Aided by Jeff Maier, the Yankees beat the Orioles in Game 1 of the ALCS. Derek Jeter ties the score in the eighth inning, homering to right. The ball was interfered with by schoolboy Jeffrey Maier, but the home run call still was in place. A Bernie Williams homer gives the Yanks an 11th inning win.

October 13: The Yankees win the AL pennant by beating the Orioles, 6–4. Bernie Williams is named the MVP of the ALCS.

October 23: Jim Leyritz homers to tie the game in the 8th inning. The Yankees go on to win in 10 innings.

October 26: The Yankees win their first World Series title since 1978, the first for Joe Torre, defeating the Braves, 3–2. Yankee Wade Boggs toured the Stadium on a police horse. The triumph foreshadows world championships in 1998, 1999 and 2000.

GAME CALL, JOE BUCK, FOX: *"Another chance to the left side, Hayes waits. The Yankees are champions of baseball!"*

1997

June 16: The Yankees host the Mets in the first regular-season interleague game between the two New York teams.

August 31: Don Mattingly has his number 23 retired and is given a plaque in Monument Park.

"A Humble Man of Grace and Dignity. A Captain Who Led by Example. Proud of the Pinstripes Tradition and Dedicated to the Pursuit of Excellence. A Yankee Forever."
—*Plaque in Monument Park*

December 10: DH Chili Davis is signed to a two-year deal.

1998

March 3: Lee MacPhail is elected to the Baseball Hall of Fame.

April 10: The Yankees draw their biggest Opening Day crowd at the remodeled Yankee Stadium (1976–2008)—56,717 and defeat Oakland 17–13.

April 13: A 500-pound steel girder falls on a seat in an empty Yankee Stadium just hours before a game, forcing the postponement of two games against the Angels. It also necessitates the Yankees playing one "home" game at Shea Stadium for the first time since September 1975.

April 27: Mariano Rivera records his 50th career save.

May 17: David Wells pitches only the 14th Perfect Game in regular season history, the first by a Yankee, besting Minnesota, 4–0, at Yankee Stadium.

July 5: The Yankees beat the Orioles, 1–0, setting a Major League record for 61 wins for the first half of a season.

July 25: Jim Bouton returns to Yankee Stadium as part of Old-Timers' Day. The former pitcher had been declared persona non grata by the Yankees since the 1970 release of his Ball Four.

September 25: The Yankees establish an American-League record with their 112th win, 6–1, over Tampa Bay at Yankee Stadium.

September 27: Beating the Devil Rays, 8–3, the Yanks set the AL record (later broken by Seattle) for wins in a season (114).

October 21: The Yankees win their 24th World Championship beating San Diego, 3–0, completing a World Series sweep. The win gives the club a record of 125–50 (114–48 in the regular season, 11–2 in postseason).

"This is a special team. The things we accomplished won't be done for a long time."
—*Paul O'Neill*

1999

January 5: George Steinbrenner ends a 14-year feud with Yogi Berra that began when he had an aide tell the Yankee legend that he was fired as manager.

February 18: The Yankees acquire Roger Clemens from the Blue Jays for pitchers David Wells, Graeme Lloyd and infielder Homer Bush. Clemens, who won two Cy Young Awards with Toronto, is coming off a 20–6, 271-strikeout year.

March 8: Joe DiMaggio, 84, passes away in Hollywood, Florida.

April 25: A monument to honor Joe DiMaggio is unveiled in Yankee Stadium's Monument Park in front of a sold-out Stadium and many of DiMaggio's former teammates. Phil Rizzuto addressed the fans, Paul Simon sang "Mrs. Robinson" while standing in Center Field. When he reached the last line, "Where have you gone, Joe DiMaggio?" many in the crowd sang along and cheered.

June 11: Mariano Rivera notches his 100th save.

July 18: On "Yogi Berra Day," David Cone tosses the only 15th regular-season perfect game. One season after David Wells accomplishes the feat. Ironically, Don Larsen—who tossed a perfect game in the 1956 World Series—throws out the ceremonial first pitch.

"You probably have a better chance of winning the lottery than this happening."
—David Cone

September 9: Jim "Catfish" Hunter dies at age 53 in Hertford, North Carolina.

October 27: Completing a four-game sweep of the Braves, the Yankees play Major League Baseball's last game of the century to win their 25th World Championship. The triumph is also the team's 12th straight in World-Series play.

December 10: Babe Ruth is voted Player of the Century by an Associated Press panel.

2000

April 23: Bernie Williams and Jorge Posada become the first teammates to hit home runs from both sides of the plate.

May 7: It is Bob Sheppard Day.

"That I should have a plaque out in Monument Park in center field. It was an incredible, memorable moment in my life."
—Bob Sheppard

July 8: Chuck Knoblauch's three-run homer keys a Yankee 4–2 triumph over the Mets at their home field in the second game of a doubleheader. The first game saw the Yankees prevail by the same score.

June 19: The Yankees romp over the Red Sox, 22–1, Boston's most-lopsided home loss ever. New York scores 16 runs in the last two innings of the game.

July 8: For the first time since 1903, two teams play two games in different stadiums the same day. The Yankees and Mets play the first game at Shea Stadium and the second game at Yankee Stadium. The Yankees win both games by 4–2 scores.

October 13: Mariano Rivera breaks Whitey Ford's record for most consecutive post-season scoreless innings—34⅓ innings.

October 14: Roger Clemens records a 15-strikeout one-hitter in the ALCS game played at the stadium.

October 22: In the first Subway World Series game since 1956, the Yankees defeat the Mets in extra innings in Game 1. The Yankees win the second game highlighted by Roger Clemens tossing part of a sawed-off bat toward Mike Piazza.

October 26: The Yankees win their third straight world championship, their fourth title in five years, their 26th overall, defeating the Mets, 4–2, in first "Subway Series" since 1956.

November 30: Pitcher Mike Mussina signs as a free agent for six years at $88.5 million.

2001

May 23: Behind Derek Jeter's five hits, the Yankees defeat the Red Sox 7–3. Ex-Yankee David Cone is charged with the loss.

May 30: Pedro Martinez is victorious over the Yankees for the first time in over a year.

"Wake up the Bambino and let me face him—I'll drill him in the ass."
—Pedro Martinez

August 1: Mariano Rivera records his 200th career save.

August 15: Roger Clemens becomes the first pitcher in 32 years to notch a 16–1 record.

September 2: Mike Mussina comes within one pitch of the 15th perfect game in Major League history, but pinch-hitter Carl Everett lines a 1–2 pitch for a base hit.

September 5: Roger Clemens wins his fifth straight game and becomes the first 19–1 pitcher in 89 years.

September 11: Within 90 minutes of the horrible attacks on the World Trade Center, Yankee Stadium was evacuated.

October 13: Down 0–2 to the A's in a best-of-five ALDS, Derek Jeter's relay shuttle-flip-throw saves the Yankees' postseason.

October 30: First time a U.S. president visits Yankee Stadium during the World Series. George W. Bush throws out the first ball in Game 3.

November 1: Yankees beat the Arizona Diamondbacks, 3–2, at the stadium. Derek Jeter's 10th-inning walk-off home run to win Game 4 earns his nickname "Mr. November," a play on former Yankees great Reggie Jackson's "Mr. October" moniker.

November 4: In Game 7 of the World Series after two dramatic come-from-behind victories, Arizona scores twice in the bottom of the ninth to beat the Yankees and deny the team from the Bronx another world championship.

November 15: Roger Clemens wins a record sixth Cy Young award.

2002

January 10: David Wells becomes a Yankee again signing a $7-million, two-year contract.

February 11: Frank Crosetti, 91, shortstop on eight Yankee World Series championship teams passes away in Stockton, California.

March 19: Yankees' YES Network is launched.

May 9: Mariano Rivera saves his 225th game, setting a new Yankee record.

August 28: Yankee pitcher Mike Mussina blanks the Red Sox, 7–0, at Fenway Park, a day after David Wells and Steve Karsay combine on a 6–0 shutout over Boston. It is the first time since 1943 that the Yankees had back-to-back shutouts at Fenway.

September 3: Roger Clemens fans ten Red Sox batters in 7⅓ innings, recording his 100th win since leaving Boston.

September 11: A pregame ceremony marks the first anniversary of the World Trade Center attack. A monument honoring those who died is unveiled in Monument Park.

October 5: The Yankees lose a 9–6 decision to the eventual World Champion Anaheim Angels. The Game 4 loss in the ALDS is the Yanks' earliest postseason exit since 1980.

December 19: Japanese professional baseball star Hideki Matsui is signed to be the new Yankee left fielder.

2003

April 8: In his Yankee Stadium debut, Hideki Matsui paces a 7–3 Yankee win over Minnesota with a grand slam home run.

June 3: Derek Jeter is named the 13th Yankee captain, according to Baseball Almanac.

June 11: The most pitchers used in a no-hitter in MLB history stymies the Yankees, 8–0. The Houston hurlers are: Roy Oswalt (1 inning), Peter Munro (1⅓), Kirk Saarloos (1⅓ inning.), Brad Lidge (2 innings), Octavio Dotel (1 inning) and Billy Wagner (1 inning).

June 12: Mariano Rivera records his 250th career save.

June 13: Roger Clemens records his 4,000th strikeout and 300th victory.

"To have these two milestones that I was able to attain on the same night here, it couldn't have worked out any better."
—*Roger Clemens*

October 16: An 11th inning leadoff home run by Aaron Boone off the Red Sox's Tim Wakefield helps the Yankees win the pennant.

October 25: Behind Josh Beckett, the Marlins defeat the Yankees, 2–0, in Game 6 of the World Series. The loss marks the first time since 1981 that New York is eliminated at the Stadium in postseason play.

November 4: Yankee icon Don Mattingly joins Torre's staff as hitting coach.

December 17: The Yankees sign Atlanta slugger Gary Sheffield to a three-year, $39 million contract.

2004

February 16: Alex Rodriguez, with the richest contract in sports, is traded by the Texas Rangers for Alfonso Soriano and a player to be named later.

April 11 and 14: Mike Mussina and Kevin Brown record their 200th victories in back-to-back games, becoming the first teammates in Major League history to do so.

April 16: The Yankees and Red Sox meet in the first game of a four-game series at Fenway. A-Rod goes 1-for-17 and is booed constantly by the hometown crowd during the series. Boston wins six of seven games over the Yankees in two weekends.

May 28: Mariano Rivera saves his 300th game.

July 1: Derek Jeter makes his most famous catch, diving into Yankee Stadium's stands off third base, nabbing a 12th-inning Trot Nixon popup. While the injured Jeter is on his way to the hospital, New York rallies in the 13th inning expanding its AL East lead over Boston to 8½ games with a 5–4 victory.

July 4: American League manager Joe Torre selects seven of his players—nearly one-third of the Yankee roster—for the All-Star Game in Seattle: Roger Clemens, Andy Pettitte, Mariano Rivera, Mike Stanton, Derek Jeter, Bernie Williams and Jorge Posada.

July 13: Joe Torre manages the American League to victory in the All-Star Game in Houston, improving his record to 5–0–1 in the midsummer classic.

July 24: In a 3-hour-54-minute thriller the Yankees nip the Red Sox, 11–10. A bench-clearing brawl breaks out when Alex Rodriguez is hit by a pitch.

August 18: New Hall of Famer Dave Winfield is honored by the Yankees. His number is not retired.

August 25: Paul O'Neill becomes the oldest player to record 20 home runs and 20 steals in a season.

2005

January 11: The trade to bring Randy Johnson to New York is official. The five-time Cy Young winner. Johnson will post a 17–8 record in his first season in pinstripes.

April 3: On Opening Day Randy Johnson and the Yankees defeat the defending World Series champion Red Sox.

April 26: Alex Rodriguez drives in 10 runs in one game bashing a grand slam, a three-run and a two-run homer. His 10th RBI came on a single. The Yanks romped, 12–4, over the Angels.

June 8: Smacking to two home runs against the Brewers in Milwaukee, Alex Rodriguez becomes the youngest player in Major League history to reach the 400-homer plateau.

August 30: A-Rod hits his 40th homer of the season, becoming the first Yankees right-handed hitter since Joe DiMaggio in 1937 to reach that mark. A-Rod went on to hit 48 homers and drive in 130 runs, earning his second career AL MVP award.

October 1: In the 161st game of the season, the Yankees prevail over Boston at Fenway Park clinching their eighth straight AL East crown title.

December 23: The Yankees make a move to bolster their own lineup while hurting the rival Red Sox. They sign center fielder Johnny Damon to a four-year, $52 million contract.

2006

August 16: George Steinbrenner helps break ground for the new Yankee Stadium, dubbed by some as "The House The Boss Built."

August 18 to 21: After four days of punishing the Red Sox, the Yankees were 5–0, outscoring Boston 47–25.

"This ranks right at the top because it was for the fans. So many guys delivered."
—*George Steinbrenner*

August 31: The Yankees suffer the worst loss in their history, a 22–0 flailing at the hands of the Cleveland Indians. It cuts the New York lead over Boston to just 3½ games in the AL East.

September 30: A two-run walk-off home run by Bernie Williams enables the Yankees to trim Minnesota, 6–4 to clinch their seventh straight AL East title. The Bombers advance to the playoffs for a 10th consecutive season.

October 20: The Red Sox did what no team had ever done before—overcoming a 3–0 postseason series deficit, ripping the Yankees in a 10–3 Game 7 shocker. The Yankees drop their fourth consecutive game, becoming the first team in baseball history to lose a best-of-seven series after winning the first three games.

October 27: George Steinbrenner calls together his top executives to Tampa, Florida for meetings less than a week after the Yankees lost the ALCS.

2007

May 6: Roger Clemens signs as a free agent with the Yankees.

May 29: The Yankees, a season-low eight games under .500 on May 29, go 73–39 in the stretch run leading the Majors in wins and winning percentage.

June 7: Recording his 2,000th career victory with a 10–3 win over the White Sox, Joe Torre becomes only the 10th manager to reach that mark. Torre also becomes the first to have 2,000 or more hits as a player and 2,000 or more wins as a manager.

August 4: Alex Rodriguez records his 500th career home run. It comes off the Royals' Kyle Davies in the 16–8 New York win. Just 32 years and eight days old, A-Rod becomes the youngest in MLB history to accomplish the feat, joining Babe Ruth and Mickey Mantle in the Yankee "500" club.

August 13: "The Scooter," Phil Rizzuto, dies at age 89.

September 5: Roger Clemens sets a Yankees record with his 15th straight victory becoming baseball's first 19–1 pitcher in 89 years as the Yankees defeat Toronto, 4–3.

September 5: Bob Sheppard works his final game as Yankees Public Address Announcer, a 3–2 win over Seattle.

October 30: Joe Girardi is named the 32nd manager in Yankees history.

2008

June 7: Johnny Damon goes 6-for-6 in the Yankees' 12–11 win vs. Kansas City matching the franchise record for hits in a nine-inning game (see June 6, 1934: Myril Hoag) becoming the only Yankee in original Yankee Stadium history to record six hits in a game of any length. His final hit is a "walk-off" single.

July 15: The fourth midsummer classic is staged at the "House That Ruth Built."

September 19: Roger Clemens becomes the first Major League hurler to post a 20–1 record.

September 21: The Yankees play their last ever game in the original Yankee Stadium. Julia Ruth Stevens, daughter of Babe Ruth, throws out the ceremonial pitch.

October 15: The Yankees are the first team to win a best-of-five series after losing the first two games at home, beating the Athletics 5–3.

2009

April 16: The Yankees play the first regular season game in the new Yankee Stadium. They lose, 10–2, to Cleveland. C. C. Sabatha tosses the Stadium's first official pitch. Johnny Damon records the first hit and Jorge Posada hits the first home run.

"It was memorable to get the first one hit. That's something I will definitely always remember." —Johnny Damon

September 11: Derek Jeter becomes the all-time hits leader in Yankees franchise history, passing Lou Gehrig in the record books with his 2,722nd career hit.

November 4: The Yankees win their 27th World Series defeating Philadelphia in Game 6.

2010

April 13: Steinbrenner attends the home opener, his final appearance at a Yankee game. Prior to the game, Derek Jeter and Joe Girardi present him with his 2009 World Series ring commemorating the seventh title won by a Steinbrenner-owned Yankee team.

July 11: Beloved Public Address announcer Bob Sheppard passes away at age 99.

July 13: George Steinbrenner dies of a heart attack at 80 in Tampa, Florida.

August 4: Alex Rodriguez becomes the youngest player in Major League history to hit 600 home runs. The circuit blast is off Blue Jays' Shaun Marcum.

September 20: A monument is dedicated to the late George Steinbrenner.

2011

July 9: Derek Jeter's 3,000th hit is a home run off Tampa Bay's David Price. He was the first player to collect his 3,000th hit for the Yankees, the first to do it in Yankee Stadium.

"Hopefully, I might be able to enjoy it the next few days."

—Derek Jeter

August 25: Yankees became the only team in history to hit three grand slams in a game. Robinson Cano, Russell Martin and Curtis Granderson all go deep in a trouncing of the Athletics 22–9.

September 19: Mariano Rivera notches his 602nd career save to become the all-time Major League leader. He works a perfect ninth inning to preserve a 6–4 triumph at the Stadium against the Twins.

December 13: Alex Rodriguez signs a 10-year contract for a guaranteed $275 million.

2012

July 23: Ichiro Suzuki is traded by the Seattle Mariners to the New York Yankees.

June 12: Alex Rodriguez ties Lou Gehrig's 74-year-old record with his 23rd career grand slam in a 6–4 victory over Atlanta. Gehrig hit his 23 grand homers in 17 seasons; A-Rod was in his 19th.

Card celebrating Derek Jeter's 3,000th hit, July 9, 2011.

2013

July 28: Hideki Matsui Day is celebrated at Yankee Stadium.

August 21: Ichiro Suzuki records his 4,000th career hit, a total combining his play in the Major Leagues and Japan.

September 11: Joe Girardi wins his 557th game as manager of the Yankees, passing Billy Martin for sixth place on the team's all-time list.

September 20: Alex Rodriguez hit his 24th career grand slam passing Lou Gehrig and powering a 5–1 Yankee victory over the Giants.

"I'm a huge fan of Lou Gehrig, everything he's done. He's become like the gold standard for a Yankee. It's a special moment. I'll think about it someday."
—Alex Rodriguez

2014

April 17: At Tampa Bay, the Yankees turn the 24th triple play in team history.

September 7: Derek Jeter Day is staged before a capacity crowd at the stadium.

September 21: Brett Gardner hits the 15,000th home run in franchise history.

September 25: Playing his final home game Derek Jeter's walk-off hit in the bottom of the ninth nipped Baltimore 6–5. The ovation was long, loud, loving.

September 28: Derek Jeter plays the last game of his career at Fenway Park against Boston.

2015

April 11: The longest game, 19 innings, six hours and 49 minutes, in the history of the new Yankee Stadium is played. The Red Sox eke out a 6–5 win.

May 24: Bernie Williams' Number 51 retired and he received a plaque in Monument Park.

June 19: Alex Rodriguez records his 3,000th career hit, a home run off Detroit's Justin Verlander.

October 1: The Yankees become the first American League team to record 10,000 victories and clinch a berth in the playoffs.

December 28: The Yankees acquire hard-throwing reliever Aroldis Chapman from the Reds.

2016

April 9: Yankee second baseman Starlin Castro notched his 1,000th career hit.

"One thousand hits feels good. I feel excited, but I came to New York to win a championship."
—*Starlin Castro*

May 15: Carlos Beltran becomes just the fourth switch-hitter in baseball history to hit 400 home runs.

"It's a great accomplishment."
—*Carlos Beltran*

July 3: Mark Teixeira becomes the ninth to hit his 400th home run as a Yankee joining Ruth, Gehrig, Mantle, Jackson, Sheffield, A-Rod, Soriano and Beltran.

August 14: Top closer in history and key part of five Yankee World Series winners, Mariano Rivera is awarded a plaque in Monument Park.

July 16: Aroldis Chapman ties his own record throwing the fastest pitch in MLB history—105.1 mph.

July 25: Aroldis Chapman is traded to the Chicago Cubs for four players.

August 5: Mark Teixeira announces he will retire at the end of the season. A Yankee since 2009, the first baseman said injuries had made the decision for him.

"I gave you everything I had. It wasn't always enough, but I tried my best."
—*Mark Teixeira*

August 5: Fourteen-time All-Star, Alex Rodriguez announces his retirement. A-Rod, who was a three-time MVP, a member of the 3,000-hit club and four home runs shy of 700, packs it in to be an advisor with the Yankees. His career is tarnished by his steroid scandal. He was a Yankee since 2004.

APPENDICES

Lists, tables, charts, stats, commandments and more, covering both trivia and record accomplishments.

MLB BATTING CHAMPIONS FROM THE YANKEES		
YEAR	**NAME**	**#**
1924	Babe Ruth	.378
1934	Lou Gehrig	.363
1939	Joe DiMaggio	.381
1940	Joe DiMaggio	.352
1945	Snuffy Stirnweiss	.309
1956	Mickey Mantle	.353
1984	Don Mattingly	.343
1994	Paul O'Neill	.359
1998	Bernie Williams	.339

MLB ERA CHAMPIONS FROM THE YANKEES		
YEAR	NAME	#
1920	Bob Shawkey	2.45
1927	Wilcy Moore	2.28
1934	Lefty Gomez	2.33
1937	Lefty Gomez	2.33
1943	Spud Chandler	1.64
1947	Spud Chandler	2.46
1952	Allie Reynolds	2.06
1953	Ed Lopat	2.42
1956	Whitey Ford	2.47
1957	Bobby Shantz	2.45
1958	Whitey Ford	2.01
1978	Ron Guidry	1.74
1979	Ron Guidry	2.78
1980	Rudy May	2.46

RETIRED NUMBERS		
NUMBER	**NAME**	**POSITION**
1	Billy Martin	M
2	Derek Jeter	SS
3	Babe Ruth	OF
4	Lou Gehrig	1B
5	Joe DiMaggio	OF
6	Joe Torre	M
7	Mickey Mantle	OF
8	Yogi Berra	C
8	Bill Dickey	C
9	Roger Maris	OF
10	Phil Rizzuto	SS
15	Thurman Munson	C
16	Whitey Ford	P
23	Don Mattingly	1B
32	Elston Howard	C
37	Casey Stengel	M
42	Mariano Rivera	P
42	Jackie Robinson	2B
44	Reggie Jackson	OF
49	Ron Guidry	P
51	Bernie Williams	OF

ROOKIES OF THE YEAR		
YEAR	NAME	POSITION
1951	Gil McDougald	3B
1954	Bob Grim	P
1957	Tony Kubek	SS/OF
1962	Tom Tresh	SS/OF
1968	Stan Bahnsen	P
1970	Thurman Munson	C
1981	Dave Righetti	P
1996	Derek Jeter	SS

CY YOUNG WINNERS		
YEAR	NAME	POSITION
1958	Bob Turley	RHP
1961	Whitey Ford	LHP
1977	Sparky Lyle	LHP
1978	Ron Guidry	LHP
2001	Roger Clemens	RHP

MVP WINNERS		
YEAR	NAME	POSITION
1936	Lou Gehrig	1B
1939	Joe DiMaggio	OF
1941	Joe DiMaggio	OF
1942	Joe Gordon	2B
1943	Spud Chandler	P
1947	Joe DiMaggio	OF
1950	Phil Rizzuto	SS
1951	Yogi Berra	C
1954	Yogi Berra	C
1955	Yogi Berra	C
1956	Mickey Mantle	OF
1957	Mickey Mantle	OF
1960	Roger Maris	OF
1961	Roger Maris	OF
1962	Mickey Mantle	OF
1963	Elston Howard	C
1976	Thurman Munson	C
1985	Don Mattingly	1B
2005	Alex Rodriguez	3B
2007	Alex Rodriguez	3B

NO-HITTERS		
NAME	IP	DATE
George Mogridge	9.0	04-24-1917
Sam Jones	9.0	09-04-1923
Monte Pearson	9.0	08-27-1938
Allie Reynolds	9.0	07-12-1951
Allie Reynolds	9.0	09-28-1951
Don Larsen	9.0	**10-08-1956**
Dave Righetti	9.0	07-04-1983
Andy Hawkins	8.0	07-01-1990
Jim Abbott	9.0	09-04-1993
Dwight Gooden	9.0	05-14-1996
David Wells	9.0	**05-17-1998**
David Cone	9.0	**07-18-1999**
Bold = Perfect Game		

CYCLE HITTERS		
NAME	INN.	DATE
Bert Daniels	9	07-25-1912
Bob Meusel	9	05-07-1921
Bob Meusel	9	07-03-1922
Bob Meusel	12	07-26-1928
Tony Lazzeri	9	**06-03-1932**
Lou Gehrig	9	06-25-1934
Joe DiMaggio	9	07-09-1937
Lou Gehrig	9	08-01-1937
Buddy Rosar	9	07-19-1940
Joe Gordon	9	09-08-1940
Joe DiMaggio	9	05-20-1948
Mickey Mantle	9	07-23-1957
Bobby Murcer	11	08-29-1972
Tony Fernandez	10	09-03-1995
Melky Cabrera	9	08-02-2009
Bold = Natural Cycle		

100 LOSS SEASONS		
YEAR	RECORD	MANAGER
1908	51–103	Clark Griffith
1908	27–71	Kid Elberfeld
1912	50–102	Harry Wolverton

100 WIN SEASONS		
YEAR	RECORD	MANAGER
1927	110–44	Miller Huggins
1928	101–53	Miller Huggins
1932	107–47	Joe McCarthy
1936	102–51	Joe McCarthy
1937	102–52	Joe McCarthy
1939	106–45	Joe McCarthy
1941	101–53	Joe McCarthy
1942	103–51	Joe McCarthy
1954	103–51	Casey Stengel
1961	109–53	Ralph Houk
1963	104–57	Ralph Houk
1977	100–62	Billy Martin
1978	100–63	Billy Martin
1980	103–59	Dick Howser
1998	114–48	Joe Torre
2002	103–58	Joe Torre
2003	101–61	Joe Torre
2004	101–61	Joe Torre
2009	103–59	Joe Girardi

1921 World Series	1943 World Series	1962 World Series
1922 World Series	1947 World Series	1963 World Series
1923 World Series	1949 World Series	1964 World Series
1926 World Series	1950 World Series	1976 World Series
1927 World Series	1951 World Series	1977 World Series
1928 World Series	1952 World Series	1978 World Series
1932 World Series	1953 World Series	1981 World Series
1936 World Series	1955 World Series	1996 World Series
1937 World Series	1956 World Series	1998 World Series
1938 World Series	1957 World Series	1999 World Series
1939 World Series	1958 World Series	2000 World Series
1941 World Series	1960 World Series	2001 World Series
1942 World Series	1961 World Series	2003 World Series
		2009 World Series

AMERICAN LEAGUE PENNANTS		
YEAR	RECORD	MANAGER
1921	98–55	Miller Huggins
1922	94–60	Miller Huggins
1923	98–54	Miller Huggins
1926	91–63	Miller Huggins
1927	110–44	Miller Huggins
1928	101–53	Miller Huggins
1932	107–47	Joe McCarthy
1936	102–51	Joe McCarthy
1937	102–52	Joe McCarthy
1938	99–53	Joe McCarthy
1939	106–45	Joe McCarthy
1941	101–53	Joe McCarthy
1942	103–41	Joe McCarthy
1943	98–56	Joe McCarthy
1947	97–57	Bucky Harris
1949	97–57	Casey Stengel
1950	98–56	Casey Stengel
1951	98–56	Casey Stengel
1952	95–59	Casey Stengel
1953	99–52	Casey Stengel
1955	97–57	Casey Stengel

AMERICAN LEAGUE PENNANTS		
1956	97–57	Casey Stengel
1957	98–56	Casey Stengel
1958	92–62	Casey Stengel
1960	97–57	Casey Stengel
1961	109–53	Ralph Houk
1962	96–66	Ralph Houk
1963	104–57	Ralph Houk
1964	99–63	Yogi Berra
1976	97–62	Billy Martin
1977	100–62	Billy Martin
1978	100–63	Billy Martin
1981	59–48	Gene Michael
1996	92–70	Joe Torre
1998	114–48	Joe Torre
1999	98–64	Joe Torre
2000	87–74	Joe Torre
2001	95–65	Joe Torre
2003	101–61	Joe Torre
2009	103–59	Joe Girardi

(continued)

WILD CARDS		
YEAR	RECORD	MANAGER
1995	79–65	Buck Showalter
1997	96–66	Joe Torre
2007	94–68	Joe Torre
2010	95–67	Joe Girardi

HOME RUN BREAKDOWN AT HOME (REGULAR SEASON)		
PARK	YEARS	HOME RUNS
Hilltop Park	1903–1912	134
Polo Grounds	1913–1922	332
Old Yankee Stadium	1923–1973	3,654
Shea Stadium	1974–1975, 1998	93
Remodeled Yankee Stadium	1976–2008	Over 2,000
New Yankee Stadium	2009–2016	899

EAST DIVISION TITLES		
YEAR	RECORD	MANAGER
1976	97–62	Billy Martin
1977	100–62	Billy Martin
1978	100–63	Billy Martin
1980	103–59	Dick Howser
1981	59–48	Gene Michael
1994	70–43	Buck Showalter
1996	92–70	Joe Torre
1998	114–48	Joe Torre
1999	98–64	Joe Torre
2000	87–74	Joe Torre
2001	95–65	Joe Torre
2002	103–58	Joe Torre
2003	101–61	Joe Torre
2004	101–61	Joe Torre
2005	95–67	Joe Torre
2006	97–65	Joe Torre
2009	103–59	Joe Girardi
2011	97–65	Joe Girardi
2012	95–67	Joe Girardi

SALARIES, 1927	
Babe Ruth	$52,000
Miller Huggins	$37,500
Ed Barrow	$25,000
Herb Pennock	$17,500
Urban Shocker	$13,500
Bob Meusel	$13,000
Joe Dugan	$12,000
Waite Hoyt	$11,000 (plus $1,000 bonus for 20 wins)
Earle Combs	$10,500
Bob Shawkey	$10,500
Benny Bengough	$8,000
Tony Lazzeri	$8,000 (plus round-trip train fare for Lazzeri and wife at the start and end of season)
Lou Gehrig	$7,500
Pat Collins	$7,000
Ben Paschal	$7,000
Myles Thomas	$6,500
Mike Gazella	$5,000
Joe Giard	$5,000
Cedric Durst	$4,500
George Pipgras	$4,500
Ray Morehart	$4,000
Wilcy Moore	$2,500 (plus $500 bonus for completing season with club)
Julie Wera	$2,400

			BABE RUTH'S 60 HOME RUNS, 1927			
			H = Home A = Away OB = On Base GM = Game Played			
HOME RUN	**GAME**	**DATE**	**PITCHER, CLUB**	**H/A**	**OB**	**GM**
1	4	Apr 15	Howard Ehmke (R), Phil.	H	1	0
2	11	Apr 23	Rube Walberg (L), Phil.	A	1	0
3	12	Apr 24	Sloppy Thurston (R), Wash.	A	6	0
4	14	Apr 29	Slim Harriss (R), Boston	A	5	0
5	16	May 1	Jack Quinn (R), Phil.	H	1	1
6	16	May 1	Rube Walberg (L), Phil.	H	8	0
7	24	May 10	Milt Gaston (R), St. L.	A	1	2
8	25	May 11	Ernie Nevers (R), St. L.	A	1	1
9	29	May 17	Rip H. Collins (R), Det.	A	8	0
10	33	May 22	Benn Karr (R), Cleve.	A	6	1
11	34	May 23	Sloppy Thurston (R), Wash.	A	1	0

(continued)

			BABE RUTH'S 60 HOME RUNS, 1927			
HOME RUN	GAME	DATE	PITCHER, CLUB	H/A	OB	GM
12	37	May 28	Sloppy Thurston (R), Wash.	H	7	2
13	39	May 29	Danny MacFayden (R), Bos.	H	8	0
14	41	May 30	Rube Walberg (L), Phil.	A	11	0
15	42	May 31	Jack Quinn (R), Phil.	A	1	1
16	43	May 31	Howard Ehmke (R), Phil.	A	5	1
17	47	June 5	Earl Whitehill (L), Det.	H	6	0
18	48	June 7	Tommy Thomas (R), Chi.	H	4	0
19	52	June 11	Garland Buckeye (L), Cleve.	H	3	1
20	52	June 11	Garland Buckeye (L), Cleve.	H	5	0
21	53	June 12	George Uhle (R), Cleve.	H	7	0
22	55	June 16	Tom Zachary (L), St. L.	H	1	1

BABE RUTH'S 60 HOME RUNS, 1927						
HOME RUN	GAME	DATE	PITCHER, CLUB	H/A	OB	GM
23	60	June 22	Hal Wiltse (L), Bos.	A	5	0
24	60	June 22	Hal Wiltse (L), Bos.	A	7	1
25	70	June 30	Slim Harriss (R), Bos.	H	4	1
26	73	July 3	Hod Lisenbee (R), Wash.	A	1	0
27	78	July 8	Don Hankins (R), Det.	A	2	2
28	79	July 9	Ken Holloway (R), Det.	A	1	1
29	79	July 9	Ken Holloway (R), Det.	A	4	2
30	83	July 12	Joe Shaute (L), Cleve.	A	9	1
31	92	July 24	Tommy Thomas (R), Chi.	A	3	0
32	95	July 26	Milt Gaston (R), St. L.	H	1	1
33	95	July 26	Milt Gaston (R), St. L.	H	6	0
34	98	July 28	Lefty Stewart (L), St. L.	H	8	1
35	106	Aug 5	George S. Smith (R), Det.	H	8	0

(continued)

			BABE RUTH'S 60 HOME RUNS, 1927			
HOME RUN	GAME	DATE	PITCHER, CLUB	H/A	OB	GM
36	110	Aug 10	Tom Zachary (L), Wash.	A	3	2
37	114	Aug 16	Tommy Thomas (R), Chi.	A	5	0
38	115	Aug 17	Sarge Connally (R), Chi	A	11	0
39	118	Aug 20	Jake Miller (L), Cleve.	A	1	1
40	120	Aug 22	Joe Shaute (L), Cleve.	A	6	0
41	124	Aug 27	Ernie Nevers (R), St. L.	A	8	1
42	125	Aug 28	Ernie Wingard (L), St. L.	A	1	1
43	127	Aug 31	Tony Welzer (R), Bos.	H	8	0
44	128	Sep 2	Rube Walberg (L), Phil.	A	1	0
45	132	Sep 6	Tony Welzer (R), Bos.	A	6	2
46	132	Sep 6	Tony Welzer (R), Bos.	A	7	1
47	133	Sep 6	Jack Russell (R), Bos	A	9	0
48	134	Sep 7	Danny MacFayden (R), Bos.	A	1	0

HOME RUN	GAME	DATE	PITCHER, CLUB	H/A	OB	GM
\multicolumn{7}{c}{BABE RUTH'S 60 HOME RUNS, 1927}
49	134	Sep 7	Slim Harriss (R), Bos.	A	8	1
50	138	Sep 11	Milt Gaston (R), St. L	H	4	0
51	139	Sep 13	Willis Hudlin (R), Cleve.	H	7	1
52	140	Sep 13	Joe Shaute (L), Cleve.	H	4	0
53	143	Sep 16	Ted Blankenship (R), Chi.	H	3	0
54	147	Sep 18	Ted Lyons (R), Chi.	H	5	1
55	148	Sep 21	Sam Gibson (R), Det.	H	9	0
56	149	Sep 22	Ken Holloway (R), Det.	H	9	1
57	152	Sep 27	Lefty Grove (L), Phil.	H	6	3
58	153	Sep 29	Hod Lisenbee (R), Wash.	H	1	0
59	153	Sep 29	Paul Hopkins (R), Wash.	H	5	3
60	154	Sep 30	Tom Zachary (L), Wash.	H	8	1

Credit: www.baseball-almanac.com/teamstats/roster.php?y=1927andt=NYA

GENERAL MANAGERS		
NAME	TENURE	NUMBER OF YEARS
Ed Barrow	1921–1944	24
Larry MacPhail	1945–1947	3
George Weiss	1948–1960	13
Roy Hamey	1961–1963	3
Ralph Houk	1964–1966	3
Dan Topping, Jr.	1966	1
Lee MacPhail	1967–1973	7
Gabe Paul	1974–1977	4
Cedric Tallis	1978–1979	2
Gene Michael	1980–1981	2
Bill Bergesch	1982–1983	2
Murray Cook	1984	1
Clyde King	1985–1986	2
Woody Woodward	1987	1
Lou Piniella	1988	1
Bob Quinn	1988–1989	2
Harding "Pete" Peterson	1990	1
Gene Michael	1991–1995	5
Bob Watson	1996–1997	2
Brian Cashman	1998–present	

YANKEE CHRONOLOGY OF RESULTS									
SEASON	TEAM	LEAGUE	W	L	PCT	GB	PLACE	ATTENDANCE
2016	New York Yankees	American League	84	78	.519	9.0	4	3,063,405
2015	New York Yankees	American League	87	75	.537	6.0	2	3,193,795
2014	New York Yankees	American League	84	78	.519	12.0	2	3,401,624
2013	New York Yankees	American League	85	77	.525	12.0	4	3,279,589
2012	New York Yankees	American League	95	67	.586	-	1	3,542,406
2011	New York Yankees	American League	97	65	.599	-	1	3,653,700
2010	New York Yankees	American League	95	67	.586	1.0	2	3,765,807
2009	New York Yankees	American League	103	59	.636	-	1	3,674,495
2008	New York Yankees	American League	89	73	.549	8.0	3	4,247,123
2007	New York Yankees	American League	94	68	.580	2.0	2	4,271,083
2006	New York Yankees	American League	97	65	.599	-	1	4,243,780
2005	New York Yankees	American League	95	67	.586	-	1	4,090,440
2004	New York Yankees	American League	101	61	.623	-	1	3,775,292
2003	New York Yankees	American League	101	61	.623	-	1	3,465,600

(continued)

SEASON	TEAM	LEAGUE	W	L	PCT	GB	PLACE	ATTENDANCE
2002	New York Yankees	American League	103	58	.640	-	1	3,465,807
2001	New York Yankees	American League	95	65	.594	-	1	3,264,847
2000	New York Yankees	American League	87	74	.540	-	1	3,227,657
1999	New York Yankees	American League	98	64	.605	-	1	3,293,259
1998	New York Yankees	American League	114	48	.704	-	1	2,919,046
1997	New York Yankees	American League	96	66	.593	2.0	2	2,580,325
1996	New York Yankees	American League	92	70	.568	-	1	2,250,877
1995	New York Yankees	American League	79	65	.549	7.0	2	1,705,263
1994	New York Yankees	American League	70	43	.619	-	1	1,675,556
1993	New York Yankees	American League	88	74	.543	7.0	2	2,416,965
1992	New York Yankees	American League	76	86	.469	20.0	5	1,748,733
1991	New York Yankees	American League	71	91	.438	20.0	5	1,863,733
1990	New York Yankees	American League	67	95	.414	21.0	7	2,006,436
1989	New York Yankees	American League	74	87	.460	14.5	5	2,170,485

Table title: YANKEE CHRONOLOGY OF RESULTS

YANKEE CHRONOLOGY OF RESULTS									
SEASON	TEAM	LEAGUE	W	L	PCT	GB	PLACE	ATTENDANCE	
1988	New York Yankees	American League	85	76	.528	3.5	5	2,633,701	
1987	New York Yankees	American League	89	73	.549	9.0	4	2,427,672	
1986	New York Yankees	American League	90	72	.556	5.5	2	2,268,030	
1985	New York Yankees	American League	97	64	.602	2.0	2	2,214,587	
1984	New York Yankees	American League	87	75	.537	17.0	3	1,821,815	
1983	New York Yankees	American League	91	71	.562	7.0	3	2,257,976	
1982	New York Yankees	American League	79	83	.488	16.0	5	2,041,219	
1981	New York Yankees	American League	59	48	.551	2.0	4	1,614,353	
1980	New York Yankees	American League	103	59	.636	-	1	2,627,417	
1979	New York Yankees	American League	89	71	.556	13.5	4	2,537,765	
1978	New York Yankees	American League	100	63	.613	-	1	2,335,871	
1977	New York Yankees	American League	100	62	.617	-	1	2,103,092	
1976	New York Yankees	American League	97	62	.610	-	1	2,012,434	
1975	New York Yankees	American League	83	77	.519	12.0	3	1,288,048	

(continued)

SEASON	TEAM	LEAGUE	W	L	PCT	GB	PLACE	ATTENDANCE
YANKEE CHRONOLOGY OF RESULTS								
1974	New York Yankees	American League	89	73	.549	2.0	2	1,273,075
1973	New York Yankees	American League	80	82	.494	17.0	4	1,262,103
1972	New York Yankees	American League	79	76	.510	6.5	4	966,328
1971	New York Yankees	American League	82	80	.506	21.0	4	1,070,771
1970	New York Yankees	American League	93	69	.574	15.0	2	1,136,879
1969	New York Yankees	American League	80	81	.497	28.5	5	1,067,996
1968	New York Yankees	American League	83	79	.512	20.0	5	1,185,666
1967	New York Yankees	American League	72	90	.444	20.0	9	1,259,514
1966	New York Yankees	American League	70	89	.440	26.5	10	1,124,648
1965	New York Yankees	American League	77	85	.475	25.0	6	1,213,552
1964	New York Yankees	American League	99	63	.611	-	1	1,305,638
1963	New York Yankees	American League	104	57	.646	-	1	1,308,920
1962	New York Yankees	American League	96	66	.593	-	1	1,493,574
1961	New York Yankees	American League	109	53	.673	-	1	1,747,725
1960	New York Yankees	American League	97	57	.630	-	1	1,627,349

SEASON	TEAM	LEAGUE	W	L	PCT	GB	PLACE	ATTENDANCE
					YANKEE CHRONOLOGY OF RESULTS			
1959	New York Yankees	American League	79	75	.513	15.0	3	1,552,030
1958	New York Yankees	American League	92	62	.597	-	1	1,428,438
1957	New York Yankees	American League	98	56	.636	-	1	1,497,134
1956	New York Yankees	American League	97	57	.630	-	1	1,491,784
1955	New York Yankees	American League	96	58	.623	-	1	1,490,138
1954	New York Yankees	American League	103	51	.669	8.0	2	1,475,171
1953	New York Yankees	American League	99	52	.656	-	1	1,537,811
1952	New York Yankees	American League	95	59	.617	-	1	1,629,665
1951	New York Yankees	American League	98	56	.636	-	1	1,950,107
1950	New York Yankees	American League	98	56	.636	-	1	2,081,380
1949	New York Yankees	American League	97	57	.630	-	1	2,283,676
1948	New York Yankees	American League	94	60	.610	2.5	3	2,373,901
1947	New York Yankees	American League	97	57	.630	-	1	2,178,937
1946	New York Yankees	American League	87	67	.565	17.0	3	2,265,512
1945	New York Yankees	American League	81	71	.533	6.5	4	881,845

(continued)

SEASON	TEAM	LEAGUE	W	L	PCT	GB	PLACE	ATTENDANCE
YANKEE CHRONOLOGY OF RESULTS								
1944	New York Yankees	American League	83	71	.539	6.0	3	789,995
1943	New York Yankees	American League	98	56	.636	-	1	618,330
1942	New York Yankees	American League	103	51	.669	-	1	922,011
1941	New York Yankees	American League	101	53	.656	-	1	964,722
1940	New York Yankees	American League	88	66	.571	2.0	3	988,975
1939	New York Yankees	American League	106	45	.702	-	1	859,785
1938	New York Yankees	American League	99	53	.651	-	1	970,916
1937	New York Yankees	American League	102	52	.662	-	1	998,148
1936	New York Yankees	American League	102	51	.667	-	1	976,913
1935	New York Yankees	American League	89	60	.597	3.0	2	657,508
1934	New York Yankees	American League	94	60	.610	7.0	2	854,682
1933	New York Yankees	American League	91	59	.607	7.0	2	728,014
1932	New York Yankees	American League	107	47	.695	-	1	962,320
1931	New York Yankees	American League	94	59	.614	13.5	2	912,437

YANKEE CHRONOLOGY OF RESULTS								
SEASON	TEAM	LEAGUE	W	L	PCT	GB	PLACE	ATTENDANCE
1930	New York Yankees	American League	86	68	.558	16.0	3	1,169,230
1929	New York Yankees	American League	88	66	.571	18.0	2	960,148
1928	New York Yankees	American League	101	53	.656	-	1	1,072,132
1927	New York Yankees	American League	110	44	.714	-	1	1,164,015
1926	New York Yankees	American League	91	63	.591	-	1	1,027,675
1925	New York Yankees	American League	69	85	.448	28.5	7	697,267
1924	New York Yankees	American League	89	63	.586	2.0	2	1,053,533
1923	New York Yankees	American League	98	54	.645	-	1	1,007,066
1922	New York Yankees	American League	94	60	.610	-	1	1,026,134
1921	New York Yankees	American League	98	55	.641	-	1	1,230,696
1920	New York Yankees	American League	95	59	.617	3.0	3	1,289,422
1919	New York Yankees	American League	80	59	.576	7.5	3	619,164
1918	New York Yankees	American League	60	63	.488	13.5	4	282,047
1917	New York Yankees	American League	71	82	.464	28.5	6	330,294

(continued)

SEASON	TEAM	LEAGUE	W	L	PCT	GB	PLACE	ATTENDANCE
					YANKEE CHRONOLOGY OF RESULTS			
1916	New York Yankees	American League	80	74	.519	11.0	4	469,211
1915	New York Yankees	American League	69	83	.454	32.5	5	256,035
1914	New York Yankees	American League	70	84	.455	30.0	7	359,477
1913	New York Yankees	American League	57	94	.377	38.0	7	357,551
1912	New York Highlanders	American League	50	102	.329	55.0	8	242,194
1911	New York Highlanders	American League	76	76	.500	25.5	6	302,444
1910	New York Highlanders	American League	88	63	.583	14.5	2	355,857
1909	New York Highlanders	American League	74	77	.490	23.5	5	501,700
1908	New York Highlanders	American League	51	103	.331	39.5	8	305,500
1907	New York Highlanders	American League	70	78	.473	21.0	5	350,020
1906	New York Highlanders	American League	90	61	.596	3.0	2	434,700
1905	New York Highlanders	American League	71	78	.477	21.5	6	309,100
1904	New York Highlanders	American League	92	59	.609	1.5	2	438,919
1903	New York Highlanders	American League	72	62	.537	17.0	4	211,808

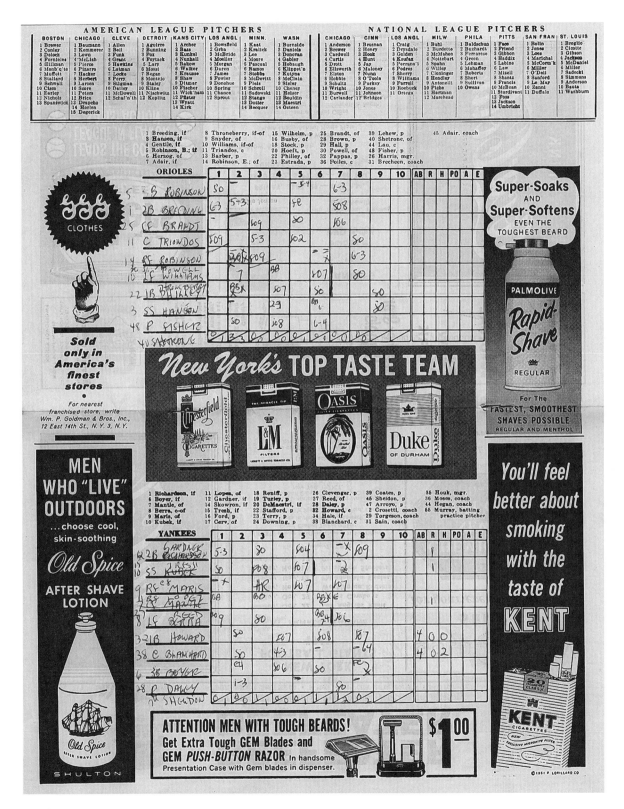

Handwritten archival scorecard from a Yankees-Orioles game, 1961, a collectible.

SELECTED SOURCES

I am in the debt to so many sources who have focused on the Yankees over the years. More books have been written about the New York Yankees than any other team. That is probably true for magazine and newspaper articles and web presence. What follows is just a small inventory of references I consulted. I especially want to recognize how useful BaseballAlmanac.com and UltimateYankees.com were in informing my research.

BOOKS

- Abbott, Jim. *An Improbable Life.* Ballantine Books, 2013.
- Achorn, Edward. *Fifty-nine in '84: Old Hoss Radbourn, Barehanded Baseball and the Greatest Season a Pitcher Ever Had.* HarperCollins, 2010.
- Alexander, Charles C. *John McGraw.* Viking Penguin, Inc., 1988.
- Allen, Maury. *Yankees: Where Have You Gone?* Sports Publishing, LLC, 2004.
- Allen, Oliver E. *The Tiger: The Rise and Fall of Tammany Hall.* Addison-Wesley Publishing Co., 1993.
- Appel, Marty. *Munson: The Life and Death of a Yankee Captain.* Anchor, 2010.
- ———. *Now Pitching for the Yankees.* Sport Classic Books, 2001.
- ———. *Pinstripe Empire: The New York Yankees from Before the Babe to After the Boss.* Bloomsbury, 2012.
- Araton, Harvey. *Driving Mr. Yogi.* Houghton Mifflin Harcourt, 2012.
- Armour, Mark L. *Joe Cronin: A Life in Baseball.* University of Nebraska Press, 2010.
- Armour, Mark L., and Daniel R. Levitt. *Baseball Operations from Deadball to Moneyball.* University of Nebraska Press, 2015.

- Barber, Red. *The Broadcasters.* The Dial Press, 1970.
- Barber, Red, and Robert Creamer. *Rhubarb in the Catbird Seat.* Doubleday and Company, 1968.
- Barra, Allen. *Mickey and Willie.* Crown Archetype, 2013.
- ———. *Yogi Berra: Eternal Yankee.* Norton, 2015.
- Bashe, Philip. *Dog Days: The New York Yankees' Fall from Grace and Return to Glory, 1964—1976.* IUniverse, 2000.
- Borelli, Stephen. *How About That! The Life of Mel Allen.* Sports Publishing, 2005.
- Bouton, Jim. *Ball Four (20th Anniversary Edition).* Wiley, 1994.
- Bowman, John S., and Joel Zoss. *Pictorial History of Baseball.* Smithmark Publishers, 1987.
- Castro, Tony. *DiMag and Mick.* Lyons Press, 2016.
- ———. *Mickey Mantle: America's Prodigal Son.* Potomac Books, 2002.
- Clavin, Tom. *The DiMaggios: Three Brothers, Their Passion for Baseball, Their Pursuit of the American Dream.* HarperCollins, 2013.
- Clavin, Tom, and Danny Peary. *Roger Maris: Reluctant Hero.* Touchstone, 2011.

- Cohen, Robert W. *The 50 Greatest Players in New York Yankees History.* Scarecrow Press, 2012.
- Cramer, Richard, and Richard Ben. *Joe DiMaggio: The Hero's Life.* Simon and Schuster, 2001.
- Creamer, Robert W. *Babe: The Legend Comes to Life.* Simon and Schuster, 1974.
- ———. *Stengel, His Life and Times.* Fireside, 1984.
- Dawidoff, Nicholas, ed. *Baseball: A Literary Anthology.* Library of America, 2002.
- Donnelly, Chris. *Baseball's Greatest Series: Yankees, Mariners, and the 1995 Matchup That Changed History.* Rivergate Books, 2010.
- Doutrich, Paul E. *The Cardinals and the Yankees.* McFarland and Company, 1926.
- Durant, John. *The Yankees: A Pictorial History of Baseball's Greatest Club.* Hastings House, 1949.
- Fisher, David. *Derek Jeter.* Andrews Mcmeel, 1999.
- Fitzgerald, James. *A-Rod: American Hero: An Unauthorized Biography.* Razorbill, 2004.
- Frommer, Harvey. *New York City Baseball,* Macmillan, 1980.

- ———. *Big Apple Baseball.* Taylor, 1995.
- ———. *The New York Yankee Encyclopedia.* Macmillan, 1997.
- ———. *A Yankee Century.* Berkley, 2002.
- ———. *Five O'Clock Lightning.* Wiley, 2007.
- ———. *Remembering Yankee Stadium.* STC/Abrams, 2008.
- Frommer, Harvey, and Frederic J. Frommer. *Red Sox Vs Yankees—The Great Rivalry.* Sports Publishing, 2004, 2005.
- Gentile, Charles. *The 1928 New York Yankees.* Rowman and Littlefield, 2014.
- Gluck, H. *The Mick by Mickey Mantle.* Jove, 1986.
- Goldstone, Lawrence, and Vernona Gomez. *Lefty—An American Odyssey.* Ballantine, 2013.
- Golenbock, Peter. *Dynasty.* Prentice-Hall, 1975.
- ———. *Number 1.* Dell, 1981.
- ———. *Wild, High and Tight: The Life and Death of Billy Martin.* St. Martin's Press, 1994.
- Golenbock, Peter, and Graig Nettles. *Balls.* Pocket Books, 1985.
- Graham, Frank. *The New York Yankees: An Informal History.* G.P. Putnam's Sons, 1943.
- Gross, Ben. *I Looked and I Listened.* Random House, 1954.
- Halberstam, David. *Sports on New York Radio: A Play-by-Play History.* Master's Press, 1999.
- ———. *Summer of '49.* William Morrow and Company, 1989.
- Howard, Arlene. *Elston and Me: The Story of the First Black Yankee.* University of Missouri, 2001.
- Jackson, Reggie, and Kevin Baker. *Becoming Mr. October.* Doubleday, 2013.
- James, Bill. *The New Historical Baseball Abstract.* The Free Press, 2001.
- Jensen, Don. *The Timeline History of Baseball.* Palgrave Macmillan, 2005.
- Jeter, Derek, and Jack Curry. *The Life You Imagine: Life Lessons for Achieving Your Dreams.* Broadway Books, 2001.
- Kahn, Roger. *October Men: Reggie Jackson, George Steinbrenner, Billy Martin, and the Yankees' Miraculous Finish in 1978.* Harvest Books, 2004.
- Kaat, Jim. *If These Walls Could Talk.* Triumph Books, 2015.
- Koppett, Leonard. *The Man in the Dugout.* Temple University Press, 2000.
- Kurkjian, Tim. *America's Game.* Crown, 2000.
- Leventhal, Josh. *Baseball . . . the Perfect Game.* Voyageur Press, 2005.
- Levitt, Daniel R. *Ed Barrow: The Bulldog Who Built the Yankees' First Dynasty.* University of Nebraska Press, 2010.
- Lieb, Fred. *Baseball As I Have Known It.* University of Nebraska Press, 1996.
- Light, Jonathan Fraser. *The Cultural Encyclopedia of Baseball.* McFarland, 1997.
- Luisi, Vincent. *New York Yankees: The First 25 Years.* Arcadia Publishing, 2002.
- Lyle, Sparky, with Peter Golenbock. *The Bronx Zoo.* Triumph Books, 2005.
- Madden, Bill. *Pride of October: What It Was to Be Young and a Yankee.* Grand Central Publishing. 2004.
- ———. *Steinbrenner: The Last Lion of Baseball.* HarperCollins, 2010.
- Mahler, Jonathan. *Ladies and Gentlemen, The Bronx Is Burning.* Picador, 2007.
- Mantle, Mickey, and Mickey Hershkowitz. *All My Octobers.* HarperCollins, 1994.
- Montville, Leigh. *The Big Bam: The Life and Times of Babe Ruth.* Doubleday, 2006.
- Murcer, Bobby. *Yankee for Life.* HarperCollins, 2008.
- Negron, Ray. *Yankee Miracles: Life with the Boss and the Bronx Bombers.* Liveright, 2013.
- Nemec, David. *Baseball, More Than One Hundred Fifty Years.* Sam Wisnia Publications International, 1997.
- Nikola-Lisa, W. *The Men Who Made the Yankees.* Gyroscope Books, 2014.
- O'Connor, Ian. *The Captain: The Journey of Derek Jeter.* Mariner Books, 2012.
- Olney, Buster. *The Last Night of the Yankee Dynasty: The Game, the Team, and the Cost of Greatness.* Harper, 2004.
- Peary, Danny. *We Played the Game.* Black Dog and Leventhal, 1994.
- Pennington, Bill. *Billy Martin: Baseball's Flawed Genius.* Houghton Mifflin, 2015.
- Pepe, Phil. *61: The Inside Story of the Maris-Mantle Home Run Chase.* Triumph Books, 2011.
- ———. *Core Four: The Heart and Soul of the Yankees Dynasty.* Triumph Books, 2013.
- Perry, Dayn. *Reggie Jackson: The Life and Thunderous Career of Baseball's Mr. October.* William Morrow, 2010.
- Pessah, John. *The Game: Inside the Secret World of Major League Baseball's Power Brokers.* Little, Brown and Company, 2015.
- Pietrusza, David, Matthew Silverman, and Michael Gershman. *Baseball: The Biographical Encyclopedia.* Total Sports Illustrated, 2000.
- Pitoniak, Scott. *Memories of Yankee Stadium.* Trumph Books, 2008.
- Randall, Ed McMillan. *Ten Amazing Tales from the Yankees Dugout.* Skyhorse Publishing, 2012.
- Rivera, Mariano, and Coffey Wayne. *The Closer: My Story.* Little, Brown and Company, 2014.
- Robinson, Ray. *Iron Horse: Lou Gehrig in His Time.* W. W. Norton and Company, 2006.

- Robinson, Brooks, ed. *Inside the Baseball Hall of Fame.* Simon and Schuster, 2013.
- Rosen, Charley. *Bullpen Diaries: Mariano Rivera, Bronx Dreams, Pinstripe Legends, and the Future of the New York Yankees.* HarperCollins, 2011.
- Rosengren, John. *Hammerin' Hank, George Almighty and the Say Hey Kid: The Year That Changed Baseball Forever.* Sourcebooks, 2008.
- Ruth, Babe, Mrs., and Bill Slocum. *The Babe and I.* Prentice Hall, 1959.
- Shaughnessy, Dan. *Reversing the Curse.* Houghton Mifflin, 2005.
- Sherman, Joel. *Birth of a Dynasty: Behind the Pinstripes with the 1996 Yankees.* Rodale, 2007.
- Simon, Mark. *The Yankees Index: Every Number Tells a Story.* Triumph Books, 2016.
- Smelser, Marshall. *The Life That Ruth Built.* Bison Books, 1993.
- Smith, Curt. *Voices of the Game.* Fireside, 1992.
- Smith, Ron. *The Ballpark Book: A Journey Through the Fields of Baseball Magic.* Sporting News, 2003.
- Solomon, Burt. *Where They Ain't.* Doubleday, 1999.
- Spatz, Lyle. *1921: The Yankees, the Giants, and the Battle for Baseball Supremacy in New York.* University of Nebraska Press, 2012.
- Spatz, Lyle, ed. *Bridging Two Dynasties: The 1947 New York Yankees.* University of Nebraska Press, 2013.
- Surdam, David G. *The Postwar Yankees: Baseball's Golden Age Revisited.* University of Nebraska Press, 2008.
- Tan, Cecilia. *The 50 Greatest Yankee Games.* John Wiley, 2005.
- Thorn, John, ed. *The Complete Armchair Book of Baseball.* Galahad, 2004.
- Thorn, John, et al., eds. *Total Baseball, 7th edition.* Total Sports Publishing, Inc., 2001.
- Tofel, Richard J. *A Legend in the Making: The New York Yankees in 1939.* Ivan R. Dee, 2003.
- Torre, Joe, and Tom Verducci. *The Yankee Years.* Anchor, 2010.
- Tuite, James, ed. *Sports of the Times: The Arthur Daley Years.* Quadrangle, 1975.
- Wagenheim, Kal. *Babe Ruth: His Life and Legend.* Praeger, 1974.
- Weintraub, Robert. *The House That Ruth Built.* Little, Brown, 2011.
- Wells, David, and Chris Kreski. *Perfect I'm Not.* It Books, 2004.
- White, Bill, with Gordon Dillow. *Uppity.* Grand Central, 2011.

ON THE WEB

- http://articles.latimes.com/keyword/mickey-mantle
- http://articles.latimes.com/keyword/ralph-houk
- http://baseballguru.com/hfrommer/analysishfrommer13.html
- http://baseballguru.com/hfrommer/analysishfrommer56.html
- http://baseballhall.org/hof/Berra-Yogi
- http://baseballhall.org/hof/Combs-Earle
- http://baseballhall.org/hof/Gordon-Joe
- http://baseballhall.org/hof/dickey-bill
- http://baseballhall.org/hof/dimaggio-joe
- http://baseballhall.org/hof/gehrig-lou
- http://baseballhall.org/hof/huggins-miller
- http://baseballhall.org/hof/jackson-reggie
- http://baseballhall.org/hof/keeler-willie
- http://baseballhall.org/hof/lazzeri-tony
- http://baseballhall.org/hof/mccarthy-joe
- http://baseballhall.org/hof/ruffing-red
- http://baseballhall.org/hof/stengel-casey
- http://baseballhall.org/hof/torre-joe
- http://bronxbaseballdaily.com/2011/02/classic-yankees-lefty-gomez/In Pursuit of
- http://bronxbaseballdaily.com/2012/04/classic-yankees-dave-righetti
- http://bronxbaseballdaily.com/2012/04/classic-yankees-joe-page
- http://bronxbaseballdaily.com/2012/05/classic-yankees-johnny-sain
- http://bronxbaseballdaily.com/2012/05/classic-yankees-red-rolfe
- http://bronxbaseballdaily.com/2012/09/classic-yankees-wee-willie-keeler
- http://bronxbaseballdaily.com/2012/12/classic-yankees-ralph-terry
- http://bronxbaseballdaily.com/2013/02/classic-yankees-ralph-houk
- http://espn.go.com/espn/feature/story/_/id/11583279/derek-jeter-plays-last-game-yankee-stadium
- http://espn.go.com/mlb/news/story?id=4704135
- http://espn.go.com/newyork/photos/gallery/_/id/6221106/image/12/40-rickey-henderson-espn-ny-50-greatest-yankees
- http://newyork.yankees.mlb.com/nyy/history/gehrig.jsp
- http://newyork.yankees.mlb.com/nyy/history/hall_of_famers.jsp
- http://newyork.yankees.mlb.com/nyy/history/rare_feats.jsp
- http://nypost.com/2014/02/01/chicago-journalist-debunks-babe-ruths-called-shot
- http://sabr.org/bioproj/person/165bef13
- http://sabr.org/bioproj/person/db1a9611
- http://sabr.org/bioproj/person/f12c897a
- http://web.yesnetwork.com/news/article.jsp?ymd=20130726andcontent_id=54358762andoid=36019
- www.backtobaseball.com/blog/cat/7/post/26/#Chronological
- www.baseball-almanac.com/articles/george_steinbrenner_biography.shtml

- www.baseball-almanac.com/articles/press.shtml
- www.baseball-almanac.com/mgrtmny.shtml
- www.baseball-almanac.com/players/player.php?p=gehrilo01
- www.baseball-almanac.com/players/player.php?p=huggimi01
- www.baseball-almanac.com/players/player.php?p=richabo01
- www.baseball-almanac.com/quotes/hank_bauer_quotes.shtml
- www.baseball-almanac.com/teams/baseball_uniform_numbers.php?t=NYA
- www.baseball-almanac.com/teams/yank.shtml
- www.baseball-almanac.com/teams/yankcapt.shtml
- www.baseball-reference.com/teams/NYY/uniform-numbers.shtml
- www.baseballinwartime.com
- www.complex.com/sports/2012/04/the-50-greatest-moments-in-new-york-yankees-history/jeter-breaks-all-time-yankee-hits-record
- www.encyclopedia.com/topic/Lou_Gehrig.aspx
- www.historicbaseball.com/players/r/richardson_bobby.html
- www.HistoryOfTheYankees.com
- www.lougehrig.com/about/bio.html
- www.newsday.com/sports/baseball/yankees/yankees-retired-numbers-in-monument-park-1.1826858
- www.newsday.com/sports/baseball/yankees/yogi-berra-statistics-and-career-numbers-1.10881524
- www.newyorker.com/news/sporting-scene/the-del-webb-yankees
- www.nonohitters.com/new-york-yankees-no-hitt
- www.nydailynews.com/archives/sports/baseball-gabe-paul-dies-88-article-1.790060
- www.nytimes.com/1985/08/15/sports/sports-of-the-times-pete-sheehy-yankee.html
- www.nytimes.com/1989/02/18/obituaries/vernon-lefty-gomez-80-dies-starred-as-a-pitcher-for-yankees.html
- www.nytimes.com/1990/05/24/obituaries/charlie-keller-73-an-outfielder-and-slugger-for-yanks-in-the-40-s.html
- www.nytimes.com/1994/12/28/obituaries/allie-reynolds-star-pitcher-for-yankees-is-dead-at-79.html
- www.nytimes.com/1998/05/18/sports/baseball-rarest-gem-for-yankees-wells-a-perfect-game.html
- www.nytimes.com/2012/04/28/sports/baseball/bill-skowron-slugger-who-helped-yankees-win-7-pennants-dies-at-81.html?_r=0
- www.nytimes.com/2014/07/26/sports/baseball/robinson-cano-is-thriving-with-the-mariners.html?rref=collection%2Ftimestopic%2FCano%2C%20Robinsonandaction=clickandcontent-Collection=timestopics&ion=streamandmodule=stream_unitandversion=latestandcontentPlacement=8andpgtype=collectionand_r=0
- www.nytimes.com/interactive/2013/09/23/sports/baseball/mariano-rivera-career-timeline.html?_r=1and
- www.nytimes.com/packages/html/sports/year_in_sports/09.30.html
- www.pinstripealley.com/yankees-history-trivia
- www.pinstripealley.com/yankees-history-trivia/2013/11/18/5119884/the-pinstripe-alley-top-100-yankees-of-all-time
- www.travel-watch.com/lougehrig1.htm
- www.ultimateyankees.com/oldtimers-day.htm
- www.ultimateyankees.com/trivia.htm
- https://en.m.wikipedia.org/wiki/List_of_New_York_Yankees_managers
- https://en.m.wikipedia.org/wiki/Old-Timers'_Day
- https://en.wikipedia.org/wiki/List_of_New_York_Yankees_no-hitters

WEBSITES

- Baseball Hall of Fame: www.baseballhalloffame.org
- Baseball Library: www.baseballlibrary.com
- Baseball-Almanac www.baseball-almanac.com
- Baseball-Reference: www.baseball-reference.com
- Behind The Bombers: www.allsports.com/mlb/yankees
- Lou Gehrig, The Official Site: www.lougehrig.com
- Major League Baseball: www.mlb.com
- New York Yankees: www.yankees.com
- The Pinstripe Press: www.angelfire.com/ny5/pinstripepress
- Society for American Baseball Research: www.sabr.org
- The Sporting News (Vault): www.sportingnews.com
- USA Today (Sports): www.usatoday.com

ELECTRONIC MEDIA

- *100 Years of the New York Yankees.* Hart Sharp Video LLC, 2003. DVD.
- *61*.* HBO Studios. 2001. DVD. ASIN: B00005M20J.
- *Babe Ruth—The Life Behind the Legend.* Warner Home Video. 2004. DVD.
- *Mickey Mantle: The Lost Stories, The American Dream Comes to Life, Special Edition,* Directed by Lew Rothgeb and Richard Hall. Baseball Legend Video, 1999. DVD.
- *When It Was a Game—Triple Play Collection.* Warner Home Video, 2001. DVD. ASIN: B00005B32G.
- *Yankeeography, Vol.* 1. Hart Sharp Video LLC, 2005. DVD. ASIN: B0001KL5J4.

ACKNOWLEDGMENTS

An exhaustive and exhausting opus like this could never have been created without a good team behind me, a trio who served as fact checkers, proofreaders, critics and major sounding boards. A special thank you for all of them.

Family first. My son Fred Frommer showed off his sharp eye proofing, adding and subtracting as he has done so capably for many other books of mine.

Paul Doherty, Yankee expert extraordinaire. What did I ever do to deserve to have him on board as friend, confidant and oral history voice in the book? He took time out of his busy schedule as partner with CESD Talent Agency in Los Angeles to fact check, suggest content and be my friend throughout the whole run of this ambitious project. I am, as always, in his debt.

The third member of my "coaching staff" is Brad Turnow, elementary school teacher and webmaster of one of the best of the best of New York Yankees websites, UltimateYankees.com. He was invaluable as oral history voice and coaching critic.

Baseball Almanac webmaster Sean Holtz and his site were of invaluable assistance.

If there were a Hall of Fame for literary agents, Al Zuckerman would get my vote as the first to go in. He knows the drill. Thank you, Al.

Will Kiester of Page Street Publishing had the smarts to offer a contract for this book. I am sure its reception and sales will prove him, and me, correct.

Special thanks to my editor Karen Levy: attentive, involved and a true partner in this venture. Thanks to all-star fact checker Katie Mitchell and all-star copyeditor Patricia Kot for their fine work on the book's manuscript.

A tip of the cap to Benjamin R. Vonderheide, "the Captain," for providing invaluable technological help and good humor.

All those who have been part of the New York Yankee story and are now part of my story in this book, thank you.

ABOUT THE AUTHOR

One of the most prolific and respected sports journalists and oral historians in the United States, author of the autobiographies of legends Nolan Ryan, Tony Dorsett and Red Holzman, Dr. Harvey Frommer is an expert on the New York Yankees. He wrote for *Yankees Magazine* for 18 years and has arguably written more books, articles and reviews on the New York Yankees than anyone. In 2010, he was selected by the City of New York as a historical consultant for the reimagined old Yankee Stadium site, Heritage Field. A professor in the MALS program at Dartmouth College, Frommer was dubbed "Dartmouth's Mr. Baseball" by their alumni magazine. He lives in Lyme, New Hampshire, with his wife, Myrna Katz Frommer.

OTHER BOOKS BY HARVEY FROMMER

HARDBACK BOOKS

- *When It Was Just a Game,* Taylor, 2015
- *It Happened in Miami,* Taylor, 2015
- *Remembering Fenway Park,* STC/Abrams, 2011
- *Remembering Yankee Stadium,* STC/Abrams, 2008
- *Five O'Clock Lightning,* Wiley, 2007
- *Where Have All Our Red Sox Gone?,* Taylor, 2006
- *Sports Junkies' Book of Trivia, Terms, and Lingo,* Taylor, 2006
- *Red Sox vs. Yankees: The Great Rivalry,* Sports Publishing, 2004, 2005
- *A Yankee Century,* Putnam/Berkley, 2002
- *It Happened in Manhattan* (with Myrna Katz Frommer), Putnam/Berkley, 2001
- *Growing Up Baseball* (with Frederick J. Frommer), Taylor, 2001
- *It Happened on Broadway* (with Myrna Katz Frommer), Harcourt Brace, 1998
- *The New York Yankee Encyclopedia,* Macmillan, 1997
- *Growing Up Jewish in America* (with Myrna Katz Frommer), Harcourt Brace, 1995
- *Big Apple Baseball,* Taylor, 1995
- *It Happened in Brooklyn* (with Myrna Katz Frommer), Harcourt Brace, 1993
- *Shoeless Joe and Ragtime Baseball,* Taylor, 1992
- *It Happened in the Catskills* (with Myrna Katz Frommer), Harcourt Brace, 1991
- *Holzman on Hoops* (with Red Holzman), Taylor, 1991
- *Behind the Lines: The Autobiography of Don Strock,* Pharos, 1991
- *Running Tough: the Autobiography of Tony Dorsett,* Doubleday, 1989
- *Growing Up at Bat: 50th Anniversary Book of Little League Baseball,* Pharos, 1989
- *Throwing Heat: the Autobiography of Nolan Ryan,* Doubleday, 1988
- *Primitive Baseball,* Atheneum, 1988
- *150th Anniversary Album of Baseball,* Franklin Watts, 1988
- *Red on Red: the Autobiography of Red Holzman,* Bantam, 1987
- *Olympic Controversies,* Franklin Watts, 1985
- *Baseball's Greatest Managers,* Franklin Watts, 1985
- *National Baseball Hall of Fame,* Franklin Watts, 1985
- *Games of the XXIIIrd Olympiad,* International Sport Publications, 1984
- *Jackie Robinson,* Franklin Watts, 1984
- *Baseball's Greatest Records: Streaks and Feats,* Atheneum, 1982
- *Baseball's Greatest Rivalry,* Atheneum, 1982
- *Rickey and Robinson,* Macmillan, 1982
- *Basketball My Way: Nancy Lieberman* (with Myrna Katz Frommer), Scribner's, 1982
- *New York City Baseball,* Macmillan, 1980
- *The Great American Soccer Book,* Atheneum, 1980
- *Sports Roots,* Atheneum, 1980
- *Sports Lingo,* Atheneum, 1979
- *The Martial Arts: Judo and Karate,* Atheneum, 1978
- *A Sailing Primer* (with Ron Weinmann), Atheneum, 1978
- *A Baseball Century,* Macmillan, 1976

PAPERBACK BOOKS

- *Jackie Robinson* (2nd edition), Lyons Press, 2017
- *Baseball's Greatest Managers* (2nd edition), Lyons Press, 2017
- *Old-Time Baseball* (2nd edition), Lyons Press, 2016
- *Remembering Yankee Stadium* (2nd edition), Lyons Press, 2016
- *Five O'Clock Lightning* (2nd edition), Taylor, 2015
- *Rickey and Robinson* (2nd edition), Taylor, 2015
- *Red Sox vs. Yankees* (2nd edition), Taylor, 2014
- *Red Sox vs. Yankees* (with Frederic Frommer), Taylor, 2013
- *Manhattan at Mid-Century* (Myrna Katz Frommer with Harvey Frommer), Taylor, 2013
- *New York City Baseball: The Golden Age, 1947–1957,* Taylor, 2013
- *It Happened in the Catskills* (with Myrna Katz Frommer), SUNY Press, 2009
- *It Happened in Brooklyn* (with Myrna Katz Frommer), Suny Press, 2009
- *Shoeless Joe and Ragtime Baseball,* Taylor, 1992; University of Nebraska Press, 2008
- *Yankee Century and Beyond,* Sourcebooks, 2007
- *Red Sox vs. Yankees: The Great Rivalry,* Sports Publishing, 2005

- *A Yankee Century,* Berkley, 2003
- *Rickey and Robinson,* Taylor, 2003
- *Growing Up Jewish in America* (with Myrna Katz Frommer), University of Nebraska Press, 1999
- *It Happened in the Catskills* (with Myrna Katz Frommer), Harcourt Brace, 1996
- *It Happened in Brooklyn* (with Myrna Katz Frommer), Harcourt Brace, 1995
- *Shoeless Joe and Ragtime Baseball,* Taylor, 1993
- *New York City Baseball,* Harcourt Brace, 1992
- *Running Tough: the Autobiography of Tony Dorsett,* Berkley, 1992
- *Throwing Heat: the Autobiography of Nolan Ryan,* Avon, 1989
- *Red on Red: the Autobiography of Red Holzman,* Bantam, 1988
- *New York City Baseball,* Atheneum, 1985
- *Baseball's Greatest Rivalry,* Atheneum, 1984
- *Basketball My Way: Nancy Lieberman* (with Myrna Katz Frommer), Scribner's, 1984
- *Sports Lingo,* Atheneum, 1983
- *Sports Genes* (with Myrna Katz Frommer), Ace, 1982
- *The Sports Date Book* (with Myrna Katz Frommer), Ace, 1981

BOOKS IN TRANSLATION

- *Throwing Heat: the Autobiography of Nolan Ryan,* Kaoru Takeda (Japan), 1993

INDEX

Italicized page numbers indicate photographs and illustrations. **Bold** page numbers indicate primary information about a person.

A

Aaron, Hank, 79, 102, 149, 189
Abbott, Jim, 154, *154*, 239
Allen, Mel, 14, **34–36**, *35*, 58, 92, 97–99, 130, 136, 137, 139, 147, 169, 171, 178, 197, 239
Anderson, Sparky, 111, 237

B

Barber, Walter Lanier "Red," 14, **36–37**, 62, 63, 97–98, 204, 230, 232
Barnes, Frank, 117, 228
Barrow, Ed, 29, **37–38**, *38*, 75, 96, 101, 116–117, 131, 166, 187, 221, 224–225, 228
Bauer, Hank, **38–39**, *39*, 79, 88, 97, 111, 118, 140, 166, 229–230
Baylor, Don, 81, 238
Berra, Lawrence Peter "Yogi," **39–42**, *40*, 48, 58–62, *61*, 67, 75, 81, 83, 91–92, 94, 97, 106–107, 110, 112–113, 139–140, 143, 153, 161, 171, 175, 176–180, 182–184, 190, 194, 196, 204, 227, 229–232, 234
    Yogi Berra Day, 157–158
    Yogi-isms, 42
Blanchard, Johnny, 14, 59, 171
Blomberg, Ron, 14, 233, 234
    as first designated hitter to bat, 147
Boggs, Wade, 87, 114, 151, 156, 196, 239, 240
Boone, Aaron, 115, 159–160, 242
Bouton, Jim, 93, 112, 166, 178, 180, 240
Boyer, Clete, 60, 87, 111, 118

Brett, George, 56, 194, 236
    and pine tar episode, 152–153
Brown, Bobby, 76, 92
Burke, Michael, 30, 36, 37, 60

C

Carew, Rod, 92, 235
Carey, Andy, 111, 140
Carney, Don, 14, 35, 97, 98
Carrierri, Joe, 14, 97
CBS, 30, 36, 108, 191, 232
Cerone, Rick, 98, 236
Chambliss, Chris, **42–43**, 72, 106, 150, 170, 182, 194, 235
    pennant-winning home run of, 147, *148*
Chandler, Spurgeon Ferdinand "Spud," **43**, *43*, 88, 115, 166, 171
Chase, Hal, **43–44**, *43*, 169, 174, 179, 183, 201, 219
Chesbro, Jack, 23, **44**, *44*, 168, 179, 184, 186, 201, 219, 220
    wild pitch of, 124
Claire, Fred, 14, 109
Clemens, Roger, **44–46**, *45*, 50, 51, 90, 158–159, 176, 183, 196, 240–244
Coleman, Jerry, 14, 35, 42, **46–47**, *46*, 50, 70, 97–98, 106, 111, 116, 166, 187, 204
Collins, Pat, 38, 62, *84*, 168
Combs, Earl, 38, **47–48**, *47*, *84*, 118, 168, 169, 173, 178, 182, 186, 201, 223, 238
Cone, David, 68, 156, 175, 177, 181, 239, 241
    perfect game of, 157–158, 194
Cosell, Howard, 98, 108, 148, 149, 166, 170
Crosetti, Frank, 16, *33*, 38, **48**, 51, 71, 96, 129, 132, 139, 143, 167, 179, 185, 224, 226, 242

Crystal, Billy, 78–79, 105–106, 180
Cuomo, Mario, 14, 16, 51, 102

D

Daley, Bud, *192*
Dent, Bucky, 89, 194, 196, 235–238
    home run against Red Sox, 150–151, *151*
Devery, William Stephen, 21–25, 219
Dickey, Bill, 38, 40–41, 43, **48–49**, *48*, 53, 76, 91, 100, 129, 132, 169, 175–177, 179, 182–183, 186, 196, 226
DiMaggio, Dom, 14, 16, 137, 196
DiMaggio, Joe, 9, 16, *32*, 38, 39, 41, 48, **49–51**, *49*, *50*, 55–56, 58–59, 70–71, 76–77, 79, 83–85, 88, 92, 96, 99, 103, 106, 108, 110, 113, 118, 121, 132, *133*, 138, 168, 171, 173, 175–180, 183, 184, 188, *195*, 196, 203–205, *218*, 224–228, 232–233, 235, 240–241, 243
    appreciation day for, 136–137
    56-game hitting streak, 133
Doherty, Paul, *14*, 197
    quoted, 30, 36, 37, 51, 56, 63, 72, 74, 75, 76, 87, 89, 90, 98, 106, 108, 109, 117, 118, 133, 135, 137, 147, 148, 155, 158, 174, 204, 205, 225, 230, 232, 233
Dukakis, Michael, 14, 196
Durante, Sal, 14, 141, 142, 143, 188
Duren, Ryne, 59, 111, 118, 166
Durocher, Leo, 74, 165, 169, 176, 186

E

epic moments, streaks and feats, 123–164

F

Farrel, Frank J., 21–25, 219
Figueroa, Ed, 89, 93, 167
Fishel, Bob, **51**, 106
Flynn, Joe, 14, 27
Ford, Edward "Whitey," 14, **52–53**, *52*,
    57–58, 70, 76, 90, 93, 111–112, 161,
    166, 170–171, 177–178, 182, 184,
    196, 228–229, 231, 234–235, 241
Frazee, Harry, 28, 101
Frick, Ford, 115, 126

G

Gallo, Bill, 14, 238
Gamble, Oscar, 89, 91, 236
Garagiola, Joe, 37, 39, 146, 204, 232
Gehrig, Lou, 16, 29, *33*, 38, **53–54**, *54*,
    68, 71, 75–76, 84–85, *84*, 99, 103,
    105, 126, 128, 132, 147, 166,
    168–169, 171, 175–179, 182–190,
    196, 201, 205, 220, 222–226, 239,
    245
    Appreciation Day for, 130–132, 226
    four homeruns against Athletics, 127
Girardi, Joe, 82, 87, 155, 161, 179, 244
Giuliani, Rudy, 14, 16, 158
Gomez, Vernon "Lefty," 38, **54–55**, *55*,
    69, 86, 100, 129, 132, 134–135, 168,
    175, 178, 182, 224, 226, 234
Gooden, Dwight, 82, 109, 176, 239
    no-hitter against Mariners, 154, *155*
Gordon, Joseph, 23, **55–56**, *55*, 76, 88,
    92, 132, 167, 185, 226, 236
Gossage, Richard Michael "Goose," **56**,
    56, 74, 81, 94, 152, 161, 168, 171,
    180, 194, 196, 236
Greenwade, Tom, 76, *77*
Griffey, Ken, 81, 238
Griffith, Clark, 23, 186, 219
Guidry, Ron, **56–57**, *57*, 92–93, 153,
    161, 168, 177, 183, 196, 236
    eighteen strikeouts in one game, 150,
    150

H

Hamey, Roy, 59, 60
Harris, Bucky, 76, 88, 168, 227
Hawkins, Andy, 153–154

Hemingway, Ernest, 49–51, 108
Henderson, Ricky, 81, 161, 180–181,
    183, 237, 238
Henrich, Tommy, 29, **57–58**, *58*, 70, 77,
    88, 103, 135, 168–169, 228
Highlanders, 23–24, 69, 186, 219
Hilltop Park, 23, 25, 124, 182, 219, 220
    pocket schedule from 1903, *23*
    ticket stub from 1903, *23*
Holzman, Red, 95, 109
Houk, Ralph, 14, 41, 53, **58–60**, *59*, *60*,
    72, 74, 87, 146, 169, 231, 232, 234
Howard, Elston, 41, 58, **60–62**, *61*,
    62, 67, 91, 106, 111, 117, 147, 161,
    166–167, 175, 179, *192*, 228–229,
    232–233, 237
Howard, Frank, 14, 105
Howser, Dick, 106, 236
Hoyt, Waite, **62–63**, *63*, 100, 166,
    169–170, 186, 202
Huggins, Miller, 29, 31, 37, 48, **63–65**,
    64, 71, 83–84, 89, 101, 103, *125*,
    131, 169, 186, 194, 202, 223, 224
Hunter, Jim "Catfish," 30, **65–66**, *65*,
    72, 81, 89, 105, 109, 168, 171, 205,
    234, 236, 238, 241
Huston, Tillinghast L'Hommedieu,
    25–29, 63, 101, 169, 186, 190,
    220–221

I

Idelson, Jeff, 14, 87
Irvin, Monte, 14, 29, 35, 50, 60
Isaacson, "Big" Julie, 14, 142

J

Jackson, Reggie, **66–67**, *66*, 68, 80, 88,
    89, 92, 106, 109, 148, 161, 163, 169,
    171, 179, 194–196, 235–237, 239, 245
    hits three homers in four swings,
    149–150, *149*
Jeter, Derek, *10*, **67–69**, *68*, 81, 90–91,
    114, 160–161, 166, 169, 173–174,
    177, 178, 179, 182, 185, 188, 190,
    191, 196, 205, *206*, 239–245, *245*
    Derek Jeter Day, 161–163
    and Jeffery Maier, 155
    as "Mr. November," 158–159
Johnson, Ban, 21, 23

Johnson, Walter, 44–45, 102, 176, 186
Jones, Sam, 125

K

Kahn, Roger, 14, 111
Kay, Michael, 85–86
Kaze, Irv, 14, 56
Keane, Johnny, 60, 232
Keeler, "Wee Willie," 23, *34*, **69**, *69*,
    134, 171, 178–179, 186, 201, 219, 226
Keller, Charlie, 58, **69–70**, *69*, 88, 168,
    181
Kelly, Roberto, 87, 182
Key, Jimmy, 87, 239
Koenig, Mark, 38, 64, *84*, 100, 126,
    186, 201–202, 239
Koppet, Leonard, 14, 16
Krichell, Paul, 29, 37, 52–53, **70**, 76,
    86, 88, 96
Kubek, Tony, 41, 58–59, **70–71**, *70*, 93,
    111
Kucks, Johnny, 111, 230

L

Larsen, Don, 59, 79, 111, 118, 157,
    158, 168, 229, 241
    perfect game of, 14, 106, **139–141**,
    140, 152, 181, 188, 190, 194, 230,
    231
Lazzeri, Tony, 38, 70, **71**, *71*, *84*, 169,
    186, 201–202, 223
legends, leaders, and luminaries, 33–122
Lemon, Bob, 67, 81, 236, 237
Leyritz, Jim, 153
    World Series comeback of, 155–156,
    156, 240
Linz, Phil, 15, 41
Lomax, Stan, 15, 111
Lopat, Eddie, 15, 35, 51, 70, **71–72**, *72*,
    92, 110, 168, 171, 178, 229
Lopez, Hector, 40, 58
Lyle, Albert Walter "Sparky," **72–74**, *73*,
    87, 93, 151, 161, 166, 234–235

M

MacArthur, Douglas, 68, 108
MacPhail, Larry, 38, 40, 60, **74–76**, *75*,
    84, 113, 115–116, 149, 166, 190,
    194, 200, 227, 240

Maier, Jeffrey, 69, 155, 240

Mantle, Mickey, *8*, 16, *34*, 38–39, 51, 53, 58–59, *59*, 62, 70, **76–79**, *78*, *79*, 81, 85–86, 105–106, 111–112, 117–118, *122*, 140–141, 161, 166, 168–169, 171, 173–189, *192*, 195–196, 204, 228–234, 239–240, 244–245

500th homerun, 146, *146*

Mickey Mantle Day, 147

tape measure homerun, 139

March of Time, 219–246

Maris, Roger, 37, 39, 58, *59*, **79–80**, *79*, 86, 88, 91, 106, 111, 118, 142, 161, 168, 175–176, 178, 181, 183, 188, 190, *192*, 194–196, 230–231, 232, 237–238

61st home run, 141–143

Martin, Billy, 41, 57, 66–67, 72, 74, 79, **80–81**, *81*, 91, 93, 97, 105–106, 108, 111, 117–118, 139, 152, 166, 168, 171, 173, 175, 184, 188, 194, 196, 228–230, 234–238, 245

Martinez, Tino, 114, 159, 161, 163, 190

Matsui, Hideki, **81–82**, 160, 163, 168, 180, 184, 194, 242, 244

Mattingly, Don, 68, 81, **82–83**, *82*, 91, 121, 153, 167, 175–180, 182, 188, 190, 196, 238, 240, 242

Mays, Willie, 77, 117, 170, 235

Mazeroski, Bill, 93, 111

McCarthy, Joe, 29, 54–55, 76, **83–84**, *83*, 86, 88–89, 99, 103, 127–128, *131*, 132, 169–171, 185–186, 224, 226–227, 229, 235

ten commandments for major league success, 84

McCovey, Willie, 93, 146, 194, 231

McDougald, Gil, 58, 70, 93, 111, 140, 170

McGraw, John J., 62–63, 110, 112, 127

McMullen, John, 41, 108

McNamara, John, 15, 102

Mears, Walter, 15, 151

Messer, Frank, 98, 151, 177

Meusel, Bob, 38, **84–85**, *84*, 125, 169–170, 174, 186, 202

Miller, Jon, 15, 158

Mize, Johnny, 97, 106

Mogridge, George, 124, *220*

monikers and nicknames of Yankees, 165–172

Moore, Wiley, 38, *84*

Munson, Thurman, 81, **85**, 91, 161, 169, 171, 175–177, 196, 234, 236

Murcer, Bobby, 15, 81, **85–86**, 91, 98, 161, 194

Murphy, Johnny, 29, 70, **86**, 132, 168, 226

Mussina, Mike, 68, 159, 161, 241–242

near-perfect game of, 158

N

Nettles, Graig, 72, 74, **86–87**, 99, 150, 170, 176, 235, 237

New York American Baseball Club, stock certificate for, *22*

New York Yankees. *See* Yankees

Niekro, Phil, 94, 168, 238

numerology: Yankees by the numbers, 173–191

O

O'Neill, Paul, 45, **87–88**, 114, 118, 161, 163, 171, 175, 178, 240, 243

owners and playing fields, 21–32

P

Page, Joe, **88–89**, 168

Parnell, Mel, 15, 196

Paul, Gabe, 30, **89**, 108, 167

Pearson, Monte, 130

Pennock, Herb, **89–90**, *90*, 168, 171, 186, 193

Pettitte, Andy, **90**, 91, 113, 166, 179, 180, 183–184, 188, 243

Piazza, Mike, 45, 118

Piniella, Lou, 15, **90–91**, 99, 103, 171, 174, 196, 234, 237, 238

Pipp, Wally, 54, 183

Polo Grounds, 25–26, *38*, 62, 101, 190–191, 220

Posada, Jorge, 68, 90, **91**, 160–161, 163, 166, 175, 177–178, 183, 188, 241, 243

R

Ramos, Pedro, 78, 139, 230

Randolph, Willie, 15, 89, **91–92**, 105, 149–150, 161, 176, 178, 186

Raschi, Vic, 72, **92**, 106, 117, 171, 196

Reynolds, Allie, 56, 72, 76, **92**, 94, 171, 173, 178, 180, 196, 229

two no-hitters of, 138–139, *138*

Rice, Jim, 67, 110

Richardson, Bobby, 15, 58–60, 70, **93**, 116, 171, 177, 178, 182, 185, 231–232

"the catch" of, 146

Richman, Arthur, 15, 114, 141

Rickey, Branch, 74, 116, 220

Righetti, Dave, 80, **93–94**, 105, *152*, 178–181, 184, 236–238

no-hitter against Red Sox, 151

Rivera, Mariano, 90–91, 93, **94–95**, *95*, 113, 158–161, *162*, 163, 166, 169–170, 177, 179–180, 185, 188, 191, 196, 239–243, 245

all-time save record of, 161

Rivers, Mickey, 89, 165, 169, 171

Rizzuto, Phil, 15, 16, 37, 40, 47, 50–51, 66, 70, **95–99**, *96*, 106, 110, 112, 117, 137, 141, 143, 148, 153, 161, 168, 170, 176, 179, 190, 196, 197, 204, 228, 230, 237, 239, 241, 244

Robinson, Brooks, 15, 106

Robinson, Jackie, 37, 62, 66, 94, 117, 140, 229

Robinson, Wilbert "Uncle Robbie," 63, 110

Rodriguez, Alex "A-Rod," **99**, 165, 174, 176, 184–185, 188, 196–197, 242–245

Rolfe, Robert "Red," **99**, 103, 132, 175, 226

Ruffing, Charles Herbert "Red," **99–100**, *100*, 132, *183*, 224, 226

Ruppert, Jacob, 21, 25–30, *27*, *32*, 37, 63–65, *64*, 75, 83, 101, 116, 124, 166, 169, 190, 196, 220, 224, 225, 226, 227

Ruth, George Herman "Babe," 16, 26, 29, *35*, 37, 44–45, 47–48, 53–54, 62, 71, 79, *79*, 84, 87–88, 99, **100–103**, *101*, *102*, *104*, 105, *105*, 125, *126*, 127, 149, 156, *164*, 165, 167–169, 173, 176–178, 180–186, 188–189, 193–196, *195*, 200–202, 205, 221–225, 227–228, 241, 244–245
  Botch'em Up and, 125
  called shot of, 128–130, *128*
  retiring of number of, 135–136, *136*
  sixty homeruns in 1927, 261–265

S

Schang, Wally, 48, 124, 221
Selkirk, George, **103**, 132, 171, 175, 186, 226
Shawkey, Bob, **103**, 125, 166, 174, 223
Shea Stadium, 42, 72, 175, 190, 234, 240–241
Sheehy, Pete, 15, 59, 98, **103**, **105**, *106*, 127, 137, 175, 177, 238
Sheppard, Bob, 15, *15*, 60, 68, 72, 74, 90, **105–107**, 141, 148, 158, 160–161, 171, 188, 197, 205, 228, 241, 244
Sinatra, Frank, 19, 108–109, 137, 161, 196
Skowron, Bill, 15, 79, **107**, 111, 169, *192*, 230, 231
Smith, Al, *27*, 124, 135
Smith, Red, 71, 99
Soriano, Alfonso, 99, 179, 242, 245
Sousa, John Philip, 28, 124
Stanley, Mike, 15, 196
Steinbrenner, George, 21, 30, 41, 56, 60, 62, 65, 67–68, 74, 80–81, 85, 87–89, 91, 94, 98, **107–110**, *108*, 114–115, 121, 153–154, 161, 166, 169, 170–171, 174, 177–178, 188, 191, 194, 200, 205, 234, 236, 238–240, 243–244
Steinbrenner, Hal, 31, 109
Steinbrenner, Hank, 31, 109
Stengel, Casey, 15, *19*, *34*, 39, *39*, 40–41, 46, 51–52, 53, 58–62, 70–72, 77, 79–80, 88, 92–93, 95–97, 100, 107, **110–112**, *110*, 114, 116, 118, 138, 140, 142, 166, 169, 176, 179, 183, 185, 222, 227–233

Stobbs, Chuck, 78, 139, 229
Stottlemyre, Mel, **112–113**, *113*
Swoboda, Ron, 15, 103

T

Tannehill, Jesse, 23, 219
Terry, Ralph, 59, 93, 111, 112, 118
Thomson, Jim, 15, 116
Tidrow, Dick, 89, 93
Topping, Daniel, 21, 30, 37–38, 60, 74, 76, 84, 111, **113–114**, *114*, 115–116, 190, 193, 203–204, 227, 231
Torre, Joe, 68, 82, 88, 94, 113, **114–115**, *114*, 118, 156, 159, 163, 168, 175, 184–185, 239, 243
Turley, Bob, 111, 118, 166, 229
Turner, Jim, 92, 166, 169
Turnow, Bradford, 15, *16*, 45–46, 53, 80, 85, 90, 94, 113, 114, 118, 120, 130, 158, 194

U

Ultimate Yankee Quiz, 207–218

W

Wagner, Honus, 29, 95, 186
Webb, Del, 30, 38, 75–76, 84, 111, 113, **115–116**, *116*, 190, 227, 231
Weiss, George, 29, 37, 50, 59–60, 72, 75–76, 80, 97, 110, 112, 114, **116–118**, *117*, 169
Wells, David, 44, 160, 166, 175, 181, 240–242
  perfect game of, 156–157, *156*
Wetteland, John, 94, 118
White, Bill, 98, 148, 177, 234
Williams, Bernie, 114, **118–120**, *119*, 156, 158, 160–161, 177, 179–180, 191, 204–205, 238–241, 243, 245
Williams, Ted, 71, 72, 97, 98, 100, 113, 134, 138–139, 196, 203–204, 225–227, 230
Winfield, Dave, 81–82, 88, 109, **120–121**, *120*, 163, 167, 169, 171, 173, 185, 236, 238, 243
World Series
  Bush throws out first ball at 2001 game, 158

fans waiting to buy tickets for 1938 game, *172*
list of Yankee wins, 255
program from 1927, *84*
ticket from 1921, *38*

Y

Yankee Doodle Dandies, 193–206
Yankee Stadium (new), *7*, *9*, *11*, 31, *189*, 190
Yankee Stadium, (old), *16*, 26, 28–29, 31, *52*, 72, 75, 77–79, 105–107, 190–191, *198*, 221, 234
  final game at, 160
  opening of, 124, *124*
  rain check for field box at, *208*
  as "Ruppert's Folly," 27
  Ruth's death and, *105*, 136
Yankees
  American League pennant wins of, 256–257
  archival scorecard, *275*
  cycle hitters, 253
  Cy Young award winners from, 250
  East Division titles, 259
  ERA champions from, 248
  general managers of, 266
  homerun breakdown by park, 258
  MLB batting champions from, 247
  MVP winners from, 251
  no hitters of, 252
  one hundred loss seasons of, 253
  one hundred win seasons of, 254
  program for 1939 All-Star Game, 132, *132*
  program from 1961, *141*
  retired numbers of, 249
  rookies of the year from, 250
  salaries in 1927, 260
  scorecard from 1903, *22*
  scorecard from 1968, *233*
  team picture from 1926, *63*
  wild card wins of, 258
year-by-year results, 267–274

Z

Zimmer, Don, 81, 115, 169, 196